HOW TO
JUDGE
A
NATIVITY

Titles in the Alan Leo Astrologer's Library

———

THE ART OF SYNTHESIS

———

ASTROLOGY FOR ALL

———

CASTING THE HOROSCOPE

———

THE COMPLETE DICTIONARY OF ASTROLOGY

———

ESOTERIC ASTROLOGY

———

HOW TO JUDGE A NATIVITY

———

THE KEY TO YOUR OWN NATIVITY

———

THE PROGRESSED HOROSCOPE

How to Judge a Nativity

by

ALAN LEO

DESTINY BOOKS
Rochester, Vermont

Destiny Books
One Park Street
Rochester, Vermont 05767

First U.S. Edition 1983
This edition reprinted in 1989 by Destiny Books

Library of Congress Cataloging-in-Publication Data

Leo, Alan.
    How to judge a nativity / by Alan Leo.
        p.   cm. − (Alan Leo astrologer's library)
    ISBN 0-89281-177-3 :
        1. Natal astrology.   2. Houses (Astrology)   I. Title.
    II. Series: Leo, Alan. Alan Leo astrologer's library.
    BF1719.L464   1989
    133.5−dc20   89-16934
                                                            CIP

Printed and bound in the United States

10 9 8 7 6 5 4 3 2 1

Destiny Books is a division of Inner Traditions International, Ltd.

Distributed to the book trade in the United States by Harper and Row
Publishers, Inc.

Distributed to the book trade in Canada by Book Center, Inc., Montreal, Quebec

PREFACE

In *Astrology for All*, the first book of this Series, a considerable amount of information regarding the zodiac and the planets has been given, while in the succeeding volume the method of casting the horoscope was thoroughly gone into with full minuteness in every detail. The present work will consist of the methods used in judging the horoscope when it has been accurately cast.

The books comprising this Series have been so arranged that the student may have a special book dealing with each stage of his study, and thus avoid confusing the mind with that which does not directly belong to the department under consideration. In all former books on Astrology too much has been attempted in one volume, and no branch of the subject has ever received the full elucidation it deserves ; though in fact no book ever will or can contain all that is to be known concerning this science. For Astrology is the most comprehensive study conceivable, a science which no mortal mind could invent, being the direct work of immortals who came from other worlds to instruct our infant humanity.

Astrology is one of seven keys required to unlock the door of the inner temple, but it is not the Astrology that is universally practised, for although this is a wonderful and useful study, it is only a key to the outer temple through which the aspirant must pass and the lessons of which he must learn ere he can prepare for the wisdom that is to be his when he shall pass into that inner temple to which the many may be called but only the few are chosen. Our world has never been without teachers ready and willing to instruct those who make the necessary conditions by fitting themselves to receive that knowledge, which is carefully guarded until humanity has grown strong enough to receive it. The divine mysteries are only for those who are ready to renounce the material world and claim their divine right to be heirs to the knowledge the Teachers have to impart.

v

In dealing with the general rules for judgment in the following pages, an attempt is made to strike a higher note than has hitherto been struck, and although it is not the highest, it is quite high enough for the present. What is here written has not been copied from other books, a practice which seems to have been adopted by the majority of writers on Astrology, but is the result of deep thought and practical experience, which I am anxious to share with my fellow students; and to those who like myself have become absorbed in its study this fragment of learning is offered in the hope that it will help them to judge a horoscope more correctly than would otherwise be the case. For it strikes the note of the New Astrology, the foundation of which has been already laid by the establishment of *Modern Astrology*, the desire of which is to purify and re-establish the ancient science of Astrology, which, through planetary symbology, seeks to explain the One Universal Spirit in its varied manifestations.

ALAN LEO.

PREFACE TO THE THIRD EDITION

SINCE the issue of this series of Astrological text books, many students have expressed their desire to have a Short History of Astrology, with a list of the famous names of those who are known to have been its sincere students. This, not merely to satisfy idle curiosity, but to add more weight and dignity to the science and to meet the sceptical minds of those who in this present day of uncertainty and doubt require evidence of this kind; and also, where necessary, to relieve the anxiety of those who have more faith in traditions and historical data than belief in original and first hand thought. For such as these the following remarks are made in this edition.

THE HISTORY OF ASTROLOGY.

Astrology has undoubtedly been known to all nations throughout the world from time immemorial and its history appears to be coeval with that of the earth, since it can be traced through every existing nation and through them again to the great nations of the past whose glory and splendour we are only just beginning to realise.

Through Egypt and ancient Chaldea ; through Japan and ancient China, and from Thibet to early Hindustan we find Astrology has passed round the globe always retaining the same symbology, the same zodiac, and also the same ancient traditions. Who invented it ? NO ONE KNOWS.

Egyptian history is full of Astrological lore, and there is now very little doubt that it was *the* religion of the Chaldeans. From Clemens Alexandrinus we learn that : 'The Egyptians follow a certain peculiar philosophy of their own, which may be best declared by setting down the order of their religious processions. First therefore goes the *Precentor*, carrying two of Hermes his books along with him ; the one which contains the Hymns of the gods, the other Direction for the kingly office. After him follows the *Horoscopus*, who is particularly instructed in Hermes his *Astrological* books, which are *four*. Then succeeds the *Hierogrammateus*, or sacred scribe, with feathers upon his head, and a book and rule in his hands, to whom it belongeth to be thoroughly acquainted with the Hieroglyphics, as with Cosmography, geography, the order of the Sun, and Moon, and five planets, the chorography of Egypt and description of the Nile,' etc.

The whole of the Egyptian philosophy was evidently based upon Astrology. The existence of Egyptian Astrologers in the time of Joseph is beyond question, and in those days there is no doubt that Pharaoh had faith in his wise men, or astrologers, to interpret his dreams.

"In our own Scriptures, both Old and New Testaments, we find abundant evidence of the knowledge of the Science of Astrology. Knowing as we do that the Chaldeans were the great teachers of historical times, and that their religion, science and art was Astrology, we can readily understand that Abram living in Ur of the Chaldees, Isaac married to a Chaldean wife, Jacob, who lived 21 years in Padam Aram, and his sons brought up by Chaldean mothers, were all thoroughly acquainted with the ideas and terms of Astrology. In those times, the twelve signs of the Zodiac were the twelve typical things, and so we find Joseph in his dream likening himself and his family to the Sun, Moon and twelve Stars (or Zodiac.) Likewise, Jacob blesses his twelve sons, and in those blessings we find a very striking analogy to the characteristics of the twelve signs of the Zodiac.

"If we take the account written by Moses, an Initiate, of the Creation, Fall, Flood, etc., we find that it sets down for the people the traditions of the faith as received from Mesopotamian sources and couched *in Astrological terms*. For example : 'And God said Let there be lights in the firmament of heaven . . . and let them be for *signs*, and for seasons and for days and for years.' (Gen i.) Again 'And God made two great lights, the greater light to *rule* by day, and the lesser light to *rule* by night.' (Gen. i.)

"Later we find the Israelites soon after leaving Egypt being met by Balaam, a Chaldean of Pethor, an Astrologer and prophet in communication with the angel of the Lord who had been engaged by Balak the enemy of Israel to curse Israel. (Numbers xxii.) The Chaldean custom on such ceremonial occasions, was to build altars and sacrifice to the seven planets. Thus we find that Baalam three times built seven altars, on each of which he offered sacrifices and then prophesied of the *Star* which was to arise out of Jacob.

"In the prophetical books we find frequent mention of the Star worship of Israel. Zephaniah speaks of 'Them that worship the hosts of Heaven upon the housetops.' Isaiah speaks of the multitude of Astrological consultations. Jeremiah speaks of the 'cakes to the queen of heaven.' These prophets and others utter warnings against the use of the lower side of Astrology, but those who understood the higher teaching not only used it but defended it. Of these the accounts given in the books of Ezekiel and Daniel give wonderful examples. The Book of Daniel is a remarkable instance of the assimilation of Chaldean knowledge by a faithful Jew, and we find Daniel's proficiency immediately attributed to God. 'As for these four children God gave them skill in all learning and wisdom, and Daniel had understanding in all visions and dreams.' In Daniel's visions there are several references to Astrological ideas, and in the Apocalypse in the New Testament, we find many allusions to the Astrological visions of Daniel and Ezekiel.

"In no part of the Christian Scriptures do we find Astrology mentioned disapprovingly, and nowhere is the study of Astrology forbidden though we *do* find warnings as to its proper use. On the contrary we find from the Song of Deborah and Barak a victory attributed to the courses of the Stars for in Judge v. we read 'They fought from heaven ; the stars in their courses fought against Sisera.'

"Coming to the New Testament, the story of the Magi, those of the Birth of Christ, and of the events accompanying the Crucifixion, show that the people of that time had a star lore which perfectly harmonised with their theology, and therefore could not fail to look for Astrological accompaniments to such great events as the Birth, Life, and Death of the Messiah. Chaldean learning was also diffused among the early Christians, and it has been said that the writer of the Apocalypse must have been an Astrologer of the Chaldean school, who used terms with which Asiatic Christians were familiar, and who could turn to the books of Ezekiel and Daniel for confirmation to convince his Hebrew readers. The Book of Revelation which has been the greatest of all puzzles to theologians and divines has been said to be a great horoscope of the World's Destiny and to contain within this vast horoscope the smaller horoscopes of the nations."

Long before the Christian era astrology was known, not only as a science but also as a religion. Zoroaster, the greatest legislator of the Magi or wise men of Chaldea was also an Astrologer. Zoroaster means a 'Son of the Stars.' Belus who reigned over Babylonia was for some time reputed to be the founder of the science of the stars, his wisdom in this direction being so great. There is now no doubt that Astrology was more studied and understood in Chaldea than in any other country in the world, and there is now abundant evidence that the Chaldeans were star or sun worshippers and believed in the spirits and intelligences ruling over the stars. Calisthenes who accompanied Alexander when he conquered Babylon found that astronomical calculations had been made for many thousands of years of the past dating as far back as the great Atlantean flood.

In ancient Persia there were many celebrated astrologers whose fame still lingers, one of these Gjamasp was surnamed Al Hakim—the Wise. He was a brother of King Gustasp, and is said to have predicted the coming of the Messiah. Dr Thomas Hyde in his account of the famous Persian doctors writes of him as follows :—Of these, the sixth was Gjamasp, an Astrologer, who was counsellor to Hystespis. He is the author of a book entitled 'Judicia Gjamaspis' in which is contained his judgment on the planetary conjunctions, and therein he gave notice that Jesus should appear ; that Mohammed should be born ; that the Magian religion should be abolished, etc.

Major-general Sir Thomas Malcolm, in his History of Persia writes :— 'They (the Persians) study astronomy chiefly for the purpose of becoming skilled in Judicial Astrology ;—a science in which the whole nation from the monarch to the peasant has the greatest faith.'

From Egypt Astrology was carried into Greece. As early as the thirteenth century before the Christian era, the position of the stars with regard to the circles of the spheres was established with great exactness, and it has been said that during the century when the Egyptians were measuring and observing the heavens for astrological purposes, the Greeks were ruthless barbarians.

One of the earliest and most famous of the Astrologers of Greece was Anaximander, the friend and disciple of Thales. He was born 610 B.C. and introduced the sphere, sundials and geographical charts brought from Egypt. He taught that the fixed stars were centres of other Solar systems perhaps more extensive and glorious than our own. He also regarded the planets as the homes of great intelligences.

Pliny tells us that Anaximander was an able astrologer and foretold the earthquake which overthrew Lacedæomon.

Of Thales it is stated by Seneca, that he was an astrologer, and that foreseeing there would be a dearth in that region of the country, where olives were principally cultivated, bought them up and enriched himself at the expense of those who would not believe him.

Anaxagoras, also an astrologer, who said that he preferred a grain of wisdom to heaps of gold, was preceptor to Socrates and Euripides and gave the greater part of his life to the study.   Many fulfilled predictions are related of him.

Pythagoras also practised Astrology ; Plato was learned in it, so also were Porphyry and many other intelligent Greeks.

Proclus believed in it, and Hippocrates the father of the art of Medicine declared that the man who did not well understand Astrology was rather deserving to be called a fool than a physician.

Coming down to the Roman empire we find a long list of great men who were firm believers in Astrology and amongst them are Propertius, Pliny, Galen, Macrobius, Virgil, Horace, Nigidius, Figulus, and Cicero.

In Arabia Astrology flourished for many centuries and all the eminent men of the time appear to have been believers in Astrology.   The sixth Caliph Mamoonorrasheed appears to have had many ancient works on Astrology translated into Arabic.   Then we have the famous Albumazar of Bulah, a pupil of Alkurdi a Jew who was a professor of Judicial Astrology at Bagdad.

Amongst the great names of intelligent men who were renowned Arabian astrologers we find Messahala, Albategnius, Alfaganus, Hely, Holy Aben Rodoan and Alphero.   No one can go through the histories of China, India, Siam, or Ceylon without being struck with the facts that Astrology has flourished in all ages before the materialistic period of our times.   Even Dr. Brewster had to admit that in China from the days of King Fohi, about two thousand seven hundred and fifty two years before Christ, astronomy was solely studied for astrological calculations, and that their Emperors were chosen on account of their attainments in Celestial Philosophy.

So far as Indian history is concerned we may go back three thousand one hundred and two years B.C., and the Tirvalore Tables, used solely for Astrological purposes.   It is even stated that the religions of the Siamese and the Buddhists have been founded upon astrology.   Coming down to our own times we find such a remarkable list of names of those who actually openly confessed their belief in astrology that it will probably be as well that a list is now given of more modern astrologers.   Roger Bacon, Cardan, Nostrodamus, Tycho Brahe, Lord Napier, Kepler, Cornelius Agrippa, Valentine Naibod, Bishop Robert Hall, Sir Edward Kelly, Dryden, Sir George Wharton, Placidus de Titus, Sir Christopher Heydon, George Wichell Astronomer Royal, Vincent Wing, William Lilly, Dr. Salmon, Flamstead, Le Duc de Volney, George Digby, Earl of Bristol, Elias Ashmole founder of the Ashmolean Museum, Culpeper, Milton, Dr. Dee, Dr. Starkey, Dr. Partridge, Dr. Moore, Sir Richard Steele, Colley Cibber, Guido Bonatus, Emerson, Worsdall, Sir Kenelm Digby, Sir Robert Holburn, Mr. Blake, Sir Thomas Gresham, Rt. Hon. W. Pitt, Wilson, Melancthon, Sir Matthew Hale, Lord Bacon, Archbishop Usher, Dr Richard Garnett of the British Museum and a great many others whose names may not be mentioned.   Indeed there are people living to-day whose names would come as a great surprise to many, who are very earnest and loyal students of astrology, but from what has been said in this brief sketch it will be seen that if some devoted student with the time at his disposal could go through the world's history it would be found that there has always been a universal belief in Astrology, and quite sufficient evidence to establish the truth of the statement that Astrology is in a word the history of the world.

ALAN LEO.

DETAILED TABLE OF CONTENTS

(The numbers refer to the pages)

CHAPTER V

CHAPTER VI

CHAPTER VII

CHAPTER VIII

CONTENTS

THE SIGNS OF THE ZODIAC

	NORTHERN	*opposite to*	SOUTHERN	
Spring	1. ♈ Aries (+ *c.* F.)	(A. *c.* +) Libra ♎ 7		*Autumn*
	2. ♉ Taurus (− *f.* E.)	(W. *f.* −) Scorpio ♏ 8		
	3. ♊ Gemini (+ *m.* A.)	(F. *m.* +) Sagittarius ♐ 9		
Summer	4. ♋ Cancer (− *c.* W.)	(E. *c.* −) Capricorn ♑ 10		*Winter*
	5. ♌ Leo (+ *f.* F.)	(A. *f.* +) Aquarius ♒ 11		
	6. ♍ Virgo (− *m.* E.)	(W. *m.* −) Pisces ♓ 12		

F., Fiery   E., Earthy   A., Airy   W., Watery

c., cardinal   *f.*, fixed   *m.*, mutable

+positive   − negative

1, 2, 3 = *Intellectual Trinity*   7, 8, 9 = *Reproductive Trinity*
4, 5, 6 = *Maternal Trinity*   10, 11, 12 = *Serving Trinity*

Parts of the body ruled by the Signs

♈ *Aries*	HEAD	♎ *Libra*	LOINS AND KIDNEYS
♉ *Taurus*	NECK AND THROAT	♏ *Scorpio*	GENERATIVE SYSTEM
♊ *Gemini*	ARMS AND LUNGS	♐ *Sagittarius*	THIGHS
♋ *Cancer*	STOMACH	♑ *Capricorn*	KNEES
♌ *Leo*	HEART	♒ *Aquarius*	LEGS AND ANKLES
♍ *Virgo*	BOWELS	♓ *Pisces*	FEET

Cardinal Signs	HEAD	*Fiery* Signs	VITALITY
Fixed „	TRUNK	*Earthy* „	BONES AND FLESH
Mutable „	LIMBS	*Airy* „	BREATH
		Watery „	BLOOD

[*Should there be found in this work technical expressions with which the reader is as yet unfamiliar, he should refer to the Comprehensive Glossary in Manual No. 7 (Shilling Series) entitled ' Horary Astrology.'*]

INTRODUCTION

A LITTLE practice only is necessary to become proficient in casting horoscopes. The judgment of the map when cast, however, is an entirely different matter, and it may be safely stated that there are very few competent to judge a horoscope, although nearly every one is competent to make all the calculations necessary for that judgment, and while it is true that practice will in time bring a certain amount of proficiency, there will always be a certain number of horoscopes which will baffle the understanding of the student, and the beginner will sooner or later come to a dead wall, so to speak, which for a time bars all further progress. In all probability this will arise from lack of experience, or the failure to blend certain positions and aspects which no reference to text-books or former study will elucidate.

This statement, that anyone can cast a horoscope but few can read it, at once marks the fundamental difference between the astronomer and the astrologer; the former can do all the work of observing, tabulating, calculating, etc., but appears to be quite unable to make a practical application of the observed phenomena.

The secret of this great difference lies in the fact that while the one is careful to study the objective and external state of things, the other pays more attention to the subjective or internal conditions. Now *both* of these aspects of Nature demand due study, and the true scientist is he who possesses the faculties which enable him to appreciate this truth ; but to find these two qualifications in one person is, at our present stage of evolution, a most difficult task. It seems almost impossible to convert an astronomer into an astrologer ; for this reason,—that he uses the mind that is confined for its functioning to the concrete brain, and he is thus limited to the objective world for his information. This explains, then, the reason why comparatively few are able to judge a horoscope ; for the cause-seeking faculty needs to be developed in the astrologer, whilst the perceptive organs alone need to be well-developed in the astronomer.

None save those who have well-developed reason coupled with clear perception and a good memory, can ever hope to become competent astrologers. The very name of the science suggests such a requirement, for Astrology means 'the reason of the stars.' Astron = star : Logos = reason.

To those who really *think*, there is nothing in the least unreasonable in Astrology, but they must think for themselves and not allow others to think for them if they would find out where the reason lies. They must also be prepared to take a far wider view of life than those who are still bound by custom and the personal opinions of others. The why and wherefore must ever be uppermost in the mind, and not the lazy indifference which drifts on aimlessly and carelessly, trusting to fate, or what is so often miscalled Providence, to carry them safely through their difficulties.

It will thus be seen that only those who are awakening to their responsibilities in life are likely to become interested in such a subject as Astrology, and it usually happens that the first step that is taken towards a study of the science is caused by an enquiry concerning the inequalities of life. The awakening soul prompts the question *Why?* and the mind is sent in search of an answer to the problem. *Why am I here?—What have I come to this earth for?—Why are some persons born poor, others rich, some weak, others strong?*—asks the soul rising above the illusions it sees mirrored on every side. The mind then goes in search of the answers to these important questions. For a time it will find comfort in various ways, sometimes in philosophy or religion, but no answer comes that entirely satisfies, for the simple reason that the answer must eventually come from within the man himself.

The Soul of every human being is immortal ; it is a fragment of the eternal Being Who is the spiritual essence at the root of all manifested life, therefore, without an actual beginning or ending. Each Soul in the far past began a pilgrimage through which it was destined to become a separate and fully self-conscious individuality. It has reached the present stage of evolution after many lives spent in various physical bodies, sowing and reaping for the purpose of experience and to become perfectly and fully individualised; so that instead of being at the mercy of circumstances in the future it may guide and direct its own evolution and, rising above the matter in which it has been ensouled, and using the various vehicles it has acquired, consciously and with set purpose, it may eventually transmute all external forces coming from the ONE GREAT LIFE and use them for future development in the grand scheme of evolution that lies before the soul in its upward journey toward self-perfection.   Then, possessed of all powers like unto the 'Father in Heaven' who sent it forth, it will become eventually like unto Himself, all-wise, all-powerful, and all-loving.   Each horoscope marks a step in that glorious evolution, and by representing the character and environment of the Soul shows the stage reached by the Ego in that particular birth.

If the fact of reincarnation be doubted the following questions should be asked: Is it not more reasonable to suppose that a soul requires many earth lives in order to learn all that the earth has to teach, rather than to think that one earth life only is necessary to fit it for eternal damnation or everlasting bliss ?   No person who has ever carefully pondered the matter, can see love or justice in causing a soul to be once born into a wretched, diseased and immoral family, where no opportunity is offered for spiritual development, and then condemning it to unceasing punishment for its unwise actions while in the body.   Why should one soul be born of moral and pure parents, and another of evil and corrupt parents, if only *one* life on earth is given it in which to grow and develop ?

In no other system of thought is this problem so reasonably answered as in that known under the title of Astrology.   The Sun, Moon, and planets are symbols conveying ideas to those minds able to appreciate what they mean.   The symbols connected with Astrology constitute the most simple and beautiful imagery we can conceive, and in them has been preserved from the beginning of our solar system to the present day the truth of man's past and his future.   The Sun is the body of the Lord and ruler over the solar system, therefore not only the symbol of life and light, but the actual source of all vitality, heat and motion in the system of which it is the centre.   The planets are the reflections of the seven spirits before the Throne, they are His messengers and the agents who carry out His will.   The Zodiac is the medium through which are transmitted the vibrations coming from the Sun as centre and reflected, or modulated, by the planets.

As each soul comes into the world the note which belongs to it is struck upon the celestial harp, and the heavens reverberate with its sound. Not a soul is born but an angel or Deva ministers to its birth, and just as no sparrow falleth to the ground without the Father in Heaven knowing it, so doth the Father know the life and manifestation of each individual. Each soul is attracted unto its appointed place, and each has its own special mission to fulfil and its own particular lesson to learn; all souls are one in *essence*, fragments of the great Soul; in manifestation all souls are different, some are older in manifestation, some are younger, some have grosser and others finer bodies or vehicles, each taking the one best suited for the work in hand.

Each soul manifests through a body of activity, or Physical Body; a body of feeling and emotion or Astral Body; and a thought or Mental Body. These three bodies St Paul has mentioned in 1 Cor. xv.

The nativity indicates what we have sown in the past and how we shall reap what we have sown. It is a chart which should be used as a guide in life. In it are concealed our capabilities, and our character, therefore our destiny. There is no study so interesting, instructive or useful as this, to those who are blending the objective with the subjective, or to those who would set their feet upon the path of the occultist or mystic, for it dispels all doubts with regard to the evolution of the soul and helps us more easily than any other known method to a scientific comprehension of ourselves and others.

Every student of Astrology should be thoroughly familiar with its symbology, for in the symbology we have all the required aid to help the intuition. Having committed to memory the opinions of the various writers upon the subject, and fully grasped the general meaning of each symbol, the student would do well to concentrate the mind as often as possible upon one of the symbols, trying to extract all the knowledge he can from the thought currents originally set in motion connected with that symbol; then gradually light will come into the mind, and more will be known in this way than can ever be obtained from books.

The first map for a student to study should be *his own*.

HOW TO JUDGE A NATIVITY

CHAPTER I

THE TWELVE HOUSES OF THE HOROSCOPE

THE earth revolving upon its own axis once in twenty-four hours causes
the sun to be viewed from the earth in various positions from sunrise to
sunset; and in order to obtain a clear conception of the twelve houses it
will be convenient to treat the matter, for the moment, as though the
earth were the centre instead of the sun, although we know very well
that the Sun is really the centre of our planetary system.

DIAGRAM No. 1

NOON

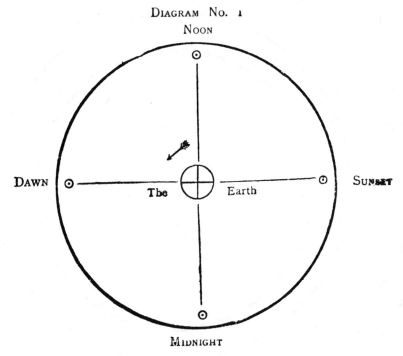

DAWN

The   Earth

SUNSET

MIDNIGHT

Adopting this course of regarding the earth as the centre for our present purpose, we will imagine the sun at daybreak rising on the eastern horizon, or, as we say, upon the Ascendant; with the earth's revolution, as the day wears on, at noon the sun will arrive at the zenith or what is called the Mid-heaven; and as the earth continues to revolve the sun will be carried to the western horizon at sunset. These three important positions in apparent time and space are produced by the sun's rising, culminating, and setting, and they mark the three cardinal points through which pass the cusps of the first, tenth and seventh houses. (See fuller explanation given in pp. 5 to 10 of *What is a Horoscope?*)

At midnight the sun will be directly under the earth at the furthest or lowest cardinal point, the whole making the four cardinal points or 'angles,' as they are termed. These four successive positions of the Sun, making the four quarters of the day, are shown in Diagram 1; they are *really* due,

DIAGRAM No. 2. DAWN

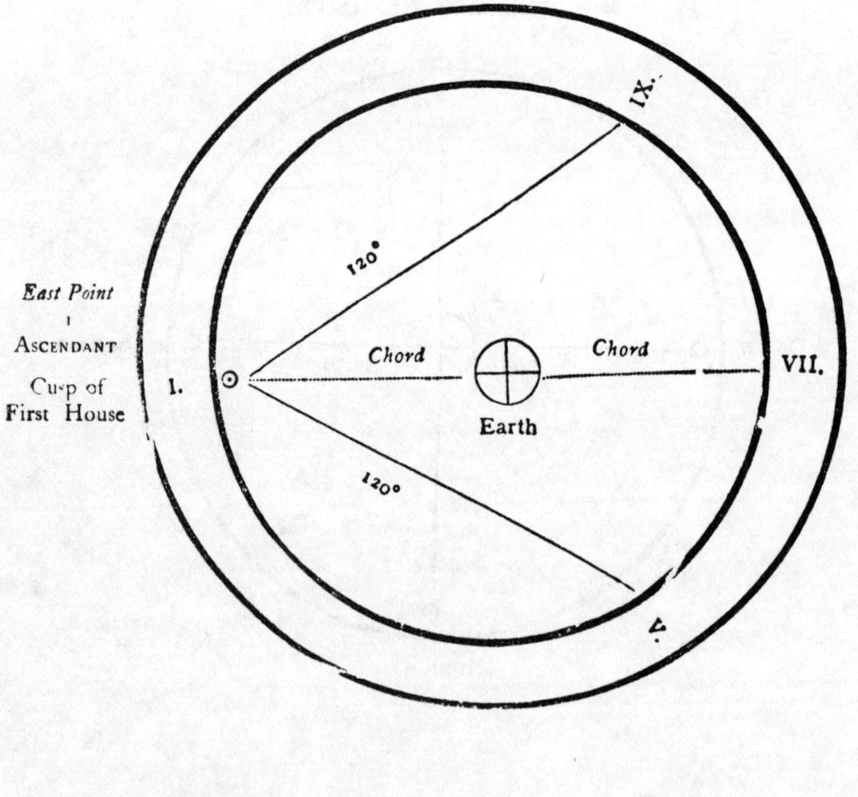

of course, to the rotation of the earth on its axis in the direction indicated by the arrow.   Out of these angles all the other divisions are obtained.

When the sun rises, the *chord* of the solar arc will pass through the earth to what is known as the 'cusp' of the seventh house or western angle.   The solar rays will also form a triangulum, and each side of this triangle will measure 120° of the circle, which is a third of the whole 360°. The Divine Archer takes his bow and *shoots:* what we have termed the 'chord' may be called His arrow of light and the 'triangulum' the bent string of His bow, quivering with the impulse.   The rays of this triangle will pass over and under the earth, the lower ray marking off the cusp of the fifth division or the Fifth House, and the upper the ninth division or Ninth House, as illustrated in Diagram No. 2, in which roman numerals indicate the house cusps.

Each of the cardinal points will, in a similar way, be connected with the other divisions, the two 'chords' together forming the Mundane

DIAGRAM No 3.   SUNSET

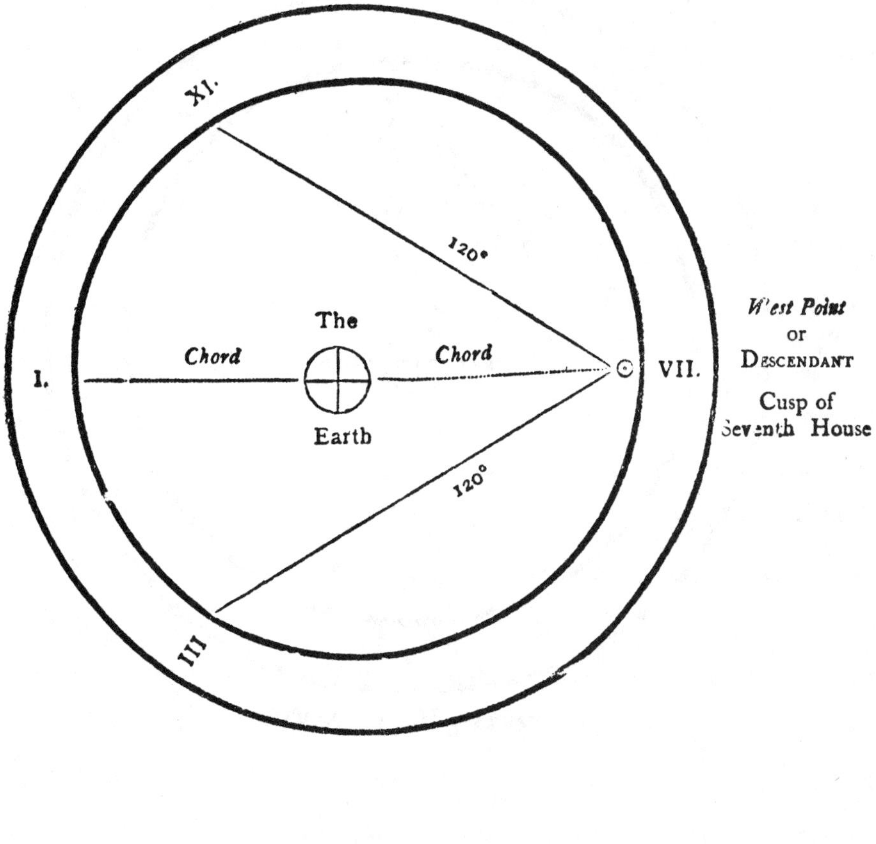

Cross which squares the circle, forming an aspect of opposition and discord, whereas each triangle forms the trine, an aspect of peace and harmony.

The divisions formed from the First House or ASCENDANT are of the nature of the Fiery triplicity, the first house being of the nature of the vital heat, the fifth the generative fire, the ninth the mental or spiritual fire. The whole key to the nature of the twelve houses and indeed to the twelve signs as well, is beautifully expressed in this symbology.

At noon the solar chord passes directly to the northern angle, the cusp of the fourth house, and the triangle is formed in the second and sixth houses. This triangle is related to the Earthy triplicity, denoting hereditary honour, fame, worldly position, finance and service (Diagram 4).

The chord from the western angle unites with the chord from the ascendant and the triangle is formed in the third and eleventh houses.

South Point or MID-HEAVEN, Cusp of Tenth House

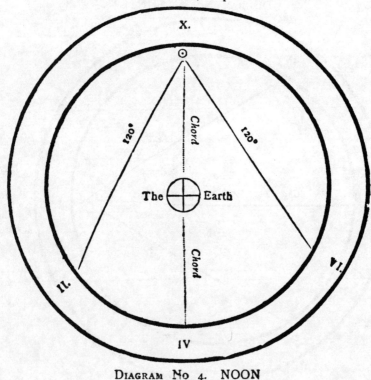

DIAGRAM No 4. NOON

This angle is of the nature of the airy triplicity, the seventh house denoting relation, such as marriage and partnership, brethren and kindred, friends and acquaintances. (See Diagram 3, facing Diagram 2.)

The fourth angle returns the chord to the mid-heaven, and the triangles are formed in the eighth and twelfth houses. This triangle is of the nature of the Watery triplicity, the fourth house denoting the psychic conditions, and that which has to do with the end of life, also death and the withdrawal from the material world. (See Diagram 5.)

It will be seen by the foregoing that the whole of the twelve houses have a symbolical basis, the succedent and cadent houses having their root in the cross of the four angles, representing what are known in the East as the three 'Gunas'—Tamas, Rajas, and Sattva—interpreted as Stability, Activity and Rhythm respectively. If these four diagrams are

DIAGRAM No. 5.   MIDNIGHT

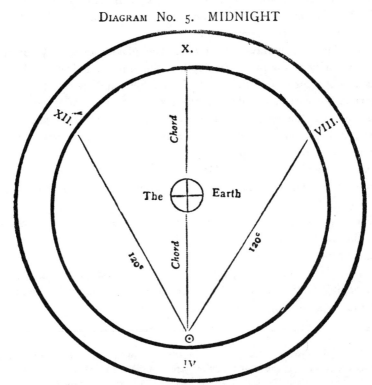

North Point or NADIR, Cusp of Fourth House

carefully traced or copied out on thin tracing paper and then superposed, the manner in which this cross is formed, and the inter-relationship of the Twelve Houses, will be shown in a very striking manner.

Every nation in the past has held the cross in the highest reverence. It is the geometrical basis of religious symbolism in connection with all the great world saviours.   On the cross of matter spirit is crucified.* The cross in motion forms a wheel, or circle, called the Svastika; from the centre of the cross the sacred fire or Fohat crosses the circle horizontally and vertically, like two lines of flame.   The Sun at the centre of the solar system represents the spiritual point in the universe to which all humanity is being drawn, the denser matter, or the physical, being farthest removed as it circles round the Sun.   But regarding the earth as the centre for astrological purposes, humanity is shown as chained to the cross of matter until the spirit of the Christ is born within, which entirely reverses the spheres.

To understand the mysteries hidden behind astrological symbology, not only purity of life but great depth of thought is required, for in it is concealed the history of the races of this globe, and in fact the whole history of our earth as a planet; but for the purpose of more clearly understanding the nature of the twelve houses we may see in its geometrical symbology three great activities connected with human destiny, as we will now explain.

Kama, Kama-Manas, and Manas are three Sanskrit words which denote the character of the three angles connected with the first, tenth and seventh houses.

Kama presides over the first house or ascendant, being concerned with the birth of the animal man, his desire nature, love of life and physical conditions.

Kama-Manas, presiding over the tenth house or meridian, denotes the blending of the mind with the desire nature, the animal with the god, thus representing the animal-human soul.

----

* In mystic writings, Enoch, the representative of the spiritual and physical or dual nature in man, is the centre of the astronomical cross : at the upper point or apex of the triangle is the Eagle, at the base of the lower angle on the left stands the Lion and on the right the Bull, these being the four fixed signs ♒, ♏, ♌, ♉ .

Manas, ruling over the seventh house, denotes the pure mind or reason and the clear intellect of the human soul.

The first angle, corresponding to sunrise, suggests spirit, life and force made subject to matter, the circle under the cross; consciousness blinded by matter.

The second angle, corresponding to the culmination of the Sun upon the meridian, suggests the native balanced half way between spirit and matter, neither wholly one or the other, the cross over the *half* circle; self-consciousness.

The third angle, corresponding to the setting of the Sun, denotes the triumph of the spirit over matter, the union of the life of the separated one with the consciousness of the spirit, the circle over the cross; super-consciousness.

The fourth angle is the great mystery, the occult centre in which all the forces are gathered together for work in the unseen worlds.

From each of these angles the other houses receive their value, the cardinal points denoting the root of the life to be expressed.

The ASCENDANT or First House shows the quality of the life forces, the material brought to the front, so to speak. The personality with the desires are shown by this house. The Fifth House will find its expression through the stream of natural fire coming from the first, and so governs offspring, enterprise and emotional impulses. The Ninth House shows the life forces running upward toward the highest thought of which the nature is capable, and signifies all matters connected with science, philosophy and religion. From the idea of the mind being able to transmit itself away from the brain limitation this has come to be the house of travel, dreams, and metaphysics, also of thought-transference, etc.

The Tenth House or MID-HEAVEN, or Upper Meridian, the apex of the earthy triangle, denotes the fame and honour and worldly status of the native, the parentage and hereditary tendencies, and governs all matters connected with profession, business, employment, and worldly occupation. The Second House shows the outcome of the labour or profession in financial advantage, remuneration and monetary condition generally. The Sixth House shows the service required, and governs all matters connected with servants and helpers and those who are often inferiors. It is the house of employment and ceremonial magic.

The Seventh House or DESCENDANT denotes relation. All partner-ships and unions of every kind are shown by this house, and thus it is the house of marriage, and of the Individuality. The Third House denotes relatives and kindred arising from unions, and also the expression through the brain of the union with the subjective and objective mind. It has also come to have some relation to *short* journeys, owing to its connection with the concrete or brain mind, which cannot travel far from the objects with which it is connected. The Eleventh House denotes the friends and acquaintances arising from unions, etc. Hopes and wishes are also indicated by this house.

The Fourth House, or NADIR, or Lower Meridian, denotes the environment, the life of the householder, also hidden and secret matters either connected with parentage or domestic affairs, and shows the conditions at the close of life. The Eighth House denotes death, and all matters connected with dissolution, and indicates the nature of the death the native will meet, and all expectations connected with the death of others; also re-generation or re-birth, or the raising of any faculty signified to a 'higher octave.' The Twelfth House is the house of confinement, or matters that, having their root in the fourth, spring out of parentage, inheritance and unseen affairs connected with the inner or psychic life; it is therefore called the house of occultism and (physical) 'self-undoing.'

The Cardinal or 'Angular' houses or angles show all things that must be expressed outwardly, such as physical matters connected with the external life; (*Rajas*—activity). The Fixed or 'Succedent,' *i.e.*, second, fifth, eighth and eleventh houses, indicate matters connected with the feelings and emotions, not yet ripe for physical expression, but maturing for future development; (*Tamas*—stability). The Mutable or 'Cadent,' *i.e.*, third, sixth, ninth and twelfth, show all matters latent in the mind and affairs brought over from past lives and not yet ready for final expression in the physical world; (*Sattva*—rhythm).

In the reverse order of the above, the Cadent, Succedent and Cardinal divisions may be said to represent thought, feeling and action, or spirit, soul and body.

The houses to the left of the meridian are called *oriental,* easterly or rising; those on the right are called *occidental* or descending. They represent respectively the objective and subjective. The six houses above the horizon, 7th to 12th, correspond to the 'life' side of the universe: the six below, 1st to 6th, correspond to its 'form' side.

Having partially explained the rationale of the twelve divisions, each house will now be seen to have a definite meaning, out of which a greater number of minor influences will arise.

The following is the general nature of each house :—

I.   *First House.*—Personality, natural disposition, worldly outlook generally. Physical experiences as obtained through the five senses. The parts of the body denoted are the *head* and *face.*

II.   *Second House.*—Finance, monetary prospects. Desires caused by tenth-house influence affecting moral growth. The parts of the body denoted are the *throat* and *ears.*

III.   *Third House.*—Relatives and kindred, travelling, intellect derived from education and study, and minor impressions made upon the physical brain. The parts of the body denoted are the *neck, arms* and *shoulders* and the *lungs.*

IV.   *Fourth House.*—Hereditary tendencies ; home and domestic life ; parentage, environment, and the general state of things at the close of life. The parts of the body denoted are the *breasts, stomach* and *digestive* organs.

V.   *Fifth House.*—Offspring ; generative powers, sensations and pleasurable emotions arising from the senses, worldly enterprise and energy. The parts of the body denoted are the *loins, heart* and *back.*

VI.   *Sixth House.*—Service and attachments arising from the expression of the tenth house, therefore servants and inferiors in social rank. This house also denotes sickness arising from worry and anxiety. It is also the house of phenomenal magic arising from the powers of the southern angle. The parts of the body denoted are the *bowels* and *solar plexus.*

VII.   *Seventh House.*—Unions, marriage, partnerships, individual character and humane tendencies. The parts of the body denoted are the *veins* and *kidneys.*

VIII.   *Eighth House.*—Death, all matters pertaining to legacies or affairs connected with death. It is also what is termed an occult house, owing to its relation to the fourth, which denotes the psychic tendencies. The parts of the body denoted are the *secret parts* and the *generative system.*

IX.   *Ninth House.*—Higher mentality, scientific, philosophic and religious tendencies. It also denotes long journeys, dreams and the image-making power. The parts of the body denoted are the *thighs* and *hams.*

X.   *Tenth House.*—Profession, business ability, fame, honour and material reputation. All worldly activities and moral responsibilities are shown by this house. The parts of the body denoted are the *knees.*

XI.   *Eleventh House.*—Friends, acquaintances, hopes, wishes and aspirations. The parts of the body denoted are the *legs* and *ankles.*

XII.   *Twelfth House.*—Occult tendencies. Its connection with the fourth house shows the psychic thought inheritance from the past and the result as either joy or sorrow. This may be said to be the most critical house of the twelve. The parts of the body denoted are the *feet* and *toes.*

These twelve houses or divisions are like spokes of a great wheel running from the hub at the centre, which represents the nucleus of the experiences gained from each of the twelve houses. The nature of the particular experience will be shown by the sign of the zodiac occupying each house, and the quality of these signs we will study in the next chapter; but the nature of each house should be understood apart from the signs, and then it will not be difficult to comprehend what follows.

When the mind has retained a clear picture of the nature of each house the student may endeavour to imagine a line running from each of the twelve divisions or houses to the centre of the map, endeavouring to think of the native as remaining in the centre with all these forces playing around him, with a natural tendency always to be drawn more toward the *first house* and grasp at this spoke of the wheel more than any of the others, while at the same time being drawn in other directions and influenced by the outside conditions affecting each spoke of the great wheel.

It must be understood that the manner of describing the formation of the Twelve Houses which has been adopted in this chapter is symbolical or *figurative*. It has been chosen because the Sun exerts a special influence when at each of the four angles of the heavens related to the four quarters of the day, an influence specially related to that of the houses concerned. But the Twelve Houses are always simultaneously present, and exert their several influences according to the signs and planets which occupy them, whatever may be the hour of the day or night, no matter whether the Sun is upon an angle or not, though of course the presence of the Sun in any house will accentuate the influence of that house.

It should also be thoroughly grasped that there exists the most intimate correspondence between the signs and the houses, between Aries and the First House, Taurus and the Second House, and so on. Hence the influence of a planet in Aries will *correspond* to that of the same planet in the First House—will correspond to it, though it will not be exactly the same. Perhaps a hint as to the difference may be given in the suggestion that the *houses* relate to physical matter, and the *signs* to astral matter. But it must be kept in mind that the influence of the signs is greater than that of the houses, and that the former will overbear the latter.

Thus spring 'corresponds' to sunrise, for it is the dawn of the year, even as sunrise is the dawn of the day. But there are many days during the year.

CHAPTER II

The Twelve Signs of the Zodiac

In the previous chapter we were concerned with the twelve mundane houses, or the twelve equal divisions of the circle of observation, an imaginary circle drawn round the earth from East to West and passing overhead and underfoot through the zenith and the nadir, the observer being in the centre.* We shall now proceed to consider the twelve signs of the zodiac. The word zodiac means a group of animals, and the twelve signs are really so many types of beings, symbolised in various ways among various nations.

We have now to consider the movement of the earth from the standpoint of the sun as centre; that is, we have to regard the annual revolution of the earth *in its orbit round the sun;* whereas in our first chapter we merely considered the rotation of the earth *on its axis* by which movement the Sun appears to pass round the earth once daily.

Now the earth completes its circuit round the Sun in one year, or twelve months; and hence the space passed through by the earth in one month—that is, one-twelfth of the circle—is analogous to one of the Mundane Houses (in fact there is an exact correspondence between them, as has been said already). These twelve divisions are called the Twelve Signs of the Zodiac; so we can see that practically the Zodiac is really the orbit of the Earth, as explained in Chapter XII of *Casting the Horoscope.* But as we are obliged to view everything from the Earth, we have to consider how this will appear from our standpoint. This is fully explained in the first chapters of the book just referred to, but it may be briefly put as follows:—

As the earth pursues its yearly course round the sun, an observer

---

* This description of the mode of reckoning the twelve houses requires some qualification, it is true, but it would lead us too far from our present purpose to go into the matter fully here ; it is thoroughly explained in the second book of this series, *Casting the Horoscope.*

on our globe seems to see the sun changing its place among the stars to the rate of about 1° per day, and thus describing one complete circle in the year. Now it is this circle of the ecliptic, or the sun's apparent path round the earth, which is what the western astrologer means when he speaks of the zodiac. It is divided into twelve equal parts, the signs of the zodiac, which correspond as just stated to the twelve mundane houses; the first sign to the first house, the second sign to the second house, and so on. The zodiac commences at that point at which the Sun crosses the equator in its northern path, which it does about March 21st each year.*

The Twelve Houses of the Horoscope govern the physical frame-work, and the fate connected with environment; that which may be overcome by the inherent will of the native. The Twelve Signs of the Zodiac are the covering of the twelve houses and give the colouring and quality to the twelve divisions of the horoscope, being more related to the psychic and inner nature. Their relation to each other may be understood in this way: if we think of the *houses* as transparent vessels, each having its own shape and pattern according as it is angular, succedent or cadent, oriental or occidental, above the horizon or below,—then the *signs* will supply the contents of such vessel, giving a special substance, colour and quality to each house.

Everywhere throughout Nature there is analogy, or rather, a reflection of attributes, from that which is above to that which is below—*As above So below* runs the Hermetic axiom. Thus we find

---

* The *signs* of the zodiac must not be confused with the *constellations* of the zodiac. The constellations are groups of fixed stars, the twelve central groups being called by the same names as the twelve signs, although they do not cover the same areas of the heavens. The Hindus and some other oriental nations work by these constellations, but the western astrologer always calculates in terms of the signs, and when he speaks of 'the zodiac' he always means the ecliptic or Sun's path. In the Tetrabiblos of Claudius Ptolemy, (Ashmand's translation, published 1822, 1896) we read on page 32 : 'The beginning of the whole zodiacal circle . . . is . . . the sign Aries which commences at the Vernal Equinox,' and the translator goes on to say :—'This shows the futility of the objection raised against Astrology, that the signs have changed and are changing places. It is clear from this sentence that Ptolemy ascribes to the 30 degrees after the vernal equinox, that influence which he has herein mentioned to belong to Aries ; to the next 30 degrees, the influence herein said to belong to Taurus ; and so of the rest of the Zodiac . . . Ptolemy himself seems to have foreseen this groundless objection of the moderns, and has written, in the 25th chapter of this book, what ought completely to have prevented

the division of the twelve signs into the three primary qualities, or quadruplicities, has its correspondence in the twelve houses, the Cardinal or movable signs corresponding to the angles, the Fixed signs to the succedent houses, while the Mutable or common signs will be similar in nature to the cadent houses. Again the four triplicities correspond to the four angles, while the four quarters of the day, dawn, noon, sunset and midnight, have their similitude in the four seasons, Spring, Summer, Autumn and Winter. The fiery signs are related to spring by Aries, the middle of summer by Leo, and the end of autumn by Sagittarius; the beginning of summer is signified by the watery sign Cancer, the middle of autumn by Scorpio, and the end of winter by Pisces; the commencement of autumn by the airy sign Libra, the middle of winter by Aquarius, and the end of spring by Gemini; the entrance of winter by the earthy sign Capricorn, the middle of spring by Taurus, and the end of summer by Virgo.*

The signs, like the houses, also govern the various parts of the body, as follows: Aries, head and face; Taurus, throat and ears; Gemini, neck, arms, shoulders and lungs; Cancer, breast and stomach; Leo, heart and back; Virgo, bowels, liver and pancreas; Libra, groin and kidneys; Scorpio, secret parts; Sagittarius, thighs; Capricorn, knees; Aquarius, ankles; Pisces, feet.

The zodiac is also divided into thirty-six decans or decanates, each sign containing three decanates. But these must be considered later, for it will be first necessary to understand the nature of each of the twelve signs before we can comprehend their parts.

Taking the circle of the twelve signs and dividing them into angles or triplicities in a similar manner to that adopted in the last chapter, we shall find a deeper meaning attached to each sign than has hitherto been explained by astrological writers.

The main classes into which we shall divide the twelve signs will comprise the 'triplicity' and 'quality,' uniting as far as possible the quality belonging to each triplicity. In each of the four triplicities or trigons the three qualities are harmoniously blended, and hitherto no clear explanation has been given as to the nature of either triplicity or quality; and yet upon a correct understanding of these factors rests the fundamental basis of Natal Astrology.

---

* These are for the northern hemisphere.

The four triplicities are Fire, Air, Water and Earth—Spirit, Space, Time and Matter—and in this order we shall study them.

The three qualities are Cardinal or movable, Fixed, and Mutable or common.

These seven tendencies or powers are each governed by a lord, angel or Deva.

The four triplicities govern the four castes. They are also the indicators of the force, active and energetic, represented by the fiery signs; the quality of solidity and stability denoted by the earthy signs; powers of extension and expansion indicated by the airy signs: and finally the plasticity and mobility shown by the watery signs.

The three qualities or quadruplicities, cardinal, fixed and mutable, represent what are known by the Hindus as Rajas (activity), Tamas (stability) and Sattva (rhythm). They may be likened to the three phrenological temperaments, the motive, the vital, and the mental.*

These three qualities in terms of consciousness may be described as consciousness in general, instinctual consciousness, and self-consciousness; or again as activity (Rajas, cardinal), stability or will (Tamas, fixed), and wisdom (Sattva, mutable).

There are also three modes of motion that may be compared with the three qualities and three groups of signs : Translation, Rotation and Vibration. Of these, translatory motion means movement from one place to another, but the real idea underlying it is that the motion is continually tending to go onward without stopping, as indicated by Newton's law of motion ; and this pairs off with Rajas and the cardinal or movable signs. Rotary or vortical motion is the most stable of the three and compares with Tamas and fixed signs. Vibration, of course, is movement to and fro, like a pendulum or clarionet reed; Sattva, rhythm, mutable signs.

---

* The phrenological ' temperaments' are quoted by way of a guide as to what is meant, since the other words will convey little meaning to the reader at present. But they should not be taken in too rigid a sense, since different writers apply these terms somewhat differently. In fact, it would appear that some phrenologists, studying humanity from the 'life' side, see the three *qualities* in manifestation, and name them : others, studying humanity from the 'form' side, see the four *elements* represented, and name them. Unfortunately the latter class use the same terms as the former, plus a fourth ; and consequently, since each class is unconsciously viewing mankind from a different standpoint, considerable confusion arises. At least, this would seem to be the explanation of the discrepancies that prevail.

The Cardinal signs govern the head as a centre of consciousness in the same manner as the angles. They divide the circle of the zodiac into four quarters, answering to the four quadrants of the horoscope. Their chief characteristic is activity, which shows out in any department of life to which it may be directed, physical, emotional or intellectual. In each of these directions they are signs of external contact, bringing the native into continual touch with the outer world, and *vice versâ*, directing constant impacts from the environment upon the native. They bring the greatest amount of outward experience; they are the most diffuse and the least concentrated. In a way their influence may be regarded as continually passing from angle to angle or from cardinal point to cardinal point, across the four fields of their unceasing motion.

The Fixed signs are associated with the heart and desire. They contain the same amount of motion as the former signs, but tend to gather it into a fixed centre, and so make less outward show. Inertia and stability characterise them. They bring experiences evolving out of themselves, repetitions of the same conditions taking place over and over again until turned outward by the movable signs or modified and harmonised by the common.

The Mutable or common signs are associated in the animal body with limbs, lungs, and bowels. Just as vibratory motion passes from one point to another and back again, linking together the two extremes of its motion, so these signs stand for everything whether in the body or in consciousness that is intermediate between the head or intellect and the heart or will. They correspond, as we have seen, to cadent houses, which stand for means of communication, servants, agents, journeys, and for other matters in which the idea of an influence uniting two extremes can be plainly discerned. They are dual in nature and fluctuating in character, as are the men that are born of them.

These three qualities, operating through three groups of signs, correspond to the three phases of man's own being: will in motion, or action; feeling, emotion, passion, intuition, or instinct; and thought or reason. But this correspondence must not be applied in too hard and fast a manner, for each quality can operate on each plane. Thus we have the slow-moving will, the extremely active will, and the balanced or harmonised will; and so with the other two classes, the feelings and the thoughts.

The student will find it an interesting task to trace this symbology out in planetary and zodiacal positions. For instance, taking the Sun as will, its position in fixed, cardinal, or mutable signs indicates the three types just mentioned, and there is a good and a bad interpretation of each. Then the Moon may be taken as an indicator of the feelings, which would have three corresponding classes, each with a good and a bad side. Finally, the Ascendant may be taken as signifying the type of mental activity most natural to the body through which the soul acts while functioning in this world; and here would be the same three modes, according to the sign rising.

TABLE OF HOUSES, ELEMENTS, QUALITIES AND POLARITIES

House	Sign	Symbol	Element	Quality	Polarity
1.	ARIES	♈	Fire	Cardinal or movable	Male
2.	TAURUS	♉	Earth	Fixed	Female
3.	GEMINI	♊	Air	Mutable or common	Male
4.	CANCER	♋	Water	Cardinal or movable	Female
5.	LEO	♌	Fire	Fixed	Male
6.	VIRGO	♍	Earth	Mutable or common	Female
7.	LIBRA	♎	Air	Cardinal or movable	Male
8.	SCORPIO	♏	Water	Fixed	Female
9.	SAGITTARIUS	♐	Fire	Mutable or common	Male
10.	CAPRICORN	♑	Earth	Cardinal or movable	Female
11.	AQUARIUS	♒	Air	Fixed	Male
12.	PISCES	♓	Water	Mutable or common	Female

The column here for convenience headed Polarity refers to the division of the signs into two groups. The odd signs are all positive male day signs, and the even are negative female night signs. They refer to the duality shown everywhere in nature. Thus the words *positive, male,* and *day* convey precisely the same idea only expressed differently, and refer to the force or life side of things; while the words *negative, female,* and *night* signify the matter or form side.

We will now consider the signs separately, taking them in groups as just described.

THE FIERY SIGNS

I. ARIES, THE RAM   I.

First sign of the zodiac; first fiery sign; first cardinal sign

This sign represents undifferentiated consciousness. It is a chaotic and unorganised sign, in which impulse, spontaneity, and instinctiveness are marked features. Its vibrations are the keenest and most rapid, but without what may be called definite purpose, except towards impulsiveness and disruption. It signifies explosiveness, extravagance, and all kinds of excess. Its influence is more directly connected with the animal kingdom, in which life is full and without the directive power of fully awakened self-consciousness. It is a sign of force, combat, strength, energy and vigour. Its tendencies are always diffusive, periphrastic, superabundant, changeful and digressive. Its natives are enthusiastic, pioneering, ambitious, militant, enterprising, independent, assertive, and self-willed. The influence of Aries needs the steadying and controlling power of the fixed signs in order to make it practical and bring it within bounds. When blended in this way it is greatly improved. When combined with the common signs it is less practical and methodical than with the fixed but is very rapid, comprehensive, and subtle. Its most distinguising characteristic is *activity*, with a desire to be at the head, and to command. It is the sign of ambition, and projective energy.

V.   LEO, THE LION   V.

Fifth sign of the zodiac; second fiery sign; second fixed sign

This is the sign of the central will, the inner consciousness, beyond the brain mind. The life forces of the fiery triplicity starting in Aries are in this sign matured, directed, and controlled, and the chaos and disruption of the life energies brought into more harmony and order.

Stability of the life currents, and the transmutation of consciousness from head to heart, is shown in this sign; the work of nourishing, preserving and sustaining being one of the chief Leo characteristics. This is the sign of power, vitality and organising ability. It is the principal focus of the Prana or Solar Breath, hence gives the greatest stability of life and more 'Vril' or *Vim* than any other sign.

In contrasting the two fiery signs, Aries is the centre of heat and the creative forces, and Leo that of vitality and generation. Its most distinguishing characteristic is the desire to give, or to rule, with a fondness for lavish outlay, and the instinct of *loyalty*. It is the sign of organisation, and concentrative energy.

IX.   SAGITTARIUS, THE ARCHER   IX.

Ninth sign of the zodiac; third fiery sign; third common sign

This is pictorially represented by a man who is half horse shooting an arrow from his bow. This sign suggests the passage of consciousness from one state to another. It is a sign of vibration, transmutation, and interchange, on any plane to which its energies may be directed; and all the activities tabulated in the books as belonging to this sign and its corresponding house may easily be interpreted by applying this method. The diffusion and differentiation of Aries are unified and centralised in Leo, and transmuted into mental light in Sagittarius. Leo is the fifth zodiacal sign, and oriental works describe five 'Life Breaths' or currents of vitality flowing through the body, each one associated with a planet. Sagittarius is the ninth sign, and the nine Muses of the Greeks are so many modes of mind, the higher mind which manifests as genius and transmutes consciousness from the abstract mental state to the manifested physical brain, or which bridges over the gulf between life in the body and life out of the body. Hence this is the sign of the prophet. In its best interpretation, the activities of this sign are directed towards a higher state of existence, in which aspiration and devotion are the keynotes. The dual nature of the sign shows the objective and subjective halves of the intuitional consciousness, and between these two states the life forces are constantly vibrating. Its most distinguishing characteristic, perhaps, is its love of sport and travel, having the attribute of *sympathy*.

Aries is the architect, the pioneer, Leo the organiser, the vitaliser, Sagittarius the builder, the executant.

THE WATERY SIGNS

IV.   CANCER, THE CRAB   IV.

Fourth sign of the zodiac; first watery sign; second cardinal sign

Cancer is the fourth sign of the zodiac. It is symbolised by the crab, which can live equally as well in water as on land: it also goes through a metamorphosis in the earlier stages of its existence. This sign is at the head of what may be termed the psychic trinity, and to this psychic basis all expression of this sign may be related. It has the tendency to retain and hold the effect of the vibrations made upon it, and like a lake it reflects all that is mirrored upon it. This sign is concerned with sensation, and all consciousness that affects the feelings and emotions, from the most external physical sensation to that internal sensitiveness which is the first germ of the astral senses. It is a sign of receptivity and assimilation, and memory, in which impressions are retained, each wave creating a greater oscillation under the vibrations awakening the inner sensitiveness belonging to this sign. Its most distinguishing characteristics are its keen desire for sensation, power, or fame, and its power of *insistence*.

Of the three watery signs, Cancer presides over the ocean, Pisces over rivers, and Scorpio over lakes, ice, and stagnant waters. In another interpretation Cancer stands for the great restless stream of astral matter, formative and plastic, changeable as the Moon, the mother of all living, and Proserpine, the queen of the dead.

VIII.   SCORPIO, THE SCORPION   VIII.

Eighth sign of the zodiac; second watery sign; third fixed sign

Scorpio is the eighth sign of the zodiac. It is symbolised by the serpent or scorpion and sometimes by the eagle. This sign presides over all liquids of a thick and heavy nature, viscid oils, poisons, sewage, stagnant pools, chemicals, mineral waters, ice, etc. This will at once convey the idea that it is a sign in which liquids are solidified, the rotary motion connected with the fixing quality being very marked in this sign. The psychic germ born of the vibrations in Cancer is brought to the solid state corresponding to awakening consciousness, and thus all the feelings and sensations of the sign are made potent and persistent. Both vice and virtue are very pronounced in this sign and nothing with which Scorpio is actively concerned is weak or 'milk and water.'

Just as rotary motion makes firm and stable an otherwise unstable body, such as a top, so the kind of soul that belongs to Scorpio gathers its experiences into a very clearly marked kind of personality, fixed and emphatic, whether for good or for evil, strong and unyielding. Along the evil side there are seen pride, jealousy, malice, personal ambition, envy and hatred; and along the good side perseverance, courage, both physical and moral, and practical ability. When the inner psychic side is awakened it brings out in a very remarkable way the mystical, occult, and higher sensitiveness shown in the sign, and the soul becomes as keenly active on the virtue side as the personal is capable of being in the vice tendencies. Its most distinguishing characteristic is intensity, or, as it might be put, 'passionateness.'

Cancer as the head of this triplicity sets quivering in a semi-conscious manner the sensations that are to be constantly repeated and made stable in Scorpio, therefore, in common with the central or fixed sign in each triplicity this is one of the critical signs, in which either will or desire is the strongest element.

XII.   PISCES, THE FISHES   XII.

Twelfth sign of the zodiac; third watery sign; fourth mutable sign

Pisces is the twelfth sign of the zodiac. It is symbolised by two fishes swimming in diverse directions. This sign may be compared to the Waters of Lethe, or oblivion. As a sign of the transitory order it denotes the transference of consciousness once again to the physical body, or—to higher planes of being. It is the end of the watery signs and represents the ocean in connection with the watery element to which it belongs. This sign is the 'Universal Solvent.' In Cancer sensation and feeling are awakened; in Scorpio they are concentrated and intensified; and in Pisces all is turned into emotion, which like the ocean is deep, silent, and inexpressible, except in what may be called universal love and sympathy. As the feet are lifted from the ground, so is the emotion denoted by Pisces lifted from the earthy taint and made more universal. Some idea of the nature of this sign may be gathered from the fact that Pisces is a sign concerned with hospitals and philanthropic institutions, wherein sympathy and benevolence are expressed.

The dual nature of the sign shows us what we might expect, namely, that failure to reach the higher sympathies produces emotional derelicts and those whose psychic nature attracts the lowest entities and thus opens the way to obsession, melancholia and hopeless despondency. It denotes either passive or active sympathy, a negative and mediumistic tendency to fruitless and wasted emotion, or a positive, active sympathy, the ideal of which is conveyed in the sentence 'Love your neighbour as yourself,' and if asked Why? the answer would be: 'Because he is yourself.' Its most distinguishing characteristic is *permeability*.

THE AIRY SIGNS

VII.   LIBRA, THE BALANCE   VII.

Seventh sign of the zodiac; second airy sign; third cardinal sign

Libra is the seventh sign of the zodiac. It is symbolised by a pair of scales or the balance. It is the first of the extensive or expansive signs, vibratory in its action, and volatile or diffusive in its nature. Like all the cardinal signs it marks the beginning of any tendency to vibrate in a particular manner. The fiery signs are connected with energy, the watery signs with mobility and sensation, the airy signs with expansion and mentality. The airy signs are distinctly connected with mind and mental experiences, and the human tendencies apart from the animal are the marked features of all expressions from this triplicity. The sign Libra separates by its mode of motion the mind from the senses, and balances the one against the other, the vibrations between the two tending to equalise and balance the consciousness in this direction. It is also the sign in which neither higher nor lower mind predominates, the subjective and objective mind being equalised and causing the mind to tend more toward comparison and justice than toward any definite bias. Its most distinguishing characteristic is conjugality or 'unifiableness' usually manifesting as the desire to please, or in its highest aspect as *devotion*.

XI.   AQUARIUS, THE MAN   XI.

Eleventh sign of the zodiac; third airy sign; fourth fixed sign

Aquarius is the eleventh sign of the zodiac. It is symbolised by 'The Man,' who is pictorially represented as pouring water from a vase on the earth. As a fixed air sign it represents concentration of mind and the attempt to fix the mental vibrations received through Libra. The human and mental nature of this airy sign is shown by the

symbol 'Man,' Sanskrit *man*—to think.   In the order of the zodiac it
shows that point where the circle is left for the spiral and man begins
his mental ascent, having attained to that stability which the fixed
quality produces.   The inertia of this sign is, at our present stage of
evolution, more in evidence than the stable and permanent expression
of the man who has controlled the lower nature ready for the higher
self-conscious ascent into the entirely human conditions.   The most
characteristic feature of Aquarius is its love of *human nature* ; and there
is always some attempt to blend art and science in this sign.   As the
last of the fixed signs it has been symbolised by two serpents, the one
the serpent of wisdom and the other the old Adam or serpent of the
earth.   In this symbology lies the mystery of human destiny.

III.   GEMINI, THE TWINS   III.

Third sign of the zodiac ; first airy sign ; first mutable sign

Gemini is the third sign of the zodiac.   It is symbolised by the
twins, which signifies its dualistic nature.   Being an airy sign it is
connected with a mental expression of the zodiac, and through its
mutable nature we see the transference from one state of mind or
consciousness to another, the objective or concrete to the subjective
and abstract, and *vice versa*.   It is often symbolised as two upright
columns, denoting the gateway to knowledge and the hall of learning.
In its objective expression it denotes material education and brain
intellect ; subjectively it is concerned with higher thought and sometimes the super-conscious mind.   In its esoteric symbology it is represented by two apes, one of which is the chattering ape and imitator,
the other the divine ape in whom thought is more superhuman and
transferred from the concrete to the sublime and transcendental ; or,
in other words, the ordinary common worldly intellect is shown, and
also the originality of genius in which mind is working direct from the
mental plane.   The most characteristic feature of Gemini is its *duality*,
shown in a love of quick alternations from grave to gay, like a child.
In the zodiac Aquarius may be termed the Father-Man, Libra the
Mother-Woman, and Gemini the Child.

THE EARTHY SIGNS

X.   CAPRICORN, THE GOAT   X.

Tenth sign of the zodiac; third earthy sign; fourth cardinal sign

Capricorn is the tenth sign of the zodiac. It is symbolised by the goat, and sometimes by the crocodile. The vibrations connected with this cardinal sign are decidedly physical, and denote the awakening of physical consciousness through ambition and temporal power. The goat is a mountain climber, and as the apex of the earthy triangle the influence of Capricorn is strongest on the physical plane, therefore the tendency will be to bring out all practical and material experiences, which will become manifested in the outer world of action through the vibrations of this sign. It has both a benefic and malefic aspect, and can only be truly interpreted by those who see the hidden wisdom concealed in mythology and exoteric symbolism. The goat is an expression of the external nature of Capricorn, and the crocodile, which can live as well in water as on land, symbolises the internal nature of this sign. This sign marks the beginning of practical experiences and brings all things to a natural and matter-of-fact standpoint. The most characteristic feature of Capricorn is its instinct for business and politics --in fact for all things which have to do with the world at large. Its watchword is *definition*. In its highest sense it is ideals made practical.

II.   TAURUS, THE BULL   II.

Second sign of the zodiac; first earthy sign; first fixed sign

Taurus is the second sign of the zodiac. It is symbolised by the bull. It belongs to the earthy triplicity and is rotary in its mode of motion. It is a sign giving solidity and strength to the physical group of signs. The practical aims and ambitions of Capricorn are gathered up and unified in Taurus, bringing gain from labour and the fruit of action. In this sign great powers of retention, conservation, secretiveness and concentration are exhibited, the power to retain and hold being a marked feature of the sign. Of all the fixed signs, Taurus is the most retentive, the life forces being held by matter more securely than in any other sign, and speech is often the only expression the life forces can make through this sign. The most characteristic feature of this sign is its instinct for finance, and its watchword is *practicalness*. It is the sign of concentrated physical energy and its highest expression is found in song and praise, as the result of concentrated emotion. The true symbol of Taurus appears to be a serpent coiled in a circle; much latent energy and captive power is indicated by this symbol.

VI. VIRGO, THE VIRGIN VI.

Sixth sign; second earthy sign; second mutable sign

Virgo is the sixth sign of the zodiac. It is symbolised by a virgin, and sometimes pictorially represented by three ears of corn. This sign denotes the ultimate perfection of the physical experiences, which are translated and transformed into self-consciousness in common with all the mutable signs. Symbolised by the virgin, it explains the necessity of physical purity to achieve the self-consciousness connected with the sign. This is the sign of Service, the cream of Capricorn and Taurus, and the outcome of industry and labour. It is a sign connected with criticism and analysis, to finally bring forth discrimination and wisdom. When failure to bring forth the fruit of the consciousness indicated by the physical signs occurs, then subservience and weakness (Virgo), ambition and selfishness (Capricorn), or sloth and obstinacy (Taurus), may result. The discrimination of Virgo, in its best aspect, comes from mental sympathy; the good and the true within recognising the same without. This, in the undeveloped soul, may show as unintelligent repetition or servile response, the automatic echoing of good and evil, false and true alike, according to the fashion of the day or the impress of a stronger personality. One of the most characteristic features of Virgo among the cultivated types is its love for biographical details and statistics, and its tendency to quote authorities. A typical Virgo woman once wrote that her favourite recreations were 'blue books and biographies.'

The following table explains the nature of each of the signs,

Sign.	Symbol.	Characteristic.	Quality.	Element.	Description.	Ruler.
LIBRA	♎	Perception .	Cardinal .	Air .	The Balance .	♀
GEMINI	♊	Reason .	Mutable .	Air .	The Twins .	☿
AQUARIUS	♒	Memory .	Fixed .	Air .	The Man .	♄
ARIES	♈	Intuition .	Cardinal .	Fire .	The Ram .	♂
SAGITTARIUS	♐	Introspection .	Mutable .	Fire .	The Centaur .	♃
LEO	♌	Faith .	Fixed .	Fire .	The Lion .	☉
CANCER	♋	Feeling .	Cardinal .	Water .	The Crab .	☽
PISCES	♓	Emotion .	Mutable .	Water .	The Fishes .	♃
SCORPIO	♏	Attachment .	Fixed .	Water .	The Scorpion .	♂
CAPRICORN	♑	Absorbtion .	Cardinal .	Earth .	The Goat .	♄
VIRGO	♍	Circulation .	Mutable .	Earth .	The Virgin .	☿
TAURUS	♉	Secretion .	Fixed .	Earth .	The Bull .	♀

CHAPTER III

The Luminaries and the Planets

THE houses, or divisions, of a horoscope we compared to vessels, and the signs of the zodiac to their contents, giving colour and substance to each house. Metaphorically speaking, the planets in a similar manner give the aroma and quality to the whole.

Each house and each sign has a lord or ruler in the planet governing that house or sign, but the planets have more definite relationship to the signs than to the houses. So that the sign specially related to any planet is termed the 'house' of that planet, this not referring to the mundane circle but to the zodiac. Dividing the twelve signs into pairs one half becomes lunar and the other solar, each planet having one station in both divisions. Again each planet is weak in certain signs and powerful in others.

Besides the two luminaries, the Sun and Moon, there are seven planets :—Uranus, ♅ ; Mercury, ☿ ; Venus, ♀ ; Saturn, ♄ ; Mars, ♂ ; Jupiter, ♃ ; Neptune, ♆. The following table of signs and rulers shows also planets specially powerful and weak in each sign.

		LUNAR				SOLAR		
Weak	Strong	Exalted	Sign	Ruler	Sign	Exalted	Strong	Weak
♄	☿	♃ 15°	♋... ☽	☉	...♌	—	♂	♄
♃	♄	♌ 3°	II... ☿		...♍	☿ 15°	♄	♃
♂	♃	☽ 3°	♉... ♀		...♎	♄ 21°	♃	♂
♀	♃	☉ 19°	♈... ♂		...♏	—	☉	♀
☿	♆	♀ 27°	♓... ♃		...♐	♉ 3°	♀	☿
☉	♅	—	♒... ♄		...♑	♂ 28°	☿	☽

No signs have been allotted to either ♅ or ♆ as houses, but for the present they may be taken as substitutes for the Sun and Moon.

A planet has power in its own house, and in certain houses has a
stronger influence for good or ill, also a weaker influence in other signs.
The 'detriment' of a planet is the sign opposite to its own 'house';
its 'fall' is the opposite degree to its 'exaltation.'

In the column which is headed 'exalted' the number of degrees
shown indicates the particular degree at which the planet receives
exaltation. The true sense of the term 'exaltation' cannot at present be explained, but there can be no question that planets in
their exaltation signs do exert a more refined and a more powerful
influence than elsewhere. As for the exaltation degrees, they have
been handed down by tradition, and since whenever such tradition has
been traced back to its source, it is discovered to be founded upon a
truth in nature, we shall do well to accept these degrees with respect,
and endeavour if we can to penetrate the reason the ancients had in so
fixing them. Thus, the exaltation degree of the Sun ♈ 19° is very
close to, and perhaps identical with, the commencement of the Zodiac of
the Constellations.

The planets are the vitalising centres in each nativity, therefore it
is necessary to know the special influence of each planet and the nature
of their vibrations in each sign and house. When we speak of a planet's
influence, it is the vibration coming from the spirit and life of the planet
with which we are concerned, and not the physical medium through
which it is acting, the physical planet being useful only as a means by
which we may locate its position for astrological purposes. The special
influence coming through each planet has been described by ancient
astrologers who were evidently taught by those who knew, for as we
have just hinted, modern students have found by study and practice that
in the main, all that has been stated by their predecessors is true, with
regard to the nature of each planet. A few students, looking more
deeply into the esoteric side of the study, have discovered that there are
higher vibrations than those generally attributed to the influence of the
planets, but the failure of those coming under any particular planet to
respond to these higher vibrations has caused this side of the study to be
neglected. It seems incredible to those who study Astrology in the light
of philosophy that any one should be found capable of believing that
planetary influence emanates from the visible physical heavenly bodies
only, or that a materialistic explanation could ever be fully explanatory

of the multitudes of facts recorded in the experience of every astrologer. That there is a physical influence there is no need to deny, although we must also remember that no scientific explanation of it is yet forthcoming.[1] But in Astrology we have to step beyond the threshold of the physical universe and recognise the reality of that indwelling spiritual life and consciousness of which visible phenomena are merely outward manifestations, whether in the planet or the atom. We must study the subject from the philosophical and religious standpoint, and to do this with any degree of satisfaction the whole subject must be approached with a feeling of reverence and a true sense of humility.

THE SUN, we are taught by those who are seeking the Path of Wisdom, is the body of *God*, the *Logos* of this solar system, through which He gives His Love, Light and Life.

In astrologic study THE SUN gives to every living organism its *Prâna*, or life and heat, each individual *specialising* his own store from the cosmic *Prâna*.   Every living thing is plunged into a great ocean of life— God's life ; and every organism, whether great or small, appropriates to itself some of this universal life which is ever flowing from the Sun, the vehicle through which the Solar Logos is manifesting.

THE SUN, giving life, light and heat to the world, stands in each nativity as the symbol of vitality and activity, mind and intellect, love and feeling. In one word it represents the centre of each separate individual character as the sum total of himself, by absorbing into himself as much of the influence of the solar rays and the planetary vibrations as possible during his previous physical manifestations. THE MOON acts as the vehicle, or link of communication between the Sun and each living thing. In Astrology the Moon is the representation of the Personality, the portion of the individual that is manifested during the one life period, and as such the Moon's position and aspects become the most important when judging a nativity. If the Moon has no aspect whatever with the Sun, or is in much affliction with this luminary, then the life forces do not flow evenly, the mentality is not so sharp and clear, and the feelings are apt to be distorted ; but the principal effect of the affliction is to hinder the flow of the life-current and thus affect the

---

[1] Since the first Edition of this work was published, in 1903, the scientific basis of Astrology has been definitely laid down. Those who wish to enquire further into the matter are referred to *The Foundations of Physical Astrology* by G. E. Sutcliffe, member of the Leeds Astronomical Society.

general health. These two centres formed by the Sun and Moon
become very important, the Sun lighting the mind by day, and the
Moon, receiving the borrowed light of the Sun, illuminating by night.
The permanent and vital conditions of each life are denoted by the Sun,
and the fleeting and impermanent personal conditions are indicated by
the Moon, this latter luminary thus representing the focussing point of
a nativity. The five planets, Mercury, Venus, Mars, Jupiter, and
Saturn, act in the ordinary human being more or less through the
five senses. Uranus and Neptune, representing the higher octaves,
are at present not quite so much in evidence, being more concerned with
evolution at a later stage.

The planetary vibrations are allied to the senses approximately as
follows : MERCURY, sight; VENUS, touch; MARS, taste; JUPITER, smell;
SATURN, hearing; URANUS governs the inner sight (clairvoyance), and
NEPTUNE, inner touch (psychometry). It is probable that Vulcan, a
planet to be rediscovered at a future date, governs the inner hearing
(clairaudience).

As concrete representatives of the Sun and Moon in the lower world
SATURN and MARS become what have been termed 'malefic planets.'
They are the disseminators of what we consider evil thoughout the
world, and Astrology can throw considerable light upon this so-called
evil that abounds, for it is through the individual and personal manifestation of the two great forces in nature known as heat and cold, motion
and inertia, that we see the abuse of these two useful states or conditions
of matter. The wise astrologer does not recognise evil as a permanent
factor in any nativity, but fully understands how the attitude of the mind
and feeling may produce the abuse of any special planetary vibration,
which will then become vice and misfortune, pain and disease.

If the natures of the two 'malefic' planets are carefully studied from
a philosophic point of view, their exact value in each nativity will be
much more clearly understood.

MARS is the planet of focussed force, and out-going impulse. Physical
heat and motion are more under the direct influence of Mars than any
other planet. He governs the sense of taste in its widest application.
All the animal propensities, sensations, passions, desires and appetites
come under the vibration of Mars. Long and careful study and a

considerable amount of first hand experience which has been tabulated
for many years have convinced the author that Mars is the ruler over the
animal nature in man ; and the task set for humanity is not only that of
subjecting, ruling and controlling the animal nature, but also its transmutation into a higher force than that which ministers to the animal
soul.

There is an occult teaching that the whole of the animal kingdom is
under the guidance of one Group Soul, and as each animal becomes
specialised, and in time is sufficiently individualised to break away from
the Group Soul, it takes with it into the human kingdom its special
nature and peculiar characteristics as an animal ; and its evolution at the
stage of either a savage or a more highly evolved but still very young
ego is also under the influence of the planet Mars, more or less, until the
vibrations from the other planets form a greater attraction than the plane
of Mars and the purely animal nature.   It is when the war between the
animal and the God begins that the human being suffers, and the evil of
Mars through passion and the rebellious senses is recognised.   Animals
in their natural state are not evil, but when the struggle between will
and desire begins, and the personal man follows the blind impulse of his
senses, then Mars becomes truly malefic.

This requires very little demonstration, for when the animal has full
sway man becomes brutal, savage and violent, and when the gratification
of the sensational and selfish desires is the strongest incentive to action,
the animal in man, to obtain its object, becomes cruel and uncontrolled.
It is only when the God in man grows stronger that the animal is held in
check, trained and finally transcended.   Force and energy are at all
times necessary on the physical plane, and without the martial influence
humanity would be tame and inactive, therefore *use* will make the
vibrations of Mars as beneficial as *abuse* will make them evil.   Each
planet portrays a particular virtue, and that of Mars, strength, acts
more especially through the muscular system ; and we can easily see
that a good muscular system is necessary for any great display of
physical strength and energy.

Psychologically, the influence of the planet Mars is greater and
more potent through the psychic nature, acting more directly upon
the sensational and emotional nature.   When acting physically the
Solar influence also is necessary to give vitality and full life to the
whole system, but psychically the force of Mars acts directly without the

aid of the solar rays. It will be seen by the foregoing how Mars will become an evil influence in any nativity where the animal side is uncontrolled. Misfortune and disaster, accident and fever, will be the result of over-excitement, impulse, rashness and over-indulgence in sensation. In fact, to control the animal passions and appetites is to control and guide the vibrations coming from the planet Mars. Force will have its outlet in some form or other, and a man may use his forces and energy either to slay his fellows, or to save them, to become a swashbuckler, or a hero; or he may use it as an energy socially and mentally.

The strength absorbed from the planet Mars will do much to improve an otherwise weak nativity, and in no position in a horoscope can Mars be said to be an evil influence unless the nature is wholly depraved. Men who have strong and personal natures will, by transmuting the force and turning the direction of the currents, become ambitious and energetic and thus raise themselves to a higher state of refinement and progress. Knowledge of the nature and influence of Mars, the position by house and sign and the aspects, will inform the student of the direction in which the force is working; this will be illustrated later.

The next so-called evil planet is SATURN. The nature and influence of this planet is cold and binding, exactly opposite to that of the fiery Mars. Let us imagine that in the process of separation from the block essence of the Group Soul, the individualised animal, which consists of a vaporous mass of matter, is crystallised or condensed and enclosed in a film which comes directly under the vibrations of Saturn. The contents of this film impregnated by the solar ray will have all the latent qualities of the martial force, but now under certain limitations and restrictions and made the vehicle upon which the higher forces are to play. Being impregnated with the divine spark, which is now in germ, it will unfold all the latent potentialities of the imprisoned God within, through time and space, until it is strong enough to burst through the shell or body in which it was individualised.

The vibrations from Mars will ever force onward impulsively and blindly, but the vibrations from Saturn will be continuously binding and limiting. It can be seen that these two extremes of heat and cold, life and form, will be inimical to each other until the life is controlled by the form and the form expanded by the life and balance obtained as a result of the struggle between the two.   In the early stages of the contest the life will be merely conscious, but gradually *self*-consciousness will result from the limitations imposed upon the life by the form.

Saturn governs the sense of hearing, a negative or receptive sense. The listener suggests patience, forbearance, silence and caution.   The planetary vibration of Saturn restricts, limits, crystallises and binds everything; holding, restraining, fashioning and solidifying all that comes under its sphere of influence.   Sat-urn is, figuratively speaking, the *urn* that holds the *Sat*.   This Sanskrit word *Sat* signifies 'that one ever-present reality in the infinite world; the divine essence which *is*, but cannot be said to exist.'   In this sense Saturn governs the encircling limit of the consciousness, the 'ring pass not' for each individual in manifestation.

In life, impulse and outrush—ever attracted by the sensations and feelings towards external objects—are checked and restrained by the nature of the form which limits them.   It is therefore the vibrations of Saturn that cause each human personality to know itself as a separate, distinct and self-conscious entity.   Saturn, as ruler of the personal ego, is the planet of fate, for it represents the personal Will, the lower brain-mind, and is practically the ego in manifestation in the physical world, and also the next world to it, which is concerned with the state of the consciousness immediately after death.   In these two worlds Saturn and Mars have the greatest power, for Mars is concerned with all the animal tendencies and Saturn directly with the animal-human soul.

The highest states signified by the vibrations of Saturn in the physical world are physical purity and justice, which produce the virtues of chastity, economy, thrift, industry, perseverance, prudence, veneration, and love of truth.   When the vibrations of Saturn are perverted through the personality, miserliness, meanness, envy, covetousness and extreme selfishness result.

The two benefic planets are VENUS and JUPITER.   Venus and Jupiter are the respective counterparts of Mars and Saturn, and they should always be considered in nativities as such.   All the martial influence, giving force, energy and strength, is eventually to be transmuted into sympathy, gentleness and charity.   The only real difference between these two planets, Mars and Venus, arises from the special vibrations.   Mars is attracted from without through desire and impulse. Venus causes all action to come from within, and instead of feeling rushing outwards to objects and becoming captive to externals, it moves from within through the ego's direct intuitive power.   The vibrations of Venus directly affect the higher part of the nature through the human soul and higher mind.   In the physical world Venus presides over the sense of touch, which sense is not related to one special part of the body, but the whole.   All the distinctly human and refining qualities come under the influence of Venus, the whole of the tendencies of this planet's vibration being to centralise and draw in from the objective world the experience necessary to awaken the inner and more subjective centres of consciousness.   Venus is on the side of Will and the Immortal Trinity, and all vibrations that are assimilated are made permanent soul possessions.   Mars on the contrary is on the side of the Mortal and Impermanent—that is, until the force is turned inward, when it passes into the ray of Venus.   Venus preserves, nourishes, rebuilds, and all who come fully under the influence of this planet are capable of living purely and appreciating beauty and goodness to the full.   It will be necessary to avoid mistaking the vibrations of Mars for those of Venus, also to know which of these two planets has the stronger influence in each nativity.   Mars is the planet of physical generation and its influence is always acting through the senses. Venus is the planet of creation, ever tending to act through the Soul and not the senses.   The love shown by Venus always sanctifies and makes for harmony through conjugality, friendship and soul union. Mars denotes feeling that is personal and selfish, and Venus that which is impersonal and unselfish.   The influence of Mars when perverted makes men seek to injure, and never allows them to forget the value of personal importance.   Venus injures none, and those coming directly under its vibration sink the personal element in love for others, through pure love and true sympathy.   The adverse influence of Mars causes men to insult and patronise, while that of Venus always makes for protection and true charity.

In some mysterious manner a ray from Venus touched the life of the animal on its first separation from the group soul.   The 'Sons of Mind' who came from the planet Venus gave to infant humanity its first germ of that true mind which is in its essence immortal, and through this the period of man's evolution was considerably shortened, for by receiving this divine spark the seed of the human soul was implanted in the animal man, who would otherwise have spent countless ages in acquiring that which these beneficent beings through their love and compassion gave to humanity.

JUPITER is termed the Greater Fortune. Its vibrations are concerned with the form side of manifestation and like Saturn it symbolises the vehicle which holds the life. St Paul has stated that we have a terrestrial body and a celestial body. Jupiter's influence in the subjective world is just as important as that of Saturn's influence objectively, but there is a wide difference between the effects of their vibrations. Saturn contracts and acts microscopically. Jupiter expands and has no limit to its expansion. Mind and feeling are condensed and focussed in the limiting form of Saturn, and expanded, broadened, and extended through the ever-increasing form of Jupiter. In these two extremes we have all the elements of pleasure and pain, joy and sorrow, increase and decrease, bondage and freedom, expansion and contraction. The life is evolving as well as the forms, and the contraction and expansion are necessary to harden and soften and finally temper the consciousness of the evolving ego. The good fortune under the influence of Jupiter acts from the subjective world by way of the accumulated experiences, the essence or cream of which is under the guiding influence of this planet.

In the physical world Jupiter governs the sense of smell. Scent pervades the atmosphere and is dispersed through it, being expansive, as is the influence of the planet presiding over it.

The whole of our present moral and social age is more directly under Jupiter's influence. The success promised by Jupiter may be traced to the best side of the character, wherein hope and the power to expand and enlarge are prominent. Saturn gives financial gain and prosperity through economy, thrift, perseverance, and industry, but Jupiter when concerned with financial success brings gain through the social life, and those under the most favourable influence of Jupiter can accomplish more in one day than the ordinary Saturnine man could achieve in a year.

Sooner or later it must be realised that character is destiny. That is why so much stress is always laid upon the fact that the nativity must be fully understood before 'directions' can be interpreted. We each bring our character with us as a result of past efforts, aspirations and opportunity. The sum total of our past is probably indicated by the planet Jupiter. Each individual is encircled by an aura, the boundary of which comes directly under the vibration of Jupiter. - We expand and increase the size and quality of that aura during each earth life, and, whether in objective manifestation on the physical world or in heaven, in the subjective worlds, this aura is our own and contains our whole history, the result of the past and the possibilities of the future ; in this sense Jupiter is the ruler over the celestial and immortal body.

MERCURY is known as the 'convertible' planet. It is neither positive nor negative, but *both*. It is the planet of the adept, being the planet of adaptation in the widest sense of the word. Mercury is termed the Winged Messenger of the Gods, and takes upon himself the vibrations of all the other planets. It is, in one word, the planet of *Reason*. In the physical world Mercury governs the sense of seeing. It has also a very close relationship with the mind. The four planets we have been dealing with are each more or less in affinity with either the *life* or the *form*, but Mercury has an influence over both. It has also a subjective as well as an objective influence, and all planets may be said to be powerful or weak, according to the strength of Mercury. Mercury, accompanying the soul into Hades, represents the silver thread of memory, upon which are strung the beads which represent the personalities of its earth lives. In every nativity Mercury will represent the ego in physical manifestation, the actor, playing the part allotted to him during each separate earthly existence ; and at the close of each life Mercury represents the knowledge gained, as Memory, the cream of which is rendered a permanent possession of the ego as Wisdom.

The planet URANUS has less influence at the present day than any other planet except Neptune. It is the planet of the coming race, for its vibrations will then be more important than to-day. It is thought by the author to represent the fully individualised Ego, and as such is the houseless wanderer half-way between earth and heaven. Its vibrations are different from those of any other planet, governing all things that are not bound by convention or limited entirely to the form side of things to such an extent as to make the form more important than the life. It appears to govern all things that are original, eccentric, and free to act apart from any conventional groove or accepted custom. It has been found to exercise the greatest influence for good over advanced thinkers —those who act independently, and from within more than from without. It seems to have little or no effect upon those who are bound or limited by opinion or custom, and to come fully under its influence the limitations of Saturn must have been passed and the form side of life conquered more or less.   No definite or precise rules can be laid down with regard to Uranus; the most elaborate plans and calculations may be upset in an instant of time by the vibrations of this planet.   Sudden and un-expected events will occur, and act in an almost unknowable manner, which makes it impossible to judge accurately exactly what will happen under his vibrations.   It is now certain that the ancients knew of the planet Uranus, but only those who were as far removed from the ordinary humanity as the poles came under its   fluence, and that for an occult and esoteric reason that cannot be explained at present.

In the outer world of human activities Uranus appears now to be exercising more sway.   Electrical and mechanical enterprises and inventions of all kinds, railways, educational 'short cuts,' index systems, the comparative study of religions, etc., etc., are all more or less under his direct influence and illustrate his peculiar mission—to cause man to seek by the destruction of a *lesser* form the added life and intelligence dwelling in the higher form of which that lesser form was an integral though separated part; in short, regeneration as distinguished from generation.

NEPTUNE, the last discovered planet, has, on the whole, but a faint influence upon our earth and its inhabitants.   The undeveloped psychic who is unable to control the mediumistic tendencies induced from with-out, and those who are easily obsessed or of very weak will, always subject to changing impressions, will in one sense come under Neptune as will also those who are very highly advanced psychically.   Experience tends to prove that the influence of an afflicted Neptune as a rule is undesirable.   There is a possibility of there being such a thing as a lost personality, metaphorically speaking, and such may be in some peculiar manner under this influence.   Depravity and exceptional immorality seem to be under the influence of Neptune, but many years must elapse before sufficient tabulation is made to warrant a reliable opinion concerning Neptune's vibrations.

Much fuller information on these and the other planets will be found in the next volume of this series, where a separate chapter is devoted to each.   The beginner, however, will do well to leave these until he arrives at the book in the natural course of his studies; otherwise, he will find himself bewildered with a multitude of ideas for which he has not yet prepared due receptacles. What has been given above is *quite sufficient* at his present stage, and will furnish him with clear fundamental ideas regarding the natures of the planets, ideas which will form a substantial foundation upon which he can subsequently erect any superstructure which the processes of his thought, aided by further reading, and matured by his own experience and observation, may incline him to devise.

To those who have carefully studied the series of Introductory Manuals issued by the Author, this caution will not, of course, apply, as they will (or should) have already obtained a clear outline idea of the essential natures of the planets.

CHAPTER IV

In the first volume of this series, *Astrology for All*, Chapter VII, a list was given of the aspects formed between the heavenly bodies as they pass along the zodiac, and for convenience sake this list may here be repeated in the following form :—

Symbol	Name	Distance	Nature
☌	Conjunction	0° or 360°	Variable
⋎	Semi-sextile	30°	Feebly good
∠	Semi-square	45°	Somewhat evil
✳	Sextile	60°	Good
□	Square (or Quadrate)	90°	Evil
△	Trine	120°	Good
⬐	Sesquiquadrate	135°	Somewhat evil
⟇	Quincunx	150°	Feebly evil
☍	Opposition	180°	Evil

The formation of these aspects will be made clear to the mind by the following illustration. At the time of the New Moon, the Moon and Sun are in conjunction, *i.e.*, they occupy the same degree of the zodiac, but as the Moon moves faster than the Sun, they very soon separate, and in fact two-and-a-half days later the Moon is 30° further on in the zodiac than the Sun is, and five days later 60° further on; hence they are said to be respectively in 'semi-sextile' and in 'sextile' to each other at these dates. Seven days after the New Moon they are 90° apart or in 'square' to each other, this being the date of the First Quarter. Ten days after, they are in 'trine,' and when half a month has elapsed we have the Full Moon, which means that the Moon is opposite to the Sun, 180° away, or in 'opposition' to the Sun. After that, the aspects given in the above list are re-formed in the reverse order, namely, ⟇ ⬐ △ □ ✳ ∠ ⋎, until 30 days from our starting point we have the Sun and Moon again in conjunction, or, a *New Moon*. In just the same way, we find a similar cycle of aspects occurring between any two planets, the faster of the two gradually passing from the conjunction to the square of the other, thence to the opposition, and again to the conjunction once more; in fact the two series of events are precisely analogous, though we must not forget that the Moon or a planet may be in square to the Sun, or to some other planet, at the same time that it is in trine to a third and in sesquiquadrate to a fourth.

To the aspects just enumerated may be added the Parallel of Declination, when the two bodies are the same distance, whether north or south, from the equator; its nature is variable, like the conjunction. The following minor aspects are taken into account by some astrologers, but in reality their influence, if they have any, is so slight as to be negligeable.

Semi-decile, 18°   Decile, 36°   Quintile, 72°   Biquintile, 144°

Those who pay attention to them believe them to be slightly good; the ancient astrologers ignored them, and the moderns may safely do the same. Omitting these, it will be seen that the table of aspects may be divided into three sections, the good, the evil, and the variable. Let us consider the latter first.

Conjunction is when two heavenly bodies are together at the same point of the zodiac. It therefore stands, symbolically if not practically, for union, synthesis, the blending of two in one. What effect the union will have depends upon the nature of the combined planets. When two forces meet, the resultant varies according to the angle between them and the strength of each force. When two notes are sounded together upon a musical instrument, the resulting sound depends upon whether the two sets of vibrations harmonise or not. And so with planetary conjunctions. If we suppose the planets to transmit their influence by means of vibrations sent through the subtle ethers of the solar system, the effects detected by the astrologer in a horoscope will vary according to whether the waves of the one supplement or contradict those of the other.

Planets, as we know, may be divided for convenience into three classes; first those which are in the main benefic—Jupiter and Venus; second, those which are very often malefic, more or less—Mars, Saturn, Uranus, and Neptune; third, those which may be described as more or less neutral and variable -Sun, Moon, and Mercury. A benefic planet is one the influence of which harmonises and blends sympathetically with our own, the Earth. Jupiter and Venus both stand, at least in relation to our humanity, for growth, increase, harmony, balance, the avoidance of extremes; while the so-called malefics bring about exactly those extremes which it is desirable to avoid; at least that is their effect when considered as malefics, although as we have seen in a previous chapter there are various ways of interpreting planetary influence. Broadly speaking, the conjunction of a neutral planet with a benefic is good and tends to harmony both in terms of fate and of character. The conjunction of a neutral planet with a malefic is exactly the reverse: Mars tending to extremes of heat, disintegration, and impulse, Saturn to coldness, selfishness, devitalisation, and isolation; Uranus being moderately Saturnian in its degree of cold, with an added tendency to suddenness and reversal, while Neptune along with some sensitiveness and intuition gives sensuousness and instability. The conjunction of one benefic and one malefic is neither wholly good nor wholly evil, but strikes a mean between the two; and that of two benefics or two malefics is neither so good nor so bad as might be expected.

To take an illustration, when Mars is in conjunction with Saturn the result should, theoretically, be a harmonious unity, but really is not so, for the combination is in effect not unlike the influence of the planet Uranus in some respects. If we look upon Mars as heat and Saturn as cold, the effect upon the weather is less cold than Saturn and less hot than Mars, and to this extent the two may be regarded as modifying one another. But in spite of this they do not blend or unify; they act irregularly as if now one and now the other had obtained control, reminding one of a gusty and chilly day with spells of heat at intervals.

In terms of character the result is similar. If we look upon Saturn as caution and Mars as boldness the result is not that prudent balance of judgment which is to be desired: to some extent the caution is modified and the boldness restrained, but now and again one or the other will operate with an irregular vigour all the greater for having been held back. If the conjunction takes place in one of the houses of Mars or Saturn the effect is very much more harmonious.

Again, if we take Mars as the senses and Venus as the soul, when they are in conjunction and Venus is the stronger by sign, as in the earthly or airy triplicity, the soul will control and refine the senses and will gain in feeling and emotion; but if they are in a fiery or watery sign there will be more danger of the senses and passions enslaving the soul.   Jupiter may be taken as the higher mind, sympathy, benevolence, and growth; Saturn as the lower mind, separateness, caution, and limitation; and if these are in conjunction in the watery or fiery triplicity, which strengthens Jupiter's influence, the former characteristics will overpower the latter and will gain by the process in definiteness, practical application, method, perseverance, and will power; while if Saturn is the stronger through being placed in the airy or earthy triplicity, the combination will show less of the elasticity and expansiveness of Jupiter and more of the rigidity and contraction of Saturn.

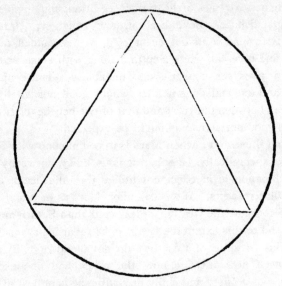

DIAGRAM No. 6

If the reader acquires a thorough familiarity with the nature of the planets, it will not be a difficult matter to see how the one must modify the other when any two are in combination; and the result may be expressed either in terms of fate or in terms of character, for these are really convertible as has been explained before.

The Parallel of Declination is generally regarded as the same in nature as the conjunction.   When, however, two planets are in parallel and in some definite aspect at the same time, it is best in practice to interpret the combination in terms of the aspect, whatever it may be good or bad. If there is no aspect, the parallel may be treated as a conjunction, but it will not be so strong, and will act rather as an inclining than a determining influence.

The remaining aspects in the table, it will be seen, are all definitely good or bad, and not variable like the conjunction and parallel.

The *Good Aspects* are all based upon a threefold division of the circle of the zodiac, as in Diagram 6. Thus the trine, 120°, is a third of the circle, the sextile, 60°, is half a trine, and the semi-sextile, 30°, half a sextile.

The *Evil Aspects* represent the circle halved or quartered, as in Diagram 7. Thus the opposition, 180°, is half the circle, the square, 90°,

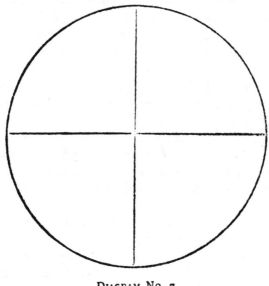

DIAGRAM No. 7

is a quarter of the circle, and the semi-square, 45°, and sesquiquadrate, 135°, are respectively half a square and a square and a half.

The question is certain to be asked here as to *why* the threefold and fourfold divisions of the circle should be the one good and the other evil? If a given planet, say Jupiter, is on the whole more good than evil, so far as its influence upon the inhabitants of this earth is concerned, why, even when it is in square to a given point in the horoscope, should its good side be entirely suppressed and only its evil side be allowed to manifest, so far as that point is concerned?

The question is not at all an easy one to answer, and we can do little more than indicate analogies. The religious philosophy of the mystic assures us that there is a basic three-fold mode of operation underlying the whole universe, and that it can be stated in terms of consciousness and in terms of force working through matter. The former aspect of it is seen in the continually recurring doctrine of the divine Trinity found in nearly all religions; and the latter side in the Hindu teaching as to the "three qualities" or modes of operation of force when involved in matter and termed Rajas, Tamas, and Sattva. If, then, three is the basic number underlying, permeating, creating and sustaining the whole universe, the astrological doctrine of the harmonious nature of those aspects based upon a three-fold division of the zodiac, falls into line with this general philosophy of things. We are apparently justified in conjecturing that the angle of 120° harmonises with the material constitution of the solar system and with the modes of opera- tion of vitality, consciousness and force. The evil aspects are based upon a wholly different mode of vibration, and start from numbers two and four instead of number three. It is philosophically impossible to suppose that there is such a thing as radical evil anywhere, evil deliberately planned and worked into the universal scheme of things by the Creator. All the evil we know of or can imagine is the result either of ignorance or of distorted free-will, which itself perhaps is only another name for a higher form of ignorance. Good is harmony, evil is discord. In music, two notes harmonise if their vibrations accord with one another; and if they do not, discord is the result. We seem, therefore, bound to suppose that aspects based upon the square represent clash, conflict and discord; and that the soul which finds itself surrounded by forces working in this fashion has itself created the discord from which it is now suffering. The effect, although temporarily painful, is spiritually good, because the soul learns by its own experience to distinguish between that which will produce discord and that which will produce harmony; so that the clash and conflict of opposition end in wisdom.

This may be illustrated in practical Astrology. The opposition aspect is when two planets are situated at exactly opposite points in the zodiac. Let us suppose that these are Venus and Mars. In this case the soul and the senses will be at war and the person will suffer. He will find it a hard task to preserve a straight course morally through life; his passions will be continually overstepping the bounds of moderation, especially in the direction of sex. When he truly realises this, and that it is a highly undesirable phase of character, he will have made a big step in the knowledge of the difference between good and evil, wisdom and foolishness. But mere knowledge will not of itsel suffice to undo the harm done ; action, will, is necessary. A strong will may gradually rein in the runaway passions, and the knowledge acquired will direct them into the right path. This may take a lifetime or even more to accomplish, but the result is good, doubly good indeed, for there is an increase of wisdom and a greatly increased strength of will brought out by the continual effort at self-control. If Venus is elevated or is otherwise the stronger of the two, the task will be rather easier than it otherwise would be.

All oppositions, and in fact all evil aspects, may be resolved along somewhat similar lines to the foregoing. In some, such as Saturn afflicting Jupiter, it is partly selfishness and partly lack of practical ability that has to be got rid of. In all those in which Mars is one of the two, trouble will arise from an excess of energy, a lack of gentleness or prudence or of consideration for others, in those matters that are signified by the other planet. When Mercury is one of the two, the reason will be at fault ; as, for instance, when Mercury opposes Jupiter, intellect and emotion clash at times and trouble will be brought about by action based upon impulse, although that impulse might be highly creditable if it were controlled by common-sense. And here, as elsewhere, the particular shade of the misfortune will depend upon which of the two is the stronger or higher up in the horoscope. With Venus it is the emotions, affections, and social qualities that contribute to the trouble and that need regulation. With the Sun it may be pride that has to be restrained, or the laws of health that must be studied and obeyed. With the Moon it may again be the bodily health that will cause trouble, or the mind may be wrongly impressionable in some direction, or the psychic and mediumistic side of the nature lacks control.

Along these lines of tendencies of character nearly all Astrology may be interpreted, that which centres round the good aspects—which will here represent balanced and wise phases of character—as well as that resulting from the evil ones—which stand for excess or defect. The planets may thus be looked upon as faculties or powers in human nature, and good or bad aspects as men's wise or foolish use of them—their

virtues and vices, in short. That these are innate in the character and
date back to birth shows, not that this view is unsound, but that the
real origin of tendencies resulting in such aspects must be traced back
beyond birth to a previous state of existence.

The question will doubtless be asked as to how we are to interpret
those aspects or directions that coincide with events which seem to be
mere fate, good or evil, and not directly brought about by any operation
of character in this life. The probability is that such events are really
fewer than it is natural for astrologers to suppose; nevertheless it
cannot be denied that they exist. An eldest son may inherit an entailed
estate; another man may be killed in an earthquake; a third may suffer
through the negligence of a parent or nurse in infancy; and none of
them may be in the slightest degree responsible for the event. Here we
must see the result of action in a state of existence preceding birth, and
in the aspects found in the horoscope merely the methods adopted by
the superhuman Controllers of human evolution to ensure that the
adequate effect should follow the cause that had previously been started,
so that the soul may reap as it has sown and learn the right lesson.
That many such lessons cannot be understood and finally appreciated
until after death, when the whole life is impartially summed up from the
point of view of the onlooker instead of the actor, does not detract from
the reasonableness of this interpretation, but only shows how long drawn
out is the evolution of the soul, and how impossible it is to compress
that evolution into a few years of existence on this physical plane.

To return to the table of aspects at the beginning of this chapter, it
may be noted that the *Trine* is by far the strongest of the good aspects;
it stands for progression and harmony, and may be compared to Jupiter,
the greater benefic. It seems to bring even better fortune than a conjunction with a benefic planet. The *Sextile* aspect is appreciably weaker,
but is nevertheless good, and may be compared to Venus. The *Semi-
Sextile* is extremely weak and may be compared to Mercury, the 'convertible' planet; not much is lost if it is omitted from consideration.

Of the evil aspects, the *Opposition* and *Square* may be compared to
Saturn and Mars respectively. The opposition separates, and causes
rivalry, antagonism, duality, in this respect being not unlike the mutable
signs in its influence. The square acts somewhat like the fixed signs;
it alternately crystallises and limits into a settled habit, and disrupts

and shatters by a sudden shock.   The *Semi-Square* and *Sesquiquadrate* are weaker than the square and not so lasting, but are similar to it in nature, and may be compared to the cardinal signs as being disintegrative or dispersive ; or to continue our planetary illustration they may be likened to a blend of Saturn and Mars, the former by square and the latter by opposition.

We have next to consider the question of 'Orbs.' In ancient times it was taught that each planet had an ' orb ' or ' sphere ' of influence which extended beyond its own body out into space in all directions ; in fact, it might be termed the ' aura ' of the planet ; and that the influences or 'rays' of the planets were mingled as soon as the peripheries of these ' orbs ' came into contact—or into aspecting distance, as the case might be. The latest researches in scientific Astrology seem to be approaching an actual physical explanation of this statement, and there can be little doubt that it is the true basis of the ' orbs ' employed by astrologers, and will thus explain why orbs should differ for each planet, as well as for every aspect. But we are here concerned with the practical application of the term, which indicates how many degrees of ' approach ' and ' departure ' may be allowed before and after any aspect becomes technically complete. In this, *experience* can be the only real teacher and the following hints must be accepted as such, and not taken as hard and fast rules.

For conjunction or opposition allow 12° when the Sun aspects the Moon, about 10° when either luminary aspects a planet, and about 8° for planets aspecting each other.

For square and trine about 8° all round may be allowed. For sextile about 7°. For semi-square and sesquiquadrate 4°. For semi-sextile and quincunx 2°. For the parallel of declination 1°.

These are the outside limits. In all cases the closer an aspect is, the stronger it is, and *vice versa*. An aspect that is only just within orbs is very weak. In some cases two planets that are widely apart by aspect may be brought closer together by a third planet ; for instance, if the Sun is at 0°♈ and the Moon at 10°♎ the aspect is a wide opposition and not very important ; but if Mars were at 5°♋ it would not only be in square to both but would render the opposition worse than it otherwise would be.

If three planets are so arranged that two of them are equally distant from the third, the effect seems to be much the same as a parallel and is therefore good or bad according to the nature of the planets.   Whether there is any limit to this kind of influence by position is uncertain.   Of course, if the three are in some recognised aspect to each other, good or bad, the effect will be according to the nature of that aspect.

The general character of the various positions and aspects will now be explained.   Before judging the nature of each aspect it should be noted which planet is the 'significator'; that is, whether the planet aspecting, or the planet aspected, is ruler of the horoscope—or of the special house under consideration as the case may be.

The influence of the planets when in conjunction is shown in the accompanying list, which is arranged in the following order, ♆ ♅ ♄ ♃ ♂ ☉ ♀ ☿ ☽.   This is the order of their distance from the Sun and hence their rate of movement; Neptune, of course, being the farthest and slowest; and it is the order that will be adopted throughout this volume.

The first column shows the influence when the significator is the *slower* planet of the two: the second column shows the influence when the significator is the *quicker* planet of the two.*

To avoid needless repetition each aspect is only given once, namely under the heading of the slower of the two planets between which it is formed, and this should be remembered when the book is used for reference.   Thus suppose we want to find the effect of an aspect between Mars and Jupiter, we look under Jupiter, since that is the slower of the two; and there we find the effect, both when Mars is significator and when Jupiter is significator.   Similarly if we want to find an aspect between Mars and Mercury, we look under Mars, if between Venus and the Moon, under Venus, and so on.

Although the influence of any given aspect will be shown out most strongly in the life when one of the two planets between which it is formed is the ruler of the nativity, yet the general nature of its influence upon the whole character will be much as here described, even when neither planet is ruler of any important house, or placed in any prominent

----

* See Important Note at end of this chapter, p. 66.

position; so that the descriptions which follow will still serve as a guide, if taken in a somewhat modified sense. Only they will represent characteristics, or events, more or less latent in the life and awaiting suitable 'directions' to stir them into activity.

CONJUNCTIONS

When slower planet is significator   *When quicker planet is significator*

NEPTUNE
*in conjunc-
tion with*

NEPTUNE *

♅ Inspirational, quaint, marvellous, antiquated, mystifying.
A dominating will.

Latent genius, ready for expression, transcendental tendencies.
Practical mysticism, intuition.

♄ Dreamy, imaginative, mediumistic.
Psychic dangers, black magic.
The mind brought under the influence of the internal will : concentration.

Intense, psychic, clairaudient tendencies.
Loss of position, scandal.
Circumscribed conditions, death-bed maledictions, curses, legacies of hate, odium, misrepresentations.

♃ Religious, philanthropic, loving.
Ceremonial magic, imagination.
Religious to an extreme, danger of megalomania. Love of financial scheming.

Devotional, poetic, artistic.
Love of beauty in colour and form.
Precocious, occult genius, recovered lore from higher planes, remembrance of former lives.

♂ Visionary, chaotic, uncertain notions.
Danger from water or drink.
Extreme egotism.

Mysterious, shady, clandestine, obscure, secretive.
Gambling instinct, marks the turfite, sharper, juggler.

☉ Paradoxical, impressionable, often clairvoyant tendencies, peculiar morals.
Clairvoyance, seership.

Psychicism, mysticism, romance.
A strange character, difficult to understand ; idealistic.
A practical mystic.

♀ Feelings expressed strangely, and liable to extremes in love attachments.

Spiritualistic, mediumistic, psychic, amorous. Ecstatic, sexual entanglements, musical inspirations, liaisons.

☿ Intuitive, sympathetic, unpractical.

Fastidious, visionary, abnormal, inquisitive, psychic.

☽ Self-deceptive, affected, impermanent moods.
Travelling, love of change, sensuous, sensitive to the poetical and humorous.

Inspirational, dreamy, mediumistic.
Superstitious, idyllic, visionary, sensitive to the finer forces of nature; active sub-consciousness; revealing through dreams.

---

* See footnote on next page.

When slower planet is significator   *When quicker planet is significator*

URANUS
in conjunc-
tion with

URANUS *

♄ Profound power of contempla-
    tion ; strongly mental.
    Ambitious, determined, re-
    served.

Inventive, imaginative, intelligent, un-
rivalled, singular.
Engineering talent, marked powers of
concentration.

♃ Original, inventive, deep musi-
    cal ability, occult tendencies.
    Peculiar religious views, imagi-
    nation.
    Eloquent, persuasive.

Inspirational, marvellous, devotional,
aspiring.
Dramatic power, sense of dignity.
True perceptions, religious interests,
catholic opinions.

♂ Extremist, enormous latent
    energy, capable of remark-
    able expressions, dangerous
    possibilities.
    Self-willed, impulsive, uncon-
    trollable.
    Egotistical, fanatical, an ex-
    tremist.

Restless, excitable, eccentric, scheming, erratic, violent, peculiar, enig-
matical.
Ability to control natural forces,
highly explosive in temper, inquisitive, restless, eccentric, wrong
headed and dangerous if not well
supported.

☉ Headstrong, socialistic or re-
    forming tendencies ; some-
    times revolutionaries.
    Strong personality, firm, power-
    ful magnetism.

Intuition, independence, originality,
This position is not good for females,
bringing trouble through peculiar
magnetic and psychic conditions.
In women, romantic marriage.

♀ Idealistic, peculiar affections,
    experimental in feelings.
    Imagination, wounded affec-
    tions, emotional, ardent.
    Hyper-sensitive, idiosyncratic,
    æsthetic, aloof. Sometimes
    deep-rooted egotism.

Mirthful, romantic, musical, artistic,
humorous, intuitive, independent,
original.
Artistic, dramatic ability, sensuous,
jealous, sex entanglements ; conduces to separation, estrangement
and divorce.

☿ Witty, intuitive, abrupt and
    critical.
    Intellectual, witty, wilful, origi-
    nal, changeable.
    Agility in all departments,
    bodily, mentally and emotion-
    ally. Somewhat of a casuist
    in argument.

Inventive, humorous, unconventional,
eccentric, profound, metaphysical,
occult.
Genius for figures, mentally alert,
inventive, rapid intuition, unconventional, progressive, mechanical
and electrical ability, embracing
quickly new ideas.

---

* The influence of Neptune and Uranus being as yet comparatively little
understood, the opinions of three students who have devoted special attention to
these two planets were invited. These, where not coinciding, are printed in
detached sentences.

When slower planet is significator	*When quicker planet is significator*
☽ Roving, enquiring, capable of forming rapid and correct judgments. Mediumistic, impressionable, nervous, subtle.	Eccentric, bohemian, erratic, nomadic. Liable to be 'swept off his feet' by some *outré* attachment or some unscrupulous friend. Peculiar in temper.

SATURN *in conjunction with*

SATURN

♃	Grave, studious, careful, acquisitive, pious, respectful, honest, placid, conservative.	Profound, contemplative, religious, thoughtful, reliable, discreet, economic, thrifty.
♂	Penetrating, intense, audacious, covetous, uncompromising, contemptuous, indiscreet.	Reproachful, absconding, avaricious, repulsive, coercive, malicious, outrageous.
☉	Deficiency of moral courage, reserve, fear, despondency, avarice, lack of sympathy, inertia, poor circulation, weak, constitution, and danger of disgrace or serious misfortune and failures.	Caution, diplomacy, austerity, economy, success through responsibility, and positions of trust. This position is not good for the general health and constitution. But it is more favourable than when Saturn is significator.
♀	Sensual, sad, variable, callous, rude, morose, greedy, pernicious.	Deception, cunning, antipathy: the nature is demoralising, mercenary, perverse.
☿	Serious, determined, austere, thrifty, apprehensive, methodical, laborious. Remarkably studious.	Subtle, diplomatic, reserved, shrewd, cautious, acquisitive, firm, patient, exacting, persevering, authoritative, zealous.
☽	Submissive, passive, fretful, repining, peevish, degenerate, sad, gloomy, melancholic, timorous, lethargic, cold, apathetic, disappointing.	Suspicious, timid, bashful, moody, sensitive, shy, miserable, hypochondriacal, unfortunate, indigent, morbid. Given to looking on the dark side of things.

JUPITER *in conjunction with*

JUPITER

♂	Extravagant, speculative, trustful, heroic, profligate, courageous, expansive.	Enthusiastic, approbative, liberal, rash, presumptive, prodigal, choleric.
☉	Pride, liberality, extravagance, love of display, conceit, ostentation, success through superiors and the favour of persons in authority.	Honesty, generosity, candour, sympathy, magnanimity, success through ambition, marriage or social advantages. This is a very favourable position.

When slower planet is significator	*When quicker planet is significator*

JUPITER
in conjunction with

♀ Ideality, chastity, piety, charity, consistency, congruity, politeness, content, peace, bliss.

♀ Harmony, elegance, munificence, refinement, gentleness, compassion, sincerity, vivacity, purity, fortune, happiness.

☿ Unsophisticated, hopeful, reliable, prudent, just, bright, humane, devoted, upright, dignified, prosperous.

☿ Judicious, philanthropic, genial, genuine, utilitarian, contented, mirthful, moral, discriminative, discreet, successful.

☽ Flexibility, exhilaration, joyous, hopeful, confident, fruitful, gracious, fortunate.

☽ Sympathetic, generous, charitable, humane, forbearing, popular. The native is fortunate.

MARS
in conjunction with

MARS

⊙ Strong character, heroism, courage, defiance, fortitude, intrepidity, resentment, indignation, anger. This position is much more favourable than when the Sun is significator, as a rule.

⊙ Bold, fearless, rash, passionate, speculative, over-assertive, dogmatic, irreverent, sceptical, exaggerative. This position gives great vitality, a strong constitution, with danger of feverish and inflammatory complaints.

♀ Passionate, fascinating, ecstatic, sensational, susceptible, propagative, impetuous, fickle.

♀ Amorous, impressionable, vain, forward, convivial, sportive, epicurean, immodest, sentimental.

☿ Enterprising, industrious, combative, pugnacious, destructive, mechanical, credulous, supercilious.

☿ Exaggerative, unsympathetic, impudent, assuming, irritable, argumentative, inconsiderate, rebellious, too sharp and deceptive.

☽ Profligate, adventurous, irascible, contentious, destructive, profane.

☽ Over-confident, rash, impulsive, restless, irritable, impudent, perverse, domineering.

SUN
in conjunction with

THE SUN

♀ Fond of pleasure, amiable, courteous, luxuriant, affectionate, easily led, cheerful.

♀ Extravagant, fond of show, pleasure and ease-loving, kind, sympathetic, amorous, apathetic, mutable.

☿ Ambitious, quick-witted, intuitive, ingenious, thoughtful, intelligent.

☿ Adaptable, aspiring, intellectual, studious, reliable. Interested in mechanics or manufactures.

☽ Aspiring, ambitious, conservative, impressive.

☽ Mutable, self-centred, harmless, inert, indifferent.

VENUS

☿   Graceful, cultured, refined, sympathetic, affectionate, charming, felicitous, chaste, cheerful.

Linguistic, musical, artistic, efficient, grateful, courteous, attractive, appreciative, idealistic.

☽   Affable, approbative, plausible, mirthful, affectionate, imaginative, inoffensive.

Ease-loving, effeminate, careless, fond of pleasure, luxury and comfort, fortunate.

MERCURY

☽   Versatility, keen wit, ingenious mind, quick perception, curiosity, intuitiveness.

Ingenuity, comprehension, mutability, quick intellect, memory, receptivity to new ideas.

These interpretations are only intended to be general indications, for much depends upon the sign and house wherein the conjunction takes place as to its action upon the character or destiny. In the above list the meaning of the conjunctions has not been given so fully nor so explicitly as one could wish, but where so many have to be dealt with it is obvious that great detail would be out of place, and that hints only can be given.

———

We now come to the evil aspects, which are the square and the opposition. The word 'evil' is only used here for convenience, since it is customary among students to divide aspects and influences into what are termed 'good' and 'evil'—by which is usually meant favourable or unfavourable from a material standpoint. It would be far better to use the words harmonious and discordant, which convey the real idea more closely. Anyone who knows anything of music is aware that discords are no less necessary in a composition than concords, and that a true artist can utilise the very harshest tones in such a way as to produce a beautiful effect. And thus also the Great Musician is capable of using all those planetary vibrations which we term 'evil' in such a way as to further His great scheme of beauty and progress. In a minor degree man has this power too, and by learning how to control the discordant vibrations playing through him he can utilise them for high purposes: in the horoscopes of great characters we usually find some powerful oppositions or squares, in addition to some of the more harmonious aspects. In a general sense the squares and oppositions give grit and energy, but in the main they give adverse conditions and trying circumstances, with an uphill fight against fate.

For the rest, it must be understood that these aspects are 'evil' only in the sense of abuse of the influence through ignorance or by a perverted expression of its true nature.

The following is the general effect of squares and oppositions when either planet is ruler, or significator.

EVIL ASPECTS: OPPOSITIONS OR SQUARES

When slower planet is significator	*When quicker planet is significator*
Neptune *in opposition or square with*	**NEPTUNE**
♅ Unreliable in feeling and action.	Erratic, strange and peculiar.
♄ Deceptive, revengeful and suspicious.	Resentful, cold and selfish; strange sufferings through enmity.
♃ Strange ill-fortune, pride, loss of friends, profound realisations.	Strong religious and mystical tendencies, deep love-nature.
	A strange emotional nature.
♂ Rebellious, discontented, contentious.	Excitable, changeable, unreliable in temper and apt for quarrels.
☉ Losses through traps, schemes, plots, frauds, tricks, enemies and psychic conditions.	Tragedies, obsessions, treacheries, vendettas, spirit voices, temptations, trances, weird dreams, low magic.
♀ Depraved feelings, lack of sympathy.	Deficient in nutritive quality, strange love affairs.
☿ Fraudential, kleptomaniacal and cunning.	Questionable habits, shifty and deceptive ways.
☽ Strange notions, changeable moods and fanciful tendencies.	Weird, morbid, fretful, hypochondriac, sensuous, strange, psychic, dreamy.
Uranus *in opposition or square with*	**URANUS**
♄ Misfortunes through lack of opportunities or the power to make use of them.	Eccentric, peculiar, faddy, liable to sudden reversals of fortune and strange fits of temper.
♃ Enthusiastic through bias or fixed opinions.	Deficient in social qualities, strange feelings, separative.
♂ Rude and rebellious, over active or diffusive, quarrelsome, unforgiving. Ever restless and unsettled.	Fanatical, defiant, erratic, irritable, fanciful, ungovernable, eccentric, odd, uncertain, dislocated, intemperate.

When slower planet is significator   *When quicker planet is significator*

URANUS
in opposition
or square with

☉ Losses through strangers, associations, societies, love affairs, marriage, partnerships and independence.

Obstacles, disappointments, abruptness, fluctuations, enmities, jealousies, liaisons, intrigues, separations, estrangements, calamities, disasters.

♀ Romantic, and liable to be affected magnetically for good or ill by others.
Strange monetary troubles.

Jealous, unrestrained in feeling, easily influenced and led astray, curious, imaginative, visionary, wonder-loving.

☿ Distorted mind, exacting and self opinionated.
Difficult to convince and apt to remain perversely indifferent to reason.

Bigoted, stubborn, unruly, wayward, rambling, deficient, notional, diffusive, sceptical, unforgiving, conceited, conventional, unsuccessful and unfortunate.

☽ Magnetic, curious, sensuous, bohemian, romantic, erratic, wilful, abrupt, irritable, independent, unsettled.

Losses through strangers, lack of balance, sudden changes, peculiar habits, and unreasonable notions. A romantic love-affair.

SATURN
in opposition
or square with   SATURN

♃ Unfortunate, wavering, liable to great opposition, liable to reversals and very heavy losses.

Unlucky, impressionable, weak-willed, indecisive, affected by circumstances and environments, mistrustful, deficient in hope and confidence.

♂ Cruel, scornful, deceptive, hostile, calculating, perfidious, fateful.

Revengeful, malicious, hasty, violent, vindictive, rash, selfish, treacherous, cowardly, uncompromising.

☉ Insincere, untrustworthy, timid, superficial, unjust, torpid, biassed, gloomy, desponding, unstable.
Losses through lack of foresight, hesitancy, fear.

Malicious, suspicious, covetous, boastful, cowardly, fearful, solitary, selfish, exacting.
Losses through land, property, inheritance, and superiors, or through governmental action.

♀ Sensual, unjust, parsimonious, hostile, covetous, jealous, exacting, weak.

Deceptive, diplomatic, avaricious, despondent, approbative, imprudent, thoughtless.

☿ Cunning, deceitful, treacherous, miserly, misanthropic, overreaching, grasping, jealous, unhappy, dull.
Losses through theft, fraud, forgery and schemers.

Narrow-minded, over-anxious, discontented, fanciful, suspicious, mistrustful, perverse, peevish, carping, envious, selfish, apprehensive.
Losses through elders, lack of enterprise, fear and over-economy.

☽ Melancholic, covetous, mean, apathetic, stupid, superstitious, ambiguous, miserly, phlegmatic, self-centred.

Unfortunate, cold, repining, resentful, peevish, discontented, listless, prejudiced, suspicious, apprehensive, deceitful, insincere.

When slower planet is significator	*When quicker planet is significator*

☽—(continued)

Losses through misfortune, fate, lack of ambition, and ill-health. | Losses through fear, mistrust, hesitancy, lack of enterprise, energy, and perseverance.

JUPITER *in opposition or square with*

JUPITER

♂ Ungrateful, unconscientious, unforgiving, unkind, unhappy, impolite, discourteous, ignorant, irreligious, cruel, vain.
Losses through impulsive action and waste. | Wasteful, prodigal, insincere, atheistical, unfaithful, proud, cynical, insolent, rash and foolhardy.
Losses through the law, wild or senseless conduct, giving way to desires and passions.

☉ Hypocritical, mistrustful, prodigal, vain, many-sided, affluent, empirical.
Losses through errors of judgment, false securities, and obstinacy. | Proud, haughty, pleasure-loving, extravagant, bombastic, fond of display and ostentation.
Losses through social intercourse, advice of friends, extravagance and legal affairs.

♀ Vain, sensual, over-liberal, dishonest, given to luxury and extravagance. | Extravagant, lavish, conceited, over-demonstrative, fond of questionable pleasures, given to flattery.

☿ Imitative, susceptible, declarative, wavering, diffusive, uncertain.
Losses through misjudgments, letters and travels. | Incompetent, deceptive, involved, satirical, lacking in true judgment, impressionable.
Losses through the law, church and social affairs.

☽ Exuberant, convivial, respectful, commiserate, liberal, impressionable.
Losses through society, the opposite sex, and speculation. | Thriftless, profuse, excessive, over-confident, affable, presumptuous, pretentious.
Losses through acquaintances, travel, and misplaced confidence.

MARS *in opposition or square with*

MARS

☉ Destructive, turbulent, gruff, irritable, overbearing, vain, disruptive, self-willed.
Losses through hasty conduct, over-liberal actions, accidents, fevers, and the opposite sex. | Impulsive, approbative, headstrong, unruly, irrelevant, arrogant, adventurous, forceful, discordant.
Losses through rash conduct, wild and unfortunate speculations and unfortunate enterprises.

♀ Vain, boastful, offensive, rude, sensual, dissipated, disreputable, indecorous.
Losses through excesses and errors of living. | Forward, intrepid, sensuous, aspiring, fickle, daring, imprudent, impulsive.
Losses through rash conduct and the opposite sex, who exercise great power over native.

	When slower planet is significator	*When quicker planet is significator*
☿	Energetic, active, artful, daring, skilful, zealous, nervous, fluent, anxious, demonstrative, shrewd, vindictive. Losses through impulse, hazardous enterprises, litigation, correspondence, and relatives.	Mischievous, argumentative, reprobate, careless, untruthful, sarcastic, resentful, defiant, fearless, impatient. Losses through wrangling, disputation, contention, strife, and mismanagement; also through abortive projects.
☽	Aggressive, proud, headstrong, obstinate, wilful, cantankerous, irritable, unfeeling, hard, severe, exacting, ardent, jealous. Losses through impolite and unsympathetic manner.	Contentious, self-confident, masterful, boastful, adventurous, indelicate, precipitate, fallacious, deceitful. Losses through rash and hasty conduct, indiscreet speech and strong opposition. Danger from savage animals.

SUN *in opposition or square with*

THE SUN

☿ ♀ Between these planets and the Sun no strongly adverse aspects can be formed; the semi-square between Sun and Venus is somewhat prodigal in effect.

☽	Mutable, changeable, irresolute, sensitive, volatile, lethargic. Losses through subordinates, inferiors, common people, and poor general health.	Ambitious, venturesome, egotistical, patronising, compelling, immoderate. Losses through disappointment, ill-health and over-confidence. Enmity with autocrats.

VENUS *in opposition or square with*

VENUS

☿ No adverse aspect between Venus and Mercury can be formed save the semi-square, which is slightly disharmonious but adverse chiefly in the sense of being unfavourable to art, to which the sextile aspect strongly inclines.

Improvident, untidy, erratic, animated, ceremonial, partial, impetuous, vain. Losses through display, contention, and pleasure.	Sensuous, careless, amorous, touchy, morbid, fickle, sentimental, pliable, comic. Losses through dissipation, loose habits, indolence, thoughtlessness.

MERCURY *in opposition or square with*

MERCURY

☽	Impressionable, mutable, opinionative, imaginative, speculative, obscure, politic, misapprehending, indecisive, dexterous. Losses through false notions, personal sensitiveness, domestic affairs and removals.	Changeable, vague, impractical, absent-minded, vacillating, tricky, fanciful. Somewhat poetical in temperament, but finding fancies running counter to ideas. Losses through the public, correspondence, litigation, sureties, inferiors, and business transactions.

Care must be exercised in using any of the above aspects, for they may be much modified and improved by sign and position, also by other more favourable aspects. In a minor degree they will apply also to the semi-square or sesquiquadrate aspect, which are as it were weaker expressions of the same influence, as explained on p. 47.

―――――

We have next to consider the 'good' aspects by which we mean those that are definitely harmonious and favourable in their action in every sense. But what has been said under the heading of 'evil' aspects should not be lost sight of when considering the nature of the 'good' aspects. Just as nothing *in itself* is evil, so nothing in itself is good, but may be perverted; and instances can be found where, in a weak horoscope, the good influences are made 'ducks and drakes of' so to speak, being used simply to minister to personal gratification or selfish indulgence. Yet such cases are comparatively rare, and, harking back to our musical simile we may say that, in a general sense, the good aspects are like the passages of smooth, sweet harmony that follow on the turbulent first movement of a symphony, where the soul appears to dwell for a while in a calm and undisturbed atmosphere, in which strength is gathered and balance restored after the turmoil of battle. Every great nation has shown its most marked periods of artistic productiveness shortly after a series of struggles for constitutional or political emancipation, the strength developed in the former being balanced by the sense of beauty cultivated in the latter: and in the same way we may think of the favourable or 'good' aspects as designed to harmonise the nature, just as the 'evil' ones are intended to stimulate it to achievement.

GOOD ASPECTS: TRINES OR SEXTILES

NEPTUNE

When slower planet is significator	*When quicker planet is significator*

NEPTUNE
*in sextile
or trine with*

♅

♄

⚹ NOTE

♃

The good aspects of Neptune
are much less powerful in
their effect than the conjunctions or afflictions, when
Neptune is significator. In a
general sense they act in much
the same way as when the
aspecting planet is significator. It is only very rarely
that either Neptune or Uranus can be regarded as the
true ruler of the ascendant
or other house.

♂

☉

♀

☿

☽

When quicker planet is significator

Deep spiritual nature and profound
occult ability. A strange life with
many vicissitudes.

Great powers of concentration and
penetration. Subtle and astute.
Tenacious and acquisitive. If cold
by nature, then *very* cold.

Kindly and genial nature, hospitable
and generous. Rather given to
pleasure and apt to be extravagant.

Abundant and agreeable magnetism.
Strong sense of colour. Inclined
towards emotionalism. Artistic and
somewhat sensuous.

Mystical tendencies and poetic temperament. Generally fortunate on
the whole. Knows the value of
secrecy.

Devotional nature very strong and
capable of great things. In a weak
horoscope this increases the sensuous tendencies.

Poetic and inspirational. Skill in
scheming, designing, or constructing
plots. Generally bestows some
literary faculty and imaginative
power.

Dreamy and fanciful nature, sensitive,
delicate and impressionable, sympathetic. Fond of the sea.

When slower planet is significator　　　*When quicker planet is significator*

URANUS in sextile or trine with

URANUS

♄
♃
♂
☉
♀
☿
☽

NOTE

The good aspects of Uranus are much less powerful in their effect than the conjunctions or afflictions, when Uranus is significator. In a general sense they act in much the same way as when the aspecting planet is significator. It is only very rarely that either Neptune or Uranus can be regarded as the true ruler of the ascendant or other house.

Intuitive, occult, mystical, altruistic, broad-minded, sincere.

Powerful magnetism, fertility of resource, contempt of danger. Remarkable love adventures.

Originality, quick perception, enterprise, intuition, talent, intellectuality. Gain through inventions, travel and antiquities.

Fascinating, magnetic, attractive, musical and pleasure-loving.

Occult, metaphysical, contemplative, studious, profound, original. Gain through inventions, antiquities and uncommon pursuits.

Adaptable, alert, scientific, firm.

Responsible, original. Gain through travel, the occult arts and mentality.

SATURN

SATURN in sextile or trine with

♃ Religious, truthful, zealous, wise. Gain and prosperity in life, good fortune, steady accumulation of wealth.

♂ Fearless, capable, temperate, vigilant.

☉ Austere, persistent, persevering, careful, subtle, circumspect, premeditative, tactful, frugal. Gain through land, property, labour and care.

♀ Calm and steadfast disposition, gentle but persevering and capable of enduring much.

☿ Reserved, slow, steadfast, suspicious, indifferent, ponderous. Gain through laborious, mental, scientific and responsible pursuits.

☽ Acquisitive, wary, remorseful, serious, particular, sedate.

Serious, profound, philosophical, contemplative, meditative, sincere, of a steady nature and capable of applying continuously to study.

Considerate, determined, self-reliant, persevering, concentrative.

Authoritative, responsible, diplomatic, sincere, just, considerate, pertinacious, methodical, conservative, gain and honour through responsible posts.

Modest, retiring, chaste, careful, sincere, frugal, unobtrusive, constant, faithful.

Steady, painstaking, thorough, determined, occult, zealous, chaste, prudent, impartial, curious, meditative. Gain through secretarial work of a responsible or political nature.

Reserved, misgiving, provident, stable, patient, apprehensive.

When slower planet is significator   *When quicker planet is significator*

JUPITER
in sextile
or trine with

JUPITER

♂ Well disposed, generous, free, earnest, aspiring, commanding.

Confident, courageous, pushful, honourable, heroic; cheerful, somewhat over enthusiastic.

☉ Unreserved, hopeful, genial, refined, confident, reliant, discriminative. Gain by investment, social affairs, public office, business, or inheritance.

Honourable, philanthropic, munificent, spiritual, trustworthy, prosperous, frank. Gain by favour of superiors and those in good social position, also through own natural and frank disposition.

♀ Kind, religious, amiable, loving, generous, well-disposed, pure. Gain, good fortune, and general success in life through peace and a noble disposition which fortune favours.

Successful, sociable, hospitable, virtuous, sincere, benevolent, good. Gain through social popularity and agreeable disposition, and through sensible judgment generally. Rather devotional nature.

☿ Eloquent, straightforward, genuine, cordial, sound in judgment, rational, explicit, expressive. Gain through the law, church or stage, prosperity and success through critical acumen.

Fertile, discriminative, fruitful, virtuous, sincere, honest, just, unaffected, lucid, intuitive, spiritual. Gain through partners and by a well-balanced judgment, also through religious affairs. Some artistic and literary ability.

☽ Fortunate, truthful, sincere, kind and social.

Successful, honourable undertakings, popular and philosophical.

MARS
in sextile
or trine with

MARS

☉ Dignity, exaltation, expansion, activity, generosity, vitality, faithfulness. Gain through enterprise, ability and courage.

Courage, ambition, enterprise, penetration, authority, determination protection. Gain through military or medical affairs. Much energy, both physical and mental.

♀ Pleasure-loving, adventurous, enterprising, sensuous, demonstrative. Gain through pleasure and that which ministers to the pleasure of others.

Vain, impressionable, susceptible, amorous, confident, aspiring. Gain through partners and those of the opposite sex and through agreeable manners. There is always some artistic feeling.

☿ Confident, industrious, bright, constructive, energetic, expeditious. Gain through the wit, speech and action.

Ingenious, shrewd, enthusiastic, diligent, expert, practical, clever, fluent, mercurial. Gain through enterprise and promptitude.

☽ Changeable, enterprising, self-reliant, competitive, imperious, contentious. Gain through self-assertion, daring, and what is called 'cheek.'

Ambitious, energetic, adventurous, intrepid, defensive, domineering. Gain through general practical capacities and enterprise. There is usually mechanical ability.

When slower planet is significator   *When quicker planet is significator*

The Sun

Sun *in sextile or trine with*

♀ Candour, willingness, felicity, devotion, love, preservation. (*Note.—This applies to the* ☌ *of course, since it is impossible for* ☉ *and* ♀ *to be in* △ *or* ✶.)

Sociability, liberality, affection, delicacy, appreciation, respect, modesty, cheerfulness. Gain through friendships, marriage, legacies, and pleasure.

☿ (*No aspect.*)

(*No aspect.*)

☽ Success, good health, recognition, ambition, sincerity, indomitable will, dignity, honour, loyalty, competence. Gain through speculation, investment, authority and position.

Favoured by fortune, noble-minded, persevering, and enterprising. Gain by the good-will of superiors and through governmental service. This is in every sense a good position and greatly improves the horoscope.

Venus

Venus *in sextile or trine with*

☿ Affable, pleasing, well-disposed, peaceful and joyous. Gain by literary or poetic gifts, and through young people.

Prudent, judicious, mirthful, artistic, eloquent, courteous, harmless, innocent. Gain through music, art, drama and pleasure.

☽ Accomplished, approbative, estimable, amiable, loving, dainty, vivacious. Gain through pleasure, females, and the negative or form side of life; a favourite with the public but changeable.

Gentle, receptive, artistic, refined, affectionate, agreeable, attractive. Gain through agreeable personality which renders native a general favourite; also through clothing, delicacies, etc., and the favour of the well-born.

Mercury

Mercury *in sextile or trine with*

☽ Dramatic, intellectual, adroit, thorough, expedient, reminiscent, comprehensive, reasonable, capable, intuitive. Gain through agencies, transit, literature and the public.

Subtle, imitative, circulative, reproductive, representative, insinuative, sensitive, anecdotal, versatile, expressive. Gain through ready wit, journalistic ability, nimbleness and general adaptability.

These aspects are not always as good as represented, since the influence will vary somewhat, according to sign and position, and other aspects may tend to counteract; but speaking generally they are harmonious and fortunate. If read in a somewhat restricted sense they may be held to apply also to the semi-sextile and quintile aspects, but though slightly good these are very weak and perhaps better omitted from consideration altogether. The quincunx or inconjunct (⚻) is by some considered good, but this is doubtful; it is better to regard it as 'resolvent' in its action, modifying and translating or transmuting the influence of one planet towards that of the other.

With regard to all aspects, particular attention should be paid to the application of the swifter moving planet, aspects in process of formation by application being far more important than aspects from which the swifter planet is separating, especially if the latter is the significator. The following explanation will illustrate this idea.

If Venus is the ruling planet, and first applies to the conjunction of Mercury while separating from the square aspect of Saturn, the application will be of primary importance, and the separation secondary, even if the separating aspect is closer than the application; for the separation indicates a lesson that has been learned and the application a lesson that is to be learned, either in this life or the next. * If the ruler has just left one aspect, and applies to another, give the principal value to the influence forming. The separating from any aspect to Saturn and applying to Jupiter is favourable for health, wealth and happiness; but if the Moon separate from any aspect of Jupiter and apply to Mars or Saturn it is unfavourable.

Several astrologers have noticed the effects of the luminaries and the planets separating from certain planets and their application to others, but the *Moon's* influence is the principal one to note in these cases, and the following separations and applications of the Moon denote the general effects of the applications.

THE MOON'S APPLICATIONS

FROM

♆ to ♅		Exceptional experiences, a remarkable life.
♆ „ ♄		Unfavourable environment, repression and serious obstacles.
♆ „ ♃		Rising fortune, social aid, powerful friends.
♆ „ ♂		Chequered career, misfortunes, failing fortune.
♆ „ ☉		Success and fame, honours and growing fortune.
♆ „ ♀		Helpful friends, prosperity and a happy life.
♆ „ ☿		A changeful life, fluctuating fortune, many struggles.

* This consideration explains the old rule that a planet is more 'powerful' when separating than when applying; for we can see that its effect, as shown in the character and actions, will of course be more pronounced.

The Moon's Applications—*Continued*

♅ „ ♆   Many enemies, deprivations, sorrowful experiences.
♅ „ ♄   Loss of liberty, danger of poverty, many disappointments
♅ „ ♃   Success in foreign lands, sudden good fortune.
♅ „ ♂   A disturbed life, misfortunes through misconduct or fateful tendencies.
♅ „ ☉   Separations, estrangements, romantic attachments.
♅ „ ♀   Strange pleasures, unexpected success, good abilities.
♅ „ ☿   Diplomatic, adventurous, liable to pass through a remarkable career.

♄ „ ♆   Danger of imprisonment, deserved or otherwise, uncertain character.
♄ „ ♅   Sudden reversals, intrigues, liaisons and many dangers.
♄ „ ♃   Good fortune, health and position.
♄ „ ♂   Accidents, disasters, ill-luck.
♄ „ ☉   Improving fortune through perseverance.
♄ „ ♀   A jealous partner, disappointments.
♄ „ ☿   Losses through deceit and treachery.

♃ „ ♆   Declining fame and fortune, many reversals.
♃ „ ♅   Romance and sudden fortune.
♃ „ ♄   Misfortunes, sickness and sorrow,
♃ „ ♂   Gain by adventure and brave deeds.
♃ „ ☉   Success, health and fortune.
♃ „ ♀   Gain and honour by marriage.
♃ „ ☿   Gain through literature, travel, the law, church, and the young.

♂ „ ♆   An uneven career, suffering through impulsive acts.
♂ „ ♅   Violent temper, grave dangers through rash and thoughtless conduct.
♂ „ ♄   Misfortune, disease and misery.
♂ „ ♃   Gain through favours and powerful friends.
♂ „ ☉   Gain through enterprise and courage.
♂ „ ♀   Dangers from the opposite sex and passion.
♂ „ ☿   Loss through fraud, deceit and bad temper.

☉ „ ♆   Forlorn hopes, sorrow through superiors, peculiar experiences.
☉ „ ♅   Peculiar episodes, sudden adventures, flashes of intuition.
☉ „ ♄   Falls, collapses, chronic complaints.
☉ „ ♃   A fortune by speculation or investment.
☉ „ ♂   Sudden disasters, strange misfortunes.
☉ „ ♀   Successful love affairs, gain through art or music.
☉ „ ☿   Gain through intellect, science and invention.

♀ „ ♆   Loss of friendships, disappointments, dual experiences.
♀ „ ♅   Extremes of fortune, remarkable experiences.
♀ „ ♄   Disappointments, disgrace, scandal.
♀ „ ♃   Noble and lofty aspirations, a peaceful life.
♀ „ ♂   Dangerous attachments, misfortunes.
♀ „ ☉   Good health, success and prosperity.
♀ „ ☿   Spiritual progress, a useful life.

THE MOON'S APPLICATIONS—*Continued.*

☿ to ♆ Mental disabilities, degenerating tendencies, sadness.
☿ ,, ♅ Latent genius, a clever mind, some original talent.
☿ ,, ♄ Cynical tendencies, pessimistic views, hard nature.
☿ ,, ♃ Intuitive, gain through application and honest endeavours.
☿ ,, ♂ Self-important, conceited, selfish, and too assertive.
☿ ,, ☉ Expanding mind, high aspirations, full nature.
☿ ,, ♀ Musical, artistic, cheerful, good nature, successful.

If the Moon separates from no planets but applies first to any aspect, the following is the general influence.

☽ to ♆ Psychic and weird experiences.
☽ ,, ♅ Sudden gain and loss through adventure.
☽ ,, ♄ Misfortune, sorrow and depression.
☽ ,, ♃ Prosperity, wealth and happiness, kind and good.
☽ ,, ♂ Indiscretion, loss through impulse and rash acts.
☽ ,, ☉ Gain from superiors, noble disposition.
☽ ,, ♀ Good fortune, social gain, nice disposition.
☽ ,, ☿ Clever, intellectual, but not over fortunate.

The above can be considerably expanded by a knowledge of the sign, house, and nature of the aspect.

Those who have realised how essential it is that any hints as to the nature of planetary influences, aspects, etc., should not be accepted too matter-of-fact and literal a sense, will, it is hoped, forgive a further insistence on this point for the sake of their fellows who have not.

It cannot be too strongly impressed upon the student that the planetary influences, aspects, etc., are primarily of a super-material nature ; so that a description of their true influence *could not* be accurately expressed in words, which are material things. And although in the progress of his study the difference between the influence of one planet and another, one aspect and another, and so on, will gradually take definite shape in the student's mind, yet he will never be able adequately to portray his idea in words,—however much he may try to do so.— any more than the effect a beautiful sunset has upon a sensitive mind can be fully expressed even in the most poetic language : for thought and feeling are always in advance of, and transcend, language. This difficulty of description, then, is more or less inevitable, but the intuitive mind will be able to grasp much of what is meant by the aid of the hints that have been given, and they will therefore serve their purpose well enough, no doubt. It is only because the author has found by experience that beginners are too apt to take what is said as a hard and fast rule, invariable in all cases, that he has felt this caution to be necessary.

IMPORTANT NOTE

It should be remembered in studying the foregoing lists that the conjunctions or aspects which appear first in each list are those formed between the slowest planets; they are therefore slow in formation and in dissolution and remain in operation for a lengthy period. Thus the conjunction of ♆ and ♅ will continue within "orbs" for a period of several years. At the last conjunction, for instance, ♅ approached within an orb of 8° of ♆ as early as April, 1817, but it did not reach completion till March 21st, 1821, and did not pass out of orbs until the end of December, 1825—a period of practically nine years, during the whole of which time these planets may be said to have been 'within orbs of a conjunction.'

From this consideration we learn two things. First, that the orbs we allow for an aspect would seem to require a certain amount of restriction in the case of the more distant planets. Second, that since during a period of four or five years (halving the above so as to be on the safe side) *every person born* would have these two planets within orbs of a conjunction, it must follow that the influence of such conjunction must be exceedingly general in its effect and must affect the community more than the individual: and we should therefore expect to find it indicating merely general tendencies rather than specific qualities: nor should we look for strong effect in the *personal* life of the native, unless (a) the aspect were very near completion, in which case it might be expected to have a marked effect on the character, and hence on the career, or (b) the planets forming such aspect occupied one of the angles, and would thus show out in the environment and personal fate. As an instance of the former, we may mention Sir Richard Burton and Mr Joseph Wallace, both born on March 21st, 1821, and both having ♆ ☌ ♅ in the second house of the nativity. The horoscopes, and incidents in the lives, of these two very remarkable people will be found in the issues of MODERN ASTROLOGY for August, 1907, and October, 1905, respectively.

These remarks will likewise apply to the oppositions and also, with suitable modifications, to the squares and trines as well. They are very important and should always be borne in mind when attempting to judge the relative values of a number of conjunctions or aspects.

It should never be forgotten that 'the greater includes the less' and 'the whole is greater than its part.' For example, suppose a conjunction of the Moon and Sun to occur during the time that the Sun is in conjunction with, say, Mars: it might in a sense be said to take place *within* the soli-martial conjunction; and all events happening during the course of that lunation would therefore be coloured by the predominant influence of the ☉ ☌ ♂, under whose ægis, as it were, it was ushered in.

It is the PRINCIPLE here outlined that is the most important thing to be taken account of, and it is not necessary to enlarge upon it; the intuitive student will readily discern how to apply it. But by way of a guide and in order to assist the mind the approximate interval, during which any conjunction or opposition between any of the superior planets ♆ ♅ ♄ ♃ ♂ remains within the 8° orb which has been given as the *outside limit*, may be stated as follows: ♆ and ♅, nine years—♅ and ♄ two years—♄ and ♃, one year—♃ and ♂, very variable, according to the position of the earth at the time, but say one month— ♄ and ♆, same as ♄ and ♅—♃ and ♅, same as ♃ and ♄—♂ and ♄, same as ♂ and ♃. These periods are only approximate, but will serve as a rough guide in dealing with ☌ s and ☍ s; for □s or △s take one third of these times.

For the other conjunctions and aspects, the Ephemeris for the year of birth will, of course, show exactly how long they remain in force.

CHAPTER V

The Three Centres. Sun, Moon, and Ascendant

Reference has already been made to the importance of the Sun, Moon, and Ascendant, three centres representing three vital points not only in the body or outer man, but also in the character and inner man. They are equalising and balancing powers, which adjust the ebb and flow or contraction and expansion in every horoscope. They have also other correspondences in religious philosophy, but here we need not follow them at present: for this side of the subject the reader is referred to *The 'Reason Why' in Astrology*, by Mr H. S. Green, which forms No. VI. of the *Shilling Series of Astrological Manuals*.

(1) The first of these centres is THE SUN, taken according to the zodiacal sign in which it was placed at birth. It represents the Individuality, or the soul of the man, divested of all outer ephemeral phases and moods. It corresponds in its highest interpretation to the very basis of the nature, the very sense of existence itself, upon which is built up that idea of *I am I* which is the root of individuality. To the character it gives power, authority, dignity, will, resolution, self-reliance. In the body it corresponds to the heart and its associated blood-vessels. It is the source of all vital energy, no matter whether coming directly from the Sun or indirectly through the Moon or the Ascendant. It is the centre of the being, both in body and soul. It corresponds to the *Fixed Signs*.

Among the planets Mercury is the messenger of the Sun, transmitting its influence outwards. In the character Mercury therefore represents the mind, which is the first outer garment of the individuality. In the body, vital energy is transmitted along the nerves: and Mercury stands for the cerebro-spinal nervous system mainly, along with such organs as the hands and tongue, which are concerned with the outward

68

expression of intelligence.   Two further degrees are seen in Venus and Mars.   Mars represents an expanding force, rushing from the centre, awakening desire and the outgoing energies.   It may be said to represent the will of the Sun definitely directed outwards; and this in the average undeveloped humanity is desire, a reaching forth after something attractive: but in the more developed and harmoniously balanced man it becomes will power, an enormous force when properly controlled and guided by intelligence and wisdom.   Venus harmonises and balances, and gives the longing for harmony and balance.   This shows outwardly as the love between the sexes, which in unbalanced and irregularly developed humanity is capable of many distortions; but in a higher degree of evolution will transcend sex completely and become universal love, pity, and sympathy—the keynote of the Saviours of the race.   The most matter-of-fact influences attributed to Venus in the books may be interpreted in this way; for the love of pleasure is only the wish to remove discords; and a fondness for society and for all beautiful and attractive things that are sources of happiness, is but the same striving after harmony, though often mistaken and ill-judged in its methods. Venus thus acts as a kind of representative of the Sun; what the planet balances and harmonises ($\simeq$) is gathered up and passed inward ($\forall$) to the solar centre, there to become a permanent possession of the soul, its own for all eternity.   Venus thus not only stands for love, peace, and harmony, but even acquires a signification in connection with property, which is seen in its rulership of Taurus, the second zodiacal sign; its other associated sign, Libra, representing harmony and balance.

(2) The second of the three centres is THE MOON, which has to be judged partly by the sign in which it is placed and partly by its distance from the Sun.   The Moon signifies all things intermediate, and hence the Personality (which is the intermediary between the Ego and the physical earth of which it desires experience); the shifting and fluctuating personality in general, with its feelings emotions passions, pleasures and pains, and the life of the senses.   In the body, it corresponds to all glandular structures and soft tissues, to the physiological life, to the power of growth, renewal, reproduction.

Looking upon the body as built up of materials obtained from all the sub-divisions of the physical plane, the Moon stands for the etheric double of the physical body, or that counterpart of the body which is built up of the ethers of the physical plane.   This double it is that forms a channel for the inflowing vital currents, signified by and derived from the first centre, the Sun; and this explains the part the Moon plays in matters of health and the hyleg. The double is in close touch with the nervous system, the Moon's influence over which is well-known astrologically, although it has probably a closer correspondence with the sympathetic than with the cerebro-spinal system. The Moon plays an important part in matters of mediumship, for the double represents the missing link between the living and the dead; we live in our physical material body, and the dead on the astral or psychic plane; and the double is a kind of link or bridge between the two. Just as the Moon never leaves the neighbourhood of the earth, so the double can never go far from the body; and its separation at all is to be deprecated; such separation is generally indicated by the prominence of the Moon, Saturn, and Neptune in a horoscope. The double has a mechanical activity of its own in sleep, as it is a kind of receiver for all sorts of telepathic thought-currents, which register themselves automatically in the brain of the sleeper and so disturb and confuse the true experiences that might otherwise come through from the soul. It has been found that remarkable dreams are most usually experienced when the Moon is rising, culminating, or setting; but sometimes Uranus or Neptune may be found in these positions.

The Moon corresponds in a general way to the mutable or intermediate signs, and may be regarded as a mean between the contraction of Saturn and the expansion of Jupiter, the two extremes already explained in Chapter III. The Moon lends itself to either of these influences. When in conjunction with Jupiter, there is the extreme of growth, fertility, and expansion, whether in terms of body, emotions, or mind; but the conjunction with Saturn, if taken alone, produces just the contrary effect, limiting the flow of the vital current in all three departments of the being. A good aspect from Saturn to the Moon, however, is of very great benefit; for the good aspects, as we have seen, signify harmony, and in this case Saturn, instead of merely limiting or suppressing, regulates and controls, and reduces that which is under its control to law and order.

(3) The third of the three centres is the ASCENDANT. It gathers up the influences of the twelve mundane houses into one, and stands for the body in general and for the head and brain in particular as the controlling centre of the body. Mind cannot manifest itself on this plane without a

physical vehicle, a brain and body; and even then it can only express what that vehicle allows it to express. There may be and often are important parts of the character that are shut out by limitations of the physical brain, and which consequently are never manifested. The brain does not make the mind, but it does limit and condition its manifestation. This vehicle, built up and handed on to the child by its parents, is represented by the twelve houses in general and the Ascendant in particular. It is the centre of inherited traits of character, inborn disposition, and parentally derived tendencies. The inner man has to take it as it is given him—for he does not fashion it for himself—and make the best use he can of it. The Ascendant thus stamps itself upon the man very distinctly. It can always be recognised very clearly in early life; but if the man breaks away from ancestral tendencies, developes self-reliance and the knowledge and power to mould his own future and to act for himself, the influence of this centre may be modified, may yield itself, so to speak, more and more, and become blended first with that of the Moon and afterwards with that of the Sun; if either luminary should be rising the 'blend' will be particularly strong.

As ruling the brain, the Ascendant has a great deal of sympathy with the planet Mercury, and therefore has much influence over the flow of the vital currents through the nervous system. It will be remembered that the sixth house, which has health and disease for one of its meanings, corresponds to Virgo and Mercury. The civilised man of to-day lives mostly in his nervous system, and whatever affects or governs the nerves has an important influence upon health. This shows why the Ascendant is of importance when considering the question of health and longevity.

The Ascendant corresponds to cardinal (movable) signs.

These three centres may be regarded in two ways. Firstly, considered as more or lest separable units, they may be arranged vertically thus:

    (1) THE SUN—*Individuality*.
    (2) THE MOON—*Personality*.
    (3) THE HOUSES (of which the Ascendant is the first)—*Body*.

In this classification the zodiac (ecliptic) would be included as part of the Sun's influence; and the planets would be grouped around either the Moon or the Sun, although in reality they are all specialised powers of that great Life that functions behind the Sun.

Secondly, when considered as three centres in a living man clothed in a physical body, they assume a horizontal classification.

BODY

Ascendant	*Moon*	*Sun*
Brain	Stomach and physiological life	Heart
Intellect	Senses	Vitality
		Will

The Ascendant is that which moves most quickly ; it corresponds to translatory motion and the guna called Rajas. The Sun moves most slowly, and corresponds to rotary motion and Tamas. The Moon is intermediate, and corresponds to vibratory motion and Sattva.

In the first volume of this series, entitled *Astrology for All*, full particulars were given of the 144 polarities of the Sun and Moon. In order to complete the subject, those of the Ascendant should, strictly speaking, be included. This, however, would multiply the above number by 12, and although much greater detail would be possible, the extent of the work obviously precludes its being undertaken here.

Any one of the three centres—the Sun, Moon, and Ascendant—may be in either a cardinal, a mutable, or a fixed sign ; and this gives 9 as the smallest number of combinations possible. If these same positions are considered in relation to each other, the number is increased to 27. If the three centres are taken not with regard to the qualities but to the elements, fire, earth, air, and water, we have 12 as the result, which would correspond to the zodiacal signs. Again, if these are considered in relation to each other, there are 84 possible combinations. All these are included within the 1728 which represent the total permutations. All should be tabulated and studied, although space will not permit of it here. The Sun and Moon in each sign, however, are severally discribed and later on the ascendant also, while the character and appearance due o each planet rising in any sign forms part of our next chapter.

THE INFLUENCE OF THE SUN IN THE TWELVE SIGNS

☉ *in* ♈   This position is generally fortunate, both   ☉ *in* ♈
for those things signified by the Sun as well as for those coming under Aries and the first house. It contributes to health, vitality, and length of life. It gives strength of will, energy, activity, self-confidence, wilfulness, and some rashness. The native will acquire some position

of authority or responsibility, no matter whether he move in a humble sphere, or in a more public one. He will be independent in manner, and capable of directing others, acting as head or chief—this not because he aims at mere popularity or notoriety, but because he feels himself capable of command, and assumes such a position naturally. Some kind of responsibility will fall upon his shoulders, either in little things or in great, according as to whether the rest of the horoscope does or does not back up this indication. There is a natural inclination to religion, though the latter is sometimes more rational than devotional ; but he will also be independent and positive in manner, enthusiastic, sometimes militant, and, if carried to excess, intolerant of opposition. He is generally magnanimous, and his anger soon passes away. There is a tendency to travel and exploration, also to scientific work. It favours a martial occupation, a pioneer, explorer, or leader. To a slight extent it is favourable to the father for the birth of sons, and for marriage and the husband in a female horoscope. If afflicted, it may cause excitability, mental over-work, insomnia.

⊙ *in* ♉ This is favourable for the acquisition of money ⊙ *in* ♉ and property generally. Such may come through business, through inheritance from a parent, through investments, stocks, and shares, or public undertakings. If a female, may gain through the husband. The children gain in money or possessions through the parents or their relatives. It is good for the acquisition of houses and lands, and for those whose occupation is connected with these, and with the earthy element generally. It is fortunate for the father, and tends towards marriage. The native is warm-hearted and amorous ; but there is some slight liability to be misled in the affections, to bestow them too readily, or to be drawn into a *liaison* He is firm, patient, obstinate ; is very set upon achieving his end ; pursues his object with great determination, even if it should lead him away from the lawful track. He is rather ambitious, and desirous of assuming a prominent position, and frequently occupies some more or less isolated or responsible position. This influence may lift the native up somewhat and give the favour of those in authority, or in a higher sphere of life. In a bad horoscope, there may be notoriety rather than fame, and bad temper rather than firmness, and it is then apt to increase selfishness. There is some inclination for poetry, music, painting, or the like. Native is usually generous and free, but sometimes quite the opposite tendency shows itself, and he is extremely careful in money matters.   This position is good for vitality, but in an afflicted horoscope may tend towards fits, convulsions, or effusion of blood on the brain.

☉ *in* Ⅱ This strengthens the intellect, and inclines the ☉ *in* Ⅱ native to the pursuit of literature, science, or art, and to following some occupation connected with these.   It favours educational, secretarial, and clerical work, writings, documents, letters; literary work of a short or ephemeral kind, such as in magazines, newspapers, pamphlets, or small books; work connected with messengers, means of transit, the post-office, etc.   The mind is versatile, and fond of change, but positive and strong.   Native is somewhat ambitious and aspiring, and may turn to public work connected with education, local politics, or public speaking and lecturing.   He is fond of moving about, of walking, and of short journeys, principally by land.   He makes friends among literary people, and others signified by Gemini, and may join some society or association, the activities of which are those of Gemini.   He may be the cleverest or best educated, or best known of his family.   It sometimes gives several brothers or sisters.   This position slightly favours the birth of twins, two love affairs, and two marriages in a female horoscope.   The children gain through their parents, relatives or friends.

☉ *in* ♋ This is good for money or property gained from ☉ *in* ♋ the parents.   Money may be gained through some occupation connected with the water or liquids, with house or land property or shipping, with acting or public performing.   To a slight extent it inclines to such occupations as detective, gaoler, policeman, worker in hospital or poor-house, or some public occupation not refined or not popular, or not in very good repute, plebeian.   At some period of his life native will live near water.   It is slightly unfavourable for a strong constitution and longevity, for the parents, and for marriage in a female horoscope, but if marriage occurs, money may be gained through the husband.   The native is attached to home and family life and the mother, and prospers with house and land property.   He is easy-going, fond of pleasure and amusements. In a bad horoscope, this position may incline to dissipation and evil courses; it weakens the will somewhat, and renders the native untrust-worthy: threatens obstacles and disappointment in life.   It favours the birth of children, but if much afflicted they may be sickly or not prosperous.

☉ *in* ♌ This position brings out strongly the qualities ☉ *in* ♌

of the Sun. The native is ambitious, aspiring, and capable of filling positions of authority and responsibility ; is fond of exercising authority and stands a good deal on his dignity, but is generous and magnanimous, affectionate and sympathetic. This position favours all who rule over, direct, or employ others ; also actors, public performers, schoolmasters and instructors, and those who follow occupations that oblige them to come to the front to amuse, instruct or direct others. The native is generally found in some more or less prominent or responsible position, whatever his sphere of life : it is difficult for him to act in subordinate capacities unless he has others under him, or unless the indications of serving are prominent in the horoscope. He is very kind-hearted, sociably inclined, and fond of cutting a figure in society ; and is susceptible in affairs of the heart. This position is fortunate for the father, for health and longevity, and for marriage in a female horoscope. It favours the birth of a son. It contributes to the manifestation of genius if other positions support it.

⊙ *in* ♍ This position is favourable for the acquisition of money through some occupation wherein the native acts as subordinate, or where he is more or less under the command of a chief or superior ; some post in which he is not the sole head, but is responsible to some master. He may be one of the rank and file, a worker, but is more likely to be a manager with others under him, but himself responsible to a head. In some cases this may take the form of partnership. He does not make a good master when left to himself ; there is some defect in his administration ; want of self-confidence, or bad judgment or some other cause. He is most fortunate when he receives advice, help, or direction from someone else. He is liable to suffer through servants or sub-ordinates, unless the Sun is well-aspected, when he may benefit considerably through them. It tends to literary, medical, or scientific work, books, reading, secretarial or clerical work ; and he may make money by some occupation connected with these. It is slightly unfavourable for health, and the constitution of the native, as well as of the father or son. It is rather unfavourable for marriage and the husband in a female horoscope, and there may be misfortune in love. ·It slightly favours money from parental relatives, and occupations of the earthly element. The disposition is rather serious or subdued, and may be melancholy at times, not sufficiently reliant, hopeful, or self-assertive, feeling disappointment keenly. He may be looked upon as either very judicial and impartial, or as vacillating and not to be depended upon, according to the nature of the horoscope.

⊙ *in* ♎ The native is rather popular and generally ⊙ *in* ♎ liked ; is sociable, affectionate and romantic ; fond of company, and easily makes friends, especially with the opposite sex. He has some taste and ability for science and the fine arts, poetry, music or painting, and may excel in one of these directions. This position tends to bring about an early engagement or marriage, unless some other part of the horoscope forbids it ; but there is likely to be some trouble connected with either or both events, such as disappointment in love or disharmony in marriage (chiefly in a female horoscope). The native can be independent if necessary, but is seldom or ever overbearing or proud. Is kind and sympathetic, and likes to awaken brotherly and friendly feelings in others, and often gives way to others for the sake of peace. Is just, sincere, and impartial ; sometimes very intuitive, and may manifest genius in some direction. There is a dash of the democratic and brotherly spirit in him, no matter what his opinions or position in life. It is favourable for joining societies, associations, companies, partnership. It strengthens the link of affection between the native and his brothers and sisters. It inclines slightly to travel, especially short journeys by land. It favours sociability, good humour, and a buoyant, hopeful spirit.

⊙ *in* ♏ This increases the vitality ; but if the horoscope ⊙ *in* ♏ shows much affliction, and other testimonies coincide, there is liability to an early or sudden death. Native is liable to accidents, illnesses and death of the nature of Mars and Scorpio, especially if the Sun is hyleg. A death may occur in his family, or among those closely concerned with it, shortly before or after his birth. This position is unfavourable for the parents (especially father) and for the husband (in a female horoscope) : it may cause the death of these, or separation or estrangement from them. It promises children, but threatens the death of one (especially son). The native may gain money or estate by marriage, partnership, or inheritance, but this position of the Sun tends to extravagance, and if afflicted native may lose heavily in any of these ways. It favours martial occupations and those coming under Scorpio and the eighth house. It tends slightly to the occult and to all mysteries and hidden things, whether those of the chemist, the physiologist, the detective, or what not. It gives firmness, determination, and obstinacy. The native resists outside influences, and all changes that do not originate with himself, though in order to carry out his own purposes he may inaugurate great and revolutionary changes, constructive or destructive. He has much pride and self-confidence, with energy and activity, and may come to the front on this account. He is sometimes passionate, with a strong temper. This position shows contradictory influences of good and bad, rise and fall, which may be seen in different horoscopes according to the aspects, and sometimes in the same horoscope at different times; the native may follow some plebeian or unpopular occupation, and rise considerably therein; or *vice versâ*, he may occupy some eminent position and not succeed therein. In some way the apparent contradiction will work itself out.

⊙ *in* ♐ The native is goodnatured, generous, judicial,   ⊙ *in* ♐ and impartial. He is naturally religious and sincere, and may be very intuitive and mystical, original in his work, an inventor or discoverer, and he becomes known for some special work he has done. Even when he does not follow the religion of his neighbours, he is generally honest and sincere in his opinions. He is restless in mind and body, hopeful and enthusiastic. He may follow more than one occupation or pursuit at a time, or change his occupation. He is suited for occupations of the nature of the ninth house. This position is favourable for health and the birth of sons, and inclines to travelling and voyaging and change of residence. It strengthens the intuition, and may exist with genius.

⊙ *in* ♑ The native is ambitious and aspiring, desirous of ⊙ *in* ♑ power and fame, and is well fitted for leading, commanding and directing others, whether for good or evil. He often makes a prominent figure in his sphere of life, or he may rise in the world and gain celebrity (or notoriety). Sooner or later he occupies some position of importance or responsibility where he has to guide others or act as head over others. He has few confidants or intimate friends, and may become isolated through fate or misfortune, and lonely. He is thoughtful and subtle, serious and reserved, may be wanting in buoyancy and hopefulness, and is somewhat conservative in his tendencies and respect for conventional opinions, although if Mars be prominent this may be altogether changed. He often succeeds well as manager for another, or in some large enterprise where he is the head or all but the head, such as in wholesale trading, banking, or in the direction of some company. He makes a good master and good servant, unless there are contrary testimonies, but prefers the position of master. There may be a good deal of self and selfishness in him. This position is not good for health or longevity, but other influences may counteract this. It is also unfavourable for marriage and the health of the husband (in a female horoscope) and threatens the ill-health or death of a child (probably son).

☉ *in* ♒ The native is popular, sociable and makes ☉ *in* ♒ friends readily. He is to some extent democratic and broad minded in his sympathies, although at the same time cautious and prudent. He often leads a more or less public life, where he comes before the many rather than the few. He is interested in educational or political affairs, or popular movements for the benefit of the many, and may follow some more or less intellectual pursuit. He is patient and persevering, skilful, humane, intelligent, and may rise considerably in life above the sphere of his birth, mainly by his own exertions. He is original and self reliant, and yet makes many friends, by whose help, advice or favour in some way he benefits. In large or in small things, for good or evil fortune, he is pretty sure to be known as a reliable worker, and to come to the front as such ; but it is necessary for him to have his own way, as he is independent and dislikes control. He will join some partner, society, association, club, or community or some movement bringing one or many others to join with him in a common cause. The position is slightly unfavourable for the father, it favours the birth of sons but brings trouble with one of them. It inclines slightly to bring about marriage, but is slightly unfavourable to the husband (in a female horoscope) and may cause some trouble in married life, or in love matters. It is slightly unfavourable for vitality and long life unless contra-indicated by aspect or mundane position.

☉ *in* ♓ This gives a restless, changeable disposition, ☉ *in* ♓ often too retiring and not sufficiently self-reliant. The native is either quiet and unambitious, or, if he essays great things and positions of importance, either does not gain them or does not retain them. He may be upheld in a high position by the influence of others or by association with someone. There is a lack of self-initiative, and he is greatly influenced by persons and circumstances instead of moulding them to his will. If he is a leader, he is to some extent a mere figure-head, expressing the views of his party rather than forcing his own upon them. It indicates the server rather than the ruler, and points out occupations which are humble or somewhat plebian, or which do not entail prominence, as well as the natural occupations of this sign and the twelfth house. There may be at some time in life a good deal of unpopularity or hostility shown to the native, or he may have moments of considerable depression and anxiety; it threatens many obstacles and misfortunes in life. He is sociable and good humoured, but rather easily influenced by others. Is usually sincere and religious, but liable to change his religion or occupation, or may have two occupations at once; is wanting in perseverance. This position is slightly unfavourable for vitality and a sound constitution, also for the father and for marriage (in a female horoscope). A child is likely to die or prove unfortunate. It is not very good for love affairs, and causes hindrances and obstacles. There may be gain by marriage, legacy or partnership.

The Influence of the Moon in the Twelve Signs

☽ *in* ♈   An enthusiast in some direction; impulsive,   ☽ *in* ♈ aggressive and militant in manner, sometimes irritable and liable to fits of anger. Insists on having his own way; disobedient to superiors; independent and self-reliant. Somewhat volatile or changeable, and depending upon impulse: disliking conventionality or discipline. May achieve popularity or notoriety. May be placed in some position in which he exercises authority over a number of people or is head over many. He will be at the head of some undertaking, or will be in some way prominent in his sphere of life. There is some liability to feverish diseases and affections of the head, especially if the Moon is hyleg. He will go more by intellect than intuition. The mother will play a prominent part in the life in some way, often not a sympathetic or fortunate one; and there is likelihood of differences between the native and his parents, or the latter may die early or be separated from him. This position favours pursuits of the nature of Mars, independent or original ventures. The native will strike out a path for himself or at least attempt to do so; and much that he does, both wrong and right, will be unexpected by his friends and contrary to their advice. Mysticism or occultism of some kind may show in his life; or the tendency may take the form of a necessity for secrecy in some of his affairs; his occupation may sometimes involve secrecy or mystery or be of low class; though this is very contrary to his nature. He may meet with unpopularity or threatened scandal of some kind.

☽ *in* ♉ Quiet and unimpulsive: persisent, determined,   ☽ *in* ♉
and not to be thwarted in his aims.   Somewhat hopeful, ambitious and
desirous of excelling.   Following established customs, conservatı ʋe by
nature, resisting change and outside influences.   This position gains
friends for the native, and favours the acquisition of money, houses, or
land.   It favours occupations of the nature of the earthy element;
dealing in land, houses, heavy goods, old established businesses; or the
native may succeed to the father's business and gain or inherit from
a parent.   In some cases the native may support the mother, or she
benefits financially through the native.   Sometimes the occupation may
be one considered low class, plebian, or unpopular, involving secrecy
or mystery; but it will generally be remunerative; and unless contradicted elsewhere in the horoscope, the native will prosper financially.
This position of the Moon is favourable for occupations of water and
liquids, and for living near rivers or on the coast; and slightly good for
money derived from companies, wholesale trading, associations, societies,
etc.   It is slightly favourable for marriage and short journeys, also for
singing, music, painting: for gaining friends and joining societies.   The
native will have more sisters and brothers, and will usually be friendly
with them throughout life.   He is somewhat sensuous and material, but
sociable and of good disposition.

☽ *in* ♊ Strengthens the intellect, and makes the native ☽ *in* ♊
a lover of books, of study, of scientific and literary pursuits; and inclines
him to some occupation of the nature of Mercury and the third house.
He is active in mind and body; changes his residence frequently, or has
more than one house; often goes on short journeys; travels, or is out
and about a good deal; is often out-doors, walking or riding, etc., or
calling on other people.   He is skilful and dexterous with his hands and
arms.   Is able to live by his wits, and may gain money as messenger,
traveller, salesman, speaker, clerk, writer, designer, journalist, engraver,
artist, sculptor, or by study and literature.   May have more than one
occupation, or may change his occupation.   May have step- (or adopted)
mother or brothers and sisters.   The mind is prone to change, and
there may be irresolution, or lack of preservance; in a bad horoscope
this may show as underhandedness, subtlety, lack of straightforwardness
and honesty, especially in matters of the second, third, and fourth
houses.   Money may be gained through the mother, or her side of the
family (or lost if the Moon is afflicted).   Native resembles the mother

mentally or bodily. If the Moon is much afflicted, will suffer through matters of Gemini and the third house.

☽ *in* ♋ The native is fond of ease and comfort at home,   ☽ *in* ♋ is homely in his habits, and attached to his home. It attaches him to his mother, whom he may take after. He is friendly and sociable in manner, is imaginative, emotional and changeable. He is influenced greatly by his surroundings, is sensitive to outside influences, and to some extent falls in readily with the ways and methods of others, adopts the suggestions of others, sympathises with the joys and sorrows of others, and takes on his colouring from outside, to some extent. He is most fortunate when acting under the direction of, or in accordance with, the advice of someone else. But this may be greatly modified if positive signs or planets are prominent in the figure; under the influence of Mars, or martial signs, especially, he may show much positiveness and independence. There is some ability for acting, mimicking, expressing the thoughts and emotions of others; also for music, painting or poetry. This position relates somewhat to mediumship, psychism, and the astral plane generally. The native is drawn to the watery element; lives near water or travels by water; deals in liquids; and is fortunate with house or land property and shipping. This is a fruitful position and increases the number of children.

☽ *in* ♌ One of the signs of rulership. It tends to uplift   ☽ *in* ♌ the native, to put him in positions of responsibility, or prominence, and to give him authority over others as head, or manager, or director. It is favourable for money matters, for inheritance from a parent, or pecuniary help from those wealthier than the native; and it gives the favour of those in higher ranks of life than the native. It may give money through any occupation of the Fifth House. It gives some love of luxuries, pleasures, perfumes, jewels, fine clothes, etc. Native is ambitious, desirous of occupying a prominent place, and does not hesitate to come before the public. He is honourable, generous in money matters, high minded, candid, and warm hearted. He is susceptible in affairs of the heart, a favourite with the opposite sex, and a sincere lover. It favours intuition and genius; it gives love of music, poetry or painting. The position is rather unfavourable for the father, and it will co-operate with any other influence in causing trouble to the father and superiors through the native.

☽ *in* ♍ The native has good intellectual powers and is   ☽ *in* ♍

capable of following some intellectual pursuit; he has a good memory and learns easily. It is good for any occupation of the nature of the Sixth House, and, to a less extent, of the Third also. It covers a great variety of occupations; servant, manager, agent, or subordinate in any capacity; any occupation connected with grain or food-stuffs, such as farmer, miller, grocer, malster, confectioner; and any connected with drugs or medicine, chemist, druggist, herbalist, analyst, doctor, dispenser, etc.; and to less extent those of the Third House. He makes a trust-worthy and fortunate servant and himself is fortunate through servants or those under him. This position, taken alone, tends to make him quiet and easy going, somewhat irresolute, not ambitious or pretentious. It does not favour sound health, and is not good for the mother; it tends to affections of the body or of that part governed by the house in which the Moon is situated. He has many friends, especially female friends. May belong to some company, firm, society, or association. There is likelihood of many short journeys and work as secretary, messenger, clerk, traveller, schoolmaster, etc.

  ☽ *in* ♎   This position favours marriage, more especially ☽ *in* ♎ in a male horoscope, and makes the native popular and attractive with the opposite sex, and it conduces to general popularity. It gives fondness for music, poetry, and the fine arts generally, and much ability in this direction. The native is affectionate, good natured, kind in manner and easily gains friends. It is fortunate for the parents, especially mother and for the inheritance from parents, especially mother; also for house and property. The native is fond of company, society and friends. Much of his fate and many events of his life will come about through his association with other people; he will be greatly swayed and influenced by other people; generally by some one person. It tends strongly to partnership, not merely in business, but in almost all affairs of life. He works with another person in nearly all undertakings; and, without necessarily being irresolute, depends largely upon some one else, and can get along best in almost all things when associated with someone. The marriage may be helped or hindered (according to aspects) by a parent, either of the native or the marriage partner. The same may be said of the occupation and position in life. There may be some difference either in age or social position between the native and the marriage or business partner.

  ☽ *in* ♏ The native is very firm and determined, self-reliant, ☽ *in* ♏

and assured, and well able to stand alone and fight his own battles. He is abrupt and plain spoken, positive, energetic and capable of hard work, though also fond of the good things of the world and of easy living. He is conservative and averse to change, especially if forced upon him from without; he is difficult to influence and may be very obstinate; and yet for his own purposes he will sometimes appear very revolutionary and changeable, and will advocate or carry out great and revolutionary changes. He is sometimes irritable, angry, and revengeful; this being a very bad position if backed up by other evil influences. This is a fruitful sign and increases the number of children, but threatens the death of, or trouble through one. If hyleg, it gives considerable vitality, but with liability to feverish diseases, especially of the lower bowel, bladder, and other adjacent parts. The position is not favourable for the mother and her side of the family. It does not favour morality, and may give habits of drinking; it often causes a coarseness in speech or manner, and threatens some scandal to the native; it rather tends against fineness of feeling and refined instincts. It inclines to medium-ship, psychism and occultism. A death occurs in the native's family, or in the ranks of their close associates, shortly before or soon after his birth or early in his life; and he has much to do with death, acts as executor, is frequently brought into relation with the dead, or may follow some occupation bearing upon the dead. It attracts to the opposite sex in any horoscope; favours marriage in a male horoscope, but threatens disharmony in the married state or in the relations with the opposite sex. It slightly favours money by inheritance, marriage, or partnership, but there is trouble in connection with it and loss through high expenditure or wastefulness, especially if bad aspects coincide; or he may be called upon to spend freely for his family or others.

☽ *in* ♐ This gives a quick, restless and unsettled manner, ☽ *in* ♐ either to the body or mind; the native is active in body and fond of physical exercise, sports, athletics, is a quick walker and worker. He is inclined to travel, and changes his abode frequently, and will probably go a voyage at least once in his life. His disposition is sincere and honourable, kindly and good humoured. There is a strong inclination to the occupation and affairs of the Ninth House, and these are sure to be prominent in the life history. The native is religious and sincere in his belief even if it be unorthodox. There is some inclination for mysticism, psychism, and the occult; he is a natural teacher or preacher, and may have something of the prophet in his nature. The intuition is increased and made more sensitive, and there may be some psychic gift, such as clairvoyance. There is a tendency to dreaming and somnambulism. There may be talent or even genius for religion, philosophy, music, poetry, etc. In the lower type of horoscope the animal side of the sign will show rather than the religious, and then occupations and amusements connected with shipping and horses will be prominent in the life. He is a faithful worker or servant, and himself benefits by servants or those under him. He may have two occupations or may change his occupation. May have a step-parent or be adopted.

☽ *in* ♑ This tends to bring the native before the public ☽ *in* ♑ for good or evil, popularity or notoriety, though it usually has some drawback attaching to it; he may achieve relative fame or notoriety, or may move in some sphere that brings him before many people. If well aspected, he may be very popular as the head of some undertaking, may attract attention as a prominent or responsible person in some way, for something he has done or with which he is associated; but if badly aspected, the publicity signified by this position may be of an unpleasant nature. It gives some degree of rulership, generalship and administrative ability, which is intensified if the Sun is in a sign or house having a similar power, or if a congenial sign is rising. There is always some drawback or difficulty attaching to the occupation or to the fame or to the position the native gains; he may raise up enemies, open or secret, or his reputation may suffer, with or without his having deserved it. There is some trouble connected with the parents; one dies, or there may be differences, inharmony, or separation, or the birth may be illegitimate, or the native badly brought up by the parents. These troubles will not all be traced in each case, but some one of them will nearly always be found. It slightly favours marriage but there is also some drawback here: the marriage partner may die, or there may be disharmony; there may be differences in age, social position, or possessions. According to aspects, a parent may help or hinder the marriage prospects. The native is rather fond of show, is rather selfish, careful with money matters, calculating and cautious, and knows how to influence others, but is often cold by nature and thinks too little of the feelings of others. If the horoscope is a good one, the more undesirable characteristics of this position may be obviated. If other influences assist, he may attain very considerable fame or prominence.

☽ *in* ♒ This gives some inclination for astrology, fortune ☽ *in* ♒
telling, dreaming, visions, mediumship, mysticism, and the occult
generally. Subjects that are unusual, original, eccentric, and novel,
attract the native. He may become a freemason, or join some secret or
mystical society, association or brotherhood. He is broad and humanitarian in his sympathies ; fraternises readily with those who are congenial
to him, is easily drawn into the company of such, and will be found in
some club, society, association, or group of those similarly minded. He
has an inclination for political, educational, and scientific work, and may
join any movement or public body relating to these ; has some inclination
for local politics and municipal affairs. He is sociable and sympathetic
in manner, and desirous of the good opinion of others, and yet may be
very independent, unorthodox, and unconventional at times. It increases
the imagination, intuition, and mental sensitiveness generally. To a
slight extent it favours benefit and inheritance from females or the
mother's side of the family, from partnership in business, and from
occupations and affairs of the nature of the Fourth House, but these will
suffer greatly under bad aspects. It is slightly unfavourable for marriage
(in a male horoscope) and for the mother. It is slightly unfavourable
for the constitution, especially the nervous system. If the Moon is
afflicted the eyesight may suffer.

☽ *in* ♓ The native is quiet, retiring, and easy going, is ☽ *in* ♓
restless and fond of variety, easily changes his mind, is irresolute and
not always to be depended upon, is rather easily discouraged, and meets
with obstacles, misfortune, and opposition in life. It favours travelling,
especially by water, and change of residence. It gives a liking for reading
of a romantic or emotional kind, for poetry and music that appeals to the
emotions and feelings. As speaker, writer, composer, the native is
fluent, copious, imaginative, and diffuse. He inclines to be religious but is
likely to be more emotional than intellectual ; his opinions being felt rather
than reasoned out. He is sometimes wanting in buoyancy and hope, is
too serious or too easily depressed, and may lack matter-of-fact common
sense and humour. There may be a tendency to intemperance or
dissipation, laudanum drinking, etc. Mediumship, clear dreaming, and
various psychic powers may manifest themselves. It softens the frame
and increases the fleshy and glandular structures and is not favourable
for robust health. The native's birth may bring trouble to the mother.
There is danger from secret enemies: the native may himself not be

quite straightforward; and there is liability to detention in hospital, poorhouse, prison, etc.; but the worst effects will not follow unless there are accompanying bad aspects or other indications.

It has been shown in a previous chapter that each house is, as it were, coloured and modified by the sign on its cusp. In considering the influence of the Ascendant, therefore, it is necessary to take into account the modifications introduced by each sign when rising. These may be, in each case, arranged under the two heads of Personal Appearance and Character. The descriptions that follow apply to the rising sign alone; when a planet rises in that sign modifications are introduced according to the nature of the planet; and in giving descriptions of personal appearance it is also usually necessary to take into account the influence of the sign containing the Moon. It has been found by experience that when the Moon is decreasing in light (going from full to new) the native is *sometimes* better described by the setting than by the rising sign, but it is still uncertain precisely when this occurs; it apparently varies according to the rules governing the pre-natal epoch, which are not as yet completely understood. If no planet is rising the sign occupied by the lord of the ascendant should be specially noted, for in any case it has a strongly modifying influence not only on the character and temperament, but even on the appearance as well.

APPEARANCE AS DENOTED BY THE RISING SIGN

ARIES, ♈.—Middle stature or rather above it; spare body; long face and neck; head broad at temples and narrow at chin; bushy eyebrows; sharp sight; eyes grey to greyish-brown; rough or wiry hair, varying in colour from dark to sandy; sandy whiskers; ruddy complexion; sometimes going bald at the temples. Motive temperament.

Mental tendencies: courage, energy, impulse, ambition, pride, combativeness, activity, ardour.

TAURUS, ♉.—Stature, middle to short, inclining to plumpness; square face and square build of body; short strong neck; forehead, nose, lips, cheeks, and mouth all full; heavy jaw; dark eyes and hair, the latter sometimes curling; often stoops; round and prominent eyes; hands plump, short and broad.

Mental tendencies: constant, persevering, determined, conservative, obstinate; can be agreeable, affectionate, sociable and loving; but can be also very unreasonable, prejudiced, and wrong-headed, and when angry will stop at nothing. Proud and ambitious of power. Are good plodding workers, but in the unrefined types sometimes very slow, indolent, and sensuous.

GEMINI, ♊.—Tall, slender, and erect figure; long face, nose and chin;

arms and fingers long; dark hair; sanguine complexion; hazel eyes, quick sight; quick and active walk. Mental temperament.

Mental tendencies: good all-round mental abilities; quick at learning, fond of reading and writing; can receive a good education; inclination for music, drawing, painting, dancing, languages; manual dexterity; active mentality; lively, ingenious, and quick-witted; good disposition. Sometimes shy and retiring.

CANCER, ♋.—Not above average height; round face; full cheeks; sometimes double chin; grey or light blue eyes; pale complexion; vital temperament; tendency to stoutness; sometimes an awkward or heavy walk; short nose, sometimes prominent at tip.

Mental tendencies: very changeable, fond of novelty, fond of travelling and yet usually attached to relatives and the home; cautious, prudent, careful with money, desirous of possessions; sympathetic; some psychic or occult tendency sometimes shows out. Usually lacking in combativeness, but if Mars is prominent may become very much the reverse.

LEO, ♌.—Tall; large bones and muscles; broad shoulders; hair light in colour, with a tendency to baldness; head full-sized and round; grey eyes; florid or ruddy complexion; upright walk; motive temperament; square build of body in middle age.

Mental tendencies: self-confident, ambitious, proud, fearless, generous, open, candid, honourable, warm-hearted, fond of power and distinction; dignified when opposed, and despising enemies; impulsive, but faithful and unchanging; determined and persevering.

VIRGO, ♍.—Average height or rather above it; face and forehead round; dark hair, eyes, and complexion; moderately plump; well-formed. Usually mental-motive temperament.

Mental tendencies: good mental abilities, in some respects very like Gemini, ingenious, active mind, sympathetic, quiet, retiring, fond of learning, methodical, critical, thoughtful; sometimes rather undecided and vacillating.

LIBRA, ♎.—Tall, well-formed body, slender in youth but tending to stoutness in middle age; hair smooth, brown to black; eyes blue or brown; round face, good complexion; features regular, often good looking. Mental-vital temperament.

Mental tendencies: cheerful, genial · fond of society, company and amusements; good-natured, humane; loving but changeable, attracted by many rather than one. Good mental abilities, but oftener showing in an imaginative or artistic direction than as pure intellect.

SCORPIO, ♏.—Average height; hair dark, sometimes growing thick and curling or waving; prominent brows and perceptive faculties: aquiline or Jewish type of nose and profile; often square type of face and build of body. Motive-vital temperament. Tendency to stoutness.

Mental tendencies: self-reliant, wilful, courageous, determined; energetic and active when roused but at other times indolent; very fixed and obstinate and difficult to influence; angry and revengeful when provoked. Some are very practical, executive and matter-of-fact, good business men and desirous of money. Others have a strong inclination for occultism or mysticism in some form. The sign also inclines somewhat to chemistry, surgery or practical scientific research as apart from theory. They make good soldiers and sailors.

SAGITTARIUS, ♐.—Tall, slender, well-formed; hair brown or chestnut;

eyes blue or hazel ; oval face ; fresh complexion ; inclining to baldness near temples. Motive-mental temperament.

Mental tendencies : generous, good-hearted, cheerful, charitable, somewhat impulsive, active and enterprising, sympathetic and humane. Fond of travelling, voyaging, out-door sports and exercises. Inclination to religion or philosophy. Just, truthful, candid.

CAPRICORN, ♑.—Stature average to short ; sometimes bony and thin ; long or prominent nose ; in profile hatchet-faced ; thin neck, long chin ; dark or black hair, usually not plentiful ; thin beard. Motive or motive-mental temperament.

Mental tendencies : ambitious, persistent ; a strong sense of self-importance and often much selfishness ; great desire for pomp or power or wealth, or self-aggrandisement ; disposition cold, sometimes despondent ; subtle, much mental ingenuity and fertility ; quiet and reserved but determined. Changeable and capricious. Ability for managing and organising ; firmness ; self-possession ; self-control. They succeed rather by perseverance and plodding than by intense or spasmodic effort. Not remarkably sociable or affectionate. ' Self' and ' mentality' characterise the sign. Children and young people often unfortunate. The sign shows out much more favourably and characteristically in middle and old age. Other things being equal, if the native lives past the middle age, Capricorn favours old age and tenacity of life ; but it is quite the reverse with infants.

AQUARIUS, ♒.—Middle stature, strong and well formed ; square build of figure ; tendency to stoutness ; good complexion ; sometimes good looking ; hair varies from light to dark ; face long and fleshy.

Mental tendencies : good intellectual and practical abilities ; good disposition ; patient, self-controlled, quiet, humane, constant, persevering ; fixed opinions, not easily altered ; ingenious, inventive, fond of knowledge ; sometimes inclining to psychic matters.

PISCES, ♓.—Stature middle to short ; fleshy person and face ; pale complexion, full eyes ; tendency to double chin ; small and short limbs ; hair plentiful, dark. Vital temperament.

Mental tendencies : easy-going and good-natured ; indolent ; uncertain, changeful ; emotional, charitable, affectionate ; sometimes diffident and reserved or secretive.

RULES FOR DESCRIBING THE PERSONAL APPEARANCE

(*a*) Note carefully the degree of the ascending sign, and modify the whole sign by the decanate rising. Remember that persons who are tall are born in the first decanate of the sign rising, those of average or medium height in the middle of the sign, and those who are short or below the average in the last degrees.

(*b*) Note the planet or planets rising in or near the ascendant ; the nearer they are to the cusp, the greater will be their modification of the rising signs' influence.

(*c*) Note the *aspects* of planets to the ascendant, for they colour or influence the rising sign.

(*d*) When several are rising in the ascendant make no attempt to give an accurate description, as it cannot be determined owing to the impossibility of combining all the varied influences.

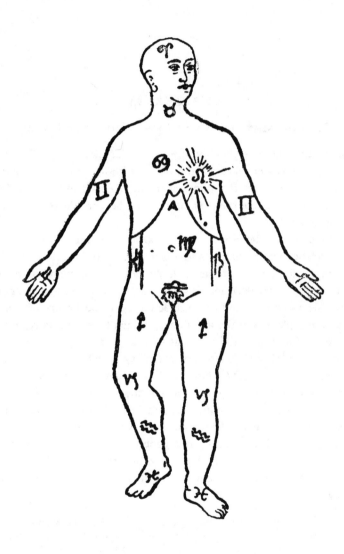

THE ZODIACAL MAN

CHAPTER VI

THE ASCENDANT OR RISING SIGN. THE FIRST HOUSE

THE sign, and more especially the particular degree, of the zodiac rising upon the eastern horizon at birth is known as the ASCENDANT. This term also embraces the whole of the first house, and in the author's opinion about 15° above the first house may be considered as included in the ascendant.*

The ascendant rules the personal appearance and to a considerable extent also the health, mind, and disposition. It is that part of the horoscope which has more to do with the physical body and its material wants than any other portion. The five physical senses find their outlet through this ascendant, and much depends upon the nature of the sign rising and any planets in the ascendant, if such there are, as regards the expression of the Ego in the physical world.

FIERY SIGNS rising denote good vitality, much force and energy, giving enough stamina to sustain life under adverse aspects and planetary positions; in a general sense they give good health. The disposition is to be hasty; impulsive; ambitious; proud; enterprising; commanding, with more desire to lead than serve; argumentative; quick-tempered; self-confident; and generally fortunate. The mind is aspiring; free; independent; acute; and penetrative.

The decanate and degree rising will show the particular mental endency.

---

* The 15° here spoken of is strictly speaking 15° of Oblique Ascension and not of the Zodiac, but in a great many cases half a sign will be near enough. A simple way of getting a good idea of the limit is to subtract *one hour* from the Sidereal Time at Birth and see in the Table of Houses what degree is then rising at the place of birth. The degree (which will at birth be found in the twelfth house, of course) may then be taken as forming the limit of influence of the first house, as above suggested.

AIRY SIGNS rising denote less vitality, and not so much robustness as the fiery signs, the artistic temperament usually predominating. The disposition is to be cheerful; amiable; sympathetic; well spoken; gentle; neat; courteous; perceptive; ingenious; and well-informed. The mind is cultured; musical; imaginative; refined; fond of reasoning and generally very well balanced, intellectual, and non-assertive.

The decanate and degree rising will show the particular mental tendency.

WATERY SIGNS rising denote less recuperative power, inability to manufacture sufficient '*Prana*,' and a tendency to weak constitution. The disposition is to be slow; effeminate; fearful; shy; backward; inert; lacking energy, and generally unwilling to act; conceited. The mind is receptive; dreamy; mediumistic; impressionable; psychic.

The decanate and degree rising will show the particular mental tendency.

EARTHY SIGNS rising denote good general health, but not too much vitality or an over-strong constitution. They give the motive temperament generally. The disposition is to be cautious; premeditative; secret; careful; stubborn; suspicious; economical; self-protective and slow. The mind is practical; objective; scientific; methodical and steady.

The decanate and degree rising will show the particular mental tendency.

Fixed Signs rising denote fixity of purpose; determination; pride; power; resolution; faithfulness; persistency; self-reliance; patience; dogmatism; independence; austerity, and reliability.

Cardinal Signs rising denote energy; enterprise; enthusiasm; activity; self-assertion; independence; ambition; changeableness; and the true pioneer spirit.

Mutable Signs rising denote versatility; sensitiveness; sympathy; impressionability; inconstancy; lack of energy; love of detail; restlessness; want of tact; aimlessness and indecision; an anxious nature.

The expression of the ascendant will be considerably modified, or accentuated, by the planets rising, positions and aspects of the ruling planet, the signs containing the majority of the planets, the aspects of the planets to the ascendant, etc. But the whole nativity, as well as the ascendant, affects the mind.

The rising sign has its own special influence upon the native's expression of himself in the physical world, though it has more relation to his environment, early surroundings, and hereditary tendencies, than to his inherent character. It is said that the rising sign influences female births more than males, also that throughout the whole of a female's life the ascendant has major influence, especially if the rising sign is a negative or feminine sign. In the author's opinion it is certain that during the first seven years the child is entirely governed by the ascendant and the lunar position, for it takes seven years for the Ego to gain control over his lower vehicles; but from this age onward environment and surroundings are gradually dominated until they are finally mastered and fresh impulses set in motion. The rising sign should be carefully studied and its ruler's influence noted, also any planets that may be rising or near the ascendant, as all these separate influences have to be synthetised by the astrologer.

THE RISING SIGN

[NOTE.—*Whatever the Rising Sign may be, pay special attention to the corresponding house; if Aries, the first house, Taurus the second and so on.*]

I. ARIES rising denotes a frank, open, out-spoken, and free-handed disposition. The fate will be precipitated by the native's impulsive and headstrong tendencies, also his fearless pioneering and progressive spirit. He will be ambitious and desirous of rising in the world and will not miss many opportunities, nor be thwarted by obstacles or failure. He will often say more than he means, being enthusiastic, energetic, enterprising, progressive, and aspiring. He will be fond of acquiring knowledge, keen in all intellectual pursuits, fond of debate and argument, and always at the front. These remarks apply to Aries as a whole, but more especially to the first decanate.*

The second decanate of Aries rising modifies the Martial element of the sign and brings more reason and sympathy into the nature, being the decanate of harmony. It strengthens the intellect and gives more fruitfulness to this otherwise barren sign. It lessens the tendency to

---

* See p. 6 of *Everybody's Astrology*. The decanate is one-third of a sign or 10°, the first is of the same nature as the sign itself and the next is of the nature of the next sign of the same triplicity; *e.g.*, Aries, 1° — 10° = ♈-♈, 10° — 20° = ♈-♌, 20° — 30° = ♈-♐; and so on with the other signs.

ambition and to rashness, but does not entirely correct the impulsiveness. The fate will be influenced by ambition and emotion, and also through speculative tendencies. The vitality is increased and the character strengthened morally.

The third decanate rising strengthens the general tendency of Aries to prevision, stimulates the ideality and adds to the impulsiveness. It adds to the desire for demonstration and expression, and brings the native to a condition in which the philosophic and religious side of life is entered upon. It makes the whole sign more fortunate, and brings a desire to travel and to see foreign lands, with success from abroad.

When the first decanate of Aries rises, study the planet Mars as ruler, noting its position and aspects carefully. When this decanate rises Mars will be very powerful in the first, fifth or ninth houses, and the aspects to Venus and the Sun must be carefully judged.

When the second decanate of Aries rises, the Sun will be part ruler in addition to Mars, and the aspects of the Sun to Mars will be most potent and of life-long effect. If either the Sun or Mars be rising, or in the fifth house, the fate will be marked and the life most eventful, but the rise and fall, honour or degradation will depend very considerably upon the Sun's position and aspects. Note also the condition of the fifth house.

When the third decanate of Aries rises, Jupiter will be part ruler of the horoscope in addition to Mars, and as these two forces are opposite in nature some contest beween materiality and religion or between the lower and higher nature will considerably affect the life. Note carefully the position and aspects of Jupiter and pay especial attention to the ninth house.

II. TAURUS rising denotes a diplomatic, secretive, obstinate and self-willed disposition. The fate will be slow to develop, as the native will not move hurriedly, tending to become fixed, and too biassed for great expansion. He will be practical, dogmatic, determined, resentful, persistent and stolid. He will evince strong likes and dislikes, take sudden prejudices and show much reserve and diffidence. He will never become over-expressive, but will maintain a silent ambition for personal success, and will act from preconceived motives with decision and perseverance. He will be physically magnetic, fond of ease, stubborn, and rather too self-centred These remarks apply more especially to the first decanate.

The second decanate of Taurus rising awakens the internal nature of the sign, giving the native more intuition, discrimination and practical business ability, but at the same time there is a tendency to be more critical as well as intuitive, and although clever the native will have many strong temptations to become selfish and over-acquisitive. The fate will be influenced by external and concrete matter-of-fact experiences. The finer vibrations of this decanate denote keen appreciation, sterling qualities, musical talent and excellent business ability. The coarser tendency makes the native too exacting and a carping critic.

The third decanate of Taurus rising denotes more ambition, with an inclination to run in a groove, or become too conventional, thus making it a laborious and over-cautious influence, but it chastens the Taurean nature, strengthening the intellectual qualities and stimulating the reason, and hence tending to lessen the intuitive nature of the sign Taurus. The fate will greatly depend upon the early environment, as there is less power to break away from early training and parental influence. The fortunes will be affected by the innate self-control and organising power which this decanate bestows upon the native. Chastity is the keynote of success for this decanate.

When the first decanate of Taurus rises study the planet Venus, her position and aspects ; also the tenth and sixth houses.

When the second decanate of Taurus rises Mercury will be part ruler, and the position of this planet must be studied in its connection with Venus ; also the condition of the sixth house, and its bearing on the general horoscope.

When the third decanate of Taurus rises the influence of Saturn will greatly affect the life. Misfortune is denoted if Saturn afflicts either Venus or Mercury, but the reverse if the aspects are good. The M.C. should be especially noticed with this decanate, and the indications of moral stamina carefully considered.

III. GEMINI rising denotes a kind, willing, humane, intellectual and expressive disposition. The fate improves when restlessness and diffusiveness are overcome. The whole life will advance through education and intellectual attainments. The native will exhibit much curiosity and a desire to learn and will show signs of cleverness with inventive abilities, which may be turned to advantage or abused, according to the horoscope. The duality of this sign signifies either the chattering ape or the divine ape of intelligence: the magpie and the parrot, or the student and the scholar.

The second decanate of Gemini rising balances the whole sign, giving perception, foresight and real artistic ability. It also gives an opportunity to blend head and heart, reason and intuition. The fate will depend upon the philosophical attitude, which will decide whether the native will become a mere imitator and copier of others, or one who awakens the spiritual tendencies which are latent within. The finer vibrations of this decanate give the tendency to cultivate clairvoyance, and the artistic abilities. The lower vibrations will show in lack of continuity and in indolence or indecision.

The third decanate of Gemini rising greatly improves the whole sign, but a great deal will depend upon the environment at birth, as to whether the finer qualities of the sign are encouraged or kept latent. The fate is generally influenced by guardians or friends, and it often happens that there is something connected with the parentage which affects the whole life. Persons born under this decanate are generally successful in dealing with the public.

When the first decanate of Gemini rises study the planet Mercury, and note especially the condition of the third house.

When the second decanate of Gemini rises study Venus and Mercury as joint rulers, also the condition of the seventh house.

When the third decanate of Gemini rises study the planet Saturn or Uranus and the eleventh house.

When either Aries, Taurus, or Gemini ascends the native belongs to what may be termed the Intellectual or forceful and assertive Trinity; hence his or her dominant keynote will be knowledge, and progression through the mind or intellect.

IV. Cancer rising denotes an imaginative, fanciful, receptive and tenacious disposition. The fate is bound up with domestic ties, family interests and impressionable attachments, and much will depend upon environment and general surroundings with regard to the progress that will be made by the native. The native will exhibit a certain amount of timidity, reserve and mistrust, which will give rise to morbid and fanciful conditions, with a liability to go to extremes and become somewhat exacting and over-cautious. The virtues of this sign are economy, receptivity, and tenacity.

This sign gives the native power to experience every kind of sensation, from the lowest physical sensation to the highest feelings of emotion, and all the misfortunes and troubles the native experiences may be traced to this emotional and hyper-sensitive nature.

The second decanate of Cancer rising awakens the psychic and mystical tendencies of the sign Cancer, but also gives a certain amount of control over the sensations. It increases the tenacity of the sign, and denotes determination, love of power, ambition, and less internal receptivity. The fate is influenced by conventional notions, acquisitiveness, and pride.

The third decanate of Cancer rising improves the whole sign and denotes a very hospitable and sympathetic nature. The native will be studious and intuitive, having a keen love of acquiring knowledge. Two distinct types are born under this decanate: the over-anxious, hysterical, and hyper-sensitive; and the kind, mentally active and useful worker for the good of others. If the Moon is afflicted at birth the former tendency is shown, with some liability to obsession, but if Jupiter is very strong the latter qualities will predominate.

When the first decanate of Cancer rises the Moon's influence will affect the nativity principally, and also in a lesser degree the fourth, eighth and twelfth houses will specially influence the life.

When the second decanate of Cancer rises the planet Mars and the eighth house must be noted. Malefics in the eighth house will then give a liability to a fatal or tragic end.

When the third decanate of Cancer rises the planet Jupiter must be noted and the twelfth house. If the Moon is much afflicted note carefully the influence of Neptune and the fourth house.

V. LEO rising denotes a fearless, frank, generous, and ambitious disposition. The fate develops rapidly, and an eventful life is the outcome of the love of power and the organising ability which the native manifests. Downfalls are the result of hasty and passionate impulses, but the native recovers his balance through firmness, endurance, and self-control. The native is generally sincere, honourable, and magnanimous, but he often displays much pride, and is generally austere and positive. If indiscreet and inclined to give way to the emotional side of his nature there is grave danger of becoming demoralised through passion and sensuality. This sign gives great vitality and a splendid physique, the body being strong, and generally very healthy. When exceptions to this rule occur it will be found that the Sun is afflicted or badly placed.

The second decanate of Leo rising denotes a liability to go to extremes, making the native more demonstrative, active, and at times very rebellious. It awakens the philosophical side of the nature when the horoscope denotes the possibility, but weakens the will-power of the sign as a whole, if the Sun is not well placed and in good aspect with Jupiter.

The third decanate of Leo rising strengthens the will-power of the sign and adds to the impulsive and persistent side of Leo. In the advanced types it gives opportunities to unite head with heart, and through the intellect strengthens the higher emotions, giving zeal and ardour to the general activities, with a quiet determination that is unequalled. The fate is to a great extent under the control of the native, whose will-power is often controlled by the reason and illuminated by the intuition.

When the first decanate of Leo ascends note carefully the first aspect to which the Sun applies, for the whole career of the native will be affected by this influence. Note also the fifth house.

When the second decanate of Leo ascends note the position and aspects of Jupiter, also the ninth house and its occupants.

When the third decanate of Leo ascends note the aspects of Mars, and its position by house and sign; give also especial attention to any planets near the cusp of the ascendant.

VI. VIRGO rising denotes a quiet, reserved, retiring, and receptive disposition. The fate depends upon opportunity. The native, although lacking in determinative ambition, is persevering and ingenious, but he rarely dominates his environment or moves entirely unaided and he'ped by others. This sign gives more than the usual amount of selfishness common to the negative signs, but it is often counteracted by sympathy for the troubles of others and by the sense of justice which the native develops when the intelligence awakens. He is very orderly, critical, systematic and often self-centred, and is rarely understood on first acquaintance. The native thrives best in a business atmosphere, and generally prefers scheming and the exercise of his ingenuity to hard work; although never lazy or afraid to work, he prefers to use his wits whenever they will serve, and to improve upon the discoveries or inventions of others.

The second decanate of Virgo rising awakens the independence of the nature, and makes the native thoroughly practical and well adapted for all business pursuits; it also gives some artistic inclinations, or musical ability. The fate is largely governed by the social element or the political world, in which distinction is generally sought and obtained. Wealth is acquired through industry, thrift, and by adopting practical common-sense methods in business organisation.

The third decante of Virgo rising accentuates all the business and practical tendencies of the sign Virgo, and adds intuition to the mental qualifications for acquiring wealth and where business enterprise is concerned. It is a fortunate decanate for the fate, and only affects the general disposition by adding determination to all the Virgo characteristics. There is usually considerable artistic ability.

When the first decanate of Virgo ascends, the ruling planet is Mercury; the fate depends largely upon the condition of the sixth house, or the aspects of Mercury, and also considerably upon planets rising, if any.

When the second decanate of Virgo ascends study the position of the planet Saturn and the mid-heaven, also the planet that Saturn afflicts; if afflicting Mercury the native is very unfortunate.

When the third decanate of Virgo ascends the planet Venus and her distance from Mercury should be considered; the nearer these planets are the better will be the fortunes; if in exact conjunction great prosperity is denoted. Note also the second house.

The signs CANCER, LEO, and VIRGO belong to the preservative and maturing or Maternal Trinity. The keynote of such natives will generally be emotion, and progression through the moral sentiments.

VII. LIBRA rising denotes a courteous, affable, kind, and affectionate disposition. The fate is largely in the hands of others, and there is very small ability to mould or alter circumstances, the natives being controlled principally by feeling and intuition more than reason. The native is keen of observation, fond of comparing, and generally very artistic, refined and truly sympathetic. There is not much energy or incentive to action, and consequently the life tends to run in a groove and the native is very much disposed to lean on others.

The second decanate of Libra rising accentuates the sympathetic side of the nature, and increases the love of approval and general adaptation of the sign Libra. The native may become remarkably intuitive, and generally takes a keen delight in social intercourse, loving and appreciating all that pertains to the social side of life. The fate is affected by friends and associates, so much so as to make the native a slave to friends and attachments. Such lives are generally bound up with others, although they may be strangers in their own homes by the peculiarity of their magnetic conditions.

The third decanate of the sign Libra rising weakens the influence of the sign as a whole, and tends to make the life more or less unfortunate. The fate is affected by the state of the mind indicated by the horoscope; when restlessness and lack of continuity are shown the native is a smatterer, and although curious and apparently intellectual is often very foolish and ignorant, lacking 'common sense.' If the horoscope is favourable there is a tendency to improve the fate through educational attainments.

When the first decanate of Libra ascends the planet Venus and the conditions of the seventh house affect the native chiefly.

When the second decanate of Libra ascends the planet Saturn decides the general welfare for good or ill, but in the horoscopes of very advanced egos Uranus influences the life, especially if the native is free from family ties or attachments of all kinds. Note the eleventh house especially.

When the third decanate of Libra ascends the aspects of Mercury and the occupants of the third house affect the native.

VIII. Scorpio rising denotes a reserved, shrewd, secretive and proud disposition. The fate is either tragic and unfortunate; or very favourable and exalted. There appear to be two classes born under this sign, the extremely ignorant and the highly mystical; the former are inquisitive, deceitful, jealous and treacherous, while the latter are prudent, self-controlled, and highly dignified. In many respects this is truly the 'accursed sign' and it generally produces natives of one extreme or the other. A great deal will depend upon planetary positions as to the class of ego attracted to this sign, the strongest and the weakest characters being born under its influence, the weakest being those who have no control over their animal senses, while the strongest are penetrative, mystical and intelligent.

The second decanate of Scorpio rising accentuates the extremes of Scorpio, as mentioned above. The fate is usually unfortunate and often disastrous. If the native is born into a poor environment under this decanate, he rarely succeeds in raising himself above mediocrity.

The third decanate of Scorpio rising wakens the sensitive nature of the sign Scorpio, and gives a keen desire for attachment, thus breaking up a great deal of the selfish side of the sign as a whole. When the horoscope denotes it the love of the occult or of psychic phenomena is very marked. Generally speaking it increases the jealous tendencies of Scorpio.

When the first decanate of Scorpio ascends note carefully the strength and position of Mars, the eighth house and its occupants. If the planet Mars is below the earth and afflicting the luminaries the character of the native is very considerably weakened. If Mars is above the earth, but not setting, it is improved. Planets rising in Scorpio will affect the whole horoscope : if the Sun rises it is considerably benefited ; if setting, the reverse. See to the fourth and twelfth houses.

When the second decanate of Scorpio ascends note aspects between Mars and Jupiter ; if in affliction the native is very unfortunate, and not well disposed. Observe also the twelfth house.

When the third decanate of Scorpio ascends note the aspects between the Moon and the planet Mars, also the contents of the fourth house. The horoscope is improved if the Moon is well placed and favourably aspected, but the reverse if much afflicted.

IX. SAGITTARIUS rising denotes an open-minded, honest, sympathetic and generous disposition. The fate is dualistic and usually divided into two extremes of fortune and misfortune. The native is highly impressionable, though fond of liberty and independence. He is often reckless, extravagant and careless. When undeveloped he is thoughtless, erratic and rebellious, but when awakened he is philosophical, a lover of law and order, peaceful, and more intuitive than imitative.

The second decanate of Sagittarius rising accentuates the impulsive and headstrong tendencies of the sign as a whole and gives great liability to go to extremes and exhaust the mental and physical energy. When the native is deficient in self-control this decanate increases the excitability, which opens the way for brain troubles and nervous disorders.

The third decanate of Sagittarius rising awakens the best half of the dual sign Sagittarius, and quickens the intuitive and inspirational nature of the sign, giving the ability to prophesy and to foresee the future. It increases the love nature of the sign and makes the native very demonstrative and ardent in affection, falling in love often and readily expressing his sympathetic, sensitive and kind-hearted nature.

When the first decanate of Sagittarius ascends note the aspects to Jupiter and the ninth house, its occupants, and aspects to them from other planets.

When the second decanate of Sagittarius ascends pay especial attention to the planets rising, and the aspects between Mars and Jupiter, also the position of Mars, and any planets near the cusp of the first house.

When the third decanate of Sagittarius ascends note carefully the planet the Sun makes first application to; any aspect to Jupiter is favourable, but if the aspect is adverse and Jupiter not well placed the native will be unfortunate though endowed with splendid abilities. See also to the condition of the fifth house.

LIBRA, SCORPIO and SAGITTARIUS denote imitative ability and the power to reform and renew, forming what may be called the utilitarian or Reproductive Trinity.

X. CAPRICORN rising denotes an ambitious, persevering, plodding and persistent disposition. The fate is affected by the moral growth and the power to organise, and to rise above the difficulties of the early environment. The native is generally reserved, firm and self-reliant and anxious to be at the head of affairs. It usually happens that some position of trust or responsibility advances the native's interests, and according to the self-possession, tact and prudence displayed the native advances and makes successful progress, gaining recognition and fame or honour.

The second decanate of Capricorn rising tempers the ambitious tendencies of Capricorn and gives more plodding persistency, and inclines towards conservative and orthodox conditions. It adds to the firmness and reserve of the sign as a whole, which however unbends in social life.

The third decanate of Capricorn rising modifies the self-reliance of the sign, but quickens the intellectual and mental qualifications, and if the native has received a good education he will prove to be a most useful and important member of society. Circumstances will rule the native, however, much more than his ability to rule his own destiny. To the awakened this decanate gives a great desire to become a utilitarian and to serve others; to the unawakened incapacity and servility.

When the first decanate of Capricorn ascends Saturn is the chief planet to study. If above the earth, increase of ambition. If below the earth, persistency without ambition. If rising, self-control. If setting, misfortunes and many obstacles beset the path. Note the tenth house and any planets it may contain.

When the second decanate of Capricorn ascends note the position of Venus and the second house, also the aspects between Saturn and Venus.

When the third decanate of Capricorn ascends note the position of Mercury and the sixth house. If Saturn afflicts Mercury, lack of wit and enterprise; if well aspected, industry and patient endeavour to rise through merit.

XI. AQUARIUS rising denotes a refined, sympathetic, and humane disposition. The fate depends upon the nature of the friends and acquaintances the native gathers around him, as he is easily influenced by his associates. He has the ability to read character, and study human nature, but does not always act upon his own intuitions, and although quiet and determined, his sympathies often over-rule his reason and intuition. There are very few born under this sign that are able to reach up to its high standard of refinement and purity, and those who respond to the higher vibrations of this sign have overcome the animal nature and live in the pure mind apart from all lower sensational and animal tendencies. The undeveloped Aquarian is often harmless and true, with good and kind intentions, but easily led by companions, so often sins without the desire or wish to fall into error.

The second decanate of Aquarius rising lessens the tendency to drift, as it makes the mind active and inclines towards intellectual attainment, but does not give sufficient continuity or concentration to qualify for any literary or educational work, and favours mechanical and physical activities in the business world more than mental pursuits. The fate is often affected by relatives and companions.

The third decanate rising improves the Aquarius nature, giving more balance and a higher standard of intellect, with very refined tastes and clear discrimination. This decanate leads the native towards the occult and mystical side of life, and often awakens the clairvoyant faculty. The fate is affected by marriage or love affairs, yet the native is not *inclined* towards marriage and prefers a celibate life.

When the first decanate of Aquarius ascends Saturn is the ruling planet, but if Uranus is strongly placed this planet will also largely share in the destiny. Note well the eleventh house.

When the second decanate of Aquarius ascends note the position and aspects of Mercury and the third house.

When the third decanate of Aquarius ascends note the aspects between Venus and Uranus, if any, also the position and strength of Venus and the seventh house.

XII. PISCES rising denotes a restless, anxious, impressionable, and mediumistic disposition. The fate is rarely under the native's control, some impelling force behind the native seeming to push him on toward good or ill unconsciously. He has dual experiences of extreme nature, and is often torn between two different emotions. He is kind and just, but tends to encourage the romantic and sentimental side of his nature, and rarely understands himself or the emotions that play through him from time to time. He is easily psychologised, and suffers from varying moods, being receptive to the mental atmosphere around him. He is inclined to be secretive, is very receptive and at times inspired.

The second decanate of Pisces rising awakens all the latent sensitiveness of the sign Pisces and gives the keenest internal aspirations to become a channel through which the good forces may flow. It lessens the methodical tendency of Pisces, but increases the inclination towards economy and usefulness, giving more persistency and ability to utilise the virtues of Pisces without passing through all its vices. This decanate strengthens the whole sign, and gives more ambition, with the internal power necessary to rise through merit and adaptability.

The third decanate of Pisces rising gives a liability to encourage the weaker side of the sign, in which selfishness, jealousy, conventionality, and the material side of life are cultivated. If the horoscope is favourable there is a possibility of the personal element being modified, but if the horoscope is weak the pride of personal qualifications is apt to carry the native beyond the limits of fear for consequences, and tends to make the Pisces nature hard and unfeeling. The psychic tendencies of this decanate are unhealthy and difficult to understand.

When the first decanate of Pisces ascends note the position of Jupiter and planets near the ascendant, also the ninth house.

When the second decanate of Pisces ascends pay special attention to the Moon's place and aspects, also note the position of Neptune; if this planet is angular it will have some influence over the life. Also the fourth house.

When the third decanate of Pisces ascends note carefully the position of Mars; if this planet afflicts Jupiter the native will suffer great temptation and may wreck his life by his conduct. Note carefully the condition of the eighth house.

The signs CAPRICORN, AQUARIUS and PISCES comprise the Serving Trinity.

The Ascendant describes the native's personal appearance, his temperament, inherited brain-mind, and peculiar habit of thinking or receiving thought from the thought-sphere around him, also his personal disposition and idiosyncrasies; in short, his personality in physical form. It may be partially summed up in the word TEMPERAMENT. Any planet rising will modify the nature of the ascending sign.

The Sun rising will increase the pride and ambition, give greater firmness and stability, and raise the native beyond his sphere of birth. The Moon rising will likewise give ambition, but it will affect the mind and intellect more than the character, making it more flexible and less firm and determined. Mercury will give greater adaptability, quicker comprehension, and the power to respond to the mental requirements of the surroundings : but it will not affect the ascending sign so much as other planets, for this planet is specially liable to become coloured by the sign it is in. Venus rising will increase the cheerfulness and artistic ability, and make the disposition affectionate and responsive to the emotional side of the nature; it usually gives a more or less comely form and attractive disposition. Mars will make the personality more consequential, increasing the impulses, sharpening the intellect, and adding fire and dash to the rising sign. Jupiter rising will give more power, greater executive ability and wider sympathies, increasing the social faculties. Saturn will give more depth and meaning to the sign rising, accentuating its main characteristics, and tending to focus and consolidate the general tendencies denoted by the sign. Uranus rising will bring out all the eccentricities of the sign, and accentuate all its qualities, either for good or ill: it is dispersive in its influence. Neptune will affect the psychic side of the sign, and will awaken its talent, idealism tingeing the whole personality with a dreamy ethereality which has a peculiar fascination: it is resolvent in its influence.

PLANETS RISING

♆ *Neptune rising in the twelve signs* ♆

NEPTUNE rising gives psychic ability, and when the native is advanced he acts under inspiration; having the power to see far into the future; when perverted, however, this influence acts most disastrously, giving mediumistic and receptive tendencies which open the way for obsession and strange phantasies. The influence of Neptune is not yet fully known by modern astrologers, and much of the information current with regard to its nature is purely speculative. Its general influence tends to the *inversion of motives.*

♈ Imaginative ; subtle ; poetical ; changeable ; full of schemes and plans.
♉ Artistic ; refined ; sensuous ; musical ; some artistic genius.
♊ Humorous ; inventive ; literary ; comprehensive mentality ; poetic.
♋ Wayward ; difficult to know ; emotionally changeable ; sympathetic.
♌ Romantic love nature ; capable of going to great lengths ; enterprising.
♍ Extremely sensitive ; retiring ; mysterious : artistic ; reserved.
♎ Poetical and visionary ; gentle and refined ; somewhat sensuous.
♏ Mysterious ; elusive ; fond of self-concealment ; proud.
♐ Inspirational ; utopian in ideas ; sympathetic ; highly imaginative.
♑ Crafty ; subtle and designing ; apt to be extremely selfish.
♒ Broad-minded ; humanitarian ; deep insight into human nature.
♓ Fond of dumb animals ; sympathetic ; some crazy notions.

♅ *Uranus rising in the twelve signs* ♅

URANUS rising always causes the native to be somewhat original or eccentric, and quite different from the everyday type. It gives a keen interest in all things occult, curious, profound, or metaphysical. To the most advanced of humanity it gives genius and the power to see ahead mentally farther than the ordinary individual. Those who cannot respond to the higher vibrations of this planet are very independent, and usually rather abrupt, as it acts directly upon the nervous system, and so stirs into great activity the personal magnetism. All persons born with Uranus rising are much in advance of the period in which they live, and usually become pioneers of reform, being attuned to a higher octave of thought than the majority can understand. It tends to the *inversion of ideas.*

♈   Abrupt ; ambitious ; changeable ; inventive ; thorough.
♉   Considerate ; determined ; occult and mystical ; devotional.
♊   Curious ; fond of everything mystical, occult, and progressive.
♋   Eccentric ; restless ; peculiar ; impatient and fanciful.
♌   Liberal ; fond of freedom ; independent and aspiring.
♍   Economical ; quiet ; antiquated ; eccentric ; psychic.
♎   Romantic ; restless ; scientific ; perceptive ; refined.
♏   Artful ; secretive ; superstitious ; inventive ; shrewd.
♐   Turbulent ; rebellious ; enthusiastic ; over-generous, and free.
♑   Insinuative ; romantic ; acquisitive ; restless, and unsettled.
♒   Odd ; impressionable ; scientific or metaphysical ; clever.
♓   Novel ; fanciful ; desponding ; psychic ; silent.

♄   *Saturn rising in the twelve signs*   ♄

SATURN rising is considered to be very unfortunate; but much depends upon the sign in which it is placed, and its aspects. It gives the native industry, perseverance, thrift, and economy. It awakens the contemplative, thoughtful, and deeply religious side of the nature, giving a quiet devotion which is both unassuming and considerate. When rising it gives humility and patience, but when perverted it causes the native to be harsh and severe, stubborn and miserable. Saturn is the planet of *limitation*, and governs the form side of power, giving the ability to undertake great responsibilities, and to organise successfully.

♈   Deceptive ; stubborn : contentious ; shrewd ; exaggerative.
♉   Envious ; sullen ; conventional ; proud ; stubborn.
♊   Progressive; mathematical ; scientific ; perceptive ; occult.
♋   Remorseful ; jealous ; peevish ; discontented ; unhappy.
♌   Enduring ; cautious ; powerful ; chaste and prudent.
♍   Captious ; melancholic ; retentive ; studious, and reserved.
♎   Improvident ; opinionative ; scientific ; liable to reversals.
♏   Avaricious ; contemptuous ; jealous ; proud ; resentful.
♐   Teachable ; sensitive ; hasty ; honest ; trustworthy.
♑   Indifferent ; suspicious ; discontented ; serious ; over-cautious.
♒   Observant ; penetrative ; thoughtful ; proficient ; profound.
♓   Nonchalent ; uncertain ; indecisive ; sensitive ; unfortunate.

♃   *Jupiter rising in the twelve signs·*   ♃

JUPITER rising in the ascendant is always a more or less fortunate influence. It gives the native power and dignity and fits him to become a leader in the social and also the business world. Jupiter governs the *internal power* in which the Will is exercised and the motive, strengthened by the moral and religious, element. It gives fortune and success when free from affliction, but even when afflicted its influence is not wholly evil. The worst tendency of Jupiter is to make those who pervert its influence hypocrites and deceivers, especially in the social and religious world.

- ♈ Judicious ; ambitious ; enterprising ; determined ; successful.
- ♉ Upright ; just ; sincere ; compassionate ; attractive.
- ♊ Reverential ; well-disposed ; refined ; literary ; mathematical.
- ♋ Intuitive ; ambitious ; fortunate and sympathetic.
- ♌ Social ; magnanimous ; proud ; powerful ; prudent.
- ♍ Dictatorial ; covetous ; aspiring ; industrious ; deceitful.
- ♎ Intuitive ; obliging ; considerate, and a great lover of justice.
- ♏ Conceited ; determined ; haughty ; overbearing, and careful.
- ♐ Truthful ; humane ; social ; refined ; courteous ; kind.
- ♑ Invidious ; autocratic ; severe, and often disrespectful.
- ♒ Operative ; cheerful ; peaceful ; merciful, and very humane.
- ♓ Nutritive ; studious ; deserving ; hospitable ; mirthful.

♂   *Mars rising in the twelve signs*   ♂

MARS gives strength and courage to the native, and when rising always makes him confident of his abilities ; sometimes too consequential and assertive. This planet governs the *desire nature* and is ever eager for pursuit and disposed to destroy. It is only when the strong influence of Mars is perverted and used selfishly that Mars becomes a 'malefic' planet, and then because the animal nature is stronger than the god within. Mars and Venus are polar opposites, the one tending to rush outward and distract, the other drawing inward to nourish and preserve. When placed in the ascendant at birth much depends upon the aspects Mars meets as to what will be the influence exerted.

- ♈ Daring ; argumentative ; prone to righteous indignation.
- ♉ Inveterate ; obstinate ; fearless ; can be led but not driven.
- ♊ Severe ; tactful ; sharp ; acute, and mentally clever.
- ♋ Tenacious ; changeable ; unruly ; peevish ; unfortunate.
- ♌ Reformative ; commanding, argumentative ; generous.
- ♍ Affable ; scientific ; original ; irritable ; diplomatic.
- ♎ Captivating ; well-balanced ; courteous ; unfortunate in love.
- ♏ Tricky ; passionate ; inventive ; clever, but resentful.
- ♐ Invincible ; rebellious ; aspiring ; talkative ; generous.
- ♑ Organising ; brave ; tactful ; adventurous ; ingenious.
- ♒ Nervous ; mentally resourceful ; clever and occult.
- ♓ Satirical ; generous ; sympathetic ; mediumistic ; acquisitive

☉   *The Sun rising in the twelve signs*   ☉

THE SUN rising strengthens the *constitution*, giving abundant vitality, recuperative power, and making the general health good provided the Sun is not heavily afflicted. The Sun rising improves the carriage, adding importance and dignity to the personality; the native nearly always presents a commanding appearance, and impresses others with his innate power and authority.

It never fails to endow the native with faith and confidence, and through his natural ambition he rises to positions of trust and influence especially if the moral growth has been encouraged, and if the planetary positions are harmonious.

In a weak horoscope it denotes arrogance and pride and a great deal of egotism, but the will is always strengthened and if the Sun is unafflicted the native will desire to do right and act morally.

♈   Commanding; combative; ambitious; loyal; defensive.
♉   Over-confident; autocratic; diplomatic; resolute; solid.
♊   Noble; refined; contented; studious; thoughtful.
♋   Sensitive; receptive; conscientious; anxious; tenacious.
♌   Thorough; ambitious; just; honourable; magnanimous.
♍   Ingenious; industrious; critical; acquisitive; agreeable.
♎   Tractable; courteous; intuitive; retiring; imaginative.
♏   Unbending; dignified; contentious; diplomatic; determined.
♐   True; generous; proud; confident; inspirational.
♑   Illustrious; moral; self-controlled; practical; persevering.
♒   Obedient; cheerful; sincere; faithful; idealistic.
♓   Negative; methodical; hospitable; peaceful; honest.

♀   *Venus rising in the twelve signs*   ♀

VENUS rising refines and beautifies the *love nature*, and indeed its effect when in the ascendant is altogether beneficial and fortunate for the native. It denotes artistic or musical accomplishments, and gives an affectionate and devoted disposition. It favours the social life and makes the native attractive and desirable. It is only when afflicted that the good influence of Venus is hindered, and then it is more often owing to the simple and trustful nature engendered by this planet. Venus governs the affectional and binding side of the nature, and when the emotions are purified and refined it elevates the affections to the plane of the Soul, separating them from the senses and thus making the love of the native *immortal.*

♈ Idealistic ; impressionable ; generous ; artistic ; expressive.
♉ Nice ; kind-hearted ; sociable ; fond of pleasure and art.
♊ Thoughtful ; considerate ; inventive ; sympathetic ; genuine.
♋ Economical ; changeable in affection ; easily influenced.
♌ Romantic ; eager for popularity ; musical ; fortunate in love.
♍ Chaste ; given to extremes in affection, or intrigue.
♎ Encouraging and helpful to others ; equable in affection.
♏ Seductive ; jealous ; always liable to extremes.
♐ Sincere ; impressionable ; fascinating ; dual love affairs.
♑ Irresolute ; fickle in affection ; when attached, devoted.
♒ Obliging ; chaste ; isolated ; idealistic and romantic.
♓ Natural and thoughtful where affection is concerned.

☿   *Mercury rising in the twelve signs*   ☿

MERCURY denotes the *mental* capacities, and is therefore very potent
when placed in the ascendant. In general it gives business ability, but
being a convertible planet it is greatly affected by the influence of
aspects. It largely absorbs the nature of the sign in which it is placed,
being further modified or intensified by the influence it receives from
other planets. Its influence is most potent in the earlier part of life,
especially during the period of youth. When the mind is shown to
be more active than the senses, being given over to learning, Mercury
is very greatly affected by the influence of the first planet whose aspect
it meets in the horoscope.

♈ Clever ; optimistic ; fiery ; exaggerative ; fluent in speech.
♉ Adhesive ; obstinate ; plodding ; musical and intuitive.
♊ Perceptive ; shrewd ; mathematical ; scientific ; amiable.
♋ Adaptable ; changeable ; restless ; discreet ; versatile.
♌ Bombastic ; determined ; ambitious ; organising.
♍ Intellectual ; literary ; capable ; ingenious ; eloquent.
♎ Learned ; musical or artistic ; refined ; fine comparison.
♏ Ingenious ; fond of occult, mysticism, or secrecy.
♐ Talkative ; passionate ; inspirational ; ambitious ; aspiring.
♑ Irritable ; suspicuous ; discontented ; penetrative ; scientific.
♒ Eloquent ; gifted ; metaphysical ; fond of useful work.
♓ Superficial ; imitative ; of few ideas but many schemes.

THE MOON rising influences the temperament, making it more pronounced and having the stamp of heredity more clearly defined. It
affects the *functional arrangements* according to the sign it occupies. It
never fails to make the native ambitious or fond of fame and public
recognition and gives a desire for change, a love of novelty, and much

curiosity. The native has a very receptive and clear mind, according to the nature of the aspects which the Moon applies to from the ascendant. It lifts the native upward in life, and brings many benefits and advantages either from the public or through the social world, into which the native's domestic interests largely enter. It denotes great activity and a very eventful or changeful life.

♈ Touchy ; aspiring ; impulsive ; penetrative ; mental.
♉ Earnest ; sympathetic ; peaceful ; intuitive ; vital.
♊ Mysterious ; secretive ; ingenious ; fond of intrigue ; motive.
♋ Persuasive ; sensitive ; sociable ; capable ; attractive.
♌ Enthusiastic ; persevering ; dignified ; intuitive and orderly.
♍ Reasonable ; expressive ; analytical ; psychic ; quiet.
♎ Accomplished ; courteous ; perceptive ; mirthful and kind.
♏ Martial ; selfish ; jealous ; proud ; revengeful.
♐ Energetic ; passionate ; aspiring ; kind and generous.
♑ Notorious ; anxious for fame ; covetous ; cautious ; selfish.
♒ Tolerant ; inoffensive ; imaginative ; active ; inventive.
♓ Sympathetic ; dreamy ; inconstant ; quiet and hospitable.

DESCRIPTION OF PERSONAL APPEARANCE

As regards personal appearance the student is often in great difficulty to make up his mind as to the type of body represented by any map he may be studying. Experience will be his only true teacher, and only hints and suggestions can be given. The descriptions which follow are intended merely to form a nucleus from which the student's own powers of observation and inference may develop a fund of ideas and conceptions which will serve as a basis for judgment of this question when at any time a horoscope may come before his notice.

In studying these descriptions, which are adapted and amplified from a very complete list given in a series of 'lessons' which came into the author's possession many years ago, it must be remembered that not every one of them is founded upon the direct observation of the writer. No observer is likely to be personally acquainted with 108 different people, each born with a different planet rising in a different sign, and therefore it is clear that a considerable amount of judicious inference, added to comprehensive observation, must have gone to the compiling of this list. But that need be no impediment to its usefulness or discredit to its accuracy ; for, as his powers of observation grow and his experience widens, the student will find growing up in *his own* mind conceptions, more or less definite, but still unmistakable, of the appearance conferred by various planets in the different signs, and he will be sooner or later in a position to formulate his ideas in some similar manner. And the fact that he can do this, even in ever so small a degree, will give him confidence in accepting tentatively the descriptions now to be set down.

It may be said that in the main the Ascendant or Rising Sign furnishes the *matrix* of the whole bodily appearance; this is very considerably modified, however, by the sign occupied by the ruling planet. As an instance may be taken the late Queen Victoria, who though born with Sun and Moon both rising in Gemini, and Mercury in Taurus, displayed a markedly *Taurean* appearance, the influence of this sign becoming increasingly marked as years went on.   The general bodily type associated with each of the Twelve Signs has been given already and need not be repeated.

In addition to the Rising Sign and the sign occupied by the ruling planet, the Sun and Moon also greatly influence the appearance, through the signs which they respectively occupy.   In men the influence of the Sun is more to the front, as a rule, and in women the Moon; but *both* have their effect and may be discerned by a little attention, even when not obvious at a first glance.   Where Leo rises, the appearance inclines more to that of the sign occupied by the Sun, and the influence of the Moon is less marked.   Where Cancer rises, on the other hand, the influence of the sign occupied by the Moon is usually paramount, not infrequently obscuring to a considerable extent the sign occupied by the Sun; indeed, even the typical 'Cancer' appearance is often hardly to be traced, so strong is the influence of the Moon's sign.*

Where two or more planets are found in the ascendant the descriptions of each should be taken and the results blended.   It must be remembered that a strong aspect from some other planet will greatly modify the influence, coarsening or refining according to the inherent nature (*a*) of the aspecting planet and (*b*) of the sign in which it is placed.

---

* By 'typical' Cancer appearance is meant the contour and expression to be noted in those who have the Moon in Cancer at birth, whether in the ascendant or not : see description of Moon rising in Cancer on p. 117.

NOTE.—It is not always that a planet is found rising in the ascendant but the descriptions that now follow can be used as well for the Ruling Planet and the sign it occupies, as for a planet rising in the sign ; bearing in mind, of course, that the Rising Sign itself determines the actual *type* of body—whether tall, sturdy, thick-set, fragile, bony, muscular, etc.—the ruler's sign merely modifying this in a secondary way, much as negro blood 'peeps out' in a mulatto or quadroon. It is in the blending of these influences that the student will develop that artistic faculty which is so essential to his progress. He should note the difference produced by the several planets in any sign, and see how each modifies the inherent nature of the sign in a way that is peculiar to itself.

PLANETS RISING IN

ARIES

♅   The influence of this planet when rising in this sign modifies the   ♅ general type but little, save that it detracts considerably from the great *positiveness* of appearance and manner which Aries usually shows, giving a more dreamy or introspective look to the eyes ; sometimes the latter are very indrawn in expression. The body is somewhat slighter in build, and the complexion very delicate and the skin sometimes semi-transparent. Much depends on the position of Mars in this case. Low types are unscrupulous, ready in resource, liars, ready to do anything for notoriety.

♅   A child born under the influence thus produced becomes a tall,   ♅ thin, but well-made person, with a somewhat ruddy complexion. Disposition inventive, inquisitive, and fond of science. Extremely positive mind, not easily overcome. Conjugality slight, and prone to become selfish. A masterful person and a born leader of thought in whatever sphere he may move. Something of a revolutionist, and ever a champion of individual freedom.

♄   Medium height, with a not very handsome complexion, high fore-   ♄ head, full dark eyes, and very little beard. A wonderfully clever person according to his own estimation, and one whom it is not wise to offend ; one who will make himself a leader in some way, being exceedingly ambitious. Much depends upon the positions of the Sun and Mars, as to whether the ambition is of a noble type or otherwise ; if the Sun also rises in Aries, the disposition is much improved.

♃   A person of about medium height, rather long visage, ruddy com-   ♃ plexion, and light brown hair. He has a noble, loving disposition ; he is a benefactor to all that seek his friendship, and a despiser of discords and quarrelling, fond of travelling, and of large ideas in most matters. There is some tendency to pride or undue egotism in this position, unless the general tendency of the horoscope counteracts.

♂   Medium height ; strong, well-built, bony individual ; swarthy   ♂ complexion, red, or sandy curly hair. Disposition daring, determined, resolute a confident sort of individual, caring for nothing and nobody ; must be first in spite of any consequences ; loves war and contention, consequently there is no peace for long together where such an one is. Excellent as a pioneer in any worldly enterprise, since the native is boundless in resource with a constant flow of ideas.

☉ A strong and well-made person, of moderate stature, with light ☉ brown or gold coloured hair, a noble and commanding disposition, possessing much boldness and daring. This position, other things being equal, shows as a rule the best side of the Aries nature, and gives one who is truly a pioneer fired with noble ideals. But note the position of Mars.

♀ A person of slender form, moderate stature, rather light hair, and ♀ light grey eyes. Disposition extravagant, wasteful, fond of pleasures, company, sports and gambling, in which he is not very successful. Inconstant in love ; and ruled by partners. The inner ideals are lofty but unpractical.

☿ Short stature, or below the medium height, thin, with a poor ☿ complexion, light brown hair. Alert and 'jumpy' in manner. The disposition is rather quarrelsome, fond of disputes and contentions, will not scruple to tell any amount of falsehoods in order to accomplish his designs. In those more advanced, a very active mind incessantly busy with various projects ; idealistic and often unpractical, very discontinuous in thought.

☽ Thin, medium height, somewhat slightly built, active, mobile, ☽ changeable in the extreme : (but note position of Mars, if in a fixed sign this changeableness is much modified). Rash, eager, active, self-opinionated, 'cocksure' ; ready in ideas, too much so for strict truthfulness, bold, dauntless, enterprising. The character depends very much on the Sun's position, and the temperament upon that of Mars, also aspects. The hair is usually light, unless there are aspects from Saturn, the eyes somewhat hard, but bright and overflowing with 'magnetism.' Ambitious to lead, always in the front, and not seldom in the way. Very difficult to deal with. Always starting new things and never (or rarely) finishing them.

Planets rising

TAURUS

♆ This sign is decidedly sympathetic to the planet, which tends to ♆ add further grace and charm to its own inherent beauty. There is an indescribable charm of manner and a curiously winning smile. Rich creamy complexion, full flexible neck, soft seductive voice. Temperament musical, artistic and æsthetic, with a strong tendency to the sensuous. This is the better type. Lower types are brutal and sensual with depraved tastes and large appetite for coarse pleasures.

♅ Rather short stature, with a dull, dark complexion, a boastful, ♅ conceited person, and a great eater. This is rarely a favourable position for this planet, and the rest of the horoscope must be looked to before forming any ment ; consider especially the Sun's position and whether in favourable aspect to Uranus.

♄ Apt to be of a clumsy, awkward, ungraceful appearance ; dark hair ♄ and sallow complexion. This is not a favourable position unless very well aspected, there is a strong tendency to gratification of the senses, and a disposition to go to great lengths in securing the object of desire.

♃ Below the average height, not quite proportionate, of a dark ♃ swarthy complexion and dark brown hair, wise and judicious in his ideas, a lover of the opposite sex, and possessing an amiable disposition. This is a rather favourable position for Jupiter, especially for worldly prosperity, unless much afflicted. The disposition is as a rule excellent, however.

♂ Rather below the middle height, with an obscure, dark complexion, ♂ large mouth, broad face and dark hair. There is no peace-making about this individual ; he will be found to be a treacherous, dissembling sort of person, that is no good to himself or anyone else. This as a rule, but there are great possibilities in this position when the horoscope as a whole shows a highly developed moral character and a well-balanced nature.

☉ Broad and fleshy face, large nose and mouth, rather short stature, ☉ the hair a dull brown, grey or hazel eyes. Disposition bold, resolute, confident without reason, delights in contentions, fighting, etc., in which he is frequently successful, not that he or she necessarily joys in strife, but glories in overcoming obstacles. Much firmness and endurance.

♀ Well-proportioned, medium stature, moderately good complexion, ♀ dark brown hair, and blue or grey eyes. A good moral disposition, kind and obliging, always ready to do a kindly action to a neighbour, fortunate in most undertakings, and much respected. A very favourable position, unless ill-aspected.

☿ Middle stature, stout and somewhat corpulent, dark brown hair, ☿ dark tawny complexion. This is not a good position, unless accompanied by other planets ; a slow-witted person, with, however, some skill in weaving tales.

☽ Middle stature, sometimes quite short : body compact and usually ☽ well-proportioned ; face, at any rate, generally neat and clear-cut or 'trim' looking, with a smooth skin, sometimes dusky ; deliberate in movement, and takes very short steps when walking. This is one of the best positions, as regards beauty, for the Moon rising ; if well aspected, especially by Venus, there is often great comeliness and personal charm. The nature is personally more fixed than with the Moon rising in any other sign, and there is often great obstinacy. The feelings are strong and usually very personal, and there is a great tendency to brood over real or imaginary wrongs or insults. There is usually good health, unless badly aspected, but with a tendency to 'lock up' poisonous matters in the system unless sufficient exercise is taken, and as these natives are naturally very indolent and do not take much exercise this may result in various diseases. Plain living is essential for their health.

Planets rising in

GEMINI

♆ Light, graceful and volatile in appearance. Excellent mimics and ♆ actors. Rapid, elusive smile, many quaint conceits. Large expressive eyes, luminous skin, great vocal range in speaking, now high, now low. Very musical and with some talent for poetry. Sensuous and *insouciant*. Fond of nonsense verses, leariques, etc. Low types are irresponsible, seldom actively harmful, but sure to find their way into evil company and prone to mischievous acts, theft, etc.; chatterers.

♅ A person of tall stature, generally light hair and eyes, with an ♅ eccentric disposition ; passionately fond of science, quick and active in all his movements. Will be a genius in some direction, probably science.

♄ Rather above the average height, with black or very dark hair ; ♄ ingenious, but not always of a good disposition. There is ability for concentration in mental pursuits, if well aspected by Mercury ; but suspicion and over-carefulness are apt to prove a great hindrance to native's success. This position is sometimes an impediment to the moral nature, inclining to cupidity.

♃ Tall and well-composed person, with a kind and pleasant expression ♃ of countenance, with dark brown hair and dark grey eyes ; a really well-disposed, kind, and obliging person, of a good moral character, judicious in all things, fond of science and of female company. There is an inclination to science and philosophy and usually some literary or poetical ability.

♂ Tall, slight, active, but well-proportioned person, somewhat swarthy ♂ complexion, dark brown hair, grey or hazel eyes. Of a wandering, unsettled disposition, fond of strife, disputes, or rather arguments, but chiefly for the sake of argument more than with the desire to arrive at truth.

☉ A person of a large organisation, high coloured or sanguine ☉ complexion, and although of large stature, well composed, of uniform structure, brown hair, and generally large eyes. The disposition is good on the whole, elegant in manners, of a kind and polished deportment, possesses a contented mind, not easily offended, and rather unfortunate in his business transactions. Given to travel; strong inclination to science and art or commerce, with a tendency to blend the two ; literary ability.

♀ Slender form, tall but well-proportioned, medium brown hair, and ♀ good complexion. The disposition is loving, free, just and merciful. The native is ambitious to be charitable, which he is to the utmost of his ability ; detests mean or unjust actions and delights in good company. Is rather inconstant in love, has many 'dualistic' love-episodes and is likely to marry twice or to carry on two amours simultaneously.

☿ Mercury rising in Gemini, which is said to be the house of this ☿ planet because the nature of the planet and that of the sign sympathise with each other, consequently produces better effects in this sign than in any other, except ♍. Students should bear in mind that this is the case with all the other planets when in their own mansions, except the malefics ; hence when Mercury is in this sign and on the ascendant at the time of an individual's birth, without any counteracting influences in operation to interfere therewith, it produces a person rather tall, well composed, with nice even features, good complexion, rather light brown hair ; disposition on the whole good, very ingenious, fond of learning, particularly arts and sciences of almost any kind, extremely apt in acquiring anything that he may set his mind upon. If Mercury be well aspected with Jupiter or Saturn, it gives a superior judgment and understanding. There is often poetical and musical ability and always wit and fluency of speech, unless Mercury is badly afflicted.

☽ Fairly tall ; slight, nervous build of person, active in movement, ☽ gesticulating freely with the arms when speaking. Lively and frequent if not incessant talker, and somewhat shallow in opinions and ideas (but see position of ☿ and ♄); much given to move about from place to place, to change from one subject or occupation to another, and to go on from one task to another while the first is as yet unfinished (usually returns to it again after a time, however, in which they differ from Moon in Aries, which as a rule does not). The arms are long and the hands narrow and nervous, the fingers moving restlessly. Exceedingly receptive to ideas and equally ready either to teach or to learn.

Planets rising in

CANCER

♆ Slight, hypersensitive body, inconstant, very emotional, ever posing ♆ or assuming identity of others. Artistic, inspirational, temperament of an April day, smiles and tears readily alternating, easily impressed by others and exceedingly unreliable as to temper. Very magnetic and attractive in a subtle and unusual way. In low types, a tendency to live on others; something of a parasite.

♅ Short stature, stout, dark hair, and pale complexion. One who ♅ *will* come before the public. Difficult to rely on, very capricious as regards feeling, and rarely remaining for long in one house or locality.

♄ Rather short stature; of a pale, thin-looking countenance, with ♄ nothing pleasing in expression or form of body. The disposition is not at all to be desired, it being peevish, somewhat malicious, and much inclined to a fretful self-indulgence. There is a great love of ease and a tendency to inactivity. In low types, sottish. Business interests are sacrificed to home cares, and public convenience sacrificed for private gain.

♃ About middle height, oval face, pale complexion, and dark hair; ♃ ambitious, aspiring disposition, aiming at great and high attainments, pleasant in manners, but fond of 'having a finger in the pie.' Jupiter is exalted in this sign, so that this position may be considered in every sense favourable, unless Jupiter is greatly afflicted. If in aspect to Mars, there will be many amours. This position is favourable for public offices, as native is sure to be popular.

♂ Short stature, awkwardly formed; pale complexion, dusky brown ♂ hair. A restlessly active, 'mind-hungry' individual, a promoter of quarrels and contentions. There is a constant passion for notoriety, and a craving for position and power.

☉ Small in stature, of an unhealthy appearance, the face somewhat ☉ defective, medium brown hair. The disposition is pleasant and agreeable, fond of company, particularly that of females, delights in almost any kind of sport or pastime; generally speaking, a free, jovial, and good-humoured sort of person that does not easily take offence. There is a strong love of power, notoriety or both, and a liking for popular measures in politics: somewhat of a lover of shibboleths.

♀ Short stature, rather stout, round face, pale complexion, light ♀ brown hair, and blue eyes. The disposition is very changeable and unsettled; never to be depended upon. Somewhat vain and idle, but fond of good company. Kindly and well-disposed, and desirous of popular esteem.

☿ If without any counteracting influence, produces a small, mean- ☿ looking person, with small eyes, thin face, sharp nose, and dark hair; usually a very remarkable memory. The disposition is malicious, deceitful, knavish, crafty, etc., one that is qualified for any kind of dissimulation, particularly so if Mars has an evil aspect with Mercury at the same time.

☽ This is a strong position for the Moon, since Cancer is its own sign ☽ and it therefore is 'lord of the ascendant rising in the ascendant.' Much depends on the Moon's aspects—more perhaps here than anywhere. Appearance: small stature, small round face, crab-like or rabbit-like in expression, the septum of the nose appearing to view below the nostrils, many slight sensitive lines on either side of the nose; pale skin, pores very open. Exceedingly sensitive disposition, responsive to every breath of feeling or opinion, very sympathetic towards suffering and apt to take on other people's magnetic conditions and to absorb disease from them. Apt to repine and become peevish or querulous, fanciful and unduly careful both about themselves and those related to them. Think much of public opinion, and are eager to be in the swim, while yet timid and retiring in actual behaviour—a strange contradiction. There is great tenacity and power of holding on to a given desire or idea, and a remarkable power of memory. Very psychic nature. Fond of power and firmly bent on attaining it. Interested in ancient customs. The most noteworthy characteristic is a certain quivering sensitiveness (like an aspen leaf). Frequently become stout, or rather bulky, after middle life. Highly emotional always, and very acquisitive; fond of 'collecting.'

Planets rising in

LEO

♆ Slighter than the usual Leo build, fiery, emotional or idealistic ♆ nature, brilliant eyes, highly romantic ideas, extravagant ideals in regard to love, catholic tastes, somewhat of a 'Timon of Athens,' and something of a salamander also. In low types, unbridled passions.

♅ A large, strong, well-made individual; light hair and sandy ♅ whiskers. His disposition is very independent, but generous and resolute. There is usually some genius associated with this position, but the passions are strong and subtle. The nature is unconquerable.

♄ A firmly set, square-built, bony individual, that all the high-living in ♄ the world could not make fat. Has little personally attractive about him; his disposition, on the whole, is moderately good, but rather passionate. This gives great business capacity, if well supported in other directions, capable of managing and controlling large enterprises. Great power of concentration of mind and will.

♃ A tall person, well made, ruddy complexion, and light hair; a fine, ♃ noble-looking person, one who delights in all humane and manly actions; very ambitious of honour and with a full sense of his own importance. A good governor or magistrate, if other positions in the horoscope support.

♂ Of full stature, strong and well-built, large head and face, full eyes, ♂ light brown or flaxen hair, hot and hasty in temper, yet free and generous in disposition; delights in fire-arms, shooting, wars, surgical operations. An ardent lover, but too prone to mistake passion for love and intensity for depth.

☉ When the Sun holds this position in a nativity, it conveys at once ☉ to the mind of an astrologer a person of full and well-proportioned structure, full face, large eyes, light brown or yellow hair, and ruddy complexion. Disposition good, faithful, just, and courteous to all men to the utmost of his ability; one who is very ambitious of honour. A ruler indeed; but if ill aspected by Jupiter, proud and overbearing withal.

♀ Moderate height, well and evenly made, round face, full eyes, light brown or sandy hair, the face spotted or freckled. Disposition proud, haughty, and passionate. Generous and kindly but too fond of pleasure and hence extravagant. Exceedingly ardent in love. Fully persuaded of own abilities. ♀

☿ A person of large stature, round face, also dark hair and complexion. Disposition proud, haughty, and passionate, artistic and a good mimic. This position gives ability for the drama, also for writing romances of love and adventure. ☿

☽ This also is a strong position for the Moon, but depends almost entirely for its character upon the Sun's position. Body moderately tall, long back, upright carriage, fearless demeanour, bold and free, but not elastic movements. Eyes large and well opened, air enthusiastic and convincing, manners agreeable and entertaining. This is a good example of the blend of the fiery and the fixed tendencies; there seems a great flexibility and adaptability in these natives, for they are impulsive and enthusiastic where their projects are concerned, but this will be found to be an appearance only: for they are almost entirely self-motived and are very difficult to move either by persuasion or argument, being in reality surprisingly stubborn except where their own enthusiasms are concerned. But they are admirable workers, and when allowed to go their own way manage things excellently, putting their heart into all they do and doing everything in a way that can only be described by the word 'thorough.' They are impulsive, but their impulses come from *within*, and are not the result of contact from without (as in the case of Aries for instance). ☽

Planets rising in

VIRGO

♆ Shy, sensitive and retiring, very like the usual Virgo type but with very wistful eyes; curious tastes, fond of enquiring into ancient customs and peculiar religious rites; more sense of humour than usually displayed by Virgos. Neat appearance, brown eyes, very luminous and mobile, delicate ears, abundant hair and wavy. Medium height, tending to shortness. Demure and somewhat mysterious, full of schemes and never thoroughly to be known. In low types, deception, theft and illicit pleasures. ♆

♅ Short, dark, and thin; independent, ingenious but very eccentric. There is often genius for music with this position. In any case there is some journalistic ability, with a taste for science and antiquarianism or out-of-the-way investigations and research. A hunter-up of obscure details and statistics. ♅

♄ Tall, slight person; dark hair and dark swarthy appearance; inclined to study and reading, particularly news of a melancholy nature. He is of a quiet moody disposition, given to fits of depression. This position is more favourable for Saturn than for Virgo; but there is much ability for painstaking work where the rest of the nativity shows a refined nature. ♄

♃ A moderate-sized person, with dark hair and complexion, a scientific expression of countenance, much given to study. Even-tempered disposition, ♃

careful with money, ambitious of honour and position. Only moderately successful and rarely marries. This is a somewhat unfavourable position for Jupiter.

♂ When fully developed, of medium height, proportionately made, ♂ rather dark or swarthy complexion, brown hair. One that requires to be treated courteously, easily offended and somewhat resentful. Disposition anything but affable, but energetic and capable, a busy worker and a most useful servant when judiciously managed. A somewhat psychic type of mind, but very intellectually disposed.

☉ A large, but well-proportioned person, *i.e.*, when fully developed ; ☉ the hair dark brown and plentiful, the complexion moderately good. The disposition on the whole also good ; very ingenious, agreeable, and pleasant in company, not very ambitious, but rather severe with those who offend him. Very careful of own interests and rather apt to develop selfishness as life advances.

♀ Moderately tall, well composed, with an indifferent complexion, ♀ dark brown hair, and dark eyes. In disposition subtle, cunning, careful of own interests, artistic, very ingenious and active ; personally very fastidious in tastes, and dainty, and apt to look down on others less refined and to misinterpret their actions.

☿ A tall and slender person, well-made, hair and complexion dark. ☿ His disposition is ambitious, scientific, quick intellect ; the organ of language well developed, consequently his tongue can always find something to talk about ; it has one great advantage over many, *viz.*, it is seldom out of employment, and if Mercury is well aspected at the time of birth it will find a good deal of very useful and beneficial work to do. This position increases the talkativeness of Virgo but somewhat lessens its tendency to prudishness or fault-finding and the native is less priggish.

☽ The Moon is well placed in Virgo. These people have a medium ☽ stature, very neat appearance, colour of hair, eyes, etc., usually tending to a general *brown* tinge, the skin being as a rule yellowish-brown, with a good colour. Small features, well made, but delicate ; good eyes but wistful rather than inspiring in expression : the body movements are Mercurial. Very neat in dress, economical withal, generally cover up the neck (distinction from Sagittarius and Jupiter, which always leave it bare). Quiet and demure—'mouse-like'—in manner, trim and orderly in methods, rather prim and always very precise in ideas. Are keen to notice *differences*, and are rather hard on 'evil-doers.'

Planets rising in

LIBRA

♆ Usually of great beauty ; ethereal appearance and large liquid eyes ; ♆ taller than the usual type of Libra native. Lofty ideals and rather visionary notions, advanced ideas of altruism. Compassionate and forgiving, eloquent and poetic, intuitional. In low types, morbid cravings for sexual indulgence.

♅ Strong, well-made person, light brown hair, fair sanguine com- ♅ plexion, quick at learning, fond of science ; hot tempered and independent.

Usually unfortunate in marriage, owing to peculiar notions or extreme independence. But the eccentricity of Uranus is rendered more moderate and adaptable here than in perhaps any of the signs.

♄   Saturn, when rising in the ascendant in Libra, represents a person   ♄ above the average height, well and uniformly made, with a good complexion, high forehead, medium brown hair ; very independent and somewhat cold and reserved. Saturn is exalted in this sign and exhibits some of his best characteristics, love of justice and devotion to duty, when the character as indicated by the horoscope as a whole is good.

♃   Near the medium height, inclining to be tall, gracefully and beauti-   ♃ fully formed, with a very pleasant expression of countenance, light brown hair and blue eyes. Disposition good, loving, kind, pleasant, and obliging. A large circle of friends and admirers, particularly those of the opposite sex. This is perhaps one of the best positions for Jupiter for worldly success and popularity. But consider his aspects.

♂   Rather tall in stature, well composed, fair and sanguine complexion,   ♂ oval visage, and light brown hair ; cheerful and pleasant expression of countenance. Delights to be in the company of the opposite sex, very approbative and uxorious. Often proves a promoter of disunion and yet rarely a positively quarrelsome or disagreeable person, so that this quality appears more as a misfortune than as a fault.

☉   Moderate height, straight and upright when walking, complexion   ☉ rather fair, light brown hair, the eyes full and blue. Disposition very approbative, amiable and good on the whole ; rather unfortunate in his affairs through life. Apt to be too yielding under pressure, and inclined to lean on others. Usually a very loveable nature, but sometimes very exclusive and distant.

♀   Fairly tall, well proportioned, good sanguine complexion, with   ♀ dimples in the cheeks, and light brown hair. Disposition very good, a lover of morality and respectability, courteous, civil, obliging ; one who delights in doing good to others. This is perhaps the most favourable position of any for a female horoscope. The love-nature is polarised toward the higher emotions and is elevated to the plane of the mind.

☿   Shows the person, when fully developed, to be of moderate stature   ☿ and proportionate, complexion fair, but sanguine, blue eyes, and light brown hair. The disposition is extremely good in every respect, a person that loves justice, virtue, and morality in all their forms, very fond of learning and of good company. Fond of poetry, and very fluent, eloquent, and agreeable speaker.

☽   This position gives, on the whole, the most 'likeable' personality of   ☽ any sign in the Zodiac. Being cardinal and yet Venusian it is sufficiently definite to be interesting and yet plastic enough to adapt itself to others and willing to do so ; being airy, it is essentially refined and concerned only with the higher emotions. Graceful, somewhat undulating carriage, medium height, rather tall than short, somewhat bird-like—dove-like—in figure and movements, easy and courteous in speech (in a peculiarly graceful way that *no other sign* possesses), and willing to be interested in all subjects that please the companion. In a word, this position makes a delightfully 'companionable' person. The eyes are frequently grey—dove grey—and there is a fondness for silver-grey or light blue in the apparel. The word apparel, as distinguished from the more homely expression 'clothing,' is peculiarly appropriate in speaking of this sign, to which gracefulness and elegance so peculiarly belong. The eyes have a gentle and wistful melancholy when in repose.

SCORPIO

♅   There is a great tendency for the evil side of this planet's influence   ♅
to be shewn here, manifesting as depravity of an extraordinary kind. But in the higher types there will be a strange incomprehensible aloofness, a nature difficult to understand, silent and unexpressed ; the feelings will be subtle, deep and poignant. There is here capacity either for great suffering or for great and deliberate cruelty. Such a position is likely to produce one who has a great genius for delving into Nature's deeper secrets and for making researches into obscure byways of science, folk-lore or medicine—the latter especially. The appearance is striking and rather forbidding, the eyes mysterious and impenetrable and the brow heavy. The sex nature is exceedingly strong in such natives, but where the regenerative nature of Scorpio is enabled to overcome it, its powerful influence is exerted in probing hidden matters, psychic, intellectual or spiritual.

♅   A short, thick-set person, with broad shoulders, dark swarthy com-   ♅
plexion, dark hair and eyes. In disposition exceedingly passionate and intense. Difficult to understand or to work with ; a close and subtle reasoner and debater, ardent in research and investigation of all physiological or medical subjects and capable of attaining eminence on these lines. Uranus is by many considered to be exalted in this sign.

♄   Short stature, thick set, dark obscure complexion, and dark hair ;   ♄
of a somewhat quarrelsome disposition, one who has great difficulty in controlling jealousy and resentment, especially the latter. Proud, masterful and ambitious of power, usually possesses much psychic ability and displays an interest in occult matters, especially psychical research.

♃   Middle stature, rather fleshy and stout, swarthy complexion, dark   ♃
eyes. A boastful disposition, but fortunate in most transactions. Benefits through partners. Has great skill in achieving own ends and is somewhat resentful. A fruitful mind.

♂   Medium height, broad flat face, dark swarthy complexion, black   ♂
or very dark and curly hair. This is a revengeful, deceitful, malicious, quarrelsome person, who ought at all times to be treated courteously, for he is very ingenious in contriving means to attain his ends or purposes, also in the profession he may follow as a trade or business. In an otherwise strong horoscope this position denotes a capable surgeon where the intellectual abilities are of an appropriate character, also one suitable for position of authority as governor of a gaol, inspector of police, or other managerial capacity where strenuousness and force of personal will are necessary.

☉   Person when fully developed of middle stature, stout and well   ☉
made, full and fleshy face, swarthy complexion, medium brown hair. Of an ingenious and ambitious nature, very clever in wars and contentions, also in surgical operations, chemistry. Strong and commanding personality, resentful of injuries, and suspicious of the motives of others. A trustworthy overseer and can be relied upon to keep a secret.

♀   Middle stature, stout, and well-built ; face broad and dark, dark   ♀
brown hair, and dark grey eyes. In disposition contentious, quarrelsome,
envious ; a person rather to be avoided. This is not at all a favourable
position for Venus, but it gives strong sex control. The native will rule his
partners.

☿   About middle height, proportionate and strong body, dark curly   ☿
hair, dark eyes and complexion. Ingenious and active mind, rather too fond of
company, particularly that of the opposite sex ; a great aptitude for making
stinging speeches, when annoyed.

☽   Appearance here will greatly differ according to sex, males having a   ☽
firmer and more strongly built body than females born with this position. In
males the form tends to be somewhat bulky and in some cases coarse grained ;
features not good, the nose usually badly formed or with a broken appearance ;
temper uncertain and quarrelsome. In females, body is often slight and wispy,
with something of a moth-like appearance, eyes large and hollow and expression
unsatisfied-looking, wistful or yearning ; the nature is uncertain and treacherous,
or at least unreliable, prone to violent changes of taste or liking, fast friends one
day, bitter enemies the next. Both these indications may be greatly modified by
good aspects or good solar position ; but something of these tendencies is sure to
remain. There is often a great deal of the lower or less admirable kind of pride
in the nature ; it is hard for them to forgive, yet easy to be ungrateful. These
people always have curious experiences to pass through in regard to sex.

PLANETS RISING IN

SAGITTARIUS

♆   The planet is thoroughly 'at home' in this sign, owing to its   ♆
Jupiterian nature, and hence a fairly harmonious expression of its influence may
be expected. Tall, fine looking, with large gleaming eyes, sensitive humorous
lips, frank and engaging manners, and a genius for 'putting themselves in
another's place,' they are sure to be universal favourites. This is perhaps one of
the best signs for the expression of Neptune's influence, and inclines the native
strongly to a study of religion and folk-lore ; or he is of a mystical turn of mind.
Even in the low types, the native is as a rule nothing worse than what is termed
'an unmitigated bounder,' full of resource and wild-cat schemes, Utopian com-
munistic ideas and other frothy enterprises.

♅   A tall, straight, and well-composed person, with a noble, intelligent-   ♅
looking countenance, rather light hair, grey or clear blue eyes, large and gleaming, and of moderately good complexion ; of an ambitious disposition, yet
generous and good hearted. There is usually genius in either art, science or
philosophy. Great intuition in regard to Astrology may be looked for from this
position.

♄   A person of rather large structure, dark hair, and moderately good   ♄
complexion. A kind, courteous, benevolent person, one who will not pass by
an offence easily, but who will, nevertheless, soon be reconciled. This is a
good position for the planet and indicates a strong natural love of either science,
philosophy or religion. Rarely distinguished-looking, however ; but this is
usually true of those born with Saturn rising, except in the airy signs.

♃ This sign is one of the houses of Jupiter, and the effects produced ♃
by the great benefic when placed in this sign are better than if placed in any
other. Represents a person of moderately tall stature, oval visage, medium
brown hair, ruddy complexion ; well-formed head, organs of which are evenly
developed. Possessing a good, honest, truthful, loving disposition ; a true and
sincere friend, just in all dealings, and very fortunate in his passage through life.
There is usually a strong leaning to the church or towards military life. Fond
of sport and a great lover of horses.

♂ A person of rather tall stature, well proportioned, good complexion, ♂
dark brown hair, and dark eyes. A regular merry, jolly sort of a person, very
fond of company, rather passionate, delights in military operations, railway enterprise, etc. Fond of travel, sport and new ideas. Apt to be superficial in thought
and to profess knowledge rather than to possess it. Capable of ' drawing a bow
at a venture ' with telling effect.

☉ Tall stature, well and proportionately made, oval visage, sanguine ☉
complexion, light brown hair. Disposition proud, haughty, very ambitious of
honour, but very pleasant in manners ; delights in justice. Talkative and
argumentative, fond of travel, games, sports and pastimes of all kinds ; somewhat
religious withal, or else militantly anti-episcopal.

♀ Rather above the average height, well and proportionately built, ♀
light hair, oval visage, grey or hazel eyes. The disposition is good. A pleasant
person, possessing agreeable and obliging manners ; noble and brave ; rather
proud ; passionate, but is soon appeased. Venus has great sympathy with
Sagittarius, as has Jupiter similarly with Libra.

☿ A tall person, well composed, rather long visage, large nose, san- ☿
guine complexion, and dark hair. A very active, busy-bodyish kind of person,
loquacious and frequently shallow-minded, sharp and intelligent in small
matters, rather conceited and vain of his abilities and eager to display his talents.

☽ This is a somewhat favourable position for the Moon, and its better ☽
qualities are usually manifested. Appearance, tall, slight (sometimes bulky and
fleshy, but only when other influences in the horoscope strongly indicate this),
lithe and active, strong muscles, or rather abundant nervous force to stimulate
them into action, quick in movement, light and graceful in bearing and free and
pleasant in speech. Large well-opened eyes, somewhat dreamy and psychic
looking nevertheless, long slender neck. Particular as to clothes as a rule, given
to a certain fastidiousness regarding linen, and fond of wearing brown leather
boots, and gaiters or spats ; in fact, there is, in general, a slight tendency to
' horsiness ' of appearance, not necessarily of an unrefined type. General
bearing ' smart ' and ' well groomed.' Quick in ideas, ready and fluent in
speech though sometimes diffident, they are entertaining comrades and good
fellow-travellers. Prone to overdo themselves where exertion is concerned, and
sometimes apt to assume a knowledge they do not possess. Humorous, loving
and generous.

PLANETS RISING IN

CAPRICORN

♆ Capricorn is by some held to be the house of Neptune, but it is ♆
doubtful if at the present stage of humanity this sign offers great facilities for

the expression of its influence, being too hard and dry in its nature. The appearance is dark and magnetic, hair smoother and finer than usual in this sign, skin dusky, eyes usually of a curious dark blue or bluey grey. Temperament idealistic, full of plans for political or economic progress, or, in the less advanced types, selfish, crafty, and relentless in carrying out predetermined ambitions. In low types, sottish and slavish, given to drink and low company, but with some genius in certain directions, guileful, readily planning and cleverly executing schemes of great ingenuity.

♅   About middle height, evenly made, high forehead, short, thin neck,   ♅ light hair, and small steely eyes. In disposition self-opinionated, haughty, ostentatious, possessing a very exalted opinion of himself. This must be judged according to the other positions in the horoscope, aspects, etc., for there is the possibility of a very lofty type of mind and character here.

♄   A thin, slender person of about middle height, with a long visage,   ♄ dark sallow complexion, dark hair, and small eyes; disposition reserved, cold and indifferent, an individual of but little conversation, and when once offended not easily appeased. Very melancholy in manner, and with little self-esteem or faculty of 'hope,' but very ambitious and persistent when once decided on a course of action. Diplomatic in the extreme, and capable of political work if in an otherwise good horoscope.

♃   This sign being Saturnine is not by any means a comfortable   ♃ vehicle for the expression of Jupiter, who shows himself to much better advantage in Aquarius. The stature is moderate, carriage fairly independent, manner somewhat truculent but good natured, air grand and somewhat disdainful or condescending. Successful in public matters and capable in organisation. Rather rebellious against authority and desirous of being chief.

♂   Small, thin structure, small head, black or dark hair, and dark pale   ♂ complexion. Disposition moderately good, quick, active and ingenious mind, usually fortunate in undertakings. Very ambitious and capable, a useful worker in engineering or organising departments, but a rather questionable person to select as a subordinate, for he is apt to turn master, and will certainly scheme towards that end.

☉   Under this influence we generally find a person of small stature,   ☉ or below the medium height, pale complexion, thin and ill-proportioned, medium brown hair, long visage. Disposition determined, resolute, undaunted; possesses a good amount of morality, benevolence, etc., and is fond of female society. Persistent ambition and political ability are marked features of this position.

♀   Medium height, thin face and pale complexion, dark brown hair   ♀ and dark eyes, good features. Very ambitious of place and preferment, desirous of achieving lasting distinction, but unwilling to use strenuous means, and preferring subtlety to open contest. There are great possibilities in this position, only too seldom realised. In lower types, a person who speaks very highly of himself and what he does, which is not much worth talking about; he is fond of drink and many of the great evils connected therewith, and not very fortunate in his transactions.

☿   Indicates a little, lean, thin-faced individual, dull and obscure   ☿ complexion, brown hair. Of a nervous, irritable, peevish nature, and one that is not very fortunate. There is great ability for diplomacy, if well aspected, and in any case much subtlety of mind ; the mental outlook is often narrow, however.

☽ This is not a favourable position, except where the individuality is ☽ very strong. Otherwise the native is apt to become 'cranky,' small-natured, narrow-minded and mean, though the position of Saturn in Leo or Sagittarius would lessen this tendency. The figure is usually somewhat small and cramped, the face long and thin, peaky-looking, the nose somewhat Jewish in type, the skin sallow and unhealthy looking or parchment-like ; the corpse-like complexion to which this lunar position inclines is especially marked in ill-health and old age, giving a 'leaden' (♄ rules lead) tinge to the skin. The native is both cautious and subtle, very watchful of self-interests or, in the higher types, the interests of the community. The eyes are dull and patient, capable of a steady fire when settling down to work in the face of difficulties, for the energy and enthusiasm of Capricorn rise in direct proportion to the disappointments or rebuffs encountered. This is a fine position for those who can make a good use of it, but they have first to overcome the timidity and to learn to understand their own natures. The heads of the great Jewish banking houses furnish admirable instances of the favourable expression of the Capricorn qualities, but with this position they are usually only displayed in a very feeble and puny way, though the instinct towards them can be clearly discerned.

PLANETS RISING IN

AQUARIUS

♆ Neptune expresses itself well in this sign, which is airy and mental, ♆ yet concerned with the deeper feelings of the heart. Appearance generally fair, eyes large and luminous, middle stature, not short, body well covered, delicate complexion and abundant hair, somewhat flaxen, blue eyes of a somewhat sapphire tint. This position should, other things being favourable, produce a genius in art, music or sociology ; not so much a 'leader' as the founder of a 'school' which would endure after him. The artist and poet William Morris had Neptune in Aquarius at birth, and very probably rising, and his life was characteristic of this influence. In low types, shiftless and improvident, given to imposing on others, plausible and deceitful.

♅ One of middle stature, evenly composed, rather light brown hair, ♅ and very good features. Large and lustrous eyes. The disposition is independent, somewhat eccentric, but ingenious and given to curious pursuits and investigations. Science and art go hand in hand with this position ; and such a person, if other aspects, etc., corroborate, should be capable of contributing some remarkable sociological work of some kind for the advancement of humanity.

♄ Medium height, rather stout, very dark hair and complexion. In ♄ disposition he is kind, courteous, ingenious ; fond of science ; but he thinks more of himself than he has any right to. Self-reliant and masterful, inclined to diplomatic or secret service work if other planetary positions are in suitable agreement.

♃ This planet when rising in Aquarius has a very good effect upon ♃ the individual who is then born. The person attains to middle stature, and is well formed; **medium** brown hair, long face, and a **very good expression** of countenance. Disposition pleasant, merry, obliging, fond of good and respectable company, a feeling which is reciprocated. This position enables the native to manifest the true Aquarius nature more harmoniously than any other at our present stage of evolution.

♂ Of middle stature, proportionately made, sandy, reddish, or flaxen ♂ hair, ruddy complexion. Has a quarrelsome disposition and inclines to cultivate it. Delights in cantankerousness and peculiarity, and seems to find pleasure in proving his dissimilarity to other people. Rarely a favourite with the other sex.

☉ Produces a corpulent person, well and evenly composed, middle ☉ height, generally good complexion, round visage, light brown hair. In disposition very ambitious and aspiring, particularly for rule and authority; he must be first and foremost in everything, whatever he may be engaged in. Interested in art and science and all sociological schemes.

♀ A handsome, well-composed person, with a beautiful fair com- ♀ plexion, light brown hair and dark blue eyes. The disposition is very courteous, obliging, always ready to lend a helping hand in any case of need; naturally a perfect peace-maker, and a despiser of any kind of evil. A very favourable position, denoting one well constituted to be a helper to humanity.

☿ Person rather fleshy, of middle stature, full and long face, medium ☿ brown hair. Disposition good, kind, loving, and generous; a genius in every sense of the word, one who is much respected by all who know him. Much more steady in disposition and in mental matters than Mercurial people enerally and very humane as well as scientifically inclined.

☽ This is not a very favourable sign for the Moon to manifest in, ☽ being a sign both Saturnine and fixed, and such natives are likely to be in general unfortunate, being not well able to express the higher side of Aquarius through lack of power (unless other planets occupy the sign), and tending to be misunderstood as to their ideals, while the lower side of the sign will have a proportionately greater hold on them. In appearance, of medium height, slight in build yet resembling sturdier people in their walk and movements; long face, with high forehead and usually broad chin with considerable depth below the lips, sometimes a long upper lip, short straight nose, spreading out towards the tip; pale, colourless complexion, flaxen or sandy hair tending to brown; if strongly aspected by Saturn or Uranus, dark or coal-black. A strange nature, difficult to understand; obstinate in maintaining own way of life, at times given to perverse and wayward instincts. Curious in tastes, with out-of-the-way hobbies, interested in ancient customs, folk-lore, obscure superstitions, original and often eccentric in ideas. Well able to manage other people as a rule, having a curious instinct of human nature and an ability for playing on the feelings of others; in unfavourable types this is likely to lead to the native becoming a social parasite.

PLANETS RISING IN

PISCES

♆ Pisces is usually regarded as the house of Neptune, and therefore ♆ we should expect a harmonious expression of its influence. Quiet, order-loving and humane, sensitive and impressionable, with a keen instinct for beauty and a love of poetry and idealistic conditions generally. Inspirational and poetic. These are they who 'bring good tidings' and whose 'feet are beautiful upon the mountains.' Appearance, meditative or inspired, skin pearly, eyes deep and unfathomable, manner mild. In low types, dissolute, drunken, and lazy, but with some happy knack or gift that usually suffices to keep them from starving, either through exercise of artistic talent, or the bounty of others.

♅ When the planet Uranus rises at birth in the last sign of the twelve, ♅ viz., Pisces, it represents a person below the medium height, stout, with dark pale complexion, dark hair and eyes. He is neither a handsome nor an agreeable person by any means. Uranus is, on the whole, badly placed in this sign of the Zodiac, and the more unfavourable side of its nature is likely to be exemplified, the native being eccentric, cantankerous, wantonly peculiar and irregular, given to unnatural tastes and generally unsatisfactory. Of course good aspects otherwise may modify this or even redeem it altogether.

♄ About middle height, dark hair, dark pale complexion, and full ♄ eyes. Subtle and difficult to know, capable of dissembling and hypocrisy. In low types, inclined to vice and intemperance. In an otherwise good horoscope well disposed and devotional in mind, but very unfortunate, in worldly concerns.

♃ The native realises beneficial influences, which are much admired ♃ by those who observe them. Represents a person below the average height, of stout build, moderately good looking ; of a studious, ingenious disposition ; a lover of music, mirth, company, and pleasure. A somewhat Johnsonian character. Jupiter in this sign gives success upon the water, dealing in liquids, etc. It favours shipping enterprises, institutions, such as hospitals, asylums, hotels, and places where the public are catered for as regards their physical well-being.

♂ Below the average height, stout, rather obscure complexion, and ♂ light brown hair. The disposition is rarely good, being frequently hypocritical, dissembling, and given to associating with inferiors. This position rather inclines to vicious habits, drinking and general dissoluteness. In a strong horoscope this will of course be much modified or entirely transmuted into loving-kindness and energy in philanthropic schemes.

☉ Short stature, somewhat corpulent, round visage, complexion ☉ moderately good, light brown hair, fond of games and sports of a harmless, innocent nature, fond of the opposite sex and rather improvident. Hospitable and kind to dumb animals. Generally good swimmers and always fond of the water. Somewhat religious-minded.

♀ Venus rising in the sign Pisces at the time of birth, generally ♀ produces a person of middle stature, fairly formed, round visage, rather fair complexion, and light brown hair. The disposition, on the whole, is moderately good ; just in all transactions, ingenious, and witty in conversation ; a delighter in peace and tranquillity. Venus is exalted in this sign, and usually when rising bestows physical beauty as well as a well-balanced understanding and harmonious temperament.

☿ Mercury rising in Pisces at the time of birth, produces a person of ☿ small stature, pale thin face, dull brown hair, and grey eyes. A gossip ; fond of rather low company, particularly that of the opposite sex ; through this

latter trait he seldom rises in life.   In higher types an inspirational mind of
no great fixity or mental grasp.

☽   The Moon, being a plastic, receptive planet, is not unfavourably   ☽
placed in this sign, and bestows when well aspected a pleasing personality,
refined, sympathetic and artistic, well adapted to express the emotions by
intellectual means; much however depends upon the positions of the Sun and
Jupiter, the ruling planet.   In appearance rarely perfectly formed, the lower
portion of the body being not well shaped and somewhat clumsy in movement,
walk indifferent, feet pointing far apart, reminding one of a fish's tail.   Features
imperfectly formed, and mouth generally loose and ill-finished.   Complexion
soft, and in favourable instances of a peculiar opalescent or mother-of-pearl
tint and lustre ; eyes soft and mild.   General nature soft and yielding, passive,
more ready to suffer than to act, timid and given to forebodings.   Very sympathetic, and in the higher types truly hospitable and compassionate.   In the
lower types of humanity this position represents a 'derelict,' one who con-
sumes without producing.   Pisces has sometimes been termed, not without
eason, the 'dust-bin of humanity' ; in some cases the apparent failure means
a real advance in soul growth, but just as in other departments of life there
are some kinds of rubbish fit only for fuel, so we may at times find it in the
dust-bin.'

CHAPTER VII

THE RULING PLANET

THE 'ruling planet' is either the lord of the ascending sign, or else that planet which is strongest or most prominent in the horoscope. No hard and fast rule can be given to indicate which this will be ; and this is one of the many points that must be left to the judgment of the astrologer. Sometimes one planet seems to dominate the whole of the character and destiny ; while in other cases two or even more may have equal sway. Planets in the four angles have the first claim to consideration, as they are always important ; and of them the first house is the most important and the fourth the least. If any planet is rising, it will be part ruler ; if more than one rises, then that which is strongest by sign, or is nearest to the cusp of the ascendant. If no planet rises, the lord of the ascendant is ruler, and of considerable importance ; but attention must also be given to any planet close to the cusps of the tenth and seventh houses as well as to any that may be in close aspect to the degree rising. The planet that is in closest aspect to the Sun is always important, as will be seen from illustrations that follow.

All these points must be taken into consideration by the astrologer and carefully weighed with a view to determine which of them is entitled to rank as ruling planet, but in every case where there is the least doubt, the lord of the ascending sign should be considered as the RULING PLANET, for that planet will be the native's representative through life and no other. Experience will soon render this a matter of comparative ease. The following examples will serve to indicate how it is done :—

Gladstone (*born about* 8 *a.m.*, *29th December*, 1809, *Liverpool*) had Sun and Mercury rising in Capricorn, and they may be considered as having been approximately equal in importance. The former planet gave him vitality, dignity, ambition, and force of character ; and the latter, learning and eloquence.

King Edwa d VII (*born* 10-48 *a.m. 9th November*, 1841, *London*) has Jupiter rising in its own sign, Sagittarius. This gave King Edward

the Peacemaker that geniality and *bonhomie* for which he was so famous.
Saturn is also strong because, like Jupiter, it is rising in its own sign;
and this planet has brought gravity, thoughtfulness, and some reserve.
The best side of Saturn's influence is seldom fully seen until after
middle age.

The Right Hon. Joseph Chamberlain (*born* 2.45 *a.m.*, 8th July, 1836,
London) has Mercury rising in Cancer, a very characteristic position,
giving subtlety, adaptability, and eloquence.

The Right Hon. A. J. Balfour (*born about* 9-30 *a.m.* 25th July, 1848,
Haddington) has the Sun in Leo on the cusp of the eleventh house in
close conjunction with Jupiter and Venus. This makes a very fortunate
combination; the Sun being probably the strongest.

The Kaiser, William II (*born about* 3 *p.m.*, 27th January, 1859,
Berlin) has a very strong Martial influence in his horoscope for two
reasons. Cancer rises; the Moon ruling the ascendant is in the martial
sign Scorpio; Mars, its 'dispositor' (*i.e.*, ruler of the sign it is in), is in
the mid-heaven.

Queen Wilhelmina of Holland (*born* 6-30 *p.m.*, 31st August, 1880,
S. Gravenage) has a horoscope that illustrates the difficulty sometimes
experienced in deciding which out of several planets is the strongest;
for she has five planets in angles, and another, the Moon, dignified by
being in its own sign. Probably Jupiter is the strongest, as it rules the
rising sign, and is in the first house.

The Tzar, Nicholas II (*born noon*, 18th May, 1868, *St Petersburg*)
has Virgo rising, and Mercury in Gemini in the mid-heaven, which
makes it the strongest planet in the horoscope.

King George V (*born* 1-18 *a.m.*, 3rd June, 1865, *London*) has Neptune
rising in Aries in close sextile with the Sun; and this renders it
powerful. Jupiter is also strong from being elevated in its own sign.

Queen Mary (*born* 11-59 *p.m.*, 26th May, 1867, *London*) has
Jupiter as the strongest planet. It is in Pisces intercepted in the
ascendant in dexter square to the Sun. Venus and the Moon are also
both important.

King Victor Emanuel III of Italy (*born* 10-45 *p.m.* 11th November
1869, *Naples*) has Jupiter in the mid-heaven in aspect to the Sun; but
Mercury and the Sun are also strong.

The Emperor Franz Joseph of Austria (*born* 8-23 *a.m.*, 18th August,
1830, *Vienna*) has Libra rising, no planet in the ascendant; Venus in

the mid-heaven must therefore be considered strong. Mars is also strong because setting in Aries; and the Sun is important because in its own sign, Leo.

Alfonso XII, King of Spain (*born* 0-30 *p.m.*, 17*th May*, 1886, *Madrid*) has Virgo rising with Mars close to the cusp of the ascendant. Mercury is also important because lord of the ascendant and in mundane trine thereto from the cusp of the ninth house. Jupiter is in the lower part of the ascendant in close trine to the Sun.

Lord Rosebery (*born* 3 *a.m.*, 7*th May*, 1847, *London*) has the end of Pisces rising, and Aries intercepted in the ascendant containing Uranus and Mercury therein. Lord Rosebery is not 'lucky' enough for a Prime Minister. His best aspects come from the third house (speaking or writing) instead of the tenth or eleventh.

INFLUENCE OF SOLAR ASPECTS

When Leo rises the Sun is the ruling planet in the majority of cases; but if *any* planet rises in Leo it will be the ruling planet unless the Sun is very powerfully placed in the map. The Sun as ruler gives dignity, power, loyalty, ambition, vitality, and a very strong and powerful magnetism. When well-placed and favourably aspected it brings success in life.

The planet that is in nearest aspect to the Sun (even when the Sun is not the ruling planet, nor even angular) must always have consideration, for that planet will often denote the whole life history, and in many cases is a far more potent factor in a horoscope than the ruling planet or even the Sun's position.

The conjunction of the Sun with any planet will give it more life and force wherewith to act according to its nature.

The opposition of the Sun to any planet will also draw out the characteristics of that planet so that its influence becomes paramount. The square of the Sun to any planet denotes obstacles to be overcome, persons who have influence over the life, and vices or weaknesses in the character. The trine aspect will show the direction and nature of the fortune and success promised by this aspect. After noting the ascendant, this solar influence should be carefully considered in all nativities.

The conjunction of the Sun with the planet NEPTUNE gives a very peculiar nature, difficult to understand. There appears to be a certain inner receptivity to the psychic influences of the invisible worlds, which may show itself in the form of inspirational faculties of some kind, artistic or prophetic: but the nature of this influence is not properly understood. The nature is usually strongly magnetic, and there is in the higher types a mystical tendency of a very pure kind, but in less advanced egos the same tendency is likely to exhibit itself in adherence to strange or fantastic religious sects, peculiar and inflated ideas, especially regarding sex and marriage.

The square is very insidious in its influence, leading to peculiar involved conditions in the environment, plots, and secret machinations of unknown enemies, etc.   It has a very hampering and tantalising influence, seeming to deprive the native of the just reward of worthy efforts ; for this reason it appears to be closely associated with what may be termed the 'psychic' karma of the native.   Its influence is rarely manifested fully in the outer personal life, and appears to relate more to the inner life of feeling, emotion and consciousness.   In those less advanced it appears indicative of a depraved moral nature, and cravings for illicit pleasures.

The opposition is in its general nature similar, though here the opposing influences, instead of being diffused over a wide field, seem as a rule concentrated in some one person, family, society, or state of circumstances, and the native is, as it were, balanced between effort and failure.   There is often a high spiritual influence about such a position, the renunciation which such native is called upon to undergo, or the isolation to which he is condemned, seeming to be for the purpose of refining the inner nature.   The mystical tendency of Neptune is more especially marked under this aspect, and such characters often possess a peculiar individual charm that is quite indescribable, as shown, for instance, in the writings of William Sharp, better known as 'Fiona Macleod.'

The trine or sextile aspect is a decidedly favourable influence and usually bestows some of the charm alluded to, though it is doubtful whether such strong characters are found, as a rule, with this as with the other positions just given.   The favourable aspect of the Sun to Neptune is a good 'stand-by,' denoting a general 'good fortune' in the wider sense, almost equivalent to that of the trine of Jupiter.

The nature of Neptune is imperfectly understood at present, but a fuller account of its influence is given in a later work of this series.

The conjunction of the Sun with URANUS gives a powerful magnetism, but it is often more evil than good and there are very few born with this conjunction who do not spoil their lives either by oversensitiveness, impulse, eccentricity, and wilfulness, or by coming into contact with those who lead them into difficulties.

If the horoscope shows the power to appreciate this conjunction, it denotes the inventive faculty, love of reform, and the ability to live without being bound by convention or arbitrary restrictions, thus bringing success in exceptional and unique ways.

The square is evil, and denotes great troubles, over which the native has no control whatever.

The opposition brings great troubles in married life, separations, divorce, intrigue, illicit connections, and sad and uncommon experiences generally.

The trine aspect is very good and rarely fails to bring the native a successful career through his ingenuity and inventiveness.

The conjunction of the Sun with the planet SATURN brings responsibility into the life, but it is only when they are in a congenial sign that it is really fortunate. A great deal depends upon the actual power of Saturn in the nativity, for if Saturn absorbs the life from the Sun, and dons its golden garment, then expect much diplomacy, with quiet and persistent purpose, in which feeling has no part, but a powerful determination is gradually and progressively manifested. A conjunction of the Sun and Saturn in common signs is not good; in the fixed signs it denotes subtle pride or much dignity and a keen sense of honour and justice; in the cardinal signs intellectual pride and dignity, and a somewhat cold and unsympathetic nature, not from lack of feeling but more often from want of breadth of thought. In weak characters the native is very selfish or much bound by ignorance. In strong characters there is large tact, and a great deal of consideration for others which comes from knowledge and experience.

The opposition of the Sun and Saturn is very evil, causing many obstacles, disappointments and failures in life, and denotes a retardation of progress through separations, deaths, and loss of credit. If in mutual reception the evil is much lessened (Lord Salisbury; the German Kaiser William II).

The square aspect of the Sun and Saturn brings domestic affliction, limitations to progress through the conditions of the home life, parents and family, and through various difficulties over which the native can have no control.

The trine aspect, or even sextile, of Sun and Saturn will steady the whole nature, so that good progress may be made. It brings responsibility that is not difficult to discharge, and causes the native to make that steady progress upward which may be slow but is yet sure.

The conjunction of the Sun with the planet JUPITER gives success through hope, the advent of a teacher or helper, the favour of some powerful person, new social advantages, or exceptional opportunities. Increase of good name and fortune through philosophy, religion, or travel.

The square or opposition of the Sun and Jupiter is not altogether unfortunate, but it retards progress, and gives rather indirect than obvious success. It will bring some losses, but often gain follows the loss, in exemplification of the proverb that it is an ill wind indeed that blows *no* good. The signs from which these aspects operate will have much to do with the effect.

The trine aspect of the Sun to Jupiter is the best possible influence and assures a fortunate and successful career, acting in a more material sense than the conjunction, with all that the conjunction indicates in addition.

The conjunction of the Sun with the planet MARS gives great force of character, and a hasty and fiery temper, though not lasting; love of enterprise, fits of ambition without sufficient stability to continue ambitions long enough to make final success assured. Forceful and often rash and over-venturesome.

The opposition of the Sun to the planet Mars will bring separations, deaths, litigation, opponents that are powerful, and a career that is full of extremes. It is against any permanent success, for sudden and serious obstacles come into the life to *mar* its progress.

The square brings domestic worries, and a liability to violent changes, feverish attacks and many troubles.

The trine aspect gives success through enterprise, speculation, industry, courage, and adventure.

The Sun approaching the conjunction of VENUS gives love of pleasure; generosity; warm feelings or strong passions; a very fruitful and successful career through life, with many domestic and social advantages. If the Sun is separating from Venus, fewer social desires and a more temperate passional nature, with less liability to indulge the latter.

When the Sun is in conjunction with MERCURY, or Mercury is in advance of the Sun, there are shown adaptability, fertility of resource and the power to fit into the environment or to rise above it as required ; but in this case the Sun and Mercury must be in a sign congenial to the nature of both, and not afflicted. If the Sun had just left the trine aspect of a planet before it came to the conjunction of Mercury, give first attention to the trine (or even in a square opposition) in preference to the conjunction. If the Sun is in 15° and Mercury 20° of a sign, for instance, and Uranus in 10° of a sign forming a ✶, ☐ or △ thereto, count the aspect to Uranus as most important, although separating by 5°. The reason for this is obvious ; Mercury is convertible, and therefore not so strong as Uranus to affect the Sun. If the Sun is in advance of Mercury there is less concentration and more pliability and changeableness.

The conjunction of the Sun with *any* planet accentuates the individual character, the planet *colouring* the Sun, so to speak, and the Sun adding life and activity to the planet, making its influence very pronounced.

The square aspect brings domestic limitations which may be traced to inherited fate. The character is often altered and modified by this aspect. Persons bound by parentage, customs, habit or family ties will have a square aspect denoting the bondage.

The trine brings success into the life through the contented frame of mind which the harmony of this influence denotes. It is the aspect that fits in with the ordinary idea of 'luck,' for it corresponds to prosperity that comes without effort.

The opposition is a separative or more properly a *balancing* aspect, which often shatters the prospects by causing sudden and often unlooked for changes, separations, and disappointments.

It will thus be seen that to a great extent character is destiny.

The semisquare and sesquiquadrate are disintegrative and weakening in their effects, causing friction and waste of power, like sand in the bearings of a machine.

THE RULER'S POSITION

We may now proceed to a consideration of the ruling planet in regard to its position in the zodiac ; first, when free from affliction by aspect, secondly, when afflicted, either by conjunction or bad aspect with the malefics, or by the unfavourable aspect of the Sun or other planets.

Ruler in the Signs, and well aspected or unafflicted

♈ Independent ; ambitious ; self-willed ; intellectual.
♉ Determined ; self-reliant ; plodding ; enduring ; careful ; curious.
♊ Imaginative ; idealistic ; studious ; sensitive ; intuitional.
♋ Tenacious ; sensitive ; mediumistic ; conscientious.
♌ Generous ; persistent ; organising ; determined ; powerful.
♍ Thoughtful ; discriminative ; industrious ; retiring ; refined.
♎ Harmonious ; intuitive ; contemplative ; imaginative.
♏ Proud ; jealous ; stubborn ; acquisitive ; sympathetic.
♐ Charitable ; ambitious ; dignified ; self-reliant ; prophetic.
♑ Persevering ; practical ; calculating ; reasonable ; religious.
♒ Sympathetic ; sincere ; faithful ; honest ; intelligent.
♓ Methodical ; receptive ; philanthropic ; modest ; logical.

The fiery signs are the most fortunate and give independence and ambition. The earthly do not give such good fortune, but they cause the native to be practical and persevering. The Airy signs give more fortune and also much refinement and intellectuality. The Watery signs are the least fortunate, giving sensitiveness and often lack of energy.

The Cardinal signs show ambition, forcefulness, love of change, and reform. The fixed signs give reserve power and determination. The Common signs intellect, sympathy, and versatility, with some instability.

Ruler in the Signs, and afflicted

♈ Passionate ; hasty ; headstrong ; impulsive ; liberal.
♉ Obstinate ; jealous ; lethargic ; dogmatic ; conceited.
♊ Conceited ; diffusive ; lacking in continuity ; irritable.
♋ Sensational ; over-sensitive ; faddy ; whimsical ; peevish.
♌ Proud ; domineering ; sensual ; prodigal ; too passionate.
♍ Selfish ; over-critical ; deceptive ; shy ; revengeful.
♎ Dreamy ; fanciful ; separative ; timid ; cowardly.
♏ Vindictive ; stubborn ; very proud ; jealous ; and deceitful.
♐ Irritable ; over-assertive ; rebellious ; self-opinionative.
♑ Over-subtle ; treacherous ; unreliable ; dishonest ; sullen.
♒ Irregular ; wavering ; romantic ; scheming ; tricky.
♓ Lazy ; unreliable ; shifty ; procrastinative ; spiteful.

Care should be taken to judge accurately the nature of the affliction. A planet is weak when out of dignities and when in square, semi-square, sesquiquadrate or opposition with the malefics, in a general sense ; but the afflictions often give grit and force, though this depends upon the house as well as sign.

Ruler in the Houses, and unafflicted

I.   Success in life through merit and personal effort. Dignity and honour created by determination and strength of character.

II.   Financial successes and prosperity through increased turn-over. Noble thoughts ; also the power to make money.

III.   Success through learning, and mental abilities. Gain by travel and through relatives and kindred.

IV.   Inheritance ; heredity ; experiences at the close of life ; psychic experiences.

V.   Successful enterprises ; love of pleasure. Gain through children, enjoyment, and investments, speculation, etc.

VI.   Gain by inferiors and through own industry in employment and in business.

VII.   Gain by marriage, partnerships, and sometimes through opponents. The native is often helped by others.

VIII.   Gain through partner, marriage, co-workers, legacies, and through deaths. The native is drawn toward the occult and mystical.

IX.   Gain from foreign affairs, travel, science, religion, etc.

X.   Success in life, gratified ambition, honour and fame ; public appointments.

XI.   Help and gain through friends ; social success.

XII.   Gain through institutions, asylums, occult and mystical affairs.

Note carefully the good aspects and where they come from.

Ruler in the Houses, and weak or afflicted

I.   Loss and trouble through rash and foolish conduct, the native standing in his own light. Self-inflicted sorrows.

II.   Trouble in connection with finance. Monetary difficulties.

III.   Loss and trouble through misconception, errors in judgment, removals, and fruitless travel; trouble through brethren and education.

IV.   Domestic troubles, inharmonious home surroundings, losses at the close of life.

V.   Trouble through the opposite sex, losses through investment or speculation, and risk in enterprise.

VI.   Ill-health, troubles through inferiors, many moods, wrong employment and errors in method.

VII.   Trouble through marriage, partnerships, opponents, litigation and much opposition.

VIII.   Trouble in connection with money left by will or legacy, and unpleasant death ; relatives or friends die or separate from native.

IX.   Losses through foreign affairs, long journeys, religious matters and scientific failures.

X.   Dishonour, loss of credit, difficulties with superiors, scandal, ill-repute, trouble with profession.

XI.   Losses through friends and acquaintances, false hopes and wishes defeated.

XII.   Confinement, lack of progress, slow development, enemies.

CHAPTER VIII

HEALTH AND THE HYLEG. LENGTH OF LIFE AND THE APHETA

THERE are three factors necessary for the continued existence of a living human body.

(1) First of all comes the visible dense Physical Body, composed of solids, liquids, and gases. It is born at birth and dies at death, and is all that the average man knows anything about; it is what is meant when the word 'body' is used without any qualification. In the horoscope it is indicated by the twelve mundane houses in general, of which the ascendant is taken as the synthetic representative. Its symbol is that of 'Mother Earth,' $\oplus$, from which it is derived: (this symbol is also used for the 'Part of Fortune,' it should be remembered).

(2) Secondly, there is the so-called Etheric Double. This is composed of the subtle invisible ethers of the physical plane. It is the ethereal companion of the dense physical body, of which it is the exact duplicate, and like it is born at birth and dies and decays at death. In the horoscope it is represented by the Moon, ☽, which is its symbol; and like that body it has an important influence upon the nervous system.

(3) Thirdly comes the Vital Energy, conveniently called *prâna*. This is derived from the Sun, ☉, which is its representative in the horoscope, and is poured out through the whole solar system to animate and sustain all things. Every living body appropriates as much of this energy as it can, by means of an organ situated in the Etheric Double and corresponding to what we know in the physical body as the spleen. Its central reservoir is the brain (which it will be remembered is governed by the ascendant) and it passes all over the body along the course of the nerves. In a normally healthy person there is usually an excess of it, and the surplus is radiated away from the surface of the body in all directions; such radiation helps to drive away unhealthy emanations which might otherwise effect a lodgment and cause disease. When too little of it is appropriated by the double, various abnormalities follow,

138

from mere lack of energy and vitality up to actual disease of various kinds.

These three factors, as represented by the ASCENDANT, MOON, and SUN in the horoscope, must all be taken into account in considering the question of health. If all three are well aspected, health and a fair length of life are a certainty. If any one of the three is badly aspected, especially if the afflicting planet is a malefic or is ruler of the fourth, eighth or twelfth house, or is situated therein, ill-health of the type indicated by the afflicting planet is liable to result at some time in life, and to be severe or slight according to the nature of the affliction. Hindu writings inform us that *prâna*, after entering the body, is divided into various currents or streams, and that each is governed by a planet. At present there is too little information available, both from scientific and from occult sources, to enable us to go into much detail on the subject; but the probability is that sooner or later not only the physical body, but the ' double ' and the vital energy (*prâna*) also will be recognised as having sub-divisions corresponding to the planets; and the task of recognising the source and nature of disease will then be greatly simplified.

If the SUN is afflicted, the flow of the vital energy will be disturbed according to the nature of the afflicting planet and the signs concerned; Mars and Jupiter causing a feverish or disorderly superabundance, and Saturn and Uranus quite the reverse. Particulars under these heads have been given previously. (Chapter V.)

If the MOON is afflicted it indicates that the subtle vehicle conveying the life forces contains some abnormality that is liable to set up disease at some time in life, the precise period being indicated by the Progressed Horoscope, which forms the subject of a later treatise of this series.

When the ASCENDANT is afflicted, the health is also liable to suffer, according to the nature of the affliction and the sign rising; but in this case one of the so-called malefics in the ascendant is not necessarily bad for health *unless it is evilly aspected.*

The part of the body affected will be either that indicated by the sign and house, or else that governed by the point afflicted. The Sun governs the heart and vitality; the Moon, the breasts, stomach, glands, the nervous system in part and the feminine functions; and the Ascendant, the head, and whatever part is indicated by the rising sign.

The part of the body so governed is always liable to be more or less affected; for instance, if the Moon is in opposition to Saturn the digestive functions may suffer, quite irrespective of the part of the horoscope occupied by the Moon. But when it comes to deciding whether those portions of the body indicated by the sign and house will also suffer, and if so which, that governed by the sign or that by the house, the answer is not always easy to give. Some observations on this problem are given later on in the chapter.

Sometimes it is possible to collect testimonies from two or even three different parts of the horoscope all pointing in the same direction. For instance, although an afflicted Sun may indicate some heart affection, yet it is seldom serious unless there is also an affliction of either Leo or the fifth house (both of which have relation to the heart). Again an afflicted Mercury may indicate liability to some nervous or mental disorder; but experience shows that in cases of grave diseases of this class either the Moon or the ascendant is usually afflicted as well, (sometimes both). It is always advisable to seek for corroboration of this sort, and to balance up the good and evil testimonies against each other. For each part of the body there is more than one indicator; thus the lungs are governed by Gemini, the third house, and by Mercury (chiefly when in an *odd* sign or house). If one indicator is afflicted and the others well aspected, especially by benefics, no disease may show itself— or not until late in life. With such positions it is sometimes found that the disease is in the family and has shown out in a parent or relative, but may not affect the native. If, however, two or more of the indicators are severely afflicted, or even if one only is afflicted by two or more strong bad aspects and receives no support at all by good aspects (more especially from benefics) disease is almost certain to show itself.

THE HYLEG

The *Hyleg* is that point in the horoscope upon which health and life depend, and has to be carefully considered when estimating the probable length of life and the constitutional strength. The Ascendant, Sun, and Moon, have all three to be taken into account when dealing with this subject. It is first necessary to consider briefly the influence of the rising sign upon health.

The cusp of the Ascendant should be treated as if it were one of the heavenly bodies, and aspects should be calculated to it from each of the planets, its declination being also noted.   The declination of the cusp of the Ascendant is that which the Sun would have if it were in the same degree of the zodiac, and therefore may be found from the ephemeris.

The Ascendant is *always* an important factor in the question of health, even when it is not what is technically called ' hyleg '; and its influence varies according to the nature of the rising sign and the aspects to the cusp of the ascendant.   Good aspects preserve the health and increase the vitality ; bad aspects threaten accidents or ill-health at some period of life according to the nature of the afflicting planet and the sign in which it is placed.   The positive (odd) signs rising always tend to give a good measure of vitality, particularly Leo, Libra, and Sagittarius ; the negative (even) signs, on the other hand, are not quite so vigorous, Virgo being the most favourable for health.   Cancer, Capricorn, and Pisces give feeble vitality, more especially in infancy.   Scorpio gives much vital energy but also extreme liability to infectious diseases.   Of the children that die in infancy a great many come under Capricorn and Scorpio because, when afflicted, the former sign gives a weakly constitution, and, the latter leaves the native liable to many of the infectious disorders of childhood.

This only happens under bad aspects ; for, in general, any sign will give good health when the cusp of the ascendant is well fortified, and Capricorn and Scorpio, if receiving good aspects, may give great tenacity of life in old age.   It sometimes happens that hereditary influence may be seen in the rising sign, and that not only in matters of health but also in events.   Thus, when Scorpio rises, an important death may occur among the relatives or close associates of the parents a few months before or shortly after the child's birth ; when Libra rises, a marriage ; when Sagittarius rises, a journey, or religious matters may come prominently forward ; and so on with affairs signified by the other signs.

In matters of health, positive signs act similarly to the Sun when hyleg, and negative signs to the Moon ; but when afflicted each sign may cause its own particular type of disease according to the planet ruling it and the part of the body it governs.

Disease as indicated by the Rising Sign

♈ The head is liable to suffer and the native will be affected with tooth-ache, neuralgia, gumboils, measles, small-pox, ringworms, and vertigo.   When the ascendant is much afflicted by either Mars or Jupiter, danger of epilepsy, apoplexy, and insanity.

♉ The throat is liable to be affected, and the native suffers from quinsy,

diphtheria, sore throat, abscesses, etc.   If the descendant is much afflicted there
is danger of heart disease, fits, and sudden death.

♊ The chest and lungs are the most sensitive parts of the body, hence
the native is liable to suffer from asthma, bronchitis, consumption and nervous
disorders.   If the ascendant is much afflicted there is danger of brain fever,
hypochondria, and diseases arising from impure blood.

♋ The stomach and digestive organs are easily disordered, giving the
native a tendency to suffer from indigestion, asthma, coughs, and wasting or
chronic diseases.   If the ascendant is much afflicted there is danger of pleurisy,
gastric troubles, and dropsy, or even cancer.

♌ The loins and back are the weakest parts of the body, giving a liability
to lumbago, syncope, palpitation, fevers, and eye affections.   If the ascendant
is much afflicted there is danger of jaundice, small-pox, rheumatic fever, and
heart disease.

♍ The bowels are liable to give trouble, causing the native to suffer from
spasms, colic, dysentery, or chronic constipation.   If the ascendant is much
afflicted there is danger of consumption of the bowels, cholera, and strangulation
of the urine.

♎ The kidneys or bladder will give trouble, causing the native to suffer
from debility, weakness in the back, and ulcers.   If the ascendant is much
afflicted there is danger of diabetes, Bright's disease and spinal trouble.

♏ The secret parts are liable to weakness, causing the native to suffer
from piles, gravel, ruptures, and venereal diseases.   If the ascendant is much
afflicted there is a liability to fistulas, gravel, stone, strange blood poisonings,
and peculiar diseases generally.

♐ The thighs and buttocks are liable to become affected.   The native is
liable to suffer from blood disorders, tumours, gout, and fevers.   If the ascendant is much afflicted there is danger of accidents, rheumatism, and violent
hurts.

♑ The knees are the parts of the body that first show signs of weakness.
The native is liable to suffer from rheumatism, cutaneous complaints, eczema,
and colds.   If the ascendant is much afflicted there is danger of chronic
disorders affecting the chest and giving rise to hysteria and general debility.

♒ There is a liability to nervous disorders and affections of the blood.

♓ The native is liable to suffer from gout, impure blood, and boils; also
from ailments arising from cold or damp feet and from bunions, etc.

Disease as indicated by Planets Rising

♆ Neptune rising predisposes to melancholia, weird fancies, mental
complaints and, when much afflicted, obsession.

♅ Uranus rising gives a tendency to incurable and uncommon disorders,
chiefly affecting the nerves and psychic aura.

♄ Saturn rising gives a liability to suffer from chill, cold, poor circulation,
obstructions, constipation, and chronic disorders such as rheumatism and wasting
diseases.

♃ Jupiter rising affects the blood and liver.

♂ Mars rising affects the muscular system and increases the liability to
feverish and inflammatory complaints.

☉ The Sun rising (i.e., in the ascendant) if free from affliction, will give great vitality and strengthen the constitution, the Sun being more or less hyleg wherever it may be placed ; but if afflicted, then the recuperative power is not good.

Venus rising affects the generative and nutritive system.

☿ Mercury rising gives nervous and mental troubles, the health depending a great deal upon the general surroundings.

☽ The Moon rising gives liability to dropsical complaints, and to chronic irregularities of the system.

Fiery signs rising predispose the native to inflammatory conditions of the system, to fevers, and to sudden illnesses generally—acute, but of short duration.

Airy signs rising denote a tendency to nervous troubles, debility, and illnesses arising from over-exertion, exhaustion, etc.

Watery signs rising give a liability to tumours, cancerous growths, mucous discharges, colds, and moist humours.

Earthy signs rising denote rheumatic, gouty, and windy complaints, with a tendency toward chronic disorders.

CARDINAL SIGNS rising incline to ailments affecting the head, stomach, kidneys, and all movable or *functional* disorders.

FIXED SIGNS rising incline to ailments affecting the heart, throat, generative system, and all chronic or *organic* troubles.

MUTABLE SIGNS rising incline to affections of the lungs, limbs, breathing apparatus, and all kinds of *nervous* disorders.

The decanate rising will sometimes show the root of the disease, or the weakest part of the system: for instance, the third decanate of Libra rising denotes a tendency to nervous diseases, brain fever, etc.

The second decanate of Libra, poor circulation, flatulency, rheumatism, etc.

If the rulers of the rising sign and of the decanate are in mutual affliction then the nature of the decanate should be carefully studied, as also the house governed by its ruler.

The rules for ascertaining which point is hyleg are much in dispute among astrologers, though nearly all are agreed that the Sun, Moon, and Ascendant are the three points from which choice must be made ; but while serious affliction of any one of these three may result in disease sooner or later, yet the idea is that the length of life (apart from the liability to disease) is more dependent upon one of these points than upon the other two, and that this one (which is spoken of as 'the hyleg') varies in different horoscopes.

The oldest rules for ascertaining which point is hyleg are those of Ptolemy. According to this system, the hylegiacal places are houses I, VII, IX, X, XI. If the Sun is in one of these places it is always hyleg; if it is not there and the Moon is, the latter is hyleg; and if neither is there the cusp of the ascendant is hyleg. There has, however, scarcely been an astrologer who has not suggested some more or less important alteration of these rules. Ptolemy himself would sometimes allow the strongest planet in the horoscope to be hyleg. In our own day 'Raphael' has suggested that the Sun is always hyleg with a man and the Moon with a woman. Others have doubted whether one body ever can be hyleg to the entire exclusion of the other two, pointing out that it is not uncommon for all three to be afflicted by direction at death; and they have drawn from this the conclusion that the hylegiacal office may be shared among the three. Others would allow the lower half of the twelfth house to be a hylegiacal place, especially for the Sun.

The student may be safely left to put all theories to the test of practical experience and draw his own conclusions; but in the meantime the following summary would probably obtain the assent of a large number of astrologers.

1. The Sun, Moon and Ascendant are three centres upon which life depends.

2. The Moon governs child-birth and the feminine functions, and its position and aspects are therefore far more important in the horoscope of a woman than in that of a man. It is also alleged to exercise considerable influence with very young children of both sexes, probably for the first seven years of life.

3. The centre indicated by the Ptolemaic rule given above is always important, whether it be exclusively hyleg or not.

THE APHETA AND ANARETA

The *Apheta* is an Arabic word used to signifiy that which supports life. Generally speaking any planet is aphetical that is in good aspect to the hyleg; but aspects from planets in the first, fifth, ninth and tenth houses or from the lords of these, are especially to be desired. Jupiter and Mars impart energy and exuberant vitality when in good aspect to the hyleg, and indicate that vital force is rapidly generated. This not only causes a quick recovery after any exhausting labour or illness, but also tends to keep even infectious diseases at bay, and carries the native through dangers that would prostrate or kill other people. The good aspects of Saturn (and probably Uranus also) are extremely important to people who have passed middle age, as they regulate and harmonise the flow of the vital fluid, and, other things being equal, help greatly in carrying on the life into old age; but it is thought that they are less important with children. The same remarks apply to a well-aspected hyleg in the Saturnian signs, Capricorn and Aquarius.

The *Anareta* is that which takes away life. Generally speaking any planet is anaretic that afflicts the hyleg; but evil aspects from planets in the fourth, sixth, eighth and twelfth, or lords of these, are particularly bad for health. In this case the afflicting planets reverse the qualities that are indicated by good aspects. Mars and Jupiter in affliction of the hyleg increase heat in the system and give liability to diseases arising from fever, plethora, excesses; and this is worse in the case of the Sun than of the Moon, because the former body is naturally hot whereas the latter is cool. Saturn, and probably Uranus also, when afflicting deplete the system, lower the vitality, and lead to diseases arising from cold and from enfeebled constitution; they destroy that unity of action, that co-operation of functions, upon which the well-being of the body depends. Rheumatism, consumption, ague, cancer, paralysis, etc., have been known to be produced by them. They are worse when afflicting the Moon than when in bad aspect to the Sun, because the natural heat of the latter body can hold out against their action longer than the former.

In all these cases any planet in its own sign or house or in one in which it is well placed, has its malice very greatly lessened and its good aspects much increased in value.

The question of the probable length of life must also be considered here. It is impossible to judge this solely by directions, because if the constitution is strong the native will live through evil periods that would kill one with a weak hyleg. A general inspection must therefore be made of the hylegiacal point or points in the horoscope of birth before the astrologer takes the question of directions into account at all. In fact this careful review of *the birth map should have first consideration*, not only when dealing with health but with all the other subjects with which the astrologer is called upon to deal, such as marriage, wealth, etc. Directions are always of secondary importance to radical indications; and it is highly probable that a fuller knowledge of the subject may enable us to judge not merely the events of the life but also the times of their occurrence from the birth map alone, without needing to have recourse to any of the present-day systems of directing.

In dealing with this question of the probable length of life, it is convenient to divide natives, roughly speaking, into three classes : those that die young, in infancy or childhood ; those that live to middle age; and those that endure to old age.   These are only intended as rough approximations for the convenience of the student, and not as scientific divisions.   If the three points, Sun, Moon, and Ascendant, are all well aspected and free from affliction, or if that one of them which is ascertained to be hyleg is in this fortunate condition, old age may fairly be regarded as highly probable, and any evil directions in early life, although they may cause temporary illness, will not kill.   If the reverse positions are found, however, and afflictions by far outnumber the good aspects, then death in early life will certainly result.   But when the position and aspects of the hyleg are neither wholly evil nor wholly good ; when the affliction is not so serious as to indicate death in infancy, and yet the hyleg is not so strong as to point to old age, the life may be conveniently regarded as likely to terminate in middle age.   Considerable experience is necessary to enable the student to balance up the various indications in the way that is desirable here, for no book can possibly cover all the combinations and great variety of positions and aspects that are actually found in horoscopes.   The astrologer, too, will be wise to be extremely cautious in positively predicting death ; not merely because the subject is a difficult one, but also because such a prediction is not a little alarming to most people ; for the average person has not yet evolved to the point of regarding 'peaceful and soothing death' as a friend, and the announcement of his approach is likely to prove very unsettling, to diminish the vitality, and to increase the power of disease.

Houses *versus* Signs

Since the first edition of this book was published we have often been asked what is the difference between the influence of *houses* in comparison with that of the *signs* : for instance, say in one horoscope Saturn, afflicted, is in the second house; in another horoscope Saturn, similarly afflicted, is in Taurus : what is the similarity and what is the difference; will both natives suffer from disease of the throat, or only one : and if both, which will be the greater sufferer ?   And we have been asked to give a series of delineations of the effects of each planet in each one of the twelve houses (similar to those given in the next book of this series, where the influence of each planet in every sign is described), so that the reader can be in no doubt. Now, in the first place, considerations of space preclude the adoption of this course, and secondly, it is not quite certain whether such a series would be of much practical help after all. This for a reason which we will try to make clear.

The relationship between signs and houses, as has been repeatedly stated, is that of 'correspondence,' or analogy, being similar to the relationship of one octave to another on the pianoforte—each house corresponds to each sign only because it is, in a kind of way, 'the same thing only different'—that is, the *noumenon* behind each is identical, and only the plane of manifestation varies. That being so it is easy to see that one influence can be exalted or degraded to the other ; just as personal interests may be expanded so as to serve the community, or public needs may be sacrificed to benefit an individual—these things we see around us in daily life. Consequently, it depends very much upon the individual how the influence will work out ; thus, Saturn in Taurus may operate in one case exactly as would Saturn in the second house ; and, vice versa, Saturn in the second house may in some cases act just as would Saturn in Taurus with the majority of people.

To take another instance, Mars in Aries or in the Ascendant. Both these positions incline to impulsiveness, rashness and ardour, also to enterprise and activity—the former as a rule more individual, the latter more personal. But a strong character who has the latter position may, by living up to the best that is in him, refine this position till it corresponds more to the former, and instead of throwing away his strength in fruitless anger or passion, or in fitful impulse, may spiritualise it and exalt it into energy, enterprise and activity, turned into the direction of intellectual pursuits. On the other hand, one with Mars in Aries might, by constantly yielding to the lower impulses signified by this position, gradually reduce himself to the condition usually described by Mars in the Ascendant, fitful, passionate, egotistical and foolishly self-sufficient. These two cases are only chosen for the purpose of illustrating the principle involved, of course ; but it is true in actual life, and will be well understood by any who have made a continued study of a few characters, strong and weak, whose horoscopes are well known to them.

Now this is not only true in regard to character, but the same prin-

ciple applies also to health.   The physical plane is the plane of outward
effects, in which causes, whether physical, emotional, mental or spiritual,
work themselves out; and no ' cause,' that is, no force which has been set
in motion, on any plane, can fail to produce its effect *sooner or later* on
the physical plane.   But it may be held in suspension, either for a
shorter or longer period.

The true cause of ill-health, disease or constitutional infirmity, is
disharmony, i.e., some infraction of nature's laws (or God's laws in other
words), on some plane or other, either in this or a previous life, which
the universal Spirit of Harmony seeks to adjust by getting rid of the discordant element.   This can only be got rid of by being thrown downward and outward, by being ' precipitated,' as the chemist would say,
into the physical plane and thus filtered out of the nature—for the true
seat of disease is in the mind.

Now this process may be brought about gradually and almost
imperceptibly, or it may be hastened considerably, or it may be brought
about almost instantaneously.   Usually, the former is the case, and
ill-health manifests itself slowly ; where much activity of mind or soul
is displayed the process is expedited, as we see in the cases of those
with a predisposition to consumption.   But in some cases, as is well
known to those who are familiar with many who have had a spiritual
quickening, the turning of the inner nature steadfastly and irrevocably
towards harmony and truth, throws all the discord and disharmony
of the nature *outwards* and *downwards*, first into the mind, then the
emotions, and, as a last resort, on to the physical plane in the form of
bodily disease.   And thus that particular sickness of the soul is got rid
of for ever.

It does not follow, of course, that any such crisis of intellectual,
moral or spiritual quickening will necessarily be followed by physical
disease.   That will depend upon (*a*) the available inner discord to be
externalised, (*b*) the soul-force which expels it and the suddenness with
which it is thrown into action, and (*c*) the readiness of response, or
elasticity, of the body; also, of course, in a very great measure upon
the hygienic conditions to which that body is subjected.   Nor is
it essential that the expulsive force spoken of need be of a very high
spiritual order, for the same principle holds good where the influx is
merely one of physical vigour ; in short the whole question is merely
one of *prâna* or the life-energy, whatever be the plane of manifestation

upon which it is first called into being.   Where the revulsion is sudden
and violent, the physical body is not always able to endure the strain
and death results ; but such cases are, as may be supposed, rare.

The truth of this principle is well-known in all Natural Cure institutions, where the first symptoms of the commencement of the cure is
that the patient *feels* much worse—the latent poison in the system has
been stirred into activity, and is on its way to expulsion through the *skin*
(Cardinal Signs, physical world), usually resulting in a rash technically
known in hydropathic establishments as the 'crisis.'

Now the bearing of all this upon the reading of a nativity will not
need very much further elucidation.   Suppose we have Jupiter on cusp
of ascendant and Saturn on cusp of fourth ; this is a mundane square
and indicates misfortune and repressive circumstances.   But suppose at
the same time these planets are in zodiacal sextile, as in the horoscope on
p. 68 of *Modern Astrology* (Vol. III., New Series) ?   This we should
judge as indicating that the objective and subjective minds were in good
accord, indicating a well-balanced and well-disposed nature, truthful,
reliable, and trustworthy ; the native himself says, 'it has always seemed
to me to denote that my character is better than my circumstances,' and
by the strength of his character he has overcome the adverse circumstances.   Suppose it had been the other way about, mundane sextile and
zodiacal square, then the circumstances would have been good and the
character different, and the result would have been precisely the
reverse, in all probability ; the character, very weak and shiftless, would
have wasted excellent opportunities and squandered wealth.

In this way it can be seen how the *houses* are always (or at least as
a rule) negative, in a sense, as compared with the *signs*, the latter representing the 'life' poured into the 'form' signified by the houses.   Suppose, then, in this last illustration, the soul of the native in some way
received a great quickening so that the inner weaknesses were cast off
by the awakening spirit, then the discord indicated by the zodiacal square
would be as it were suddenly precipitated, and the disasters and misfortunes (in a worldly sense) which so often follow in the train of a
spiritual awakening would very soon make their appearance ; had the
planets ruled or been in houses specially concerned with health, this
would probably result in some disease of the stomach (fourth house).

The circle of the houses and the circle of the signs mark progressive
limitations, and also progressive powers.   As the attempt is made to

transcend the one the forces of the other at once flow in, and should
this attempt be made too suddenly, or should fixed habits and conventional states of mind prove too inelastic, disharmony and hence illness or
disease will result.   But in the history of the Soul they might be written
down as 'growing pains.'

AN ILLUSTRATION

X	XI	XII	I	II	III
♋29½	♍4	♎1	♎22	♏18	♐21

☉	☽	☿	♀	♂	♃	♄	♅	♆
♐20½	♍19½	♐7	♑7½	♐22	♋13½ R	♍2	♒27	♒2

The above is the horoscope of a female born at 2.42 A.M. 13th
December, 1835, London. The Moon in this nativity is hyleg and
afflicted by square ☉ and ♂, ∠ ♄. The Sun is also afflicted by
conjunction with Mars.

The native died 17th November, 1855, under the following
'Directions':—Ascendant ∠ ♂, bringing into action ☽ ☐ ♂ at birth ;
Mars at the time of death was transiting the place of the Moon at birth.
The Moon by secondary direction was applying to the opposition of the
Sun and Mars, and was therefore in square to its own place at birth.
The Sun had also arrived at the opposition of Jupiter's progressed
place and Venus ruler of the first and eighth was in square to Saturn
lord of the fourth.   In this case death had been predicted, the
astrologer finding it inevitable.

CHAPTER IX

THE SECOND HOUSE—WEALTH AND FINANCE, AND HEREDITARY POSITION

IN any horoscope money matters are judged largely, but not exclusively, from the state of the second house. As we have seen elsewhere, this house belongs to the triad of tenth, second and sixth: and of these the tenth house or mid-heaven is concerned to a great extent with occupation. business. profession; the sixth with servants, employees, situations, positions or spheres of activity in which money may be earned; and the second with money. In addition, the eighth house has to do with money inherited, legacies, and money coming to the native through other people (chiefly through the business or marriage partner); and in a similar way the twelfth and fourth houses may be considered to have a similar reflex influence, as it were, of the sixth and tenth houses. The question of money cannot therefore be judged *exclusively* from the second house, for these others have also to be taken into consideration and judged in their relation to each other and to the horoscope as a whole, nevertheless the second house must be allowed final voice in the matter.

In dealing with this, as with any other house, the usual order is to be followed:

(1) Consider any planet in the house, whether strong or weak, whether well or ill aspected and by what planets, also what other house or houses it rules by sign. The normal state of affairs, in theory at least, is for a planet in the second house to indicate *gain* through events, occupations, or persons signified by the planet, quite irrespective of whether it is a 'benefic' or a 'malefic.' If it is uniformly well aspected, this probability will be a certainty; but any bad aspect will be a source of difficulty, delay, or loss, according to the closeness of the aspect and the nature of the planet that throws it. For instance, if Mars is in the second house and well aspected, the native will gain money by his own exertions, through people who are born under Mars or under the planets with which Mars is in good aspect; by the dead

(legacies); and by the occupations that come under this planet, such as that of soldier, surgeon, butcher, worker in metals, chemicals, etc. But if Mars is badly aspected, there may be loss through any or all of these channels, and also through those signified by the afflicting planet. If there is a mixture of good and evil aspects, the good luck will of course come through the planets that throw the good aspects. In any case there will be a tendency to give away, spend, or in some way scatter money, owing to the inner nature of the planet Mars, irrespective of its aspects. The general influence of the planets and signs over money is given below.

(2) Secondly, if no planet is in the house, that ruling the sign on the cusp of the house is sure to be important, and must be considered much as Mars in the instance just given. Here again the natural tendency is for the native to *gain* through the lord of the second house, according to its nature, to the part of the horoscope in which it is situated, and to the planets that are in good aspect to it: and only to lose if weak by sign or badly aspected. For instance, if the lord of the second is in the third house and well aspected, there will be gain through matters signified by that house, such as brothers and sisters, short journeys, writings, mental work, and the occupations associated with the third house. The inherent nature of the planet that rules the second house must also be taken into account, and the sign in which it is placed. A gentleman born under Libra has Scorpio on the cusp of the second house; Mars, the ruler of Scorpio, is in Capricorn in the third house; he holds an appointment as Medical Officer of Health in a large health resort. Here Scorpio and Mars agree with the nature of the occupation, and Capricorn being the tenth sign of the zodiac signifies a public appointment; and the third house influence may perhaps be detected in the reports he has to issue at intervals. Another, who has Virgo on the cusp of the second and Mercury in Capricorn in the sixth, holds a scientific appointment under Government. Another, who has the lord of the second in the seventh, has benefited through his wife and is also in partnership. Another, who has the lord of the second in conjunction with the lord of the third, incurred debts that were paid by a brother. Another, who has the lord of the second in Libra in the eleventh, has received financial assistance from friends; but it is squared by Saturn from the eighth house, and he separated from his wife, to whom he had to pay an allowance which he found it very hard to earn.

Instances like these might be multiplied to almost any extent if it were necessary; but the student will soon find from personal experience that the general principles here given are reliable.

(3) Thirdly, it is necessary to take into account those planets that have a general signification in connection with money and property, whether they have any dignity in the second house or not. If Venus or Jupiter is in good aspect to Saturn or the Moon, the influence is very favourable for wealth, especially if one of them is ruler of the second or tenth. Probably the most favourable aspect for money is the trine of Jupiter to Saturn, and the least fortunate a square or opposition between these two planets. Of course, any good aspect signifies good luck of some sort, but unless one of the two planets has dignity in the second or tenth, or has some inherent signification in connection with possessions, the good luck indicated may have no financial significance. A good aspect to Venus, for instance, might give popularity and social success and bring no monetary prosperity: yet a trine or sextile from Venus to Saturn is extremely favourable for the accumulation of money.

The Moon in good aspect to the Sun, again, is a general indication of good fortune, paternal harmony, the favour of the family and of superiors and employers; but it may not produce much in the way of money unless one of the two is in the second or tenth; otherwise the success indicated will come mainly through the houses in which the two are placed. If benefics are strong, angular, and elevated, it is a good sign, also if malefics are well aspected; but whether the good signified will come through money and occupation or not depends upon their position by house and rulership. Saturn and the Moon are the two bodies that tend to accumulate and pile up money by caution, prudence, and thrift; this if carried to excess may become miserliness: but when afflicting each other they are very unfortunate, money is hard to earn, and property is lost. Jupiter and Venus bring money by good luck, popularity, relatives, and friends; Mercury, by occupations of the nature of the third and sixth houses; the Sun and Mars by personal exertions and legacies, although they both part with money easily. Jupiter or the Moon in good aspect to Saturn may also bring legacies. Jupiter and Venus are not of much use in the second house if they are seriously afflicted.

Planets and Money

Neptune denotes gain through navigation, and the sea generally also through secret service, the turf, hospitals, asylums, institutions, swimming baths and lavatories; also through public establishments in which the unfortunate and afflicted portions of humanity are confined. Money may be gained in peculiar and questionable ways, sometimes through fraud and deception, blackmail or ways that are not considered exactly straightforward. 'Bubble' schemes come especially under the influence of this planet, also misrepresentation, 'bogus count' business, etc.

Uranus denotes gain through antiquities; old and curious objects; through unique employments of a purely mental character, especially those occupations in which the occult and mystical side of things are the main feature. It is the planet which brings gain through astrology, clairvoyance, mysticism and the occult generally. Writers of extraordinary fiction in which the imagination is of an exalted kind; organists or musicians who have a touch of genius in their composition come under Uranian influence; also high-class mechanics, inventors, originators and composers. In a general sense railway employees of all grades come under the influence of the planet Uranus.

The aspects, good or ill, of Uranus to Neptune are so comprehensive in their nature as to affect rather the life as a whole (unless, indeed, the influence remain latent) than any one department in such a way as could be particularly indicated.

Saturn denotes gain by labour; method; responsibility; land; building; farming; heavy trading, such as contracts or time periods; minerals; carrying in transit; removals; storage; shipping of merchandise; public appointments; investments, stocks, shares, companies (chiefly when in good aspect to Jupiter or Venus).

Saturn in good aspect to Uranus indicates gain in connection with antiquities, archæological research, museum work, and all out-of-the-way investigations where much application is required; dealing in antique furniture or curios; also in connection with societies. Saturn in affliction with Uranus: sudden and unexpected losses in connection with societies, companies, stocks and shares, etc.

Jupiter relates to religious affairs; Government offices; managements; legal affairs; trusts; banking; churches; charity and charitable institutions; to some extent, also, to the higher forms of education and cultivation, such as philosophy, professorships in science, literature, or religion, etc. ; it also has a bearing upon voyages and shipping.

Jupiter in good aspect with Saturn or Uranus is favourable for monetary prospects, and gives good fortune and success in life if the luminaries are not afflicted at birth. Jupiter in affliction with Saturn produces many monetary difficulties and sometimes much poverty.

MARS denotes gain through strength and force; engineering; mechanics; cattle-dealing; breeding; stock farming; timber, coal, slate, iron; steel; drugs; chemicals; mining; sanitation; hygiene; surgery; soldiers, and, to some extent, sailors ; if well aspected it somewhat favours money by legacy or marriage. If favourably placed it may enable the native to earn money easily, but it will also incline him to spend freely.

Mars in affliction with Jupiter denotes loss through extravagance, over-liberality, waste, and often prodigality. Mars in affliction with Saturn : great poverty and difficulty in acquiring wealth. Mars in affliction with Uranus : peculiar and sudden losses. Mars well aspected is favourable for money matters, as it increases the personal acquisitive tendencies.

THE SUN indicates money derived from the father or his side of the family, from superiors, and from the holding of responsible positions or official appointments, also through social influence. Its occupations are mainly those indicated by the sign in which it is placed. Like Mars, it may give money through the native's own labour, but it also parts with money easily.

VENUS denotes gain through social condition ; friendships ; society; marriage ; pleasures; amusements ; finery ; domestic affairs ; jewellery ; adornments; upholstery; millinery; hosiery; wearing apparel ; hotels; restaurants. Its good aspects to Saturn are fortunate for the accumulation of money, for money invested, and for banking.

Venus in good aspect to the Moon denotes gain through social intercourse, and public gatherings and the general public. In good aspect to Jupiter : profitable dealings with friends and influential persons, also gain through travel and foreign affairs. In good aspect with Uranus : gain through peculiar and exceptional circumstances, strangers and acquaintances.

Venus in affliction with Mars denotes waste, impulsive, over-liberal tendencies, and losses through carelessness and extravagance generally.

Venus in affliction with Saturn: fear of poverty, losses which the native has no power to prevent, wasting of substance, and monetary difficulties. In affliction with Uranus: sudden and very unexpected financial losses.

MERCURY denotes gain by writing, speaking, travelling, clerks, agencies, commissions, discounts, dividends, interest, and paper money generally.

It is good for success in all commercial undertakings; scientific pursuits; trading; publishing; advertising; distributing; and circulating; also occupations in which special skill or training is required; examinations, teaching. It relates to brothers, sisters, cousins, and to some extent servants.

Mercury in good aspect to the Moon denotes gain through the general public, learning and quick perception, ability and capacity. It brings opportunity, and the necessary application to take advantage of circumstances. Mercury in good aspect to Venus: gain through refinement and good taste. In good aspect to Mars: gain through industry, skill and ingenuity. In good aspect to Jupiter: through sound judgment, intuition, and moral principle. In good aspect with Saturn: gain through tact and diplomacy, caution and perseverance, and the power of profound thought. In good aspect with Uranus: through inventiveness, originality and speculation, or unusual enterprise.

THE MOON indicates money derived from the mother or her side of the family, from females, or from inferiors through the employment of labour. It indicates subordinate positions, the employee rather than the employer, unless it is elevated or rules the mid-heaven; and it has a general signification of occupations that are connected with the water or liquids, with the masses and the general public rather than with superiors or the few. It gives more thrift and prudence in money matters than does the Sun. If elevated, angular, or well aspected, it may signify factories or businesses where many hands are employed.

⊕ THE PART OF FORTUNE ⊕

It is held by many that the 'Part of Fortune' indicates inherited wealth, property accruing, or worldly fortune in a general sense. This point is found as follows:—Add the longitude of the Ascendant to that of the Moon and subtract that of the Sun, adding the circle of 360° if necessary: the operation is best performed by expressing the longitude

in signs, degrees and minutes.   For instance : Suppose ⊙♒ 18° 4′,
☽♑ 26° 4′, Asc. Ⅱ 20° 29′ ; then say

	Signs	Degrees	Minutes
Asc.	2	20	29
+ ☽	9	26	4
	12	16	33
— ⊙	10	16	4
Part of Fortune	1	28	29	*i.e* ⊕ in ♉ 28° 29′

It is advisable here to reflect upon the metaphysical significance of
this so-called 'imaginary' point: the old rule is worded 'As the ☽
is to the ⊙ so is the ⊕ to the ascendant.'   That is, the Part of Fortune
stands in the same relationship to the ascendant as the Moon does to the
Sun.   Now we have already seen that the Moon supplies the *vehicle* for
an expression of the Solar life: similarly, then, we should regard the 'Pars
Fortunæ' as indicating the *pabulum* for the sustenance of that general
synthesis of the personal life controlled by the ascendant. Hence the
reason for allotting to the Part of Fortune chief control of the pecuniary
well-being of the native is readily seen.   This point of the horoscope is
a matter greatly neglected by many modern writers, which is regrettable.

To recapitulate :—When a judgment upon the financial prospect
indicated by any nativity is desired, a careful study must be made of the
second house in all its bearings.   First ; any planet posited therein and
the aspects it receives, also the nature of the planets whence the aspects
are derived, and their position in the nativity.   Secondly ; the sign on
the cusp of the second, its ruler, position and aspects.   Thirdly ; since
finance is not concerned *only* with the second house, the positions and
mutual aspects of the Sun and Moon, as indicators of the individual and
personal fate respectively, must be considered—also those of Jupiter and
Venus, natural significators of good fortune.

Moreover, the signs of the zodiac have also some influence over
finance. The Cardinal Signs give money through fame and public
recognition, also through enterprise and adventure.   The Fixed Signs
bring gain through government or authoritative influence, and the
Common Signs through service and ordinary means.   Should a horoscope
show the majority of planets in one of these groups, more especially if
the Sun, Moon, or Ascendant be also included, particularly the latter,
the fortunes will show out the prevailing influence.

CHAPTER X

THE THIRD HOUSE—-BRETHREN AND RELATIVES, SHORT JOURNEYS, THE MIND

THE *First House* has a very decided influence over the physical body as a whole, governing what we may term the general temperament. The *Second House* has also a decided influence in this respect, having considerable sway over the emotional and desire nature. The *Third House* in the same way has a definite influence over the mind; these three houses analogically coming under the dominant rulership of the three planets Mars, Venus and Mercury respectively.

In the THIRD HOUSE, which we are now to consider, we study all that relates to movement, transition, and change. It is also related to the seventh house, as previously shown, and thus governs relatives and kindred; but, generally speaking, it rules all affairs that seriously affect the mind, and the mental tendencies.

The planets occupying the third house will first be considered, the customary order being adopted.

NEPTUNE in the third house, imaginative, fanciful, and weird mental tendencies; fondness for spiritualistic phenomena and matters pertaining to the occult and mystical side of things; poetical fancies; dreamy state of mind.

Only a few can respond to the higher vibrations of the planet Neptune; but those who have any tendency to allow their nature to become depraved and degraded seem to come under an influence from this planet which appears to be *the inversion* of a very high moral grade. In a great number of cases already investigated, and afflicted Neptune in the third appears to denote imbecility or weak intellect, depraved tastes, and morbid fancies. Troubles of a peculiar nature appear to affect the relations, and troubles on journeys are very probable.

Up to the present the influence of Neptune does not usually appear to be favourable, and until the work of tabulation with regard to this planet is complete, no definite statement can be made with regard to its influence.

URANUS in the third house denotes an inventive, ingenious, and curious mind; given to study mystical and metaphysical subjects; unconventional and very liberal mental tendencies; fond of abstruse and profound studies. In a weak horoscope this position denotes bohemian tastes, wild and erratic schemes and projects formulated by the brain, and unaccountable and strange mental attitudes. In a progressive horoscope it widens the mental vision and broadens the intellectual view of life. In the advanced types of humanity it raises the mind into higher thought and prepares the way for altruistic ideas, and social or mental reforms. To all it gives a touch of the eccentric or a flash of genius, especially in music or oratory, with, in the latter, a distinctly epigrammatic tendency. It gives a love of Astrology and kindred subjects, power to hypnotise, heal and use the mesmeric forces for the benefit of others. It denotes the possibility of awakening clairaudient or clairvoyant faculties, and tends to make the native a distinct and unique character, especially in mental expression.

This position denotes some strange experiences with or through relatives; sudden and unexpected journeys; travels for adventure and new discoveries.

When in aspect with Neptune, especially if afflicted, these tendencies are accentuated.

SATURN in the third house indicates a despondent, slow and laborious mind; plodding, careful, cautious and fearful. It favours secrecy, and mental pursuits where tact and patience are required, but much depends upon the nativity as to how Saturn in the third house will affect the mind. In a poor horoscope it will tend to make the native deceitful, cunning and over-acquisitive, and if badly aspected will show as follows, according to the afflicting planet: $\displaystyle 2\!\!\!\!\;$, hypocrisy and treachery; δ, unreliable and prone to give way to violent fits of passion; $\,$♀, depraved tastes and lack of refinement; $\,$☿, thievish and dishonest tendencies; ⊙ or ☽, a weak intellect, inclined to fret, pine, and become very discontented.

This position gives a liability to melancholia, insanity and morbid tendencies. It is an unfavourable position for dealings with relatives, and often brings much sorrow through them. It is not good for travel and denotes loss, delay and disappointment in connection with journeys, also many unprofitable changes—unless very well aspected, when responsibility and a strong sense of duty are shown.

JUPITER in the third house shows a religious and philosophical mind, kind and sympathetic mentally, with abilities above the average; sincere and courteous in speech and writing; earnest, thoughtful and considerate in all matters of correspondence and exchange of thought. This position favours those who are naturally social and readily able to adapt themselves to all average conventional requirements. It denotes a hopeful, cheerful and contented mind, but gives no striking mental ability unless in good aspect with the Sun, Moon or Mercury, but even if no planets are in favourable aspect it is especially good for the mental faculties.

This position promises much gain, and many benefits through and from relatives; also prosperous and fruitful journeys, and generally financial success through travelling.

The position of Jupiter in the third in *Fiery Signs* is good for social success; *Earthy Signs*, good for business, commerce, and speculative enterprise; *Airy Signs*, good for the mind and mental pursuits; *Watery Signs*, good for voyages and travel by water. But it is unfavourable for all things if afflicted by the planet Mars.

MARS in the third house denotes a turbulent and forceful mind, the native being usually over-energetic and impulsive mentally, possessing a keen, alert and sharp lower mind, but apt to lack control and balance. The only aspects that moderate and temper the influence of Mars in this house are those of a favourable nature from Saturn or Mercury, and under some conditions those coming from Uranus, when great mental energy and keen inventive genius are denoted.

The afflictions of the various planets to Mars in the third house are very critical, especially afflictions from Uranus, which has a certain violent tendency. All persons with Mars in the third are liable at some period of their lives to a touch of brain-fever, or some over-balancing of the mental faculties—unless this planet is placed in the sign Capricorn, the only sign in which the fury and impulse of Mars are lessened and brought more under control.

Many troubles through relatives are denoted by this position, and dangers through travel and unfortunate journeys are very marked if the planet Mars is afflicted. The turbulent tendencies of Mars in the third are modified considerably when a negative or passive sign rises at birth.

THE SUN in the third house bestows magnanimity of mind, with some pride, and ambitious tendencies. Firm and self-reliant in all mental pursuits, always aiming at success, seeking honour and fame through mental qualifications, and ever desirous of benefiting others mentally.

When in good aspect to ♅, inventive, constructive, and reformative mental tendencies; ♄, the mind is profound and authoritative, commanding respect and obedience; ♃, religious or philosophical, very kind and considerate; ♂, militant, and at times aggressive.

This position gives success in travel, and in dealing with relatives, by whom the native is respected and sometimes feared.

If the Sun is much afflicted in the third house it denotes great pride and arrogance, and a domineering and over-ambitious mind, causing trouble and sorrow to others, according to the sign upon the cusp of the third house and the sign in which the Sun is placed.

If the native is born under any of the positive signs it is more fortunate. The Moon in good aspect with the Sun promises important beneficial changes every seven years of the life.

VENUS in the third house is very favourable, giving much love of art and refined literature, poetry, music, painting and all the higher attributes of the mind and mental faculties. The mental qualifications are of the highest, making the mind bright, hopeful, peaceful and harmonious. When Venus is in good aspect to the Moon or in conjunction with Mercury this position considerably modifies an otherwise adverse horoscope, for the mind is naturally inclined to be pure and free from vice or evil intent. When afflicted the mind is over-sensuous and inclined too much to pleasure and gay society, but not wholly unfortunate unless Mercury and the Moon are also in adverse aspect.

It is a position very favourable for travel and gives many journeys taken for pleasure, or those out of which pleasure eventually comes. It denotes favourable relatives, and success or gain through their aid.

Persons born under positive signs are favoured mentally by this position, and those born under negative signs gain more through the feelings and emotions; therefore the former may have literary and poetical ability and the latter musical talent and ability to draw or paint.

MERCURY in the third house indicates one fond of learning, studious, and generally mirthful, alert, and active mentally. Eager to investigate science, or any new thought, fond of reading, literature and all things that enlighten and tend to expand the understanding. This house is wholly mental, being (analogically) the positive station of Mercury: it therefore gives a love of writing and speaking, and tends to quicken all expressions of the mind in every form. The following are the indications when we find Mercury in good aspect to: ♆, humorous, dreamy, poetical and mystical in thought; ♅, intuition and a love of advanced thought; ♄, profound and deep thought; ♃, judgment and reason is denoted; ♂, mechanical or mathematical skill.

If Mercury is afflicted the mind is wayward and prone to worry and fret. If afflicted by: ♆, vague or morbid fancies and impracticable schemes; ♅, precipitate and 'wrong-headed,' or cantankerous; ♄, much melancholy is denoted; ♃, danger of hypocrisy and deceit; ♂, untruthfulness or exaggeration.

Much will depend upon the sign on the third as to how the affliction of Mercury will affect the mind, for in some cases this affliction denotes reform and eccentricity though with good motives; but generally it is a very unfortunate affliction, giving some liability to insanity.

Mercury in the third house denotes gain by travel through the expansion of the mind, if well aspected. It also denotes much thought or anxiety concerning the affairs of relatives.

THE MOON in the third house shows native to be changeable and inconsistent in mental pursuits; very curious and inquisitive; fond of enquiring into all kinds of knowledge, ever possessing a fund of information and superficial learning, but lacking in continuity and stability. Fond of publicity, and eager to know all that is going on under any conditions. Much depends upon the aspects of the Moon from the third house to the various planets as to whether the above will be modified or accentuated.

The Moon in good aspect with: ♆, adds a touch of genius, or insanity, according to sign and aspects to other planets; ♅, increases the love of the romantic and awakens the imaginative faculties, tending to quicken thought and lead the mind into original study; ♄, steadies and adds firmness and prudence to the mental qualifications; ♃, adds to the social inclinations and gives *bonhomie;* ♂, quickens the love of enterprise and adventure; ☉, strengthens continuity and the mental faculties; ♀, refines the mind and raises it above the average; ☿, quickens the wit and stimulates the mental ability.

This lunar position gives much concern with respect to the affairs of relatives, also gives much travel, love of change and a tendency to take many journeys.

It is an unfavourable position for the mind when the Moon is afflicted, especially by Mars or Saturn.

The sign occupying the cusp, or generally ruling the third house when no plants are therein, has considerable influence over what is known as the lower brain mind, that part of the universal mind which is imprisoned in the brain, and therefore the state of this lower brain mind when each sign of the zodiac occupies the cusp of the third house will now be considered.

♈ Acute, selfish, intellectual, impulsive, ambitious and aspiring.
♉ Obstinate, determined, receptive, jealous, acquisitive and sensuous.
♊ Intelligent, fond of detail, refined, methodical but discontinuous.
♋ Indolent, peevish, impressionable, fanciful, negative and very sensitive.
♌ Ambitious, high-spirited, passionate, enterprising and fearless.
♍ Subtle, laborious, selfish, keenly alive to own interest, fond of science.
♎ Just, well-balanced, sincere, artistic, refined and fond of comparison.
♏ Secretive, very subtle, curious, mystical, shrewd, proud, and suspicious.
♐ Cultured, prophetic, impulsive, rebellious, religious, sympathetic.
♑ Crafty, cunning, ambitious, jealous, subtle, penetrative, reflective.
♒ Refined, artistic, concentrative, constant, faithful, scientific, intuitive.
♓ Receptive, capable of understanding, but somewhat superficial or methodical in expression, and often dreamy and far too impressionable and mediumistic.

Cardinal Signs on the cusp of the third house, or if planets occupy cardinal signs in this house, the mind is ambitious, changeable, aspiring, and very enterprising.

Fixed Signs give the mind a fixed and determined attitude, persevering, plodding, persistent, proud, authoritative, and difficult to convince or impress.

Mutable Signs make the mind more impressionable, receptive, methodical, systematic, painstaking, and easily affected by surroundings.

The third house should not, however, be relied upon alone when giving a judgment of the mind and mental qualifications, for the luminaries and Mercury must also be carefully considered. Indeed, the whole horoscope may in a sense be said to represent the mind.

CHAPTER XI

The Fourth House—Environment, Home, Parents ; the End of Life

THE fourth house relates to the 'grave,' the end of life, one of the parents—usually the father, according to Western astrologers, though the Hindus say the mother, since the fourth house corresponds to Cancer—and denotes also the environment, residence and family conditions in which the native dwells.

A few words may not be out of place here in regard to both the fourth and tenth houses, regarded from a more or less metaphysical point of view. The fourth house may be briefly summarised as the personal environment, the tenth house as the individual environment. Passing in review a moment the four angles of the figure and their corresponding signs ♈, ♋, ♎, ♑, we can see very well how this is. Firstly, the oriental half of the map, fourth to tenth (reckoned backwards) indicates, as has been said in an earlier chapter, the objective side of existence, of which the ascendant, representing the personal man or woman, is the most obvious and sharply focussed expression. The occidental portion of the map, tenth to fourth, on the other hand, represents the subjective side of the nature, which finds its external concrete expression in the partners, domestic and business, to which the native is drawn. In the same way, therefore, that the fourth house represents in a general sense the centre or focus of the *personal* or domestic environment, the tenth house represents the focus of the *individual* or business environment.

Looked at in this way, a horoscope becomes exceedingly interesting when we study it from the standpoint of business or marriage. A certain humorist has hinted that 'marriage is woman's business,' but without any cynicism, real or assumed, we can see that viewed in this light there is a certain basis for the suggestion. A young man's start in life is reckoned from the time when he first sets out in business (tenth house, business, honours, ideals, ambition) ; and similarly a young woman's start in life dates from marriage, when she removes to the house provided by her husband (10th house, fourth from the seventh, *i.e.*, the husband's domestic environment). The *real* factor in both cases is the same, the personal or outer self (first house), usually domiciled in the fourth, is removed thence and commences to take up its abode in the tenth, the domicile of the individuality or *alter ego*, the (relatively) higher self, the 'better half.'

If we regard the true Man as represented by the centre of the map, we shall thus see him crucified, as it were, on the four angles of the figure; the first house representing the personal, or limited self, the M.C. the aspirations and ambitions, the seventh attraction to another self and the fourth as a synthesis of the whole carried into the invisible planes.

We can see then how the life of the average City man continually passes, as it were, round the circle, ebbing and flowing from the fourth to the tenth as he journeys (either in thought or by train) from home to business, and back again; while at the same time there is a perpetual transverse current from first to seventh, activity to rest, and from rest to activity once more. And thus the most ordinary and prosaic factors of life may become interesting when viewed as visible manifestations of universal principles.

Turning for a moment to the signs, if we call Cancer the Tent we may fitly term Capricorn the Temple; Cancer the house of the Moon, the home of the personality (♈), Capricorn the house of Saturn, the shrine of the Ego, the home of the individuality (♎). And in this connection it is interesting to note that there is a planet suspected to exist beyond the orbit of Neptune whose period is 360 years or thereabouts, *i.e.*, a year for every one of our days; to this planet, then, Saturn, whose period is thirty years, stands as our Moon is to the Sun, since he would make twelve revolutions in that time, and therefore his period would be but a 'month' in the 'year' of the other: so that, if true, this would make the analogy still closer.

Descending now from these speculations to the more practical and detailed consideration of the fourth house of the horoscope let us first consider the effect of planets, severally, when in this house. It may here be remarked that the Nadir or cusp of the fourth is the magnetic point to which all the influences below the horizon seem drawn as to a focus; any planet in this house will therefore serve as a centre for the magnetic forces, and hence the influence of such a planet tends to become progressively manifest as life advances. In any family, other things being equal, that member who has a planet in the fourth house will be the most influential in the home and will form, as it were, the pivot about which all domestic matters will turn.

NEPTUNE in the fourth house denotes an unfavourable close to the life, living under some peculiar restraint or in some especial retirement in the latter portion, or placed in unpleasant positions at the end. It denotes very unusual and unique domestic conditions. Not infrequently the native is compelled to reside in houses or localities where the magnetic conditions are unfavourable or exhausting, and he or she is always liable to a certain amount of psychic vampirisation by others. It is probable that all who have Neptune in the fourth have something in the nature of a skeleton in the cupboard in connection with their family affairs. The native may be subject to fraud or be guilty of fraudulent action toward the end of his life. If the horoscope is not a very favourable one, then troubles of various kinds are denoted by this position. It is a position which gives uncommon and exceptional events, the exact nature of which none can accurately predict.

If afflicted by the luminaries, the health suffers; and if afflicting Mercury, the mind is disordered.

The good aspects to Neptune will bring peculiar benefits and some psychic experiences.

URANUS in the fourth house denotes sudden and tragic or exceptional experiences at the end of life. It is not a good position for Uranus, and nothing definite can be predicted with regard to the close of life, for reversals and sudden changes are shown. To those who seek to lead the occult life denotes isolation or expansion of consciousness upon higher planes, but only where the horoscope shows occultism or mysticism can this be judged.

If Uranus afflicts the luminaries, danger of paralysis and sudden death is shown; if afflicting Mercury, insanity or mental shocks to the nervous system; and if Mars, tragedy and violence.

This position denotes trouble in the home life, estrangement from parents, a chequered career, and many family troubles. There is usually some peculiar source of disharmony in the domestic conditions throughout life. Uranus in any angle favours a bohemian or peculiar life, the native being unconventional and somewhat eccentric.

SATURN in the fourth house denotes the development of acquisitiveness and a desire to live a very retired and secluded life, or heavy responsibilities which bind and fetter the native to his detriment or hinder his progress. It is not good for worldly success unless well aspected. It is unfavourable for domestic or family affairs, and denotes an environment that is not altogether satisfactory or to the native's liking.

If afflicted, Saturn in the fourth house is very unfortunate, denying or preventing any gain by inheritance, and if very much afflicted denotes poverty and privation at the close of life. Nothing turns out wholly successful under this position of Saturn, and the native's life is more or less under the law of fate, in which free-will appears to be the smallest element.

If well aspected this position indicates occult tendencies and asceticism at the close of life, and turns the mind from worldly interests.

JUPITER in the fourth is a most favourable position for gain by inheritance, and denotes property, wealth and prosperity toward the close of life. It promises a happy home, very peaceful and successful domestic surroundings, and denotes favours from parents and benefits through or from them which considerably help the native. Enterprises and business undertakings have a successful issue.

If well aspected by the luminaries it will counteract many other defects in the horoscope, and shows the probability of great gain and fortune at the close of life, or great spiritual advance.

If well aspecting Mars a religious end to the life is denoted : and if Saturn or Uranus are in good aspect, occult tendencies are denoted.

If afflicted, Jupiter in the fourth house denotes extravagance, waste of money in the household, and troubles through parents and their affairs. Mercury in affliction denotes lawsuits, and the luminaries afflicting, danger of apoplexy or sudden heart troubles.

MARS in the fourth is a very unfavourable and unfortunate position, causing the close of life to be perilous and fraught with many trials and troubles. It denotes quarrels with parents, and many disputes in the home life, domestic affairs going wrong and causing much unpleasantness and many misunderstandings, with probable strife, and if Mars is afflicted by either Saturn or Uranus, danger of violence and a sudden *terminus vitæ*.

If Mars is well aspected in this house it will show energy and force, and much enterprise, but a liability of error through impulse is also shown. Mercury afflicted by Mars from the fourth house denotes feeling and passion to be in excess of thought and reason. Uranus afflicting Mars, there is a danger of suicide or insanity, which may be hereditary. This position of Mars denotes inherited tendencies, and shows a life that is more or less fatalistic. Troubles through the dwelling-house and house property ; danger of fire and accidents therein. It sometimes gives an unruly nature.

THE SUN in the fourth house shows success at the end of life, realised ambitions, hopes and desires when the life is nearing the close. It denotes a good heredity with which pride of ancestry is connected. It promises gain by inheritance or some benefits coming through, or by means of, the parentage. It is a position that favours enquiry into the secret and hidden things in nature, such as occultism, mysticism, and thoughts connected with the higher mind or individuality.

If well aspected by Jupiter or Saturn and the Moon, gain of property or financial benefits by inheritance. If afflicted, trouble through one or both parents, and obstacles in life. It also shows that the native may exceed his income and incur heavy debts through extravagance, or by living beyond the sphere of life to which he belongs.

VENUS in the fourth denotes a peaceful end to the life amid comfort, and successful achievement to hopes and wishes. It promises gain by inheritance, concord and happiness from parents, and a satisfactory home life. This is a very favourable position for all affairs of a domestic nature, and is a sure token of a good finish at the close of life.

If afflicted it is not so very disastrous, except that it affects finance and denotes grief and sorrow at the close of life when in a sign that is not congenial to the nature of Venus. If afflicted by : ♅, some sudden reversals of fortune or extraordinary experiences; ♂, carelessness and looseness of morals, or a tendency to be extravagant at the latter part of the life.

Venus in the fourth house in good aspect with the luminaries is very fortunate and makes the whole life a success, fortune favouring the termination of all transactions, tending to bring all undertakings to a successful issue.

MERCURY in the fourth denotes changes of residence, worry and anxiety concerning home and domestic affairs, and great difficulty in settling or avoiding frequent disturbance.

If afflicted by: ♅, mental distress and strange change of fortune with much difficulty in remaining for any length of time in one place; ♄, thefts and frauds; ♂, the victim of sharp practice and treachery.

If in good aspect to: ♅, denotes a considerable expansion of consciousness toward the close of life; ♄, considerably steadies the tendency to change, and brings gain from parents; ☉ or ☽, lessens the tendency to adverse change, and promises the retention of the mental faculties at the close of life. It indicates ability that lacks opportunity, but if Jupiter is in good aspect with Mercury then opportunity comes at the end.

THE MOON in the fourth house denotes much fluctuation of circumstances and many changes of residence at the close of life. It is only a favourable position when the Moon is well aspected at birth, when it denotes probable gain by inheritance and some reputation or popularity through one or both of the parents. It is a frequent indication of adoption, or early separation from the home sphere.

If the Moon is afflicted: by ♅, sudden adverse changes, unexpected turns of fortune, difficulties in the home life and a chequered career; ♄, a sure sign of poverty or much disappointment, with small ability to succeed in life and prosper; ♂, reversals of fortune through impulsive conduct and rash action; ☉ or ☿, loss through theft and deception is denoted.

If the Moon in the fourth is well aspected a peaceful end is promised but this position indicates many changes, and often frequent removals, with no certainty of a settled abode.

The fourth house in quite a general sense denotes the parents, their condition and affairs. In considering the question of parentage, with regard to the father the Sun and the planet Saturn should have careful consideration. It is difficult to convey the ideas relating to the Sun and Saturn as significators of the father to those who are not familiar with the mystical side of the subject, but to those who understand that there is a life and form side to everything the idea is expressed in the fact that through the Sun comes the spiritual heredity which is connected with the Ego, and through the limitations of Saturn are conveyed the Karmic or fatalistic and physical tendencies.

In the same way Venus and the Moon represent the mother and her conditions, Venus denoting the nutritive and preservative quality, and the Moon the formative tendencies, the habits and peculiar hereditary inclinations.

The Sun represents the father, or life and health aura, also the higher mental and moral merits; Saturn the Kama-Manas or crystallised personal legacy of the previous life: (that which is bred in the *bone*). Venus represents the feelings and higher emotions and the human qualities, the cream of all past experiences; the Moon the animal and personal inclinations, the watery and fluidic part of the personal man.

The position of the Sun and Venus will denote the moral and purely mental or human tendencies of the joint parents. The aspects to these two significators will improve or modify their conditions; if there should be much affliction it weakens the moral stamina transmitted from the parents to the native.

The position of Saturn and the Moon denotes the worldly and material condition of the parents and the early environment of the native.

The signs upon the cusps of the tenth and fourth houses, their rulers and the aspects between them, will denote the attitude of the parents toward each other and their influence upon the native, especially if the ruler of the ascendant is considered in its relationship with the rulers of the tenth and fourth.

If both the luminaries are well aspected by the benefic planets the native is usually born into a good environment. If the luminaries are afflicted by the malefic planets, then adverse fortune and more or less obscurity are denoted. Careful judgment and much practice are needed before a correct opinion can be formed regarding the parents and their affairs.

If the Sun and Saturn are very well aspected, and either or both angular, long life to the father is denoted. If these significators are better placed, or above Venus and Moon, the father will outlive the mother. The significators exalted, dignified, and well aspected, favour the parent described. If occidental (in the western half of the map) longer life to the father is denoted than when oriental.

It is never safe, of course, to judge the affairs of the parents from the native's map alone, but general ideas may be obtained as to the sympathy or otherwise existing between the native and his parents. In many cases pretty reliable results may be obtained by taking the tenth house as the ascendant of the mother, and counting the houses round in the usual manner, and similarly by treating the fourth house as the ascendant of the father, etc.

The author has known cases where the place of the Sun in the native's horoscope has represented the nativity of the father, and the place of Venus that of the mother, but in any of these cases the affairs of the parents should be judged only from after the birth of the native.

AN ILLUSTRATION

X	XI	XII	I	II	III
♊ 10	♋ 16	♌ 18	♍ 15	♎ 6	♏ 5

☉	☽	☿	♀	♂	♃	♄	♅	♆
♐ 24	♑ 8	♐ 22	♐ 5½	♊ 27 R	♍ 22	♈ 1	♈ 22½ R	♓ 2½

In the above nativity, which is that of 'Viscount Hinton,' the 'organ-grinding earl,' the unsuccessful claimant to the Poulett peerage, —'if the meridian be made the ascendant, and the nativity be turned round so that the sign Gemini is made the first house, we shall have a symbolical map of the mother, who will be represented by Mercury with the planet Mars rising in the ascendant. Students may learn a great deal by this arrangement. The ruler of the tenth is in the fourth in the planet's fall, indicating the mother's honour. The ruling planet Mercury is in opposition to the planet Mars from the ascendant. She is described as a rebellious, thoughtless and impulsive woman, high-spirited, careless and reckless.'—*Modern Astrology*, Vol. VI (Old Series) p. 49.

CHAPTER XII

The Fifth House—Children, Enterprise, Speculations. Gains, Love Affairs, etc.

The fifth house relates to pleasure, society and social inclinations also the emotions and feelings. It may be regarded as a material representation of the eleventh house, which governs hopes and wishes, and often denotes their worldly fulfilment. It shows the nature of the native's love affairs, courtships, and the affections which spring from the feeling and emotional side of the nature; it represents the seat of the physical and magnetic attractions between the sexes. It is also concerned with speculative affairs and all matters of enterprise and activity prompted by the desire nature; having a direct and what may be termed a lunar reflection from the eleventh house, which denotes the internal nature of the desires, hopes and wishes.

Neptune in the fifth house denotes strange and abnormal conditions relating to sex matters. It is not a favourable position for any who have not definitely decided to choose platonic love in preference to the ordinary love attachments. All manner of evils arise from this position in connection with courtship and matters pertaining to the opposite sex.

If Neptune is afflicted in the fifth troubles are severe, many dangers being threatened, and unless the horoscope as a whole shows an innate love of purity the animal tendencies will override the human.

If Neptune is well aspected it tends to bring experiences in connection with the opposite sex which will be beneficial to the progress of the native.

Uranus in the fifth house causes strange and peculiar experiences in connection with the feelings and emotions, romantic love affairs, and unconventional ideas with regard to sex union. This position favours free love, and gives a tendency to ignore the legal tie, and act from an independent motive. It is not good as regards children and shows separation from offspring and much anxiety through them. If afflicted many domestic troubles are shown, and some inconstancy and intrigue or liaison denoted.

Uranus in the fifth causes trouble and scandal through children, and is very unfavourable for all matters in which the senses play a prominent part. If with Venus, sometimes homo-sexual instincts.

If well aspected by the luminaries, secret love affairs of an ideal character are denoted; in good aspect with Mercury, exceptional correspondence and successful intercourse with the opposite sex.

SATURN in the fifth house denotes hindrance, delay and disappointment in love affairs and causes the native to become attracted to persons who are older and more serious in nature and disposition. If evilly aspected, death of the loved one is probable, or some heavy sorrow in connection with the object of the affections. This is not a good position for bold speculations but is much more favourable for well-secured investments, especially in land, mines, or buildings. It denotes trouble through offspring, and lack of interest in pleasures or entertainments. It considerably tempers the affections.

If afflicted by Mars or Venus, danger of unnatural affections and a lack of real sympathy or feeling is denoted. This is a very unfavourable position where Saturn afflicts the luminaries.

JUPITER in the fifth house is a very favourable position, showing reasonable and legitimate affection, in which the senses are under control and the sympathetic side of the nature is expressed. It promises much success in courtship, and gain through the opposite sex. It is a very good position for speculation, investment and financial enterprise. This position also promises good and dutiful children and much happiness through them.

In a female horoscope this position often denotes an attachment to a widower, or to a man who has had a former engagement which has affected his life to some extent. It favours love affairs with the religious minded or socially inclined.

If afflicted by the luminaries or any of the planets the good influence of Jupiter is much modified, but if well aspected the life is successful, and there are many opportunities to become prosperous and happy through gratified affection.

If either of the luminaries be in trine aspect to Jupiter in the fifth, a fortune is likely to come to the native either through speculation, lotteries, or what are called games of chance; but other influences should also be studied.

MARS in the fifth house denotes a very unsettled and inharmonious home life, in which discord and disputes are frequent. Impulsive, sudden, and unfortunate attractions towards the opposite sex, and an over-ardent, emotional nature is shown by this position. It inclines toward rash speculation, and if much afflicted shows gambling and prodigal tendencies.

If Mars and Jupiter are in evil aspect there will be a waste of the vital forces through unrestrained feelings, and if Venus is also in affliction ruin through the opposite sex is denoted.

If afflicted by Uranus, foolish and unreasonable infatuations are denoted.

Even if well aspected, Mars in the fifth shows extravagance, and excess of feeling. It is not good for children, kills one of them, and shows much trouble and danger through them.

THE SUN in the fifth house denotes success in speculation and matters of enterprise, also gain through children, pleasure, society and entertainments. It is favourable for courtships and promises a success-ful and honourable attachment. This is not a fruitful position, however, and often denies offspring or brings trouble to the native at the birth of children.

If the Sun is afflicted in the fifth it is very evil, and denotes much loss through speculation or enterprise, and trouble in courtship through pride and jealousy. Afflicted by Uranus or Mars it denotes tragedy and very sorrowful love experiences.

If well aspected it considerably improves the nativity, giving success towards the close of life, and gain through children.

VENUS in the fifth house denotes successful love affairs, the capacity to fully enjoy and extract the full measure of joy out of life. It gives ability to entertain others and much success in connection with enter-tainments, concerts and social gatherings and shows general domestic felicity. It promises gain through speculation, investment and general enterprise. This position of Venus favours a fruitful union, and gives children who are specially endowed with artistic or musical talents.

If Venus is afflicted by : ♆, strange courtships; ♅, very romantic attachments ; ♄, disappointment in love affairs and grief or sorrow in connection with the feelings; ♂, there will be extravagance in matters of pleasure, or ungratified affection.

Venus well aspected in the fifth is a sure token of a happy and successful love attachment; but much depends upon the sign ruling the fifth house as to the expression of Venus in this house.

MERCURY in the fifth house tends to bring anxiety in connection with love affairs, and shows that the mind is liable to become absorbed in feeling and emotion. It denotes some fatalistic affair in connection with children, with much worry and perplexity of mind concerning their affairs.

When well aspected by Jupiter or Saturn, however, it is very good for speculation or enterprise. If afflicted by Mars or Uranus scandal and ill-repute in connection with love affairs is shown, and danger of separation, breach of promise actions or divorce. It also denotes trouble to the object of the affections, and the mind is generally concerned about the welfare of others who minister to the feeling and emotional side of the nature.

This position of Mercury is always improved if in good aspect with the Moon.

THE MOON in the fifth house denotes much fluctuation in all speculative affairs, and much activity and change in all enterprise. It gives a love of pleasure and a peculiar aptitude to gain pleasure out of amusement. It denotes changeable and fickle affections, and an engagement with the opposite sex which may quite absorb the life even although the object of the native's affection may be not in the least worthy of the affection or attention shown. It promises a child who will have fame or notoriety, and indicates that the life of the native will be bound up in some peculiar manner with a child or children.

When afflicted this is an unfavourable position for children or love affairs, and often denotes intrigues and liaisons, the state of the morals depending upon the nature of the affliction.

The fifth house is generally an index to the state of the lower feelings, the sensations and passional tendencies, the sign upon the cusp of this house indicating the past experiences and thus denoting the nature of the emotions. The first, fifth and ninth houses represent the personal man in a very marked degree, showing his present, past and future consciousness symbolically. In the harmony of the signs with the houses, one of the four triplicities will usually be found influencing

all three of these houses.   Thus when Aries rises Leo usually governs
the fifth, and so on with each sign in succession, the sign upon the cusp
of the fifth having a direct relationship with those on the first and ninth.
The influence of each sign when on the cusp of the fifth house is as
follows :

♈   Impulse and mental realisation out of sensation.
♉   Strong feelings and sensations.
♊   Dual love affairs in which mind seeks to abstract itself from sensation
♋   Impressionable feelings, with receptivity to the feelings of others.
♌   Strong passions and ardent feelings, many love episodes and experiences.
♍   Discrimination in love affairs, and receptivity.
♎   Refined and pure emotions.
♏   Self-control in sex matters but secret inclinations towards opposite sex.
♐   Dualistic experiences with a strong desire to rule the senses.
♑   Ambitious love nature, with a tendency to absorb the feelings of others.
♒   Very constant and faithful in attachments.
♓   Plastic and impressionable love nature.

Aspects to the cusp of the fifth house, as well as to planets in this
house, should be noted, for the fifth house is very important in all
out-of-sight matters ; it shows the inner feelings, and leads from mere
sensation up to the highest emotions, to be finally expressed in the
ninth house as sublime philosophy or religious devotion.

CHILDREN

Much care is needed with regard to a judgment of the fifth house,
and although it denotes children in a general sense the joint horoscopes
of husband and wife should be considered efore any definite judgment
is given with regard to offspring.

The old astrological rule with reterence to children is that the tenth
and eleventh houses, together with the houses opposite to them, *i.e.* fifth
and fourth, must have consideration, also the aspects of planets to the
cusps of these houses and to any planets that are in them.   The Moon,
Jupiter and Venus together or singly in any of these houses promise
children, or rather a fruitful union in this respect, while the Sun, Mars
and Saturn either deny offspring or denote but few and those to be
reared with difficulty.   Mercury acts, as usual, according to aspects and
position ; if oriental he promises children, if occidental he denies them.
Malefics in the fifth house nearly always cause barrenness in a woman
or sterility in a man, and if children are born they are either too delicate
to live, or if reared cause endless trouble ; but in this case the aspects

to the malefics should be well considered. Benefics in the fifth house bring children and much pleasure through them.

The rules are as follows :—☽ in ♉, ♍, ♎ or ♒ a moderate family. If in ♊, ♋, ♏, ♐ or ♓ a large family; in this respect ♊ and ♐ are very fruitful signs often denoting twins. If in ♈, ♌, or ♑ there is small chance of a family.

Much skill is required in judging children from a horoscope and it is never safe to go by the horoscope of one sex alone, for it sometimes happens that an unfruitful horoscope in one case is made fruitful by blending with that of another.

CHAPTER XIII

The Sixth House.—Sickness, Servants, Work, etc.

THE sixth house is connected with the mid-heaven and the second house and relates to work and servants, also to sickness, and the condition of the physical body. It is an unimportant house if no planets are found in it, or if the sign upon the cusp has no definite indication relating to sixth house affairs. In some cases it is necessary to study the ruler of this house, but only when so placed or aspected as to show marked signs of importance. In all cases where a planet occupies this house it will have some direct bearing upon the work in which the native is engaged, the inferiors he contacts and the sickness or ill-health he is liable to suffer. In an indirect way it governs uncles and aunts or the relatives of the father.

NEPTUNE in the sixth house is very unfavourable for health, denoting atrophy, incurable diseases, and strange complaints that are inherited. If much afflicted it denotes serious ill-health through debauchery and evil habits, especially if afflicting Venus or Mars. It is not good for work and often brings enforced idleness or a chronic state of inertia. It inclines to mediumistic tendencies and is favourable for psychic phenomena, but there is always a danger of serious reaction resulting from this position. It is not good for dealing with inferiors and denotes hatred, or intense dislike from servants or inferiors. If well aspected the influence of Neptune may be improved but it is not a good position for this strange planet, and seems to produce very curious and peculiar disorders which in most cases seem to result from *astral* causes; that is, due to evil influences or negative conditions affecting the native directly from the astral plane.

URANUS in the sixth house denotes peculiar and exceptional complaints arising from nervous agitation and environment. Very few are sensitive enough to fully appreciate the psychic tendencies of this position. but in those who are very receptive it awakens the psychic faculties and brings abnormal development of some kind, according to the other conditions in the nativity. Nearly all the ailments may be traced to the nervous condition, for it is supposed that Uranus has much influence over the etheric double, which is the medium through which the *prâna* or vital force is conveyed to the body. If much afflicted in this house there is danger of insanity or hypochondria, epilepsy and hallucination. If well aspected diseases are curable by electricity, massage, etc., but if much afflicted diseases become incurable.

This position makes the native an unwilling servant and is not good for service of any kind, unless the soul has awakened, when the native elects to become a servant of humanity. Much will depend upon the sign ruling the sixth house as to how this influence will operate. To some it brings great opportunity, to others it is a curse, extremes ruling.

SATURN in the sixth house is very unfavourable for health and denotes much sickness, which is often the result of circumstances and conditions over which the native has little or no control. It causes sickness through privation and want or neglect, and causes many sorrows and disappointments through the state of the health. If afflicted by Sun or Moon a chronic state of ill-health is shown.

This position causes sickness through cold and inability to recuperate readily. It brings rheumatism and diseases that are difficult to cure.

This position is not favourable for work, or employment, nor is it good for servants and inferiors, through whom the native suffers losses. The good aspects to Saturn have very little effect upon this position, which often makes the life unfortunate and a burden to the native.

JUPITER in the sixth house denotes good health and little danger of sickness, except such as arises through excess and over-indulgence. If sick, the native is well and carefully nursed and sometimes gains through his sickness.

The native makes a good and faithful servant and either inherits or gains through his employer, with whom he may become partner or whose full confidence he shares. He would gain by and through servants if he employed them, for profit through inferiors is denoted by this position.

Jupiter afflicted in this house affects the blood and the liver. If much afflicted the health will suffer through intemperance and over-indulgence. This influence generally brings gain directly or indirectly through the religious tendencies.

MARS in the sixth house denotes a liability to suffer in health through carelessness or indiscreet action; there is a tendency to inflammatory complaints when Mars is afflicted by Sun and Jupiter, and danger of suicide or some fatal accident when afflicted by Uranus, this latter being a very evil influence.

This position denotes much energy in all work, and the native is generally an enthusiast where work is concerned. It is not favourable for servants, and causes the native annoyance and worry in connection with them; they gain through his generosity and often take advantage of his liberal treatment.

In this case it is perhaps best for the native to become his own master, as he is apt as a servant to do too much for others and impair his health through his energy and his impulse. If Mars is well aspected in this house it gives an abundance of animal spirits, and much rude physical health.

THE SUN in the sixth house is not good for the health of the native, the vital forces of the Sun having less power while in this house, but unless afflicted the native is careful and generally knows how to safeguard his health.

If afflicted by Saturn or Uranus the constitution is weak and the recuperative power is not good.

If in good aspect with Mars or Jupiter it favours the health, and indicates the best kind of work to be that connected with the medical profession. It denotes some promotion while in the employ of others, gain through serving others, and promises employment that is dignified and ennobled by the good that may be done to others.

It is not a position that favours opportunity, and in the case of those who work for work's sake only may show talent and ability lacking the opportunity to find a fitting or appreciated expression.

VENUS in the sixth house is very favourable for health if not seriously afflicted. The health is liable to be affected through excess of any kind, especially pleasure. If temperance is observed, especially after marriage, the health will be good and little trouble will be experienced in this direction. Should the native fall ill he will be carefully nursed, and may gain in several ways indirectly through his sickness.

This position denotes gain through servants, and brings pleasure and happiness through them. It makes work a pleasure, or rather in many cases pleasure becomes work. The native is by no means industrious but has a faculty for making his work in life a pleasure which

absorbs him.   No planet in the sixth house, not even Venus, favours
the native being his own master, but should he become so he would
obtain good and faithful servants to work for him.

MERCURY in the sixth house denotes mental troubles, and danger of
nervous breakdown.   This position affects the health when the nativity
shows much worry or anxiety, and the native is always liable to be over-
strung or easily affected physically by his surroundings and environment.

If afflicted by : Mars, there is danger of insanity through excitement
or lack of control over the impulses : Saturn, the mind becomes impaired through over-anxiety.   Uranus afflicting Mercury in the sixth rarely
fails to unbalance the native, causes him to commit rash acts and sometimes denotes suicide.   All afflictions to Mercury in the sixth house are
dangerous and tend to ruin the health through the condition of the mind.

This position denotes an energetic mental worker, but fails to bring
the best outlet for the mental energies.   The native though fitted to be
master can only hope to succeed as servant, and should be concerned
with either chemistry, writings, books or clerical work.   With this
position there is some danger of chronic dyspepsia.

THE MOON in the sixth house denotes a liability to suffer in health
through changes and fluctuating causes ; it is particularly inimical during
the infantile stage, and if much afflicted shows danger of an early death.   The
health is always liable to break down when under adverse lunar influences.

If afflicted by : Sun or Uranus, the digestion is usually impaired by
this position, and the native becomes a dyspeptic ; Mars, inflammatory
complaints ; Saturn, chronic diseases are shown.   Good aspects to the
Moon lessen the tendency to suffer in health, but it is not a good position for the Moon so far as health is concerned.

This position makes the native a better servant than master, and
shows ability to serve others and win the good fellowship of equals ; it
favours domestic service, and gives many opportunities to enjoy life if
employed as man-servant or maid in families of good position.   It shows
success in work of a light, watery, or fluctuating nature, but often gives
a strong desire to come before the public professionally.

The body is the physical medium through which we express ourselves upon the physical plane, therefore it becomes essential to know
the kind of dietary most suitable for the physical welfare of the native.
The sixth house is peculiarly related to food, and the nourishment of the

physical body; thus ill-health often results through inattention to the diet most suited to the body.

If the native has Mercury in the sixth house, it will be found that he has many fads and fancies with regard to diet, unless that planet is very well aspected or occupying the sign Virgo, when he will make a study of the laws of hygiene; but if afflicted this will be carried too far and the native become a faddist, over-dainty and lacking in common-sense with regard to diet. Saturn in the sixth often inclines the native to become too ascetic and prone to adopt periods of fasting and privation, thus going against the very necessary requirement of this indication that a generous and nourishing diet should be adopted; in such a case the room where meals are taken should be sunny and its temperature warm. Mars in the sixth has a tendency to cause the native to over-indulge and eat too much, but it generallly denotes a very healthy appetite. Jupiter in the sixth sometimes causes ill-health through surfeit and the love of feasting. Venus in this house sometimes denotes a danger of excess through a love of nice things to eat and drink, but generally its influence is temperate, especially if in Libra. The Moon will cause the native to be whimsical and fanciful in his eating, and over-fond of liquids and moist foods.

The signs occupied by the planets will in the majority of cases modify the influence, and in some cases accentuate the foregoing. In all cases where the Moon or Mercury occupies the sixth, reading, worry and anxiety should be avoided at meal times. Cases have been known where natives have suffered considerably through the magnetic conditions of those who have been present at meal times, showing the extremely psychic nature of this house. Again, persons with Saturn in the sixth, or even ruling the sixth, will be magnetically affected by the occupants at the same table during meals, while those having Jupiter in the sixth or ruling this house will be benefited by others joining at a meal probably owing to the social element that Jupiter always tends to give.

Similar remarks apply, though in a lesser degree, when by progression after birth the radical position of such planet has descended into the sixth house. In one case the progression of Saturn's place into the sixth house in this way caused the native to suffer much discomfort and annoyance from being obliged to take meals in chilly, draughty and sunless apartments and in undesirable surroundings.

When judging sickness from the sixth house care should be taken to note the general state of health, the constitution, and liability to functional disorders. No definite statement should be made from the sixth house or planets in that house with regard to sickness, unless ill-health is shown by the nativity, such as the affliction of the luminaries, etc. ; then note carefully the indications of the sixth house. Changes in the system and a liability to ill-health will arise when the planets in the sixth are aspected by the luminaries, but this may be caused by good aspects as well as those which are considered evil. A malefic may occupy the sixth house and yet the native will enjoy general good health ; but there will come a time when the health will break down, and then the malefic influence in the sixth will affect the native, either temporarily or permanently, according to the original indications.

It is generally true that the part of the body denoted by a sign of the zodiac is affected whenever the malefic planets are found in that sign of birth, but especially if in the sixth house. If the native suffer from any inflammatory complaint the sign occupied by Mars will show that a mark or scar will be left upon that part of the body after illness. Should the native suffer from rheumatic fever and Mars occupy the sign Capricorn upon the cusp of the sixth, then a mark or scar would be left upon one or both knees, and in all probability the fever would expend itself chiefly through that part of the body. If Saturn occupies the sixth then that part of the body governed by the sign holding Saturn would be the weak or fatal part. Similarly with Uranus ; if Uranus occupies Leo in the sixth there may be liability to heart disease, etc.

The sixth house may be considered a psychic house, in which the psychic tendencies of the native are indicated. All forms and ceremonies in which the native is interested are usually shown by this house, it being the house of phenomenal or ceremonial magic. It is, however, a house in which much may be said to be latent, and unexpressed. Saturn and Jupiter in the sixth incline to form and ceremony ; in the physical world this sometimes expresses itself in uniformed servants connected with the household, or the commoner types of liveried servants. The finer grades of the physical or earthy triplicity combine to operate through the influence of this sixth house.

The remarks in this chapter may be considerably amplified and usefully extended by a study of *Medical Astrology*, Manual No. 9, in which Heinrich Däath has dealt with sickness and disease in a most satisfactory manner.

CHAPTER XIV

THE SEVENTH HOUSE.—MARRIAGE, PARTNERSHIPS, ENEMIES, ETC.

MARRIAGE is the chief influence of the seventh house. The seventh house in every horoscope is the complement of the first, and represents the unifying of all that is separated or isolated in the ascendant; it indicates the subjective side of the nature as distinguished from the objective side indicated by the first house : * and successfully to unify all that is denoted by the first and seventh means an enlarged experience which can be gained in no other way. In the abstract, it means the blending of Mars and Venus, Mercury and Jupiter, or the luminaries and Saturn. In other words it signifies the transmutation of the passions into pure love, the exchange of intellect for wisdom and the perfect individualisation of the conscious Self.

Just as there is to be a divine marriage of the Personality with the Individuality when man attains to the perfection he is destined to reach; so on a minor scale, on the physical plane, the union of the sexes is a commencement of that unification which is eventually to unite the self to all other selves. The triangle that has its apex in the ascendant, when interlaced with the opposite triangle that has its apex in the seventh, symbolises the formation of the divine tetractys, or the union of opposites.

We have been considering hitherto the first half of the circle in the six houses that are under the earth, these being chiefly concerned with the Personality, starting full of life and force from the ascendant, and culminating in the sixth, where the life is either expended through sickness or work, or transmuted through the psyche or Soul into the human stage where the true individual begins. The chord from the first to the seventh houses divides the dark from the light half of the circle, the animal from the human, the latent from the active, the objective from the subjective. It is true that the one is but the reflection

---

* See remarks in early part of Chapter XI.

of the other, but from the seventh house the dividing line leads onward to the 'ascending arc' of human progress, and to the broad daylight of the solar half of the circle, which is not only less limited and restricted in its expression but more potent and real than that which is fore- shadowed by the dark and lower half.

Each house directly or indirectly affects the native in a definite manner according to a fixed law; but the house alone is not wholly responsible for the event. In the order of the signs Venus governs the seventh and the second, love and money; but although Venus is the planet most active in the majority of cases when marriage takes place no hard and fast rule can be applied in every case of marriage, and it is therefore advisable that the student should carefully study what is meant by the term marriage. In our own country, for instance, marriages take place at any time, and at any age. In India, on the other hand, marriages are arranged from birth, and in the majority of cases the native has no voice in the matter. In all parts of the world marriage laws differ, and the work of the astrologer is by no means an easy task when marriage is the subject for consideration.

If the word 'union' is substituted for marriage many grave errors will be avoided, for it is possible to see a union of the sexes when it is difficult to be sure that a legal marriage has been contracted.

In the course of practice an astrologer hears some very remarkable stories. In one instance the author was aware of a case where a highly respectable couple lived together as married, without having passed through the legal ceremony, for many years without the fact being in the least suspected. In another case a housekeeper had formed a union with her master which lasted for over twenty years. Three months before the birth of a child she was forced to marry a man she disliked to save herself from public dishonour. Cases are on record of marriage and separation taking place on the same day; and in fact the whole subject is one that requires the most careful judgment before any definite prediction can be safely made.

There are four factors concerned in all cases of union; the Sun, the Moon, Mercury and Venus.

In a male horoscope, note the planets to which the Moon, Mercury and the ruling planet make first application: they will describe the partner. In a female horoscope substitute the Sun for the Moon.

These three significators respectively represent the mental, psychic, and physical unions or attachments. If a planet is found in the seventh house it will describe the partner and give what is practically the history of any union.

NEPTUNE in the seventh house denotes peculiar and exceptional unions, and in some cases marriage to cripples or deformed persons. Extremes of good and evil seem to be the latent possibilities of the planet Neptune; therefore grave risks are run by the native who has this position. It may bring about a platonic union or one that is the very reverse; long expected happiness often meets with disappointment at the last moment, though often the seeming misfortune proves a boon, this depending on the aspects Neptune receives at birth. If Neptune is much afflicted in the seventh then marriage is inadvisable unless exceptional experiences along this particular line are required. If well aspected much of the evil is mitigated, but in all cases it is a very doubtful and uncertain position, showing marriages that are unique and out of the common.

URANUS in the seventh house denotes romantic attachments, hasty and impulsive engagements. It also denotes the possibility of marriage to a genius, or to an original character. This influence may be very good or very evil according to the horoscope. There is an element of uncertainty about this position and the unexpected usually happens to those who have this influence operating at birth. To them romantic love is always the spice of life, and they often end by marrying the last person they thought they would marry. If well aspected, the marriage partner turns out to be a true friend of the native and has original and ingenious methods of ministering to the domestic comforts. If afflicted the partner brings about ruin, and eventually separation or grievous misunderstanding.

SATURN in the seventh house shows a faithful partner or marriage to a person older than the native. Saturn is exalted in Libra, and as this sign is equivalent to the seventh house Saturn in the seventh denotes faithfulness and sincerity on the part of the marriage partner. It does not give affection of the demonstrative and emotional order, but it makes love a duty and gives stability to the affections, which become permanent and enduring. If Saturn is much afflicted in this house then sorrow and grief may be expected in the married life. If well aspected the marriage partner is prudent, steady, persevering and industrious, though not especially fortunate. If Saturn and the Moon are afflicted in the seventh the domestic happiness is spoilt.

JUPITER in the seventh house promises a good and faithful partner and much happiness in the marriage state, also success and gain resulting from marriage. It brings social advantages after marriage and financial prospects, the partner having independent means in which the native shares.

This position often denotes marriage to one who has been previously married or a partner older and more religiously inclined than the native. If afflicted lawsuits and litigation are threatened by this position, but principally when the affliction is from Mars or Uranus. Marriage is delayed if afflicted by Saturn and may be denied if the luminaries afflict. When well aspected all goes well in the marriage state, and marriage often turns the life into pleasant paths and favourable conditions.

MARS in the seventh house when afflicted denotes quarrels and unpleasant conditions in the marriage state. It is very unfavourable in a male horoscope, denoting a wife that is combative and over-forceful. In a female horoscope it is also evil and is somewhat disastrous to the husband, showing the probability of a violent death. If Mars is afflicted in the seventh, separation through the uncontrolled temper and passionate nature of the partner is denoted. Even when well aspected this is not a good position for marriage, Mars ever tending to extremes and excess, in affection as in other things. It is more favourable in a female horoscope than in a male nativity, females represented by Mars being far too masculine and forceful, while males represented by Mars express the force as energy and enterprise. Note the *sign* occupied by Mars.

THE SUN in the seventh house in a male horoscope denotes a proud but honourable partner, and progress in life through marriage. In a female horoscope it is not so important unless the Sun is 'void of course,' *i.e.*, makes *no* aspect during its progress from its place at birth before quitting the sign it is in. This position causes marriage to take place towards middle life, and denotes happiness in the married state.

If the Sun is much afflicted in the seventh, marriage will be delayed or strong opposition will be experienced. Lasting attachments and firm friendships are formed when the Sun occupies the seventh house, and when the Sun is in good aspect to the Moon or Jupiter from this house much domestic happiness is shown. If afflicted it is disastrous according to the nature of the aspect and the position of the afflicting planet.

Venus in the seventh house promises a happy marriage; the partner will be attractive and pleasing and generally fortunate. 'Venus joys in the seventh' is an old aphorism, for the seventh is the house and home of the planet Venus.

The afflictions to this planet must be very severe to cause unhappiness in the marriage state, though they may delay or hinder marriage; but the position of Venus alone is sufficient to ensure happiness, or a partner whose influence upon the life is beneficial. Success socially and financially comes after marriage and the help and assistance brought into it by the partner's influence is such as to improve the whole of the future life of the native. If well aspected the whole of the life will turn upon marriage, but the best aspects will be those of the Moon and Jupiter, even the good aspects of Mars, Saturn and Uranus tending te act adversely upon the pure influence of Venus.

Mercury in the seventh house denotes a partner who is quick-witted, clever, and not always to be relied upon. If afflicted a life of bickering and wrangling is shown. If well aspected the partner will be shrewd, active and progressive. Marriage usually takes place as the result of much correspondence or travelling, and the partner is generally younger than the native, and may be a cousin. The fact of Mercury being a convertible planet renders it important that the aspects of other planets to Mercury be considered carefully, and also the sign Mercury occupies must be taken into account. When unaspected care will be necessary in judging the influence of Mercury in the seventh house. If much afflicted legal troubles in connection with marriage are shown, and the possibility of much worry, anxiety, and difficulty arising out of misunderstandings either through speech, travelling or correspondence.

The Moon in the seventh house in a female horoscope denotes some romance in married life and a partner whose affections fluctuate. Unless the Moon is well aspected this is not a very favourable position. It should not be taken as the sole significator in a male horoscope, but it must be considered as an important factor in producing marriage.

It favours early marriage, and if alone in the seventh without aspects marriage will probably take place between twenty-four and twenty-eight. The marriage partner will be fond of change and travel and not always constant in affection. If afflicted, it denotes tragedy or an early death for the partner. The sign occupied by the Moon must be studied, for the Moon will be coloured by the sign it is in almost as much as by the aspects it receives from the planets.

Although the seventh is principally the house of marriage, at the same time it also governs legal affairs, opponents, and that which is farthest removed from the native. It is the house of partners and co-workers, and, from a still higher standpoint, the house of the Individuality during the period of manifestation as contrasted with the Personality. The blending of these two is the true marriage, of which all unions on the physical plane are but material representations.

There are several rules for judging marriage, some of which we shall now consider.

The best testimony for a marriage that will be harmonious and successful is the interchanging of the luminaries. The Sun of the native in the same place as the Moon of the partner or the Moon near the partner's Sun, is an admirable testimony of a happy union, or even a good aspect between the luminaries in the two horoscopes is very favourable.

In male horoscopes if the seventh house and its ruler do not offer a clear judgment note the application of the Moon, and in a female horoscope the Sun.

The ruler of the first and seventh houses should be in good aspect to each other; when afflicting, *especially by square*, disharmony and trouble are shown.

In a female's horoscope note carefully the Sun's application to the planets,—the planets to which the Sun applies denoting the men she will meet, favour, become engaged to, or marry. The planet, with the sign that it is in, will describe the men she will meet. Do not attach much, if any, importance to those planets from which the Sun is separating. It is not advisable to recommend marriage to the man described by the planet to which the Sun forms an adverse aspect; but this may be counteracted by a good aspect between Mars and Venus, which always hastens marriage. Saturn afflicting Venus delays and hinders it, causing much trouble in love and courtship.

The Sun's application to any planet is very important when considering female horoscopes with regard to marriage. If the Sun applies to any aspect of Uranus or Saturn, or to both, and these two planets aspect each other, marriage will tend to be unhappy or unfortunate. It denotes a late marriage, if any, or an exceptional union. This is especially evil if the luminaries are in affliction at the same time, and it denotes widowhood.

The Sun separating from a parallel of Uranus, Saturn, or Mars, is an unfavourable testimony for marriage, giving liability to widowhood. If the Sun applies to these three planets by favourable aspects it will denote several suitors, or more than one marriage.

The Sun applying to the conjunction of Jupiter, and a trine aspect to Saturn, favours more than one union. When the Sun is in a double-bodied sign, either Gemini, Sagittarius, or Pisces, and makes several applications, more than one union is denoted.

Similarly also both for males and females when the lord of the seventh or Venus occupies a double-bodied sign.

WOMEN'S MARRIAGES: Should the Sun be between the cusps of the tenth and seventh or the fourth and first, women marry early in life, or to men younger than themselves. Should the Sun be between the cusps of the first and tenth or the seventh and fourth, women marry late in life or to men older than themselves.

MEN'S MARRIAGES: Should the Moon be oriental* or between the conjunction and first quarter, or between the opposition and last quarter, men marry early in life or to women younger than themselves. Should the Moon be occidental* or between the last quarter and conjunction, or between the first quarter and opposition, men marry late in life or to women older than themselves.

With men marriage is difficult to bring about when the Moon or

---

* NOTE.—*Oriental and Occidental.* The above use of these terms, although familiar to those acquainted with mediæval writers in Astrology, may prove rather puzzling to others.

The two words literally mean *rising* and *falling*, and in a general sense planets in the left-hand half of the map (*i.e.*, in the space occupied by houses X., XI., XII., I., II., III.) are said to be oriental or rising, those in the opposite half (houses IV., V., VI., VII., VIII., IX.) occidental or falling. [LATIN: *orior, oriori*, to become visible, appear, arise; *occido, occidere*, to fall, fall down, die or perish.]

But in regard to the Sun, he is said to be oriental in houses XII., XI., X. or VI., V., IV., and occidental when in the opposite houses; the reason being that when the Sun has reached the seventh house cusp he is then *becoming visible* in the opposite hemisphere of the world, and when he has passed the fourth house cusp he has culminated and is therefore setting in that hemisphere, or *falling down.* Similarly with the Moon also.

Venus is in Aries, Leo, Virgo or Capricorn, and sometimes Gemini owing to its duality. If these signs are cadent and afflicted by Saturn, it is more difficult. The Moon afflicted by Sun, and Saturn and Moon in the occidental side of the map, results in hindrance or delay to marriage, often in no marriage at all. Planets in barren signs or cadent houses, with much affliction, are against marriage. When the Moon is in double signs, such as Gemini, Sagittarius or Pisces, then more than one marriage is shown: note also Venus the same, or a double-bodied sign on the seventh.

The kind of partner is shown by the planet the Moon applies to. Thus: if the Moon applies to Uranus, little domestic comfort; to Saturn, a partner, grave, serious, industrious, poor, careful, laborious and sometimes cold in temperament—if Saturn weak, then one of poor birth, etc.; to Mars, one who will be masterful, bold, proud, and conceited, often quarrelsome and disputatious; to Jupiter, virtuous, peaceful, harmonious, etc.; to Venus, cheerful, good-looking and happy; to Mercury, clever, sensible and witty—but if afflicted look out for tongue, for speech will be quick and fluent and not always choice.

Judge of the descriptions according to the planet occupying the seventh and the sign of the cusp thereof: if no planet in seventh, then judge by lord of sign on cusp and the sign which said planet occupies.

The Moon in any adverse aspect to, or in parallel of declination with Mars will cause discord, disruption, struggles for mastery, and a great deal of discontent and hasty speech and quarrelling; to Uranus, separation, sudden estrangement, unfaithfulness and extraordinary experiences. If either of these planets is in the seventh or in fiery signs the evil will be accentuated. The planets to which the Moon applies describe the women the native will meet, affecting or being affected, according to the aspects. The true partner is the one described by the planet to which the Moon first applies.

Uranus in particular is a very important planet to study with regard to love affairs, for this planet affects the magnetism of the native when he comes into contact with those who have the power to influence his emotional nature. Where the Moon is applying to or forms any aspect to Uranus, the native should guard against a sudden or hasty marriage, as in such a case he is almost certain to meet someone after marriage to whom he will become attached.

Marriage is best consummated when Jupiter is transiting one of the angles. The time of marriage is seen when the significators by progression form a complete aspect, when the luminaries are in aspect to Jupiter or Venus, or passing through the seventh house. In some noroscopes marriage is very clearly seen, in others it is difficult to discover. The progressed Moon, passing through the radical or progressed seventh, is sure to awaken amatory feelings on the part of the native.

The following descriptions will apply in a modified sense where the planet described is ruler of the seventh house, if there be no planet occupying the house.

NEPTUNE: usually signifies strange relations in the marriage state. clandestine attachments, seduction, or a platonic union, according to general tone of horoscope. Often marriage is unexpectedly delayed or prevented at the last moment, or an engagement from which much was hoped falls through.

URANUS: is not good for partnerships and denotes trouble through strangers and opponents. It is as a rule an exceedingly unfortunate position.

SATURN: is very evil for partnerships or litigation, and denotes some very persistent enemies or opponents, by whom the native loses. Steadiness and patience need to be cultivated.

JUPITER: should give success through partnerships, also in legal affairs, and gain, either directly or indirectly, through litigation.

MARS: very unfavourable for legal disputes, denoting much loss, trouble and annoyance, with great difficulty in bringing litigation to a termination. The native is usually somewhat turbulent or quarrelsome in disposition, and tends to get himself into trouble by truculent behaviour.

THE SUN: gives success in legal affairs, and will help the native in all litigation or matters in which the law may be invoked. It denotes opponents who will act from a sense of justice and a love of right, and although powerful they will act generously and with magnanimity. If afflicted, the opposition that the native will meet may be severe but the solar influence will help as well as make the opposition powerful. If well aspected, gain through lawsuits, and a successful issue to all affairs of a legal nature is shown. It favours settlement by arbitration or mutual consent.

VENUS: is very favourable for partnerships, and denotes success in litigation if not very much afflicted; otherwise it always gives disappointment.

MERCURY: gives a liability to much litigation if once started; trivial and petty worries and quarrels, much wordy warfare and unprofitable correspondence: law should be avoided altogether unless Mercury is well aspected by Jupiter. If afflicted this denotes much annoyance from opponents who are better ignored than noticed. Lawyers and solicitors are best avoided, especially if Mercury is much afflicted, as it denotes them to be incompetent or untrustworthy, and therefore likely to cause much trouble and loss.

THE MOON: not favourable for legal affairs, and shows danger of much loss and trouble in connection with litigation. It makes the native unpopular and denotes female enmity, and opposition of a public nature, which, if the Moon is afflicted, will bring notoriety and ill-repute. It will be well for the native to avoid law even if the Moon is well aspected, for then he would gain only fame or public notice, but would in all probability lose financially.

In considering the question of marriage it is advisable to take into account the indications afforded by the *eleventh* house as well as those of the seventh. It seems probable that good or bad aspects thrown to the marriage significators from planets in the eleventh house are respectively much better and much worse than from any other part of the map except the seventh house. Cases are known in which the marriage partner is born under the sign on the cusp of the native's eleventh house, or under the rulership of a planet in that house. The eleventh house seems to have much to do with ideal attachments and the highei side of the love nature which is less personal.

According to the old rules the Moon and Venus must be carefully considered in all cases of marriage. If the Moon and many planets are placed between the first and tenth houses or the seventh and fourth, then an early marriage is denoted, or in a male horoscope (if marriage has not taken place before middle life) men will marry women much younger than themselves. If the Moon is in any of the other portions men to marry late in life or else to women older than themselves.

If the Moon is aspected by Saturn, or if very near the Sun, marriage is delayed; also if the Sun and Moon are in affliction. **If** the Moon is occidental and afflicting the Sun marriage is rarely consummated.

Happy marriages are those where the Moon, Jupiter and Venus are all in good aspect, with the Sun free from affliction.

The Moon in Gemini, Sagittarius, or Pisces points to more than one marriage especially if oriental, or angular.

In a *male* horoscope the wife is always described by the planet to which the Moon first applies, for instance if to Saturn, she will be grave, serious, and thoughtful, if to Jupiter, cheerful and fortunate, to Mars, self assertive and hard to please, to Venus, good-looking and a pleasing companion, to Mercury, clever and sensible. In a *female* horoscope the Sun is to be taken as the Moon in a male horoscope in this respect. The description of the wife (husband) is that of the planet forming the nearest aspect to the Moon (Sun), and partakes largely of the sign which that planet occupies.

If none of these rules can be applied judge well the seventh house and the planets aspecting the cusps.

In FEMALE HOROSCOPES the Sun, Venus, and Mars are the chief significators. A good marriage is made if the Sun is in good aspect to Mars, and Mars well placed, but if the Sun has no aspect to Mars and is afflicted by Saturn, then marriage is hard to find. If the Sun is oriental a woman marries early, or to men younger than themselves as already stated, but if occidental then a late marriage or to men who are their elders. More than one marriage is shown if the Sun is in Gemini, Sagittarius, or Pisces. Venus afflicting Saturn denotes trouble in the marriage state.

CHAPTER XV

THE EIGHTH HOUSE—DEATH, AND THE DREAM CONSCIOUSNESS

THIS house belongs to the triangle of fourth, eighth, and twelfth; which have as their correspondences Cancer, Scorpio and Pisces, ruled by the Moon, Mars and Jupiter. These form the watery, psychic, or astral subdivision of the zodiac and indicate channels through which influences (good or bad) may flow down upon the man from the next interior plane of being, as well as ways by which he may himself contact that plane.

Of these three, the eighth house is generally considered to have a direct bearing upon death and all matters connected therewith, such as the goods of the dead, legacies, occupations connected with death, executorships, coroners, surgeons, medical officers of health, sanitary officers or inspectors, slaughter-houses, butchers. It also has relation to some forms of mediumship and occultism, generally of a practical executive kind.

The sign on the cusp of the eighth house, planets in the house, or failing these, the lord of the house, usually indicate the kind of death the native will die. But it is necessary to exercise the greatest caution in judging this point because it is seldom that any one indication can be trusted if taken alone. The influences of the eighth house must be considered in connection with those of the ascendant, the hyleg, and the health generally; and the principles laid down in the chapter on health must be carefully borne in mind when considering the probable duration of life and date of death. Death is usually led up to by a train of evil directions, but before deciding that those will be fatal it is necessary to ascertain whether the positions at birth promised short, medium, or long life. If the health indications at birth were good and promised long life, no evil directions in youth or early life will kill; but on the other hand if the hyleg was weak at birth a comparatively minor direction may prove fatal. When it has been decided that death will not occur until middle or old age, directions involving the eighth house and falling out in early life may act in various ways.

(1) The native's health may be temporarily upset, but not to the point of proving fatal ; and even this may not be serious unless at least two or three hylegiacal points (Sun, Moon, and Ascendant) are afflicted together.

(2) A death may occur among the relatives or associates of the native. This is a very common result of these directions, but it should be remembered that the death will not always be in the native's own family. A relative by marriage, an associate by employment, a friend, anyone whose death will decidedly affect the native, emotionally or other-wise—any of these may fulfil the direction according to the planets, signs and houses involved.

(3) Or the disturbing events may occur among those affairs, other than death, which are governed by the eighth house.

The following cases will prove instructive in connection with this point :—

A gentleman born under Scorpio, with Virgo on the cusp of the eleventh house and Mercury in the eighth house afflicted in Gemini, was greatly disturbed by the death of a college companion, and was suddenly called upon to take a short journey to attend the deathbed.

A gentleman whose Moon was progressing through the eighth house, lost a parent, and at the same time passed through some strange spiritualistic experiences.

A lady, while the Sun was progressing through the eighth house and forming bad aspects there, was involved in long continued trouble and anxiety arising out of a will, and her own health was seriously upset.

A gentleman who had the Moon in the eighth house at birth, in his twenty-eighth year (when the progressed Moon returned to this posi-tion), lost by death his mother and a female friend, both very suddenly, and within a few days of each other.

The death may be judged to be by natural means unless there are very marked indications to the contrary. When Sun and Moon are both afflicted by malefics and the latter elevated, there is a probability of violent death, although it will need no little skill to distinguish between this and a sudden but natural death, such as heart disease.

Speaking generally, the malefics are more prominent and the afflictions are heavier in cases of violent death. The malefics mixing their rays, especially Mars, with either Uranus or Saturn, increase the likelihood of suddenness or violence. Taurus and Scorpio are signs that act suddenly and violently when afflicted, and to a less extent Aries and Capricorn. When the ascendant is involved the native may be, intentionally or unintentionally, the cause of his own death; when the twelfth house, there may be treachery or assassination (if a violent death is indicated), or death may occur in a hospital, asylum, etc.; if the eleventh, it may happen at the residence of a friend, or through a love affair (especially if fifth and seventh are also involved); if the tenth, it may be a public death; if the ninth house, a death while travelling, or when at a distance from home; and so on, according to the nature of the houses involved in the affliction.

NEPTUNE in the eighth house gives liability to a very strange and peculiar death, possibly through trance, with some danger of being buried alive; or death after a long period of unconsciousness or from overdose of soporific drugs, etc. In some cases it denotes cremation after death, and when very well aspected the probability of carrying the consciousness through from the physical brain to the astral while in waking consciousness. This is not a good position for gain by marriage, although in some cases it denotes gain by a legacy or in some peculiar manner through others. When afflicted it denotes chaotic dreams and weird fancies, nightmares, etc.

URANUS in the eighth house denotes danger of paralysis, or death through epileptic fits and uncommon nervous disorders. It denotes a death quite out of the ordinary, which is often sudden and quite unexpected. Unless Uranus is well aspected at birth it is likely to cause much worry and annoyance in connection with money that may be left, and usually causes the unexpected to happen with regard to deaths. If well aspected it may bring sudden benefits and gain through the marriage partner. This position arouses a keen interest in occultism and mystical subjects, and the native is generally absorbed in some of the problems concerning the after-death state. It often causes the native to have uncommon dreams. Uranus has a natural sympathy with Scorpio, and hence is not so badly placed in this house.

SATURN in the eighth house denotes a slow and often a lingering death from some chronic, or long-standing ailment. When much afflicted fatal accidents occur and sometimes there is danger of drowning when Saturn occupies a watery sign in this house.   If well aspected this position indicates a long life, and denotes death in old age from natural causes.   This is not a good position for gain by marriage or through partners, neither does it promise gain by will or legacy, but generally disappointment with regard to any money that may be left by others. In some cases this position gives a deep interest in occult subjects.   It is not good for the remembrance of dreams.

JUPITER in the eighth house denotes a very peaceful and a perfectly natural death.   It denotes, when afflicted, heart trouble and danger of death through blood poisoning, also through tumours, cancer and consumption.   When not afflicted this is a very good position for finance after marriage, and generally denotes gain through a wealthy partner.   It also gives gain by legacy, and through the deaths of others. It generally causes the native to take a deep interest in occult subjects, especially those dealing with after-death states.   In some cases the native is able to remember remarkable dreams and can often relate the details of impressions made upon the brain during sleep.

MARS in the eighth house indicates a liability to a violent or sudden death.   If much afflicted this is a very evil position, but Mars alone in this house will not kill the native, although the end whenever it comes will be sudden and after an illness of short duration or by shock or accident.   It will be necessary to note the sign Mars occupies at birth: if a watery sign there is danger of death by drowning, if a fiery sign death by fire or violence, if an airy sign mental affliction; when in an earthy sign Mars is not so evil.   This position causes much trouble in connection with finance after marriage, either the partner is extravagant or wastes money foolishly.

THE SUN in the eighth shows that the middle period of life will be critical; and if malefics afflict, danger of violent or sudden death.   If well aspected, the life is prolonged and vitality increased.   This position is liable to affect the heart.   Death may occur through hereditary or constitutional weakness, or it may be an honourable death due to some self-sacrifice or heroic deed.   If the Moon afflicts the Sun the eyesight may be affected, and the health is liable to be disturbed by malefic transits.   If the Sun is afflicted there is some likelihood of the premature death of the father; or of the husband, in a female horoscope: if well aspected, there may be money inherited from both these.

VENUS in the eighth house denotes a peaceful and easy death, but if afflicted death may be caused through pleasure, or its pursuit. If much afflicted kidney troubles may cause death, or diabetes and obesity or urinary troubles. This position promises financial gain by marriage or partnerships. It also denotes gain by legacy or through money that may be left by will or the goods of those who have passed from the physical into the next plane of existence. This position is favourable for the progress of the native at middle life or when finally settled in the domestic sphere by marriage or otherwise.

MERCURY in the eighth house indicates a liability to brain and nervous disorders, which may be either the direct or indirect cause of death ; this is an unfavourable position if Mercury is much afflicted by either Mars, Saturn, or Uranus. It generally denotes the consciousness to be active and fully awake at the time of death, but does not appear to be the direct cause of death, the afflicting planet being the cause according to its nature and aspect. This position denotes worry in connection with partner's financial affairs, and to a female difficulty in obtaining money from her husband, or if Mercury is afflicted, quarrels in connection with finance. It also indicates an enquiring mind concerning occult subjects, and an inclination to study hidden and metaphysical problems,

THE MOON in the eighth house denotes a death of a more or less public nature, death by drowning, shipwreck, public calamity, or in the presence of many people. Afflicted by Mars, danger of sudden or violent death ; by Saturn, a lingering or very grievous end ; by Uranus, a peculiar, sudden or extraordinary death ; by Neptune, tragedy, danger from water. Well aspected, possibility of inheritance through women, or by the mother's side of the family. Some likelihood of early death of the mother, or of the wife (in a male horoscope). In a woman's horoscope it tends to increase the number of children, but threatens the death of one or more, especially if afflicted. If there is any tendency to occultism, this position will increase it and give practical ability for some form of psychism, such as clear dreaming, mediumship, etc. Every seventh year is apt to be a critical period for the life, especially if the Moon is afflicted.

In no case should death be judged by position alone ; when the native has passed the infantile stage, death is, in nearly all cases, caused by a train of evil directions. If the directions occur from fiery and airy signs the death is more liable to be violent and sudden than when the affliction occurs from earthy or watery signs.

The earthy signs are more directly connected with the physical body, the watery signs with the etheric double, which is the finer mould into which the physical was cast at birth. The fiery signs are connected with the vitality or vital forces, and the airy signs with the nervous system, the brain and the mind generally.

The planets also have a significance apart from the sign they may be in. Neptune usually signifies a very mysterious death in some way. Sometimes the native dies in an unknown manner, or disappears and is never heard of again. But these are extreme cases. Uranus denotes sudden and peculiar deaths either through some new invention, by explosion, or diseases that are incurable, or where ignorance with regard to the ailment causes the native to have wrong treatment, etc. Uranus rarely kills unless very severely afflicted, and then is most probably an indirect cause of death. Saturn, death by suffocation, falls, bruises, rheumatism, consumption, and all cold, wasting, and lingering diseases. Jupiter, death by diseases of the liver and blood, according to the sign it occupies. Mars, death by suicide, fever, inflammations, violence and accidents. The Sun when denoting death affects the vital centres such as the heart, etc. Venus, death by poison, wasting diseases, diabetes, skin disease and venereal disorders. Mercury, diseases of the brain, melancholy madness, and nervous disorders. The Moon denotes death by drowning, phlegmatic and cold complaints in which the functional arrangements are disordered.

The sign upon the cusp of the eighth house, and the signs containing the majority of the planets, must have careful consideration in all questions of death.

A critical period is always reached when the luminaries are in conjunction, square or opposition.

Much skill is required, not only to discover the time of death, but also the nature of the disease causing death, and the blending of influences is always necessary. Saturn, Mercury and Venus are directly concerned with the physical body : Saturn governing the bony structure, the skeleton ; Mercury the brain and nervous system ; Venus the flesh and generative system. It is true that each planet governs a special part of the body, but in the main Saturn, Mercury and Venus are chief rulers of the physical conditions.

AN ILLUSTRATION

X	XI	XII	I	II	III
≈29	♈2	♉19	♋4	♋19	♌7

☉	☽	☿	♀	♂	♃	♄	♅	♆
♌15	♈1	♌18½	♋11½	♈1¼	♑9 R	♌21	≈8 R	♑21 R

Cases of violent death are always very plainly shewn in horoscopes where both luminaries are afflicted by the 'malefic' planets. In the above nativity the Moon is hyleg and ruler of the horoscope of which Venus is part ruler, owing to her position near the Ascendant. It is the horoscope of a female born at 1 a.m. 8/8/30., Lat. 50.30 N and Long 2.30 W. She was executed for murder on the 20th April, 1849.

Here we find both malefics afflicting the luminaries. The condition of the mind is shown by the third house and the sesquiquadrate aspect of ☽ ♂ ♂, to ☿ ♂ ♄. Death by violence is here clearly marked by the affliction of the luminaries. The Moon is much afflicted and has no good aspects, applying to ♂ ♂ □ ♃ □ ♀ ⚹ ☿ and ♄ and separating from ⚹ ☉. The ☉ is ☍ ♅ and applies to no good aspects.

CHAPTER XVI

The Ninth House—Philosophy and Travel

THE ninth house is the house of philosophy, the higher mind, and hence of all that concerns the scientific and religious attitude of the native. It is the house of the subjective and abstract mind as opposed to the objective and concrete brain mind, represented by the third house. The third house, representing the smaller and slower mind which has its range in the physical world only, also represents short journeys and travelling by land; while the ninth house, signifying the wider and less limited mind, also represents transit that is rapid, long journeys, sea voyages, foreign travel, etc. The third house governs education and studies of the minor and more conventional order, the ninth house philosophy and deep thinking. The third is the house of perception and learning, the ninth the house of reason and intuition. The ninth house has some connection with legal matters, probably owing to its being governed by Jupiter in the natural order of the signs. It may also be taken to represent relatives of the marriage partner, and many conditions which lie entirely outside of the native's immediate environment.

· The ninth is a house that represents the future more than the past (fifth) or present (first), and in this respect it governs dreams, visions, prophecy, imagination and thought, also intuition and pure reason; these faculties are expressed in accordance with the development of the native, and also according to the planet *occupying* the house, this being, as in the case of all houses above the earth, more important than the *ruler* of the house itself.

NEPTUNE in the ninth house denotes very peculiar and generally psychic persons whose minds are absorbed in phenomena and strange theories. It is not a good position unless free from affliction; alone in this house or badly aspected it is likely to cause the native much trouble —if not in waking consciousness then in dreams or through fancies.

It gives a weird and uncanny tendency to the mind, which is impressionable, easily influenced and liable to be quickly psychologised. This position appears to act beneficially only when all the other evils in a nativity are exhausted and then from a psychic more than a material standpoint.

URANUS in the ninth house depends entirely upon the composite horoscope, *i.e.*, the horoscope as a whole. In some nativities it will denote inventive genius or intense love of metaphysical studies, and a keen delight in all occult subjects; in other nativities it will give an aversion to all that relates to metaphysics. There can be no worse position for Uranus when in opposition, square or conjunction with the planet Mars. If the luminaries afflict it will give a very eccentric and peculiar mind, much trouble through travel, law and occult arts. In the very advanced it denotes a highly original and progressive mind; in the undeveloped it denotes a 'crank' who does more harm than good with his absurd notions.

SATURN in the ninth house denotes a studious and meditative mental attitude towards all higher thought pursuits. It favours the scientific and philosophical more than the religious mind and often causes the native to investigate astrology, metaphysics, and psychic studies generally. In the unawakened it denotes some stupidity with regard to higher thought questions and tends to produce self-deception, and a very crafty and subtle mentality. If afflicted by Mars or Uranus it tends to produce madness, or grave mental affliction. This is not a good position for voyages, travels or foreign affairs. If Saturn is in good aspect with the Sun from this house it denotes the true religious spirit and makes the native faithful to whatever causes he espouses.

JUPITER in the ninth house is the ideal position for the philosopher or saint, unless afflicted, when religious fervour and devotion will take the place of philosophy of the metaphysical order. If afflicted: by Mars, a tendency to go to extremes in religious matters, also legal troubles and danger of shipwreck or accidents abroad; by Saturn, self-deception and trouble through overstepping the bounds of reason. If in good aspect to the Sun, Moon or Mercury this is a splendid position for the higher mind, giving true intuition, and the ability to forsee clearly. This position brings true dreams and a very peaceful state. It is favourable for travel and residence abroad, also for clerical, legal, philanthropic and religious affairs.

MARS in the ninth house denotes an over-enthusiastic nature with regard to religious and philosophical subjects, and tends to destroy reason or to allow impulse and desire to overrule the mind. If much afflicted it gives fanatical, irregular, bigoted or sceptical opinions on religious matters; if well aspected a zealous and enterprising mind. This is not a good position unless the native is shown to exercise self-control, when it will probably destroy any preconceived or orthodox beliefs, and give liberty and freedom of thought, which will be far from conventional or stereotyped. Much will depend upon the sign Mars occupies. In the fiery signs there will be rebellious tendencies and over-much impulse. In the earthy signs the position is better than in the watery signs, but when in the airy signs there will be grave tendency to overstep the boundary of reason. This position gives some danger from voyages, travels, litigation, etc.

THE SUN in the ninth house denotes a very austere mind, firm and self-reliant, inclined to investigate scientific subjects with an unbiassed and clear judgment. It gives success in matters connected with the church and the law, and those in which the mind is engaged in higher problems dealing with the masses rather than the few. This position promises success abroad, or residence in foreign countries, also through travel and social intercourse. The more cosmopolitan the native, the greater will be the advantages arising out of this position; if orthodox or conventional, the position shows some tendency to become bigoted in religious belief, also to become proud and over confident. May rise to some position of responsibility in matters signified by the ninth house. If afflicted: by Mars or Uranus, fanatical or extreme enthusiasm in religious faith, legal difficulties and trouble in foreign countries; by Jupiter, hypocritical tendencies and poor success in religious affairs; by Saturn, an over-bearing and hard mind, too imperious and full of false pride, which warps and hinders the progress of the native, the social benefits promised by the Sun in this house being considerably limited. If well aspected: by Mars, patriotism, courageous defence of right, and a great deal of righteous indignation when moved to expression; by Jupiter, sincere and true ideas concerning religion and a very philo-sophical spirit; by Saturn, a strong love of justice with a steady mind and power to undertake much responsibility.

VENUS in the ninth house denotes a very refined and artistic mind, loving every form of mental improvement and giving a very keen appreciation of all that pertains to mental culture. This position will improve every horoscope, for it denotes a kind and sympathetic disposition and real ability to help and assist others. It gives the native a love of music, art, high-class literature and social intercourse with intellectual persons. It denotes success abroad, gain through travel, also through shipping, yachting, boating, etc., and pleasure through these, coupled with a very contented disposition. If afflicted it denotes disappointment in connection with ideals, and creates an internal longing for the unattainable ; but very little harm will come to the native who has this position at birth.

MERCURY in the ninth house denotes a love of knowledge, an enquiring and studious mind. Unless well aspected this position is not altogether favourable, but if the horoscope indicates power to concentrate, the position is improved. If afflicted it denotes a tendency to worry, and to become engaged in too many things at one time, also to wander and take aimless journeys. It causes the native to entertain many contradictory opinions and to waver and become far too indecisive for his own good. If well aspected it gives literary ability, and a keen appreciation of art, science, and all things which help to improve the mind. If unaspected it is not likely to affect the native to any marked degree, but in this case much will depend upon the sign it is in.

THE MOON in the ninth house denotes a keen imagination, a mind receptive to higher thought ideals, and the ability to study or understand metaphysical subjects. It gives a love for travel and denotes many changes in the life and those chiefly of a beneficial and improving nature. If afflicted : by Mars, affects the religious tendencies, either giving over-enthusiasm, or peculiar and unorthodox views ; by Saturn, sorrow and grief through religious difficulties ; by Uranus, a tendency to become too romantic, dreamy and visionary. If well aspected : native is fond of investigating new subjects, and is generally penetrative and very reflective ; gains success through travel and takes a deep interest in all modern modes of transit. This position denotes an ingenious mind, inventive, full of plans and progressive ideas. If afflicted by the Sun this is an evil position, tending to cause brain troubles.

The ninth house may be said to be the home of the metaphysical and occult mind in which the subconscious mental state is concerned, and wherein are denoted dreams and all that pertains to the intangible, the subjective, and the idealistic side of life. It is the house in which the *life* side is more in evidence than the *form*, through the medium of what may be definitely known as the Higher Mind. It always denotes that which is to be the unfolding of what is possible in the future, and all planets in this house have a higher vibration than when placed in any other, but particularly so far as the mind apart from the brain is concerned. It is true that this is a cadent house and therefore not considered so important as the angles, but it denotes the unexpressed, the motive behind the act, the thought behind the speech. When it denotes the *acts* of the native's life he will have so far advanced as to become a true magician, therefore the most the majority can hope to express from this house is speech, which is thus the true *Vach*, the gift of prophecy; the power to become clairvoyant with that clear vision which sees the future will be denoted by the mysterious potency which this house gives to planets found in it at birth.

A very good illustration of the ninth house in connection with travel will be found in the horoscope of Stanley Conder, published in Manual No. 12, *My Friends' Horoscopes.*

CHAPTER XVII

The Mid-Heaven or Tenth House

This is the house of honour, reputation, profession, business or occupation, and represents the public standing or worldly position of the native. It may be taken as the apex of the horoscope, or that portion which is thrust out most prominently into the busy life of the world. Good and evil must both alike find expression, and culminate in honour or dishonour; and the culminating point is the tenth house.

An action may be said to be the child of thought and desire, which are its parents. The impulse to action first arises in one of these two, either thought or desire; the other—whichever it may be—quickly responds; but the action cannot take place until circumstances permit. It is conceived by the coming together of thought and desire; it then lies in gestation for a longer or shorter period; and when circumstances are favourable, its birth as an action is a certainty. Of the innumerable potential actions thus conceived, a few come to birth during the present life and produce their effects. A very great many, however, are thwarted or held back by circumstances; and because, when once conceived, their birth is a certainty, they are carried over by the soul into a future incarnation, and there take effect as actions, inevitable and unavoidable. Regarded as indicative of actions, therefore, the horoscope at birth may be said to be the necessary outcome of those thoughts and desires that remained unexhausted at the death of the last personality. Present action is past character coming outward; present character is future action in the germ. Every astrologer knows that the indications of future actions can be detected in the horoscope of birth; and this therefore becomes a clue to the thoughts and desires of the past. For instance, an afflicted Venus shows that the affections were selfish or badly regulated; and the same planet well placed and aspected indicates that they were unselfish and good. The cause was started in the past and the effect is found in the present. Mr Gladstone was born with the Sun and Mercury rising in Capricorn; showing in the past a mind oving oratory and intellectual pursuits, and ambitious of power and distinction : and these causes, brought over into the present, resulted in such fated actions and inevitable events as are familiar to all.

The abuse of any principle, power, or quality, will sooner or later find us labouring under the adverse side of the influence proceeding from the planet corresponding to that principle ; and this may either happen in this life or it may be delayed until the future.   There are certain streams of living 'essence' on the way down towards expression in the lower kingdoms of nature ; and there are other streams tending upward towards expression in the higher kingdoms.   The ether is permeated with this 'essence' on these downward and upward arcs, and man can absorb or be temporarily influenced by either, according to his receptivity and his mental attitude.   The world is filled with love, compassion, and beneficent influences from beings higher than man ; but it is also clouded with man's own selfish, lustful, and passionate thoughts. Everything ruled by the forceful, animal and downward activity of Mars varies sympathetically with the aspects of that planet in the zodiac ; and on certain days this force is more powerfully present in the atmosphere than on others.   It may be that we give way to a fit of anger, jealousy, envy or resentment on a day when the Moon is afflicted by Mars ; and then the passions within are reinforced and strengthened by the influence without.   On the return of the Moon to the same affliction, or even at its next aspect by Mars, we shall be liable to repeat our former action. This, if often recurring, becomes a definite tendency, mood, or habit, and even a part of our character.   But, on the other hand, if the passions are firmly reined in, the transits of Mars and the Moon's evil aspects to that planet will have no dangers for us.   If we continually give way to discontent, peevishness or melancholy, we shall find ourselves coming more and more under the influence of Saturn, until, in some future birth, Saturn will sit darkly in our horoscope.

The ordinary man is generally content to drift aimlessly along, sometimes finding himself so fortunate as to be in harmony with the surrounding influences, and at other times beaten and buffeted by adverse storms.   In each case he is slowly learning a lesson, that certain qualities and actions are to be cultivated and certain others are to be avoided.   The more highly evolved man has passed through this stage of comparative indifference, and has entered upon another in which he sets himself very deliberately to avoid or control that which tends to evil.

and to work in harmony with those influences which result in good because they proceed mediately through the great hierarchies of star angels and ultimately from God Himself. In doing so he knowingly plans his own future, rearranges his own horoscope, and controls the forces at work therein.

Planets rise, culminate, and set ; and it is the culminating point, the mid-heaven, that is the most critical so far as planetary influence in worldly life is concerned. The horoscope ' progresses ' with the lapse of each day after birth ; and the influences concentrated in the ascendant are in this way elaborated, distributed, and carried round the circle of the heavens and enabled to produce their effects just at the right time and through the channel appropriate to each.

The probability is that each horoscope is taken up afresh where it was laid down in the last life ; so that, with certain exceptions and modifications, the birth horoscope represents either the progressed map or the death figure of the past. This has not yet been definitely proved, but it is the most feasible hypothesis.

NEPTUNE in the tenth house denotes a very strange career, unless the native is very undeveloped, in which case it will have little or no effect upon the life. It is possible to obtain benefit from this position, but this planet must be well aspected, and free from any affliction ; afflicted it is likely to cause much trouble, especially affecting the honour, often bringing undeserved scandal. No definite statement can be made as to the exact manner in which Neptune will affect the native when placed in the M.C., or, indeed, in any other house, but when in an angle it is reasonable to expect its influence to affect the physical conditions more than the psychic or mental.

URANUS in the tenth house denotes a chequered career, fortune and misfortune alternately. If Uranus is free from affliction the native becomes a unique character, and invents or originates a new line of activity for himself, breaking away from limited and conventional customs. This position denotes a curious life of ups and downs with many important changes of environment. If much afflicted the native is singularly unfortunate, and must make up his mind to be content to be a 'failure' in life. It is a position indicating a critical stage in the evolution of the native, in which the 'root of merit' is either firmly established or shaken from its centre. The native follows uncommon employments, has his own code of honour, and prefers to be a law unto himself, following the dictates of a higher law than that made by man.

SATURN in the tenth house denotes a precarious condition at some period of life. Saturn is essentially the planet of fate, and to all who are born with Saturn in the mid-heaven this text may be quoted—'And Satan took Him up into a high mountain and showed Him all these things.' The elevation of Saturn gives some power, pride, ambition, and persistent desire for material objects and worldly welfare. If well aspected the native will rise by his own perseverance and industry far above the sphere into which he was born. If afflicted, he will rise only to fall again, or will over-reach himself by a lack of proportion or ability to judge the limits to which he can expand. The affliction of the luminaries from Saturn in the M.C. brings dishonour or scandal, and many obstacles to progress; good aspects strengthen the character, but render progress slow and liable to interruption and delay. Saturn has power and dignity in the M.C., but much depends upon sign and aspect, for the unfolding of Saturn is proverbially slow, though sure.

JUPITER in the tenth house denotes much success and prosperity. The moral standard is very high, and the native holds a very secure and important position at some period of his life. This is one of the best positions for financial and social success. If afflicted: by Mars, legal troubles are threatened and heavy losses at certain periods; by Saturn, the good influence of Jupiter in the M.C. is vitiated, and almost rendered nil ; by Uranus, grave reverses of fortune, and a liability to become involved in serious difficulties. If the luminaries afflict Jupiter it hinders social success, and brings difficulty in connection with travel and changes of position ; but when well aspected thereby much success is denoted, both social and financial. This position generally shows good birth, and help through relatives. Jupiter has less power in airy or earthy signs when in the M.C., and has chief potency in either fiery or watery signs, especially Sagittarius and Cancer.

MARS in the tenth house denotes an ambitious and masterful spirit. It is favourable for success in business or profession, since the energy of the native is able to carry him through the turbulent and stormy periods he will experience in the business world. The native does not prosper when in business for himself, unless in an occupation of the nature of Mars, and this planet well aspected. The animal and passional side of the nature is likely to override the intellectual, and impulse or feeling to be much more prominent than reason. The native will not escape scandal or ill-repute, whether deserved in the present life or not. If afflicted by Uranus, the native either becomes immoral or is carried away by impulse and commits some rash act. Afflicted by Saturn the native is vindictive, resentful, and unforgiving, or over-critical and sceptical. Afflicted by Jupiter, improvident and wasteful, or over-enthusiastic and self-deceptive. If well aspected the native is courageous and brave, but acts more from impulse and instinct than reason.

THE SUN in the tenth house denotes honour and success in life, a good moral heredity, and the favour of persons of power and position. It gives fortune and prosperity toward the middle portion of life; right means of livelihood, and the ability to become independent, prosperous, and successful in whatever business, profession, or occupation the native may follow. If much afflicted it denotes arrogance and pride and position held under protest or by right of birth more than by right of merit. If well aspected distinction, authority and permanent success in life. This position causes the native to occupy places of trust, important posts of honour or responsibility, which will be maintained or lost according to sign and aspect. It favours the vital temperament, governmental positions, and generally denotes good birth or favourable hereditary conditions.

VENUS in the tenth house denotes success in life and high moral stamina. It favours artistic or musical pursuits and gives general prosperity, also the favour and good esteem of exalted persons. The native has merit and ability, is generally very well disposed and succeeds through possessing a pleasant and agreeable manner. If in trine or sextile aspect with Jupiter the native will have some social distinction, or good reputation with great financial success at some period of life. If afflicted, the influence of Venus is not materially affected but there is a lack of opportunity to express ability. The adverse aspects of the Moon are not favourable to Venus, and they affect this benefic planet more unfavourably than the aspects of the planets, but on the other hand the favourable aspects of the Moon to Venus are particularly good. This position favours marriage, money and friendships, also those occupations, arts or businesses where the needs of women are catered for, such as milliner, modiste, fancy confectioner, etc.

MERCURY in the tenth house denotes success or failure according to sign and aspects.   It generally gives ability to successfully undertake commissions and agencies, or causes the native to adopt several professions and undertakings.   If well aspected this position denotes tact and a clear mind with fertility of resource.   If much afflicted, cunning and deception, with inclination to act dishonestly or indiscreetly, the moral standard being sacrificed for mental interests, while tact and diplomacy become deceit and craftiness, according to the sign Mercury occupies.   Afflicted by Mars, without any good aspects to mitigate, untruthfulness and impulsive speech are denoted; afflicted by Saturn, without other mitigating influences, tendencies to commit forgery and embezzlement.   Mercury has very little dignity in the M.C. unless very well aspected and in a good sign.   It may give fluent speech and retentive memory.

THE MOON in the tenth house denotes fame and publicity, fluctuation and change in business, or occupation.   Ephemeral success without permanent stability or assured position.   If afflicted this will bring notoriety and scandal.   If well aspected many advantageous and desirable changes.   In cardinal signs it denotes great ambition and a very active life.   In fixed signs more stability and perseverance, but less activity and change or progress.   In mutable signs less fortune and more ability without adequate opportunity.   If afflicted by Mars this position will bring scandal of a public nature or discredit which will injure the native's future.   If afflicted by Saturn, many difficulties and obstacles to overcome.   If well aspected by Jupiter, much success and prosperity. Birth is generally poor or in an indifferent environment.

PROFESSION OR EMPLOYMENT

It is not necessary to fix the attention solely upon the tenth house to discover the business, profession or employment that the native will follow.   In the present state of civilisation many persons follow professions for which they are not qualified or naturally fitted.   In such cases unless able to adapt themselves to their environment and take an interest in the occupation followed, it is likely to be undertaken either as a necessary but unwelcome means of livelihood or else from merely sordid motives.   The planet or planets in the mid-heaven will, in the majority of cases, denote the trade, business or profession, but when none are found in this part of the nativity, the houses and the signs containing the majority of the planets must be carefully considered.

The sixth house is especially related to a business or profession followed through pressure of necessity, or force of circumstances, rather than from choice or direct ambition.

A Nativity with the majority of the planets in :

FIERY signs gives ingenuity and energy, and fits the native to study mechanics and to follow any trade or profession in which fire is a necessary element in the production of the goods handled, sold, or worked with.

AIRY signs denote skill in some literary occupation, scientific pursuits or any profession wherein the mind and brain are more exercised than the body. It would make the native a lawyer, writer, mathematician, draughtsman, designer, artist, clerk, reporter, teacher, novelist, poet, etc.

WATERY signs favour all employments in which liquid is used, from mineral waters to wines and spirits, or from washing clothes to sailing yachts. Also emotional acting, elocution, etc.

EARTHY signs give employment in connection with buildings, mining, and all laborious, heavy and slow work in which time, labour and persever- ance are required. Virgo inclines to chemistry, Taurus to agriculture or finance, Capricorn to administrative or political positions.

CARDINAL signs denote ability to take up pioneer work, to engage in callings that are new, inventive, and of a public nature. It fits the native to undertake new enterprises, and also to adopt those professions that require speed, ingenuity, quick wit, tact and diplomacy. It also denotes that the native will be aspiring and ambitious, never resting until he is his own master or at the head of whatever pursuit he follows.

FIXED signs give the native ability to plod and work industriously, and to succeed best where he can exercise patience, endurance and quiet determination. It favours employment under government, civil service, ancient institutions, old-established businesses, and professions that are stable and conventional. It inclines to the medical profession, or the navy.

MUTABLE signs fit the native to become a better servant than master ; an agent, messenger, clerk, traveller, teacher, editor, speaker : but unless the nativity shows exceptional success he would do best in the employ of others. It sometimes denotes occupations in which uniform is worn, or work in institutions and public companies or where public commodities are dealt with.

The task of deciding which planet, house, or sign will best signify the occupation is not an easy one. As has been pointed out, not only do many people, perhaps most, follow pursuits they find more or less distasteful, but some change their occupation more than once, and others carry on two or more lines of activity at the same time, such as business and politics, or business and preaching. If many planets are in one sign, things signified by that house and sign are sure to be forced forward, but whether they will be fortunate or otherwise depends upon the nature of the combination, i.e., whether it is more benefic or malefic.

As a general rule people like occupations at which they succeed, and dislike those at which they fail, and whether they will do the one or the other depends upon whether or no benefic planets and aspects predominate in any given combination.   If there are not several planets in one sign, it is as well to count those in the groups of signs, cardinal, fixed, mutable, etc., as just given.   It must be remembered, however, that a smaller number of planets in an angular sign (especially first or tenth) may outweigh a larger number in a sign not angular.   The strongest planet in the map should be carefully considered, also that which is closest to the Sun or in closest aspect to the Sun; attention being paid to whether such planet is angular, whether it has dignity in tenth, or second, whether it is strong by sign and fortunate by aspect, and whether it is elevated or not.   The consideration of signs and groups of signs usually gives a better indication than the planets alone, because these may change their nature according to sign.

For instance, Mars in Scorpio may indicate a soldier or sailor: but Mars in Gemini one who fights with his mind only, a debater, political speaker, barrister, etc.

NEPTUNE appears to favour the sea in all its varied means of finding occupation and work.   It has also to do with spiritualism, psychism, etc.   In regard to business, those interested in the cotton industry are, it is said, frequently found to have this position at birth.

URANUS fits the native to follow uncommon and original pursuits, to study inventions, reconstruct, and undertake new and improved methods, to create new professions or adopt unique plans of work, etc.

SATURN fits the native to undertake grave responsibility, also to follow pursuits that require deep study or patient planning; architects, land surveyors, contractors, miners, builders, holders of public positions and offices, municipal or state officials, etc., are signified by Saturn.

JUPITER gives success as merchants, physicians, lawyers, ministers, bankers, and persons in whom much trust and confidence are placed, also in all employments of a lucrative and fruitful nature in which other people's money is principally concerned, such as trustees, stockbrokers and money-changers, etc.

MARS, employments and professions in which muscular energy is necessary, hazardous and skilful occupations in which there is always an element of risk and danger; such as soldier, surgeon, dentist, worker in metals, chemist, engineer, sailor, agitator, etc.

THE SUN will give love of power, with ability to rule and command, and will fit the native for government employment and professions or business to which much dignity and honour are attached.

VENUS, refined and artistic occupations and all business directly concerned with females, adornment, finery, jewellery, amusements, pleasure, luxury, etc.

MERCURY, literature, agencies, clerical work, and all employments requiring study, skill, and ingenuity.

THE MOON will give ability in business or employments of a fluctuating and changing nature, such as a seafaring life or travelling about from place to place, from hawking goods to advertising on the largest scale, dealing in novelties, etc.

In addition to the ruler it is necessary also to note the planet in closest aspect thereto, and also to pay special attention to the planet Mercury, which as ruler of the mental faculties has a very important influence over the business abilities and chances of success.

Mercury in conjunction with Uranus will cause the mind to be more inventive and will bring the mental conditions to those of Uranus. When partaking of Saturn's nature there will be more organising power and ability to manage others, also to study deep and grave subjects such as chemistry, science, etc. When partaking of Jupiter's nature, philosophical tendencies, and ability to put the mind into profitable undertakings. When partaking of the nature of Mars the wit is sharpened and the profession is more of the commercial and enterprising type. The following hints will be serviceable.

EMPLOYMENTS DENOTED BY MERCURY'S ASPECTS

♆ ☌ . Inclines towards some pursuit of an artistic nature, where the æsthetic instincts can have full play. There is usually ability for either music or painting.

♆ , △. Similar to conjunction, but influence not so marked.

♆ □, ☍. This is rather a deceptive influence, and natives will be vague or unpractical, or, worse still, deceitful. They usually have certain fundamentally wrong notions. Subtle and plausible, full of schemes.

♅ ☌ . Inventors, novelists, lecturers, patent agents, electricians, magnetic healers, mesmerists, astrologers and psychologists.

♅ ⚹, △. Metaphysicians, advanced scientists, chemists of the progressive order. Investigators, explorers, teachers, divines, and world reformers. Hydropaths.

♅ □ ☍. Hypnotists, antiquarians, dealers in antiquities and curiosities, astronomers, reporters, sensational novelists and those who are oddities, eccentrics and cranks, generally having distorted views and notions.

♄ ☌. Organisers, managers, solicitors, government officials, stationers, surveyors, detectives, and those who follow secretive and diplomatic occupations.

♄ ⚹, △. Architects, builders, contractors, lawyers, scientists, mining engineers, coal merchants, geologists, and those whose employment requires care, skill, and sound judgment.

♄ □, ☍. Bookbinders, printers, carpenters, potters, bricklayers, miners, and those who labour with body as well as mind, particularly with the hands and brain combined, such as dyers, etc.

♃ ☌. Ministers, ambassadors, judges; councillors, merchants, philosophers, and those who exercise judgment and combine the social element with the mental, feeling and thinking.

♃ ⚹, △. Barristers, bankers, town councillors, government officials, and all those who occupy posts of trust, distinction and honour employing their minds for social welfare and the common good.

♃ □, ☍. Clothiers, provision dealers; drapers, upholsterers, officers, and those who cater for the public, or who hold the lower government offices, where unpleasant duties are performed.

♂ ☌. Sculptors, carvers, artists in wood, engravers, cricketers, footballers, wrestlers, strong men, mechanics, soldiers, etc.

♂, ⚹ △. Chefs, stewards, publicans, and those who attend to the tastes of others. It also denotes surgical instrument makers, and all who combine skill with mental and muscular work.

♂ □, ☍. Butchers, cattle-men, tanners, masons, labourers, iron workers, and those who may be skilful, but have to follow coarse and low callings, in which grime and dirt play a prominent part, such as scavengers, lavatory attendants, etc.

♀ ☌. Musicians, painters, artists, speakers, and those who minister to the minds of others. Somewhat similar to the conjunction with Neptune.

☉ ☌ } These act largely through the sign and house in which they are
☽ ☌ } placed.

Each ruler may be joined with other planets, and combinations made according to the ingenuity of the student. Practice will suggest many occupations which will appeal to the native. Do not judge forgers, or those who live by sharp practice or by their wits, unless ☿ is afflicted by both ♂ and ♄ without any signs of moral stamina in other directions. Saturn and Mars will make the employment more practical and laborious than Jupiter or Venus, but at the same time the whole horoscope must be well weighed before a definite and decisive opinion can be given.

As a general significator of avocation, Saturn, being the ruler of Capricorn, the natural tenth house in the order of the signs, is important and should have a very careful consideration.

CHAPTER XVIII

The Eleventh House—Friends, Hopes and Wishes

THIS house is that of friends, acquaintances, hopes, wishes, aspirations. It belongs to the triangle of the seventh and third houses, and has a great deal in common with both of these. By secondary influence it stands to the seventh house as the fifth stands to the first; that is, it is the fifth house of the marriage partner, and therefore has to be taken into account when considering questions concerning children and the other affairs of the fifth house. Taken by itself, free from affliction, it may be considered a benefic house, as its natural tendency seems to be towards good fortune, pleasure, happiness and prosperity; and benefics in this house or planets well aspected will benefit the native, socially or otherwise, and lift him up in the world, according to the nature of the planet. It has a great deal of sympathy also with the tenth house; and is often found containing strong or fortunate planets in the horoscopes of persons who are prominent in politics, in municipal affairs, or who in business matters are concerned with the many rather than the few, through factories, companies, associations, stores, societies, etc.

Its connection with the seventh house is shown in the fact that, in some cases, as alluded to in Chapter XIV, the lover or marriage partner is more accurately described by the eleventh house than by the seventh, as it stands for friendships that may end in marriage. But as a matter of fact, any house under consideration should be judged along with the other two that are in trine to it. For instance, if the eleventh house is examined in a question concerning friends, its relation to the seventh will show open friends, and to the third, secret or private friends Good aspects between planets in these three houses or between their rulers are extremely fortunate in the matters governed by them; the affairs signified are strengthened and benefited greatly; friends will hold firmly to the native and he will have pleasure and good luck through them, his family ties will be strong and fortunate, and marriage will benefit him socially.

Any planet in the eleventh house, whether good or bad, has some significance in connection with the class of persons the native will be likely to meet as friends or acquaintances ; but if bad aspects prevail the acquaintanceship will be followed by trouble. For instance, if Mercury is in the eleventh, writers, literary people, learned persons, and those born under Mercury or its signs will bulk largely in the native's life. If Venus, musicians, artists, actors, etc. ; and those born under Taurus and Libra ; and many pleasant friendships and acquaintances will be made in social life. When there is no planet in the house, the sign on the cusp will often indicate the class of persons with whom the native will come in contact as acquaintances, and the position of its ruler must therefore be taken into account also. But as a rule the influence of this house is lessened when there is no planet in it.

NEPTUNE in the eleventh house denotes unfavourable attachments, which rarely produce any lasting or satisfactory friendship. If much afflicted there is serious trouble and danger from friends and acquaintances. It signifies unique friendships, good or bad.

URANUS in the eleventh house denotes peculiar and remarkable friendships ; the native will meet with those who will either benefit or injure him considerably. Sudden and unusual attachments will be formed, and also sudden and unexpected estrangements. Much will depend upon the aspects formed by Uranus, also the general planetary positions. Uranus will *benefit* the native if he is able to respond to its vibrations, for this planet has more affinity with the eleventh house than with any other of the twelve. In one case it brought a fortune to a nurse who attended a sick man on a battlefield, although it gave her a serious disappointment through a drunken lover. It requires great skill to judge the true influence of Uranus.

SATURN in the eleventh house shows few friends, and these are liable to forsake the native, or give him advice ratner than practical help ; still the native will have a few faithful friends amongst those older or more thoughtful than himself, and if Saturn is well placed this will prove of real service to him.

This is an evil position if Saturn is afflicted by the Sun, Moon or Mars. If in the Cardinal signs failure is denoted, and probably ruin through acquaintances. If in Fixed signs, the early part of the life is subject to much delay and hindrance. In the Common signs, the native rarely achieves his ambitions. This is not a good position for marriage, relatives or superiors.

JUPITER in the eleventh house denotes many true and fortunate friends, by whom the native will always benefit. This position gives a love of social life, and causes the native to do much that will bring him friends and helpers. If in conjunction or good aspect with :

♆ Mystical acquaintances and friends. Sometimes indicative of great wealth.

♅ Remarkable enlightenment and assistance by means of religious, philosophic or highly-connected people, or occultists.

♄ A lasting attachment, from which much good will come.

♂ If afflicted by this planet, a lawsuit ; whereby the native will gain or lose according to the general tendency of the horoscope.

☉ Denotes fame and renown to the native, bringing very distinguished and honourable friendships.

☿ Much intuition and splendid judgment.

☽ Many benefits through travel and the public generally.

In the Fixed signs Jupiter in the eleventh house denotes pride and egotism ; in Cardinal signs, enterprise and progress ; in Mutable signs, religious and domestic experiences.

MARS in the eleventh house shows few real friends, but several acquaintances whose influence upon the native is not in any way likely to add to his reputation. If Mars is in a watery or airy sign this position denotes friends who will turn enemies. If afflicted by :

♆ Dipsomaniacs or very questionable characters.

♅ Very tragic and fateful friendships.

♄ Violence or grievous injury.

If afflicting Jupiter, lawsuits and financial loss through friends. If Mars is strong by sign and aspect, but not the ruling planet, the native's friends will overrule and dominate him, and their advice will tend to bring about his ruin : it is an unfavourable position unless the horoscope denotes a considerable amount of mind control.

THE SUN in the eleventh house is a favourable position. It gives the good-will of elders, superiors, masters, those who are more powerful or of higher rank or standing than the native. If in business, he rises through association with these and benefits by them, even though they may not be his friends in the sense of manifesting affection for him. If in some profession or public occupation he is likely to rise in the same way and be a man of some note. Socially it gives some degree of ambition, ostentation, respect for dignitaries, superiors, and the fashions and customs of good society. The native will gain in reputation and esteem through his friends; will make the acquaintance of prominent people and those who hold important posts; will have definite ambitions and desires, and—if well aspected—sufficient strength of will or good luck to carry them out. It is a good position for material welfare and general prosperity, for increase of reputation, and for the holding of public appointments or positions of responsibility. It generally denotes a loyal mind and honesty of purpose, with a sense of self-esteem, dignity, superiority and worth, and gives success about middle life or soon afterwards.

VENUS in the eleventh house denotes much gain and help through friends, whose desire will be to forward the interests of the native, and who will help him by thoughts of kindness and goodwill, as well as by action. The planets aspecting Venus are important. If in conjunction or good aspect with:

⊙   Gain and prosperity through friends, especially women.
☽   Love of pleasure, society, amusements, popularity.

If applying to the conjunction of:

♅   A very remarkable love affair or attachment, where extreme disparity of age or other unusual features exist; platonic love.
♅   A romantic and extraordinary love attachment, the result of some great fascination.
♄   A fatalistic and very sad attachment.
♃   Great joy and happiness through friends.
♂   Passionate attachments and impulsive affections.
☿   Danger of deception through clever men.

If afflicted by Mars or Saturn, unfortunate friends. But no harm will ever come to this native through his friends unless he is inclined to go to excess in pleasure and indulgence.

MERCURY in the eleventh house denotes friends who appeal to the mind more than the feelings, also in a general sense those who are younger than the native; but if afflicted, deceitful and false friends are shown. The sign Mercury occupies will show the nature of the friends. When in:

♈   Quarrelsome and assertive acquaintances.
♉   Dogmatic and stubborn yet faithful friends.
♊   Clever and accomplished friends.
♋   Peculiar attachments to inferiors.
♌   Noble friendships and much help from others.
♍   Learned friends who are clever and well disposed.

♎   Artistic friendships and good acquaintances.
♏   Treacherous and mischievous acquaintances.
♐   Friends showy and clever but shallow.
♑   Crafty and untrustworthy acquaintances.
♒   Faithful and sincere friendships.
♓   Talkative and inquisitive acquaintances.

The native should be careful not to become surety for others if Mercury is afflicted, especially if by Jupiter.

THE MOON in the eleventh house, if fairly well placed and aspected, gives a large number of acquaintances, either of a social and domestic character, or among the general public, equals, and inferiors: more acquaintances than friends in fact. It is good for family life and for the sociable and domestic side of the nature, giving ability to fraternise and mix easily with other people: it is also good for the native's children.

It is necessary to note the sign that the Moon occupies when in this house, also the nature of the aspects formed. When in:

♈   Romances and adventures in connection with friends.
♉   Intrigues and sensuous acquaintances.
♊   Dual attachments, friendly disposed relatives.
♋   Friends in the domestic circle, strange experiences.
♌   Ardent affections, poetical and idealistic friends.
♍   Peculiar friendships, attachment to inferiors.
♎   Marriage to a friend. It favours platonic unions.
♏   Secret attachments, fatal attachments, tragedy.
♐   Loyal friendships, gain through attachments.
♑   Inconsistency and deception amongst acquaintances.
♒   Varied friendships, faithful attachments.
♓   Hospitable friends, mediumistic acquaintances.

If the Moon is afflicted by Mars or Saturn sorrows and losses through friends will occur.

Although the eleventh house in general represents friendships, yet these are not to be judged exclusively from this house, for the horoscope of another may so blend as to produce a lasting friendship that is not wholly shown by the eleventh house. The luminaries in favourable accord in two nativities will produce sympathy, while if, moreover, the ascendants be in good aspect to one another a lasting and firm friendship will result; again, acquaintance will ripen into friendship if in two horoscopes the ruling planets are in favourable aspect to each other.

Friendships will occur between two persons when the ruler of one transits the ascendant of another. Saturn's transits will bring friends who are older than the native and whose influence will be according to the nature of the aspects formed.

Jupiter will bring friendships arising out of religious or social intercourse, and which are likely to be both pleasant and beneficial. Mars and Venus friendships awaken the emotional side of the nature and, if between opposite sexes, lead to amours or attachments in which the feelings or passions are aroused. In all friendships Venus will be the planet most affected, by its own position, and by the planet which in another horoscope occupies the same place; for Venus is the planet of union and of communion.

♆ being a negative planet of the nature of Venus herself, is most affected by its opposite, Mars, and often produces a strong sympathy or affinity of a remarkable character, if only the senses are not allowed free rein.

♅ will cause strange romantic attachments which do not always end happily, unless there is great self-control, the feelings being very violently affected.

♄ will cause affinity through some sorrow, fatalistic tendency, or ties connected with the past, which will steadily cool the affections, bringing them to a critical stage from which grave issues will spring.

♃ will bring social affinity and friendship through hospitality.

♂ will produce a strong attachment in which feeling and emotion are chiefly concerned ; but this chiefly in opposite sexes.

☉ in one horoscope on the place of Venus in another will produce a happy and pleasurable friendship.

☿ will give affinity in music, art, or mental intercourse.

☽ in one horoscope will have a similar effect, tending to make friendship more permanent and lasting.

Mars on the place of Venus will produce magentic attraction in which the senses will sooner or later play a prominent part, while Saturn on the place of Venus will produce a mental fascination, in which the mind will play a more prominent part than the senses.

If the benefic planets are in sympathy in two horoscopes friendship and true affinity will result, but if the malefic planets are in adverse aspect in two horoscopes then enmity or discord will be the outcome of acquaintanceship. Similarly with the luminaries, according as they are aspected either by benefics or malefics.

In this way friends or enemies may be judged from the nativity by noting the planets in aspect to the Sun or Moon. Saturn afflicting either will denote trouble and probably sorrow from persons older than the native, or who are of the nature of Saturn (according to the sign it is in at birth). Mars afflicting the luminaries will denote trouble and pain through martial persons, according to the sign and house in which Mars was placed at birth.

The following case will illustrate this, showing how fate will punish by affinity. A lady who has Saturn elevated above all the other planets in the sign Cancer in the mid-heaven, and afflicting her ruling planet, has all her life (now fifty years) suffered through the influence of her father, and the weaker he became (♄ in ♋) the more acutely did she suffer. The bond of affection between them was the Sun in the father's horoscope on the place of the Moon in his daughter's nativity. They were alternately attracted and repelled—loving and hating each other at intervals.

Careful judgment will reveal all enemies to be overcome, by the position of the malefics, and the aspects they form to any of the planets in the nativity. It is always safe to consider true friends to be shown where the benefics in one horoscope occupy the place of the luminaries or ascendant in the other, and, similarly, enemies by the malefics. It is also important to notice that those who are seeking to rule their stars overcome their enemies by *love*, and ever seek to return good for evil; but in the less evolved this will not be the case.

In regard to attractions between two individuals—more especially, perhaps, between those of opposite sex—it must be remembered that Nature is ever seeking to supply deficiencies and to counterbalance excess. Hence, any given native, or any given portion of a horoscope, will always be most strongly attracted by his or its *opposite*, even as the seventh house is opposite to the first. We must therefore expect to find the greatest attraction between opposite planets : thus, Mars will attract Venus, and *vice versâ*; Saturn, Jupiter; the Sun, the Moon; and so on. Not only so, but one nativity, *as a whole*, may attract another as a whole, although there may be no specific points of contact discernible. For instance, when one nativity shows a strong predominance of the Martial and Jupiterian characteristics, however these may be displayed,—by the two planets rising, or in reception, or by Martial and Jupiterian signs being prominent,—such a person will be strongly attracted to one whose nativity shows a marked excess of the Venusian and Saturnian qualities. And such an attraction, being more general than particular in its nature, is likely to prove more lasting and deeper in its effects than such as are signified merely by the sympathy of one pair of planets.

In this, as in all other departments of Natal Astrology, it is ever necessary to keep a watchful eye upon the horoscope as a whole, whenever concentrating special attention on any detail.   But the above considerations will throw light on many problems of mutual attraction that are likely to come before the student, and which may puzzle him because the cause of the attraction is not immediately apparent.

It must be remembered that Nature is greater than Man, and has her own problems to solve, which are more important than his, and that she works more largely by generals than by particulars.   Thus, when it becomes necessary that the custom of inter-marriage in a clan or tribe should be broken up, some individual will be found powerfully attracted to one outside that clan or tribe, and the whole weight of tradition, custom, and tribal prejudice, with its weapons of disinheritance and ostracism, will be found powerless to prevail against this new attraction. Instances of this kind, of course, are comparatively rare, but they serve to show that Nature, 'ever careful of the type,' cares nothing for individual interest or prejudice.

This is a fitting place to state the fact of there being seven distinct types of individuals in the world, each type being directly or indirectly connected with its own planetary ray, all persons thus being more or less influenced by the planetary spirit to whom they belong.   And until this truth is recognised, and the fact known that although we are all *one in essence* as 'Divine Fragments,' yet all are 'coloured' differently, there must continue to be sympathies and antipathies.   This accounts for the pronounced Martial types having very little sympathy for the Saturnine types, and *vice versâ*.   It is difficult for the unevolved to understand that it is the decree of Nature to produce distinctions for purposes of evolution, and until the law of magnetic vibration is understood this law will continue to distress many other wise well-disposed folk.   Hatred is often the result of magnetic conditions affecting each person discordantly, while on the other hand affinities expressing true friendship are those produced by the rhythmic interblending of the rays, resulting in harmonious vibration.

The value of Astrology is here demonstrated, for true friendship is rarely found when the planets Mars or Saturn in one horoscope are found upon the luminaries or the planets Jupiter and Venus respectively in another; thus :—*Saturn* on Sun or Venus, *Mars* on Moon or Jupiter.

If it should be found impossible to agree with those who are vibrating differently or discordantly, it is always best not to *force* the friendship, or serious consequences in the end will surely result. Cultured and refined persons often sacrifice themselves, and make great effort in seeking to harmonise themselves with others with whom they find themselves in antipathy. In many cases, however, this antipathy is a true safeguard and a protection, and it is therefore rarely wise to force the good feeling until the time is ripe to blend the magnetism. This time will come, for 'to understand all is to pardon all.'

CHAPTER XIX

The Twelfth House—the 'House of Self-Undoing'

THE twelfth house is generally supposed to be the house of sorrow, enemies, imprisonment and misfortune. This is probably owing to its being one of the houses belonging to the psychic trinity; and, as the cadent houses of that triangle, it is the least fortunate of the three.

Before concluding our consideration of the twelve houses it will be as well if we analyse the value of the cardinal, succedent, and cadent houses. By doing so we shall obtain a clearer understanding as to why the twelfth house should be thought so very unfortunate.

The Cardinal houses or 'Angles' represent the physical body, and all that is expressed by action in the outer or external world; they are quick, acute, active, energetic, open. They concern the *head* chiefly.

The Succedent houses are less physical and material in their nature, being more in sympathy with the feelings and emotions. They govern principally the trunk of the body, and the *heart* is thus affected more than any other part. These succedent houses are not as plainly expressed in the outer or physical world as are the cardinal houses, but they are more closely related to the inner strength of the character.

The Cadent houses are the least expressed of any signs; they govern the mind and thought more than emotion or action, and are more closely related to the *limbs* of the body than the other signs.

In the mutable signs we may trace the birth of thought and intellectual conceptions apart from worldly knowledge or practice; therefore all influences connected with the mutable signs are, more or less, latent. The third, sixth, ninth and twelfth signs in the order of the signs are common or mutable signs and in the order of the twelve houses are the 'cadent' houses; these are 'unfortunate,' owing to their latency or lack of practical external expression.

In Natal Astrology, influences coming from these cadent houses are often accompanied by lack of opportunity and inability to bring practical worldly success or reward, no matter how great the merit or skill. In other words, they lack *power*.   In the succedent houses and signs there is more power, but it is sometimes silent power awaiting favourable expression ; while in the cardinal signs and houses whatever power or merit there is in the native is expressed.   Now in common with the other houses, the twelfth house may be either fortunate or unfortunate, but only with regard to that which the house denotes.   But, for the reasons stated, when afflicted it is most unfortunate.

The fourth house denotes psychic power, which will become occultism, 'white' or 'black' according to the status or development of the native psychically or spiritually.   The eighth house is related to the astral world, in which psychic feeling is intensified after the death of the physical body.   The twelfth house is related to the psychic mind, in which receptivity or mental sensitiveness to the unseen worlds is awakened ; therefore it is known as the house of self-undoing, which in some cases may mean the breaking up of the concrete physical condition by a leaning toward the occult side of things.   The twelfth house, then, may denote sorrow in matters of an external or purely physical type ; trouble and difficulty in matters of an emotional character ; annoyance, worry and anxiety in matters intellectual or mental—but in *this* relation it may also bring joy and peace.   It is the house of the voluntary recluse as well as of the pauper, the invalid and the prisoner. It is also the house of enemies, or may show the native to be his own worst enemy.*   It is the most mysterious of all the twelve houses.

NEPTUNE in the twelfth house exerts an influence which is very difficult to foresee when good, or to guard against when evil.   When afflicted, the native is in danger of all sorts of secret enmity, underhand conduct from others, and treachery.   When well aspected he benefits through affairs that are kept secret, and through matters that even his friends do not suspect ; its influence is then good for all secret concerns and occupations, detective work. private agencies, etc., as well as for occultism.   This is not altogether a bad position for Neptune, being related to the sign Pisces, with which this planet has much sympathy.

URANUS in the twelfth house is unfavourable for all except those who are inclined to act from occult or from psychic motives, in which case it favours mysterious, romantic, and out-of-the-common actions. For those who have unfortunate horoscopes it is evil, denoting confine-

* This may be generally judged when the same sign is on cusps of both twelfth and first.

ment in hospitals or public institutions, etc., and threatening somewhat similar dangers to those indicated by Saturn in this house. If much afflicted there may be trouble or danger from psychic sources, and the native may lose money or reputation, or both, if he follows a Uranian occupation. He should be very careful as to his methods of investigating psychic matters.

SATURN in the twelfth house denotes one who is very reserved and fond of solitude, with strong inclinations to become a recluse. It is an unfavourable position for all save those who love to work in secret and live by themselves. If much afflicted the native easily makes enemies, and may suffer imprisonment or enforced confinement at some period of his life. If afflicted by :

♅ Persistent enmity of powerful persons, loss of honour and reputation, social degradation.
♂ Danger of suicide or other tragic end.
☉ or ☽ Sorrow through death of loved ones, and a tendency to despond and suffer from melancholia.
☿ Danger of hypochondria or mental delusions.

The good aspects in this position give acquisitiveness and a love of secretly hoarding money.

JUPITER in the twelfth house denotes success in occult studies, and a respect for the sacred and ancient beliefs. It also gives success in a quiet and mysterious manner of which the general public are unaware. It enables the native to gain either directly or indirectly through his enemies, or to turn them into friends, even against their will. This position gives dual love affairs ; or some peculiar experience in connection with the affections which is evidently beneficial to the native. It will bring success toward the middle or latter portion of the native's life, and tends to bring him secret aid and help from good friends, even when afflicted. It makes him charitable and philanthrophic and willing to help others. It is good for physicians, clergy, officers of public institutions, hospitals, etc. The native is benefited through the philanthropy of others and by public institutions. It is unfavourable when Jupiter is in Scorpio or Virgo.

MARS in the twelfth house denotes strange and unfortunate adventures, in which grave dangers to the native are to be apprehended if he is shown to act more from impulse than reason ; to decide this the position and aspects of Mercury must be studied. The native is liable to false imprisonment, treachery through misplaced affection, and

Injuries from enemies. In some cases this position denotes poverty, or a difficulty to make headway, especially if Mars is placed in Libra or Pisces. Those having this position would do well to avoid spiritualistic seances, mediumship, etc., for there may be danger of obsession. If afflicted by :

♅	Detention in an asylum ; tendencies to violence.
♄	Imprisonment is shown.
♃	Ruin financially and socially.
☽	A sad end to the life.

The good aspects of the Sun and Venus improve this position; but it is more unfortunate than favourable, unless Mars rules the fourth, in which case the native may create his own dignity.

THE SUN in the twelfth house denotes that one-third, if not more, of the native's life will be unfortunate and liable to obscurity ; but from misfortune and sorrow he will rise to success, principally by his own efforts. He will have strong leanings towards the occult and psychic side of life, will be estranged from his parents, and will be one apart from his family. If the Sun is afflicted by Mars, Saturn or Uranus, the whole life will be one of sorrow and affliction, but if well aspected by Jupiter or Saturn the native will be capable of much self-sacrifice and endurance. Care must be taken to note the sign the Sun occupies ; if in a watery sign the mediumistic tendencies are accentuated. Sorrow through things indicated by the sign generally comes to the native. Thus, when in :

♈	Trouble through persons in authority, and tragedy.
♉	Occult ability, indirect gain through secret enemies.
♊	Misfortunes through relatives and in travel.
♋	Gives a keen interest in all occult studies.
♌	Secret love affairs, trouble through the opposite sex.
♍	Psychic tendencies, a love of magic and phenomena.
♎	Painful separations, loss of honour and credit.
♏	Powerful enemies, long voyages, a tragic end.
♐	Sorrow through death of loved ones, enemies.
♑	Misfortune in marriage and in love affairs.
♒	Occult tastes, keen intuition, ill-health.
♓	Strange enemies, fondness for spiritualism.

The Sun gives faith, and generally denotes faith in matters concerning the house in which the Sun is placed. If the Sun is not afflicted by the Moon, the native generally emerges from obscurity and makes the latter part of the life very eventful and fortunate; but all persons born with the Sun in the twelfth house are more or less eccentric, or possess uncommon tastes and inclinations.

VENUS in the twelfth house inclines to romance, and denotes obscure or clandestine love affairs. The native will be involved in a strong attachment, which will escape the notice of others unless the planet Venus is afflicted by Mars or the Moon; if well aspected, a fortunate love affair will lend interest to the native's life. This position often causes an early marriage, but brings the native into contact with those who may have power to influence the affections after marriage; where Venus is afflicted by Saturn, divorce or separation will result as the outcome of this second attachment, but if well aspected the native has the power to love unselfishly, and will do much for those he loves. This is a dangerous position if Venus is in either Scorpio or Capricorn, and also in some cases, when in Aries or Cancer.

MERCURY in the twelfth house denotes a peculiarly subtle mind, one loving risks and dangerous adventures of a secret nature; if well aspected the native has ability for occultism, and is well able to investigate mysteries or to follow unusual modes of thought. If afflicted, the native, although possessed of undoubted ability, will lack opportunity; in fact this position usually gives efficiency and practical knowledge which it is found difficult to express. In many cases the native underrates his own powers and is sadly lacking in self-esteem and this, if Mercury be afflicted by Mars or Jupiter, will lessen his conscientiousness. The sign Mercury occupies will considerably modify its influence.

THE MOON in the twelfth house denotes a life in which restrictions and limitations play a prominent part. This is the ideal position for a monk or nun, a hospital surgeon or nurse, for it favours all out-of-sight sympathy or work. The native will either carry the secret of another, or have some secrets of his own which would injure him if known to others. This position gives a love of occultism, mystery or romance. Unless the Moon is very well aspected it is not good, causing the native to be lacking in firmness or stability of character and hence far too easily led by others; it somewhat inclines to mediumship or interest in spiritualism. If under any spell of the opposite sex, he or she will be indiscreet in love affairs and inclined to allow the senses to dominate the reason; this causes the native to act foolishly, and to suffer financial loss thereby. If the Moon is afflicted by Mars or Uranus, much worry and trouble will be caused by the native's own folly.

GENERAL REMARKS ON CHAPTERS VI TO XIX

As a conclusion to this detailed consideration of the Twelve Houses, it will be well to draw the student's attention to the relative values of (*a*) houses, (*b*) signs, and (*c*) rulers of signs, when judging a nativity.

Those people who come solely or chiefly under the influences of (*a*) the houses and their rulers alone, apart from the signs occupying them or the planets governing those signs, are such as are entirely bound by heredity and environment and who live more or less the life of the *senses* —who, in fact, are utterly 'conventional'; while on the other hand those who move with the progressive nature of things are not so much limited by the houses, being more influenced by the nature either of (*b*) the *desires*, indicated by the signs of the zodiac, or (*c*) the *mental conditions*, described by the planets in those signs; or even, in the case of the truly original, by the planets themselves, apart from all reference to the signs they occupy. The latter will be more fully treated of in the second part of this work.

The following table will well repay study; it indicates the true value appertaining to each house of the horoscope:

+	☽	☉	Nature	Element
I.	V.	IX.	Individual	△
II.	VI.	X.	Temporal	☐
III.	VII.	XI.	Relative	⚌
IV.	VIII.	XII.	Terminal	▽

This table represents the whole scheme. The cross denotes the body ☽, denotes the soul, and ☉ the spirit. The elements fire, earth, air, and water, are respectively shown by a triangle, a square, horizontal lines, and the triangle reversed. There are many other considerations arising out of this plan of the twelve houses, which the intuition of the reader will discover.

NOTE:—*The First Edition of* How to Judge a Nativity, Part I, *ended with this Chapter; the remainder is additional*

CHAPTER XX

A COMPENDIUM OF PLANETARY POSITIONS AND ASPECTS *

THE readings here given of the Destiny and Influence of the several Planets in each of the Twelve Signs, and their mutually modifying effect when in aspect, are based on the assumption that the planet in question is angular, well-aspected, or otherwise dignified in the horoscope, more especially when either rising or culminating; and particularly, of course, when ruler of the nativity. If, on the other hand, the said planet is weak by position, or much afflicted by aspect, its influence is so restricted and hampered thereby that the descriptions given can only be said to apply, if at all, as regards their less desirable characteristics.

It is just in such cases that the faculty of *judgment* must be brought into play; to determine, for instance, how far bad position or aspects will debilitate the favour of a 'benefic,' or to what extent favourable aspects and a powerful position will moderate the misfortunes attaching to a 'malefic.' This faculty, however, has to be acquired by each student *for himself*; it cannot be imparted by another.

Little useful purpose would be served by giving the influence of the two distant planets Neptune and Uranus in this chapter, which would only take up space which can ill be spared. Moreover, they have been already given in *Astrology for All*, (*pp.* 191 *to* 200), to which work the reader may be referred for further information. The aspects to these planets will be given, however, since they are not given in that work.

THE ASPECTS OF NEPTUNE

The whole question of Neptune's influence is at present in such an uncertain condition that the following notes on the planet's aspects do not profess to be other than tentative suggestions, to be corrected and added to as future experience may dictate.

The conjunction appears to be neither wholly good nor wholly evil.

---

* These were originally printed in *How to Judge a Nativity, Part II*.

♆ *and* ♅. This influence is very difficult to elucidate; for, apart from their obvious influence upon matters signified by mundane house and zodiacal sign, there does not seem to be much effect other than that upon mystical and occult affairs and out-of-the-way subjects and occupations. When in good aspect, the native will benefit through these, or will be favourably inclined to them or will come in contact with other people who follow such pursuits.

In bad aspect, he may be interested in such matters, but there will be obstacles and trouble of the nature of the signs and houses involved. The intuition is increased considerably, especially if the aspect is from the third or ninth houses, and various psychic gifts may be cultivated. It increases thoughtfulness and seriousness and may give some inclination to religion: it bestows ingenuity and originality of mind. The good aspect is decidedly favourable for those who actually study psychic matters.

♆ *and* ♄.—In good aspect the influence is not unlike that of ♅ just mentioned, especially if ♆ is the more elevated of the two. It is good generally for occupation, worldly standing, preserves the goodwill of acquaintances and the public, and wards off enemies. It increases concentration, intuition, depth and clearness of thought. Benefits those who follow psychic or unusual occupations, also those connected with the water; sensitives, psychics, etc., may meet with considerable success not only in developing their gifts but also in utilising them practically. It inclines somewhat to the company of serious or elderly people, and benefits through them. It controls and sobers the instincts and passions, such as drink, sex, etc. It seems probable that it may favour money, property, investments, shares, legacies.

In bad aspect, the above indications will be more or less reversed, and trouble or danger may attend any of these matters, generally acting through the signs and houses occupied by the two planets. Disrepute, ill-favour, scandal, are to be feared.

♆ *and* ♃.—In good aspect this refines and purifies, but at the same time strengthens, the feelings and all the social and emotional side of the nature. It favours courtesy, honour, candour, sincerity, gentlemanly feeling benevolence, sympathy. It increases the devotional and religious aspirations, although these may be directed into psychic, semi-occult, or unusual channels. If the aspect is close or the planets prominent some marked psychic experience, dream or vision, etc., may be met with ; astral travellings out of the body ; pre-natal reminiscences. It somewhat favours travelling. It improves the artistic, poetic, æsthetic side of the nature, and, if other positions co-operate, may aid in giving a touch of genius in matters pertaining to religion, poetry, music, art, or the stage. It increases the imagination ; and its general tendency is towards growth, increase and fertility in whatever department of the horoscope it may influence.

The bad aspects between these two planets are probably not very serious, but they may throw obstacles in the way of any of the matters mentioned above or cause some little trouble through them, as well as through those signified by house position.

♅ and ♂.—This influence is not easy to determine, as the two planets do not seem to have a great deal in common ; in fact they appear in some respects almost polar opposites, the one typically negative and the other extremely positive. When in bad aspect they are apt to increase the instincts, emotions, and passions too much ; to give undue tendency towards pleasure, sensation, self-indulgence ; and to slightly coarsen the nature. There may be danger arising out of the relations with the other sex, scandal and disrepute ; danger from the water and liquids, also of poisoning and contagious diseases. If the native dabbles in psychism, there will be astral delusions and deceits and risk of obsession. He will be liable to foolish ideas and habits from which no reasoning can free him. But if Mars be dignified by sign or well placed, none of these dangers need be at all serious.

The good aspects seem even more difficult to interpret than the evil ones. The feelings and emotions are apparently quite as much stimulated, but they operate through benefic and legitimate channels. There are activities, ardours, and enthusiasms manifesting through matters signified by sign and house. It is good for sailors and for occupations connected with the water. It increases generosity and kindly impulses. It has a bearing upon occult powers of the practical or ceremonial kind.

♅ and ☉. In good aspect this must tend to bring good fortune through whatever occupations may be signified by the planet ; but, unfortunately, very little is known of these. It probably influences pursuits connected with the water, travelling, speculating ; also activities that give amusement and pleasure, theatres, concerts ; and is beneficial for events of the fifth house generally, and perhaps for legacies. It intensifies but also refines the feelings and emotions; there is love of pleasure, but it runs in legitimate channels; love of refinement, luxury, elegance. The aspect tends towards generosity, kindness, sympathy.

When in bad aspect there is some instability and danger of reversal in matters of occupation, power, rulership. The favour of superiors and those in authority is not to be depended upon; the reputation may suffer; the native's schemes collapse, perhaps through no fault of his own, his ambitions are thwarted, his efforts come to nought. Events signified by the houses containing the two are sure to suffer seriously. Native may fill posts of responsibility but is seldom at the head of his department, and is often subordinate to others, by whom he is liable to be opposed and checked. It tends towards excesses and lax morality. Its influence upon health seems also in the direction of excess, plethora; but it is alleged to cause fainting, syncope, and sometimes coma or trance.

♆ and ♀. In good aspect, the native is easily moved to admiration of the opposite sex, and is emotional and romantic in love affairs, and easily caught by beauty. There may be more than one love affair or marriage. It is good for partnership and general prosperity, and contributes towards benefit and pleasure through friends, associates, popularity. There is love of beauty in art, music, the stage, etc., with a strong emotional or sensuous element in it. May contribute towards genius if other positions concur. Good for occupations of Neptune.

In bad aspect, fickleness or deceit in love or marriage on the part of one or other of the parties; danger of scandal; instability or want of good faith on the part of marriage or business partner. Loss of money through false confidence, deceit, fraud; obtaining of money by false pretences.

♆ and ☿. In good aspect a versatile mind, changeable, embracing many subjects and not lingering long over one; ingenious, inventive, intuitive, fertile in resource. Gives aptitude for psychic studies, ability to get ideas from astral sources; crystal-gazing, psychometry, automatic writing, trance or inspirational speaking. Gives some understanding of interior planes of being, and attraction to subjects connected with them, and success in practising them. Attracts to unconventional healing and hygienic methods, faith-healing, curative mesmerism, etc. The pleasures and the emotions are chiefly mental in character. There is clear dreaming and ability to remember dreams. If any ability for poetry, music, etc., exists, this aspect will support and increase it.

In bad aspect, any or all the above subjects may attract quite as much, but will be attended by obstacles and misfortune. The memory is apt to be poor, and the native in some respects unpractical. He changes his opinions, vacillates, or even holds contradictory views. Danger of trouble, duplicity, underhand conduct. Trouble through servants and possible dishonesty, slander, libel or scandal. Both aspects promote changes and travelling.

♆ and ☽. In good aspect, increases the imagination, makes the emotional side of the nature active and fertile. The native lives largely in the emotions and feelings, is swayed by passing moods and impulses, lives in them, learns from them, and expresses himself through them. Fortunate for acting, music, art, etc., and for most psychic studies and occupations, mediumship, crystal gazing, etc. Gives sympathy with the mother and possible benefit through her. Favours offspring.

Any aspect increases the impressionability, and this may blend with the higher side of the mind in emotional, imaginative, or devotional activities ; or may show as love of the things of sense—luxuries, exquisite tastes, colours, odours, etc. ; while in bad aspects and in a severely afflicted horoscope, may tend from the sensuous to the sensual. Serious affliction brings trouble through any of the above sources, largely depending upon the house in question ; bad luck from females ; hinders marriage in a male horoscope ; threatens incurable diseases ; brings trouble at the close of life ; danger from deception, fraud, or slander.

These influences will be accentuated should either planet be the ruler. (Neptune, however, is very rarely the ruler of any horoscope—see p. 37.)

The Aspects of URANUS *

♅ and ♄. Any good aspect will deepen and intensify the nature in some respect, but this may vary according to the type of horoscope. With some, it increases the strength of the will, gives a very fixed and unchanging nature, one that can form its plans a long way ahead and spend a lifetime in carrying them out. It concentrates the mind, gives thoughtfulness and seriousness, ability to plan and control, formulate and reduce to order and method. This general tendency may operate either through the feelings and emotions (fire and water), or the reasoning mind (air and earth), according to position by sign and the type of

---

* The influence of aspects between Uranus and Neptune is given on p. 233.

horoscope; its good influence giving control and orderliness in either direction. Whether the inward power thus shown will be carried out into actual practice in daily life, depends a good deal upon whether the influences in the horoscope are chiefly positive or negative. It attracts somewhat in the direction of psychism and occultism, and gives some success in these matters; but here either angular position or the good aspects of the Moon or Mercury are usually necessary if the influence is to amount to much in actual life. The effect as regards health is to conserve the vitality and prolong life, especially after middle age; but probably this will not operate greatly unless one or both are in good aspect to the luminaries or the ascendant. If favourably placed, its power of concentration and control may be brought to bear upon business and worldly affairs with fortunate results.

In bad aspects these planets are extremely likely to affect the health injuriously, either sooner or later, according to directions. Their mere presence in the same sign, even if not in conjunction, is liable to weaken that part of the body ruled by the sign or the house, unless well aspected by Sun, Moon, or Ascendant. Their diseases are long-continued, complicated, and frequently incurable. The general tendency under bad aspects will be much the same as under good ones, but misapplied, wrongly-used, inverted, or attended by bad luck. For instance, when in opposition or square, there may be as much strength of will, control, and force of character as when in trine, but the result may be continual bad luck in those matters signified by whichever is the weaker of the two; or, in a thoroughly evil type of horoscope, the powers may be deliberately used for wrong ends, producing a dangerous criminal; or, again, in an unevolved nature, the outcome may be indolence, sloth, tâmasic inertia that never progresses, never improves. This may show mentally or morally, according to sign, or, if angular, in practical life: but the evil effects are not usually serious except when other testimonies concur, either by radical position or by direction.

♅ and ♃. In good aspect it is fortunate for all matters signified by the two planets. The higher side of the mind is opened, and there may be an impulse towards philosophy, the higher sciences, and originality of thought. The religion is of a mystical, poetic, imaginative or occult type. The native may succeed in or receive worldly benefit from pursuits bearing upon any of these matters, depending upon position by sign and house. If Uranus is angular, there may be success through following one of the Uranian occupations or studies. The influence is believed to be good for money, legacies, and general worldly success, as well as for all affairs arising out of the ninth house, either those connected with the churches and religious movements, or with law, philosophy, and mystical affairs, or foreign travel.

In evil aspect, these same concerns and tendencies are to the fore, but they occasion trouble and loss, and entail suffering.

♅ *and* ♂   In good aspect, energy, impulse, activity, and power, manifesting through matters signified by the houses involved, qualified by the signs.   The mind is generally very alert and quick to act ; the will is vigorous and emphatic ; a good deal of determination and energy are thrown into whatever is undertaken.   The tendency is to increase the mental pride and self-will.   The native is original, enterprising, resourceful, and practical in those matters involved by the aspect ; ambitious, difficult to turn aside or thwart, and in general gets his own way.   The aspect increases the will-power, mental activity, and positiveness of character.   It is allied to wit, sarcasm, irony, and destructive criticism.   In psychic matters it interferes with the development of those gifts that are promoted by passivity, such as mediumship, clairvoyance, trance, etc., but inclines to those requiring mental activity and a positive will.

In bad aspect, there is the same energy, will-power, and positiveness, but acting erratically, unwisely, imprudently.   There is apt to be much spasmodic self-will, lack of mental balance and sobriety of judgment, intolerance of opposition or control, dislike of all restraint.   It signifies unfortunate events that come about with startling suddenness ; and it tends to disturb and upset all matters signified by the houses involved.   This position strongly predisposes to physical violence if either planet is angular, and is in any case of a turbulent character, needing strong self-discipline on the part of the native to overcome its evil influence.

♅ *and* ☉.   In good aspect is fortunate for any of the Uranian occupations, bringing good luck and success through them.   It is also said to be fortunate for public appointments, and for matters connected with national or municipal public bodies, membership in those bodies, or offices held under them.   It is good for societies, associations, and brotherhoods.   It preserves the health in old age and lengthens the life.   It gives benefit through uncommon methods of healing, such as electricity, hypnotism, etc. It somewhat increases the positive side of the nature, self-reliance, independence of character. If mental signs are involved it may co-operate with any other indications in an intellectual direction, giving originality and a fertile mind.

In bad aspect, it tends to upset the health, according to the sign and house involved. There may be quite as much inclination for Uranian matters as with the good aspects, but the influence acts unfortunately and in an erratic, unbalanced fashion, much as with the evil aspects from Uranus to Mars. It endangers domestic (especially parental) harmony; is bad for public position, popularity, the good will of the world generally; and causes broken ties of all sorts in business, marriage, and friendship.

♅ and ♀. In good aspect, gives many friends and acquaintances, increases the popularity, and sometimes gives an attractive and magnetic personality. The love of beauty is increased, the emotions are lifted up towards the intellect, and there may be ability for music, poetry, art, etc., or liking for any of these. It brings good fortune through friends and the public, and success through any occupation or pursuit signified by either planet. The love nature is increased, and it tends to promote happiness in marriage if other testimonies concur. It conduces to worldly prosperity in a general way, but mainly through such matters as are governed by the two planets.

In bad aspect, friends and acquaintances and especially the opposite sex cause trouble. Love matters are involved, marriage hindered, and sometimes scandal threatened. There is, in some cases, fickleness in love, broken promises and vows; or the native may suffer from these at the hands of the lover or marriage partner. It tends to bring trouble or loss through the occupations governed by either planet.

♅ and ☿. In good aspect, the mind is active, original, quick, fertile, inventive, and intuitive. Intellectual power is increased, and there may be success and good luck in following any of the Mercurial or Uranian occupations, studies, or activities. The mind does not always pursue the beaten track, but makes its own rules, follows its own laws, and obeys its own inner nature. Wit is increased, ingenuity promoted, and a tendency given to discoveries and inventions, intellectual or practical. It gives benefit from study, education, mental pursuits, and travelling. It often inclines strongly in some Uranian or semi-occult direction.

In bad aspect the mind may be just as active and the tendencies similiar to the above ; but there will be an irregular or erratic action, and all matters signified by position and rulership will be hindered and liable to result unfortunately.

♅ *and* ☽. In good aspect, generally inclines to one or more of the Uranian studies or occupations, and brings considerable success through them, whether followed as a private hobby or a public occupation. When the native does not take up such matters himself, he is generally brought into contact with those who do, and the result is for his interest or profit. If in a man's horoscope, he may marry a wife having these tastes, or form friendships with such people. In a woman's horoscope, she may benefit in health from uncommon methods of medical treatment, mesmeric or otherwise. It favours travelling.

In bad aspect and in a man's horoscope, the influence is bad for marriage and the family ; troubles and irregularities of all sorts follow, from mere disappointment in love to separation or the formation of irregular attachments. In a woman's horoscope, it is not good for health and if the Moon is in a hylegiacal position, it is bad in this respect with either sex. With females, it is bad for childbirth and the children and home life ; and the emotions and feelings are apt to be erratic, fickle, changeable and irregular. There will be trouble, bad luck, or loss from any Uranian occupation that may be taken up. It will unite with any other influence in upsetting the nervous system and causing mental distı.rbances of various kinds, from mere nervousness up to more serious irregularities. It tends to upset the stomach and digestive system. There is trouble or danger from the water and any place or occupation of the Moon. Any aspect is likely to cause either travelling or changes of residence, good or bad, and perhaps also changes of occupation.

THE FATE OF SATURN IN THE TWELVE SIGNS

[The following refer to Saturn as ruler of the nativity or when the strongest planet by position, etc., as well as applying in a general sense to ALL who have the position at birth, since Saturn is the planet of FATE.*]*

♄ ♈. Troubles, difficulties and obstacles in the first half of life. Sorrows in connection with finance, friends amongst relatives, honour or dishonour in connection with domestic affairs according to environment. Gain or loss through the death of uncles and aunts, according to house and aspects of Saturn. A jealous partner, or marriage to an elder; danger of poverty through marriage. Strange diseases of an internal nature, with suicidal tendencies if Mercury is afflicted at birth. Some religious experiences. Reserve and acquisitiveness at close of life, retirement with a competence if Jupiter is well placed: few journeys, and those few fraught with danger. Ambition for success, with the promise of prosperity through industry and perseverance.

♄ ♉. Economical, reserved, fond of solitude, prudent and diplomatic. Gain by industry and frugal methods. Sorrow and loss through relatives : brethren occult or mystically inclined : a few faithful friends in the domestic circle : anxiety through children and their affairs. Aunts and uncles abroad, from whom there are expectations with faint prospect of realisation. Death of marriage partner, or financial troubles through marriage. Liability to treachery, and secret opposition. Sickness through foreign travel. Gain through judicious investment. Peculiar domestic experiences : disinclination to travel · fondness for mysticism and secret societies.

♄ ♊. Dual experiences; liable to self-deception; subtle and resourceful. Liable to false imprisonment or treachery through domestic attachments : deceitful friends : trouble through relatives, and dishonour through inferiors or common and public pursuits. Marriage to a foreigner, or an alliance made abroad. A strange death : liable to violence or to succumb through the jealousy of others. Unfortunate in legal affairs and fated to suffer through lawyers or solicitors. Sickness through profession or employment, and sorrow through children and their affairs.

An unfavourable end, hastened by the action of relatives or powerful opponents. Gain from two sources and by questionable means.

♄ ♋. Peevish and somewhat discontented nature, repining and fretful disposition, always liable to domestic trouble and family discords. Anxiety, grief and disappointment through love-affairs, and sorrow through children. Unfortunate and unprofitable experience with inferiors, and sickness caused by impure magnetism. Honour or dishonour through marriage, according to position and aspects : a partner who rises through merit or industry. Death in a foreign land, or by drowning. Occult tendencies or sincerity in religious affairs. Opponents who affect the honour or reputation. Trouble in partnerships; griefs through the loss of a relative : sickness of friends and acquaintances. Pleasure from psychic sources. Difficulties at the close of life. Gain through the occult arts.

♄ ♌. Disregardful of pleasure, enterprising, ambitious, determined : overcomes obstacles by perseverance and by will-power. Sorrow and secret enmity from inferiors; treachery of servants and hatred from them. Marriage to a friend, and the realisation of hopes and wishes through the partner. Honour through deaths and secret or governmental positions, gain from foreign affairs, and philosophic tendencies. Liable to death through overwork or heart-disease; and death of employers. Partnership with friends and acquaintances who turn to opponents; a few faithful and sincere friends amongst equals or superiors in birth. Psychic ailments and danger of infection, (crowds should be avoided). An enterprising and speculative tendency, with prospects of a fortune by speculation or gain through domestic affairs. A powerful intellect and good judgment, with faith in religion or the subjective world.

♄ ♍. Discriminative, discreet, and cautious : suffers through psychic conditions, and by bashfulness or excess of reserve; fond of science or occult studies. Difficulties in the first portion of life; disinclination to marry, troubles and misfortunes through marriage. Occult friends and secret alliances; gain through religion, philosophy, or employers who are religious, also from foreigners. Death of friends and acquaintances, unfortunate partnerships, liability to headaches or to mental diseases. An occult mind, fond of all deep and scientific studies; more intuitive than intellectual. Romantic courtships, and gain by investment or enterprise.

♄ ♎. Refined tastes, intellectual tendencies, and ability to compare, arbitrate, and unify; if much afflicted at birth a fatality to cause separations and destroy unions, especially if Venus is afflicted or weak in the nativity. Sorrow or grief through the death of a secret friend, or of a female to whom there was a deep attachment; female enmity at some period of the life, particularly at the ages of 21, 35, and 42. Religious or philosophical friends: strange experiences through friendships made abroad: fickle fortune through marriage, and opposition in profession or employment. Liability to a tragic death, producing notoriety or fame according to environment. Career considerably affected by marriage and the marriage partner's influence: gain by labour or through employment rather than by luck or ability: speculative and imaginative intellect. Serious domestic troubles and misfortunes at the close of life; occult pleasures, and gains and losses thereby. Emotions should be easily balanced by the mind.

♄ ♏. Acquisitive, passionate, self-willed, the selfish instincts being well developed; jealous, independent and resourceful, shrewd and cautious. Great tenacity and love of life. Disregard for religion except in form: fond of secret and hidden things: generally bound by religious heredity or custom. Friends amongst elders, or ambitious persons who have power: secret alliances and intrigues. Honour through friendships, and the realisation of hopes and wishes through cleverness and subtlety. Voyages or foreign residences: success after difficulties. Liability to sudden death; gain through partnerships or through opponents, also losses through determined opposition. Psychic intellect: shrewd, rather than intellectual, mentality. Gain or loss through speculation in public companies and popular enterprises, or through life policies and the death of others; careful in investments. Sad love affairs and secret domestic ties; inferior kindred, poor and jealous. A solitary end, full of mystery.

♄ ♐. Philosophical, religious, honest, fearless, and plain spoken. Dual life of popularity and seclusion, according to environment. Troubles through public affairs, honour and reputation. Occult tendencies, humanitarian views, and many public friends and supporters. Promotion and advancement in life from unassuming conditions, ability to create own dignity, and prophetic insight with regard to future welfare. Death amid good surroundings, with religious thoughts at the close of life. Opponents in mental pursuits; capacity to overcome

mental conditions by intuition, or by a philosophic attitude.   An inclination towards public service and the welfare of others, or towards labour
for domestic welfare.   An independent worker, free from influences of
inferiors in thought.   Gain by judicious investment : fortunate children :
liable to nervous breakdown or failure at close of life.   A religious mind,
free from mercenary taint or sordid motives.

    ♄ ♑.   Ambitious, careful of self-interest ; melancholic, cautious
and apprehensive.   Fated to be treacherous or unfaithful to friends, and
destined to sorrows through acquaintances : easily influenced through
inferior friendships.   Anxious to rise in life, and through tact or
diplomacy generally succeeding, if Saturn is not heavily afflicted at
birth ; but will gain more financial success abroad than in native land.
Liable to death through some chronic ailment affecting the mind.
Opposed to marriage, or unfortunate in choice of partner through lack
of correct judgment in love affairs : liable to attachments to inferiors or
the opposite sex and to become seriously entangled.   Losses through
speculation or investment, and sufferings through selfish children.   An
unfortunate end to existence, in which many painful realisations are
borne home : the mind is liable to taint from hereditary tendencies, and
there is danger of tragic mental states at the close of life.

    ♄ ♒.   Refined, reserved, intellectual, humane, serious, thoughtful
and well disposed.   Suffers at the hands of others passively without
much resistance : makes friends without effort, and is faithful to those
selected.   Gains through profession or employment by quiet and persistent determination, and generally secures good financial prospects.
Refines the mind by study and appreciative observation, and is
thoroughly practical in all mental states of consciousness : is inclined to
join societies for mutual benefit.   Faithful in love affairs ; generally
marries well.   Avoids sickness through a study of the laws of hygiene,
or by temperance and food reform.   Generally forms some pure romantic
attachment or lasting tie.   The end of life is generally better than the
beginning, and takes place amid refined surroundings, the intellect
having been improved by experience and study.

    ♄ ♓.   Sorrows and disappointments in life : forms unfavourable
ties and is seriously handicapped by attachments generally beginning
romantically and ending tragically, or with misfortune and disaster : the
native is usually himself the cause of his bad luck and trouble through
lack of hope or true courage, and proves to be his own enemy through-

out.   He acquires a disregard for money or suffers losses through friends and acquaintances.   He rarely creates his own dignity; and cannot maintain it when gained, unless the horoscope is very favourable.   He has occult leanings, and rebels against orthodox religion.   His death is often tragic, and sometimes occurs through suicide or grief.   He is unfortunate in marriage or has an ailing partner; servants cause trouble after marriage.   He is separated from his children, or they suffer in health.   His end is spent in retirement or seclusion, his mind being engrossed with psychic matters.

The Aspects of Saturn *

♄ *and* ♃.   This combination of influences is most difficult to elucidate clearly.   In good aspect, it is good for the occupations, pursuits, and general affairs of the four signs ruled by the planets, and for the houses in which they are placed, as well as those on the cusps of which the four signs are situated.   It is fortunate for money and possessions derived from any of these sources, and gives some desire for respectability and for the good opinion of the world.   The native wishes to stand well with superiors, elders, and those around him, and will generally succeed in this.   He will have independence and originality, and yet defer a good deal to custom and formality.   He is likely to rise in religious or political spheres, and he has considerable ambition, but unless Jupiter is very strong there is some likelihood of his religion being tinged with unorthodoxy, which may have its origin from a variety of sources—doubt, indifference, self-seeking, ambition, worldliness, deep thought, or pessimism.   It gives much strength of character, and ability to overcome obstacles.   There is likelihood of long journeys or voyages, and of acquaintances or friends abroad; his occupation will take the native abroad, or he will have to do with a foreign country; he may also travel with or for friends, or on account of matters rising out of the twelfth house.   It upholds the native's credit and reputation, helps to uplift him in the world, and to give honour, esteem, and general prosperity: there is a good deal of 'self' in the aspect, although it is modified by the justice, benevolence and devotion of Jupiter.   He gains through the father, or sometimes the father through him, and it tends

---

* The aspects of Saturn to Neptune and to Uranus are given on pp. 233 and 236 respectively.

generally to make the relations of the two to one another satisfactory. He gains the respect of friends, who are usually honourable and of good class. His fortune through societies, associations, and companies is good, both pecuniarily and otherwise. The effect of this aspect varies, being in some horoscopes democratic and others aristocratic; but it is a very good influence for any man holding a public position or appointment, whether among the classes or the masses. Similarly, the native may follow either a great and public career, or one just the reverse, obscure, humble or plebeian; but in either case he will acquit himself worthily. It diminishes the likelihood of enemies and of harm from them, and upholds the native in adversity. He will receive or bestow, according to the station in life, charity and benevolence; and good arising out of homes, hospitals, and other medical, religious or charitable institutions will form a feature in his career. To a less degree it is good for matters in the third house, in so far as these are not contradicted by the four signs ruled by the planets. It inclines slightly to travelling; and is also slightly good for writings, mental ability, capacity for education, etc. Whether the aspect makes for a public and honoured, or merely an obscure but worthy existence, must of course be judged, in this, as in other cases, by the horoscope *as a whole*, and by the solar aspects, etc.; also according as the aspect in question comes from cardinal, succedent, or cadent houses, and according to which planet (if either) is above the horizon.

The conjunction is generally considered benefic; but it seems open to doubt whether it is uniformly so under all circumstances; and a good deal must depend upon which planet of the two is the stronger by sign.

In bad aspect this combination brings obstacles and misfortune through the four signs ruled. It is unfortunate for money and occupation, especially any coming under these signs, more particularly if either sign is on the cusp of the second house. It threatens a downfall in the world through loss of money or credit, and trouble, pecuniary or otherwise, through the father. There will be social difficulties and trouble through societies, companies, friends, and matters of the eleventh house. The native is never or seldom orthodox in religion, and there are troubles indicated in connection with study, education, travel, voyaging; also matters of the twelfth house, enmity, opposition, treachery. In some cases he will be in danger of prison, or will be supported by charity or be the inmate of a workhouse or charitable institution.   He will be the victim of dishonesty, or will himself be not quite straightforward in money matters.

♄ *and* ♂ .   It is more than usually difficult to disentangle the good and evil effects in the aspects of these planets ; and very much will depend upon the sign rising, and the general state of the horoscope, whether tending to good or evil.   The trine is, of course, the best of the good aspects.   Some consider the square the worst of the evil aspects, while most incline to the opinion that the opposition is worse than the conjunction ; bearing in mind what has been said of Saturn representing the mind and Mars the senses, the reason of the latter judgment will be at once apparent, for here they are in conflict, and discord must inevitably arise.

In conjunction or bad aspect there will be much ambition, and notoriety in some form, accompanied or followed sooner or later by danger, difficulty, and trouble to life and honour.   It is bad for the parents : the death of one or both under painful circumstances is threatened ; and there may be separation from, or disputes with, a parent.   Wounds and accidents are threatened, and danger of sudden or violent death, either to the native or a parent.   Danger of death from enemies or during war, or at the hands of the State, or while in the service of the State.   The honour and reputation are imperilled : the native will meet with some great reversal or downfall ; he will encounter hostility, opposition and criticism, even from his own friends, and the chances are he will not hold for long an honourable place in public opinion.   He may not succeed at his occupation, and is sure to meet with serious difficulties in it.   He either has few friends, or they ¬lay him false.   There will be some severe complaint of any part of the body ruled by the four signs, or by the signs and houses in which the two planets are placed, and death may result from it.   It is bad for peace of mind ; the native is hot-headed and rash : the temper may range from mere recklessness or irritability (which may be partly hidden or overlaid by the influence of benefics) to anger, passion, and uncontrollable rage.   If unmodified by other influences, the native is indifferent to the feelings of others, and will be hard, cruel, spiteful, and revengeful.   It is bad for legacies (except perhaps the conjunction in a favourable sign) and brings trouble through companies, associations, societies, etc. : if either planet be well placed by sign or in a favourable house, however, much of the malice may be abated. In some cases, instead of the native suffering in the ways indicated above, he will himself be the cause of such suffering in others, *e.g.*, instead of suffering from false friends, he may himself be a false friend, etc. In all cases note must be taken of the houses ruled by Saturn and Mars, since they will afford the key to the manner in which the latent disharmony will eventuate.

In the case of a good aspect, the worst results of the bad aspects will not be seen, but there will be a good deal in the character that is undesirable. It promotes ambition in the native, love of rule and mastery, bravery, carelessness both of his own safety and that of other people. Will face danger recklessly, either because he does not see it or has a contempt for it. It hardens the nature somewhat, but gives great energy of a more or less turbulent and overbearing kind. If influencing the religion, this may make the native militant or fanatical, whether for or against. In mental signs similar characteristics will show, and if Saturn is strong by house or elevation, much subtlety will be added to the power of the aspect. Subtle to scheme, and quick to execute, the native will combine quickness or apparent changeableness with dogged perseverance. He will be a leader, a pioneer, daring and, it may be, over-bearing and contemptuous of others. This may help to lift him into fame, power, or prominence of some kind, but it is attended by undesirable circumstances or danger.

Most of what is here attributed to the good aspect may be seen in the case of bad aspects also, if the benefics are strong or elevated so as to tone down the more undesirable effects.

♄ *and* ⊙. In any aspect tends to give a strong personality, one who goes his own way irrespective of the feelings or desires of others, who is not affected by the protests or opinions of others, and who is with difficulty thwarted or turned aside. He is capable of organising, controlling, governing and directing others. He is to some extent a natural leader; is subtle, often most so when seeming to be frankest, and does not mind isolation or positions of responsibility. He is ambitious, and if the fire and energy of Mars are added to the subtlety and controlling power of Saturn, nothing can turn him aside; he will work out his purposes successfully in the face of the greatest obstacles, and is certain to obtain leadership or mastery over others and positions of prominence or responsibility, even though in a small sphere. There is a tendency to pride, dignity and isolation, and to whatsoever lifts a man up or separates him from his fellows.

In good aspect, his schemes, plots, and ambitions meet with success; he has much self-control, and the more undesirable Saturnian qualities may avoid expression. It brings the favour of superiors; the native will rise in life and associate with those somewhat above himself; he will be pretty sure to join some society or association or to form one of a group of persons banded together for a common purpose. In money matters it inclines to companies and rings, and slightly to partnerships; the native may be in partnership with his father or with one of his own sons; but if his own master he will rule autocratically, and take the advice of none. It brings benefits to sons, but limits the number of children. It favours money from the father. The native may obtain municipal or similar local honours.

In conjunction or bad aspect, the native is frequently confronted with obstacles and delay, and unless in mutual reception * it is very unfortunate for all things signified by the two planets, bringing misfortunes in business, loss of public favour, likelihood of the father's death, loss of father's money or separation from or disagreement with him; and the same of a child (probably son): the native incurs opposition, enmity and jealousy; his ambitions are frequently thwarted, and he meets with reverses or downfall: he will be autocratic, boastful, selfish, or careless of the feelings of others, cold and unsympathetic. It has an injurious influence upon the heart and the vitality generally. It may bring the disfavour of others, social unpopularity, and the enmity of superiors and those in high positions.

Any aspect may incline to marriage or a love affair with one in a different position of life (probably higher, but sometimes lower). If bad, lack of sympathy and disharmony in love and marriage; the parent (probably father) may intervene to delay or break off a love affair. In any case there will be some little difference in age between husband and wife.

♄ *and* ♀. In good aspect this is very good for money matters, giving a tendency to prudence, thriftiness, economy, and carefulness. It

---

* 'Mutual reception' is when each of two planets is in a sign governed by the other—*e.g.*, ☉ in ♒, ♄ in ♌, which was the case with Lord Salisbury.

favours the accumulation and prevents the wasting of money. In some cases it will go rather too far in this direction, and result in a lack of generosity and a hoarding up of money approaching miserliness. Money or property is acquired through the native's father, by his own exertions, or by marriage; also through occupations of the tenth and eleventh houses. There is considerable business ability and tact, and the native makes the best financial use of any occupation he may follow, or any opportunity he may have. He may be very successful as a financier, in either a small or a large way, depending upon the environment of birth. He gains through companies, societies, associations, banking, investments, etc.; generally speaking, through the aged, or those considerably older than himself, and through superiors in position. His gains do not come so much by favour as by method, by business instincts, prudent manipulations, or by mere inevitableness. There will be some little difference either in age or social position, or both, between the native and the marriage or business partner. The union will probably be with one in a higher social position: it may be for money or position or ambition; and will be brought about or assisted, directly or indirectly, by a parent, guardian or superior. There will be gain of friends by marriage. It is an aspect favourable for pleasure, social intercourse, and popularity; and it gives faithfulness in friendship and love. To a less extent, moreover, it favours the gain of money by superior positions or occupations coming under the ninth house; through friends of the mother, and through careful speculation for financial ends rather than for pleasure, though there may also be gain through occupations of the fifth house and of the earthy element; success in business or occupation through partnership or association with another person; partnership with the father or association with him in some pursuit or purpose; marriage with a relation; membership in societies or associations coming under the ninth house; good fortune, pecuniary and otherwise, for the children.

In bad aspect, all matters referred to under the good aspect suffer, and, generally speaking, all things signified by the four signs also. Money is lost through the parents (father) and occupation; little or none is inherited; severe loss in business, or even bankruptcy, is threatened. If the moral sense is deficient, which must be judged from the horoscope as a whole, there will be dishonesty: or if otherwise, the native will suffer through the dishonesty of others. Money is lost through investments, speculations, financial operations, companies, societies, farming, building, gardening. To a less extent, too, it is bad and brings loss through all occupations and matters of the fifth and ninth houses. It threatens unpopularity or hostility from some quarter: reversal, downfall, misfortune through elders, seniors, parents, and relatives: trouble in partnership and marriage; interference of parents, guardians, or seniors; marriage delayed or not contracted until over twenty-eight: trouble in marriage through difference in age or social or pecuniary position: trouble, financial or otherwise, through children and friends.

The conjunction is partly good and partly bad, and exhibits influences and characteristics from both; Venus benefiting Saturn, while Saturn impedes Venus.

♄ and ☿. In good aspect this will make the native very successful at some occupation of the third or sixth houses; he will gain power, responsibility or fame through writing, speaking, or in connection with intellectual work, drugs, hygiene, medical works. He will occupy some responsible post as agent, traveller or servant, or may himself have many such under him; and will exercise a good deal of power or authority in this way according to his position in life. Either he himself or one of his brothers or sisters will rise considerably above the ordinary in capacity for education, intellectual ability, or some matter of the third or sixth houses. This is a good influence for the mind, memory, and reasoning powers; it gives orderliness and method. The native will make friends and acquaintances among people whose character or pursuits come under the third or sixth houses, and to a less degree the ninth. He will belong to, or be associated with, or start, some club, society, association or union coming under the third or sixth houses, or to a less degree the ninth, and may be of some importance therein: will be secretary, servant, agent, or representative in some way for his father, or will be associated in occupation with a brother or sister; but if so there is unlikely to be equality between them, for one will dominate the other. He may derive benefit from drugs; will be cleanly in habits, and observant of sanitation; and very particular with regard to food. He will have others under him; will pull the strings and direct others. May own or have to do with merchant vessels, means of transport by short journeys, vehicles, post-office, telegraph, and general affairs of the third house, also the distribution of food-products, drugs, and affairs of the sixth house. He will be a vigorous and capable master of his servants and those under him, exercising both persuasion and compulsion.

In a slighter degree such aspect gives the possibility of a legacy from brethren or friends, or money by association with them, and from societies, clubs, etc. It inclines slightly to travelling, more especially in connection with business, but chiefly to intellectual pursuits. The native is an investigator of mystical or occult subjects ; may possess psychic powers of some kind, more or less mental; and may gain some eminence, responsibility or mastery in religious matters or affairs of the ninth house, probably as agent or superintendent for another. Will study or write on subjects coming under the ninth house, and will travel because of eleventh house matters.

The conjunction is partly evil but not wholly so, and is distinctly beneficial for the mind, making it concentrative, careful and precise. Two planets like these that have their houses in trine cannot be altogether evil when in conjunction. This influence would seem to be intermediate between the good and evil aspects. The same remarks apply to the conjunction of Saturn and Venus.

In bad aspect, matters signified by the four signs ruled by the planets suffer; misfortune, hindrances and obstacles attend these activities. Native will be very ambitious in spheres of activity coming under the eleventh, third and sixth houses, and may exhibit much selfishness and desire for mastery. His desires in these respects are frequently thwarted and often entirely overthrown. He meets with much criticism and opposition, open or hidden, and will suffer from slanders, false reports, back-biting, forged letters or documents, unfriendly writings, etc. ; or may himself descend to these methods. There will be trouble in his education and all matters pertaining to school, study and books. The death of father or brethren, or their ill-health, or separation or estrangement from them, will occasion him sorrow or loss. The aspect is bad for digestion, and may cause affections of the bowels or digestive tracts, or, to a less degree, of any part of the body signified by the houses of these planets. It causes trouble between master and servant; the native will be for long in a relatively subordinate position, or, if a master, will suffer through those under him : he will be a strict and harsh master, or will suffer under one himself. It brings trouble through false friends, societies, associations ; also from servants, messengers, travellers, and generally through people following any occupation of the four signs ruled by the planets; and to a less extent from the ninth house.

♄ and ☽. In good aspect, is good for the parents, brings benefits to the native from them, and *vice versa*. It gives prudence, caution and circumspection; respect for law and order, with somewhat conservative tendencies. The native possesses the ability to organize and systematise; he combines self-reliance with subtlety and diplomacy; and influences other people easily, more by tact and method than by force. It is favourable for public advancement, for success in the occupation, for the attainment of posts of responsibility, and for gaining the respect of people generally. It is beneficial for matters and occupations of the fourth, tenth and eleventh houses. To a less extent it favours marriage and partnership, in which the approval or help of parents, seniors or friends, public repute or official position play a part: but there will be some difference in age, tastes or position between the native and his partner. It slightly favours legacies from parents.

In conjunction or bad aspect, it is bad for parents and for the native's associations with them, whether natural parents, step-parents, or those of the marriage partner; one of them may be sickly or may die early, or there may be separation or differences of opinion or tastes, either between the parents themselves or the native and one or both of the parents. (In some cases it accompanies illegitimate birth, although if taken alone it would not be a sufficient indication, of course.) It is very unfortunate for affairs and occupations of the fourth, tenth and eleventh houses, and trouble is certain to arise through them. The native's good name will be in danger at some time of life; he may suffer from slander or public attacks or open opposition or persecution; something will be done or said by himself or others to bring him into disrepute and obloquy, and he may be in danger of imprisonment. He meets with frequent reversals and rebuffs; his undertakings do not succeed; he incurs the disapprobation of seniors, and may meet with a great downfall, while the latter part of life is likely to be unfortunate or full of disappointment. His greatest success or highest rise is quickly followed by failure or down-fall, or is thwarted by death. There will be a good deal of selfishness, strong personal ambition, and love of mastery in his character, and he will work subtly and sometimes unscrupulously or dishonestly. In some cases this influence merely keeps the native relatively in the background or in obscurity, often afflicting him with despondency and self-mistrust;

while in others he will be lifted up in the world, and for a time may attain his highest ambition, though this is generally quickly followed by reversal; which of these two will occur must of course be judged from the sign occupied, the other lunar aspects, and the horoscope as a whole. It may produce a disorder of some part of the body according to the signs or houses in which the planets are placed: it sometimes causes cancer. It may bring trouble through friends, societies and companies. To a less extent it is unfavourable for marriage and legacies.

THE INFLUENCE OF JUPITER IN THE TWELVE SIGNS*

[*Jupiter's primary influence in the world is connected with the social and the refined domestic element : success is brought about through favour or influence and by everything arising out of favourable social standing, either in one's own or a higher sphere.*]

♃ ♈. Ambitious, enthusiastic, aspiring, fortunate. Gain by voyages, also by shipping and secret means. Intellectual friends and fortunate acquaintances made through travel; honour and fame gained through family ties and domestic relationships. Successful speculation or investment in foreign securities, success in law and gain through children. Legacies from aunts or maternal side of the family. An ambitious partner, and an heroic death. Pleasure from religious associations. Honour and position at the close of life. Friends amongst relatives, and gain from enemies.

♃ ♉. The nature is peaceful, dignified, reserved and firm. There is sorrow through relatives, but on the other hand gain through friends connected with the family circle. Position obtained through investment and speculation, or through the care of children. Health is affected by travel abroad, also financial prospects. Gain by marriage, the partner being moreover interested in mystical subjects. A faithful worker for religious, philanthropical or philosophical causes; chaste in affection, gaining socially through love affairs and individually through personal efforts. The friends in the domestic sphere of life are spiritually minded.

♃ ♊. A high-minded, prophetic nature, successful in attention to perfection of detail. Occult thoughts, domestic concerns, and friends of noble birth all play a great part in the life, and honour is achieved through modest undertakings or obscure pursuits. Marriage to a cousin

---

* NOTE :—Jupiter does not act upon the life with any appreciable power until the fortieth year and onwards : if above the earth at birth its influence begins earlier than when below. The particulars here given refer of course to its normal influence unafflicted ; they will naturally be subject to the *least* modification when Jupiter unafflicted is either lord of the horoscope or otherwise powerfully placed.

or distant relative : clear dreams (leading to clairvoyance or inner perception) : religious opponents : professions that are either unprofitable
or unpopular : joy in friendships and sorrows in the domestic sphere ;
mental culture through self-education ; and psychic tendencies at end of
life.

♃ ♋. The native is sympathetic, loving, kind and popular, or
indeed famous, overcoming enemies by love and an enterprising spirit ;
makes friends of inferiors and those willing to serve.   Fame or reputation and social success through marriage : mystical in religious thought.
Public approval and renown through public work : work in accordance
with hopes and wishes.   Pleasure through psychic or occult studies or
interests.   Gain through intellectual ability or exercise of mental power.
A notable end ; death occurring abroad, peacefully and with honour.

♃ ♌. Proud and powerful, but loyal and noble-spirited.   Joy in
overcoming enemies.   Marriage to a friend having influence.   Successful
in secret service and diplomatic pursuits ; fitted for detection or judgment
of criminals, and dealing with strange occurrences.   Generous opponents
who become friends.   Capable of a great degree of natural enjoyment.
Fortunate in all speculative and especially in mining affairs.   An
intuitive mind and strong religious principles.   Success in domestic
affairs.   An honourable death.

♃ ♍. Common parentage.   Discriminative in choice of friends,
prudent in speech and successful in business pursuits.   Secret love
affairs and a marriage in some way peculiar.   Friends among mystics
or strange characters.   Honour in religious or philosophical studies.
Foreign associations or travels abroad on business undertakings.
Legacies from friends and marriage to a social inferior.   Love of service.
Gain by investment and in mercantile pursuits, also literature and
speculative dealings in second-hand things.   A philosophically critical
mind.

♃ ♎. Compassionate and harmonious, a steadfast lover of justice
and mercy.   Involved in trouble through death, and in the sorrows of
others from good motives.   Conscientious and pure-minded friends, or
friends amongst those who are scientists, philosophers or divines.   Gain
through partnerships or by marriage.   Gain also by joining with others
in connection with some profession.   Lasting friendships made abroad,
and legacies from strangers; or gain through public institutions, hospitals
and asylums.   A well-balanced mind ; a happy marriage and fruitful

union. Gain from inferiors or through servants; good children. Gain from commerce and science, or the employ of agents. Successful enterprise through clear perceptions; and a peaceful end, united with family, and amid good domestic surroundings.

♃ ♏. Pride of birth; deep emotions; powerful will; jealous enemies, and peculiar intrigues with superiors. Connections with Government or Government officials. Entrusted with secrets in connection with the profession, or with information that affects the honour of others. Possessing power with associations and societies. Gain through litigation or by marriage: also through arbitration or by death of partner, and through public investments, mining, etc.: singular family experiences. Liability to gout, blood-poison and hereditary diseases: heart troubles at the close of life. Notoriety through children. Unsound or questionable speculations. Curious mental fascination for chemical experiments. A friendship of a critical and peculiar nature; long voyages and strange adventures abroad, and a liability to a tragic death through social or political connections.

♃ ♐. Prophetic, sympathetic, impressionable; philosophical or religious. Unfortunate in profession or business pursuits where social interests are involved. Gain in common pursuits where detail is concerned more than principles; gain also through legacies or marriage partner, or through a sick relative. Fond of speculation and games of chance. If afflicted there is danger of a gambling spirit. Two love affairs or marriages, one probably to a relative. Gain through deaths. A peacemaker.

♃ ♑. Ambitious; somewhat orthodox; a lover of organising and management. Creates his own dignity or social sphere. Concerned by and involved in the sorrows of friends whose misfortunes have caused their confinement in some way. Gains through (orthodox) religion or by foreign affairs and the death of relatives or kindred. Opposed to or unsympathetic towards mystic or occult thought. Finds pleasure in physical service and the idea of 'duty,' obtaining in this way joy out of work. Gains credit and honour through commercial enterprise. Parents are concerned in some way with the marriage; and the domestic sphere in general largely affects the honour and profession. Somewhat conventional in mind, and enthusiastic for education on materialistic lines.

♃ ♒. Social and humanitarian views, and a broad and philosophical mind, tolerant and sympathetic. More philosophical than religious. Much concerned with public institutions. Many friends gained through own personal influence. Gain by profession and employment in associations, societies, etc.; also by inheritance. A marriage of love. A student of the laws of hygiene. Takes a pleasure in public work. A somewhat sudden end.

♃ ♓. Hospitable, fond of all dumb animals, deeply interested in all philanthropic work, work for the sick and suffering, etc. Gain through hospitality to friends. Elevation through kindred, hereditary influences in a religious direction; interested in spiritualistic phenomena. Generous to opponents. Marriage to an inferior. Hazardous and risky investments. Gain through associations and public companies, or through mining speculations. Mentally very concerned regarding honour and profession. Quiet and religious end.

The Aspects of Jupiter *

♃ *and* ♂. In good aspect, a great deal of energy and enterprise are thrown into all occupations signified by Jupiter's signs. There is some degree of self-reliance and originality in matters signified by the planets : the native launches out into new undertakings or lines of thought; does not hesitate to forsake the beaten track; and may be, if only in a small way, a pioneer in his work : is a lover of freedom and justice, and one likely to espouse the cause of the weak, the poor, or those suffering from injustice. This will especially be noticed in religious affairs, but more or less in all matters of the ninth and twelfth houses. Fond of travel and exploration, he will succeed well in any occupation connected with sailing, shipping, travel; also in the mechanical occupations connected with the ninth house. There is some degree of pride, ambition, and jealousy of position; but the native will ever be open-handed, free and straightforward. A legacy or money through the relatives of the marriage partner or through the marriage partner of a brother or sister is likely. Native arouses others to activity, seeks to lead, guide, or teach them for their good; champions others, whether a forlorn hope or not. The aspect in general inclines somewhat to irregular forms of religion, and slightly to the occult : it frees from captivity, servitude or bondage.

---

* The aspects of ♃ to ♅, ♆, and ♄ are given on pp. **233**, **237** and **245** respectively.

The conjunction is partly good and partly evil.

When in bad aspect, this position tends to irreligion, unorthodoxy, lack of devoutness and carelessness of established forms of religion. Its general influence is injurious for religion, morality, law, order, honesty, and upright living. Much will, however, depend upon which planet is the stronger, and whether by elevation, house, or sign ; for if Jupiter is elevated or otherwise strong, the extreme evil results need not be expected. There is a liability to feverish diseases, diseases of the blood and blood-vessels and of any part of the body ruled by the four signs concerned. Trouble will come through religion, and any matter or occupation allied thereto ; and through any affair or calling relating to the eighth, ninth, and twelfth houses ; shipping, voyages, the goods of the dead, any occupation connected with the dead, prisons, asylums, charitable institutions. He will suffer from dishonesty, treachery, underhand dealing, desertion, severance of bonds and ties, misrepresentation ; or in some cases (according to the relative power of ♂ over ♃) he may bring about these himself, or be accused of these things, perhaps unjustly. He is often himself the cause, indirectly perhaps, of the misfortunes that befall him under this aspect. There is some danger of death by drowning, or on a voyage, or while absent from home, or in a distant country. In past ages this might have signified death through religious persecution ; but there is little likelihood of things proceeding to such extremity in modern times. Mediumistic or psychic practices may injure health, or such power may appear during or result from ill-health. The native will be in great danger of death once, or more than once, during his life. There is danger of trance being mistaken for death, death by misadventure, by enmity or treachery ; death during restraint, imprisonment, or in a charitable institution. To a slighter extent it signifies loss of a legacy : extravagance in money matters ; loss of money, sometimes through dishonesty or deception either on his own part or at the hands of someone else ; loss of money through affairs or occupations of the twelfth house. Trouble and loss through pleasures and speculations arising out of the fifth and ninth houses, horse-racing, boating, travelling, etc. Death or danger to health may occur in connection with any of these. Danger of psychic diseases, obsession, etc. The tendencies to the latter are, however, very slight.

♃ and ☉. In conjunction or good aspect, it conduces to kindness, sympathy, sincerity and honesty. It inclines somewhat to religion, and may give some degree of prominence or eminence therein, as well as good fortune in affairs of the ninth house generally, occupations or amusements connected with religion or places of worship, travelling, shipping, horses, amusements and games. It increases the vitality—almost too much so, inclining to plethora, in the case of the conjunction, —the most vitalising aspects in general being those of Mars and Jupiter to the Sun and Moon, when the luminaries are free from bad aspects from other planets. It slightly favours legacies, either to the native or to his father or children; he benefits by any occupation of Leo and the fifth house, and is likely to rise to some position of responsibility in whatever occupation he pursues. It increases the social and benevolent instincts and humanitarian feelings, and is favourable to the prosperity of father and children, or for help received by the native from them. It is somewhat beneficial for love and marriage, but more for love than marriage. It is good for nursing, and all charitable work such as that connected with hospitals and charitable institutions; also for work connected with the poor and the lower classes generally.

In bad aspect, it is less good for health; it may weaken the heart and bring about any of the Jupiter diseases; but unless the horoscope is a bad one for health these will not be important, or may not appear until the latter part of life. It introduces obstacles and misfortune into all matters signified by the two planets and by the fifth and ninth houses. There will be trouble in love, trouble connected with children, religion, travelling, shipping, horses, amusements, games; but none of these need be very serious unless backed up by other influences in the horoscope. It is slightly unfavourable for the life of the children (sons especially) and father; one may die, or there may be disagreements or unavoidable separation. The native's religious opinions will prove at variance with those of his superiors, father or son. He may require charitable assistance, or at some time of life may be the inmate of a charitable institution, and if other influences coincide this may help to bring the native to a prison, hospital, asylum, etc., at some time in his life; but here much depends upon the general state of the horoscope. If a nurse or doctor, may suffer from some disease contracted from a patient. It inclines somewhat to duplicity or a double life, which need not necessarily be of the native's own seeking; in some cases it may be forced on him against his will. It may co-operate with other influences that tend towards dishonesty, irreligion, or lack of straightforwardness, or the native may suffer from these qualities in others rather than possess them himself. In this respect the predominance of the Sun or Jupiter, as the case may be, will afford the clue. None of Jupiter's bad aspects are very serious, however, unless there are other influences or indications, pointing in the same direction.

♃ and ♀ In good aspect all four signs ruled by the planets benefit. Money and possessions come through ninth house activities, by religion and occupations relating in any way to it or to the Church ; by travels, journeys, shipping, or occupations relating to these ; by intercourse with foreign countries or people from a distance ; by activities of the twelfth house and matters connected with prisons, hospitals, asylums, nursing, charitable institutions, etc. The native is honest, sincerely religious, pious, virtuous, sympathetic, and honourable. There is genius of some kind, imagination, and the love of beauty ; but in what form, whether sensuous, intellectual, artistic, spiritual, poetic, or musical, etc., depends a good deal upon the signs and houses the planets are in, and also very largely upon the Mercurial and Lunar positions. It inclines to partnership, association, or marriage with a person coming some way under the ninth or twelfth houses by birth, character, or occupation ; or with a person from a distance, or of a different nation. It gives social and general popularity, esteem, and respect, and is extremely fortunate for love and marriage. It inclines to acts of charity, and the native will be fortunate in receiving charity or the help of sympathetic benefactors when needed. To a slighter degree there may be money by legacy by matters connected with the dead, or with what may be called religio-occultism, and by any matters that are a combination of seventh and ninth houses, by the brethren of the business or marriage partner. Money will be gained through two different occupations or sources, either both at once or successively by a change in the occupation, or from two businesses ; also from trade-unions, companies, associations, etc., chiefly those that are local or limited in their scope and that do not appeal to a great number of people, or that bear upon activities of the twelfth house. There is a likelihood of two love-affairs, attachments or marriages ; of a love-affair or marriage with a relative or with a relative of the business or marriage partner ; also of third or ninth house activities carried on in connection with someone else (such as literary collaboration, etc.) ; and of a secret marriage or love-affair, or of one with someone very different to the native in station (probably lower).

When in bad aspect, the native suffers through matters signified by the four signs, and trouble may come through anything referred to under the head of the good aspects. There will be either loss of money or money troubles of some kind arising directly or indirectly out of the ninth and twelfth houses, their occupations and mental characteristics. Money may be lost through easy good-nature, through fondness for ornaments, fine clothes or luxuries, through deceitful friends or acquaintances, through companies, societies, or associations, through carelessness and lack of business instinct, or through fraud and deception ; the aspect is also slightly unfortunate for money as related to the third, sixth and eighth houses. There will be similar troubles through partnership and marriage, or arising out of the ninth and twelfth houses, such as religion, voyages, foreign countries, etc., and due to deceit, concealment, treachery, desertion, persecution, abandonment or separation ; to a less extent, also out of the third and eleventh houses. The fact of Jupiter's houses being both double will cause various troubles, such as loss of money through divided interests, through carrying on two occupations at the same time, or through change of occupation ; while in seventh house affairs, flirtation, jilting, two or more love-affairs or marriages—or even, in a bad horoscope, faithlessness, breach of promise, bigamy or divorce— will figure in some way.

♃ and ☿ . In good aspect, and in the world of mind, this harmonises the influences of intellect and devotion, or science and religion, bringing the one to the support of the other and smoothing away antagonism, and will develop its influence in many ways according to the native's station in life. According to the general status of the horoscope it will give a profoundly religious temperament, accompanied by a broad intellect and a philosophical mind, or by much learning ; or, it may merely eventuate in ability to aim, steer or drive well : in any case, however, the power of *judgment* will be well marked (unless other aspects contradict, that is), and whatever his course, the native will steer it with both skill and ease. It inclines to tolerance and broad-minded views in the domains of religion and intellect, strengthening both the intellect and the religious sentiments, and inclining to honesty, straightforwardness, candour, conscientiousness, mental balance, equanimity, good judgment. It enables the native to see all men as his brothers, to see the germs of truth in the most diverse opinions ; and thus it may act in various ways between the two extremes of a large-hearted toleration and philosophical indifference. It gives harmony and good will between brethren and relatives, with mutual good fortune or good offices to or from either. It broadens the mind out towards general principles instead of confining it to details ; it tends to versatility and the study of many subjects rather than one, and helps the native to be in some measure all things to all men. It may be one of the factors in genius and intuition ; and somewhat inclines to the mystical or philosophical aspects of religion, and slightly also to dreams, visions, psychic-writing, astral wanderings out of the body, and various forms of occult powers. It gives journeying and travelling, and changes generally, both physical and mental. There is the possibility of the higher cultivation of the mind, the perception of beauty in its higher aspects, and copious yet well-ordered imagination. It is good for health and digestion, and generally for any matter or occupation signified by the four signs ruled by the planets.

The conjunction is mainly good, but it may vary a good deal according as to which of the two planets is the stronger ; it adds much to the native's self-confidence and *may* be found associated with overweening conceit.

In bad aspect, the various meanings of the combination may be brought out just as clearly as with the good aspects, but they will generally be accompanied by obstacles and trouble in various degrees. The third and ninth houses, in short, will be found more or less at variance : and this may vary from a very pronounced religious scepticism or even atheism to ʾ much milder questioning spirit which requires reason or evidence before believing, but which believes sincerely when it has them. Much will depend upon which planet is the stronger ; if Mercury, doubts of some kind will assail ; if Jupiter, there may be a blind unquestioning faith bordering on unreasoning superstition. The native will take his religion too severely, from the point of view of a student rather than a devotee, or it may be tinged with Calvinistic gloom if Jupiter is otherwise afflicted. There will be third or ninth house troubles connected with the parents or brethren. Any matters signified by the four signs involved will be accompanied by more or less misfortune according to the nature of the planets. There will be some tendency to vacillation of mind, and the native may throw over old opinions and adopt new ones more than once in his life. It tends to weakness of any part of the body ruled by the four signs, and there will be a good deal of journeying or travelling at some time of life. The native is liable to suffer from libels, slanders, false reports, or any kind of deceit affecting matters signified by Mercury. He may suffer from visions or hallucinations due to an over-active mind, or brought on by the use of drugs.

♃ *and* ☽. In good aspect, increases the imagination and intuition, and is sometimes the accompaniment of genius. It increases vitality and fertility, both of mind and body. It inclines to honesty, religion, justice, compassion and sympathy. It is fortunate for all matters of the fourth, ninth and twelfth houses, and for things connected with the watery element; also for the mother and her attitude to the native. It gives children, possibly twins. If there are inclinations to psychism or occultism, this will lend its influence for good. Money is gained through the ninth house or by legacy from the mother's side of the family. It is good for friendship and all social feelings; and it greatly improves and ripens the character. The conjunction is almost wholly good, but somewhat inclines to excess, either in love of pleasure or in enthusiasm and 'go.'

In bad aspect, it may bring illness of mother or lack of sympathy between her and the native, or separation from her. Possibility of a step-mother or of adoption. It is unfavourable for offspring, and puts obstacles in the way of all matters and occupations of the fourth, ninth and twelfth houses. The native will show duplicity and deception, or lack of straightforwardness, or may perhaps suffer from them in others, in matters signified by the two planets. In extreme cases, if the rest of the horoscope accords, the native will either be dishonest or suffer from the dishonesty of others. There will be trouble through religion, voyages and the watery element; moreover the native may suffer from slander, or be accused of wrongdoing he has never committed. This aspect is unfavourable for health, especially in women.

THE INFLUENCE OF MARS IN THE TWELVE SIGNS

[The following refer more particularly to Mars as ruling planet, or when angular and a strong planet in the nativity, also in a general sense as indicating the instinctive impulses of the native. The special influence of each decanate is indicated.]

♂ ♈. Positive, idealistic, enthusiastic, loyal and independent. Secluded or obscure means of livelihood. Gain from private sources. Intellectual friends. Employment in connection with the home. Pleasure in religious activity. Financial losses through marriage, and difficulty to consummate union. Liability to inflammatory and mental complaints. An enterprising and philosophical spirit. Troubles through parents. Self-interest strongly marked. More favourable for males than females. The above remarks apply to the whole sign generally, and in a more particular sense to the first 'decanate' (space of 10°). Mars in the second decanate gives amours, intense feelings, heroism, love of adventure, and a fearless disposition, fond of argument, enterprise and pleasure. In the third decanate, fluency of speech, impulsiveness, enthusiasm and much independence; love of sport or active outdoor pleasures, with a keen sense of enjoyment and love of travel.

♂ ♉. An enterprising spirit. Acquisitive, determined, reserved, proud and resentful. Keen instinctual consciousness. Suffers keenly through relatives and legal affairs. A friend of famous or notorious persons. Liability to loss of honour through love affairs. Both gain and pleasure from occupation. Peculiar religious views, more mysacal than orthodox. Unfavourable unions or partnerships ; tragic or unfortunate marriage, and ill-health through religious enthusiasm. An early love affair. Strange experiences concerning children. Some connection with associations at close of life. Gain by efforts and perseverance; but the native will have many powerful opponents. These remarks apply to the whole sign generally, and in a more particular sense to the first decanate (space of 10°). Mars in the second decanate gives a quick wit, tactful methods, a keen sense of self-interest, and good business foresight. In the third decanate, diplomacy and quiet ambition, with power to organise, manage and direct.

♂ ♊. Keen mentality, and an acute intellect, with strong educational leanings. Sorrowful home episodes. Pleasure-loving friends by whom the native is greatly influenced. Scandal or discredit caused through inferiors or confederates. Marriage to a relative or to a religious-minded partner. More than one union. Liability to death from lung troubles. Better fitted to serve than rule. Involved in two attachments at the same time. An unfavourable end, surrounded by adverse relatives. Quickwitted, and a gainer by 'wits' or sharp perception. The above applies to the whole sign generally, and in a more particular sense to the first decanate (space of 10°). Mars in the second decanate gives clear perceptions, ability to undertake legal actions with skill and success, but is unfavourable for love affairs, and unions with the opposite sex. In the third decanate sharpens the insight, and gives ability to study science or chemistry to advantage; it inclines towards humanitarian tendencies, and refines the senses.

♂ ♋. Ambitious and industrious, but unfortunate and changeable, though very domesticated. Many worries and sorrows. Romance in speculation: unfortunate children: friendship of servants. Power to resist sickness. Scandal or ill-repute through marriage. Struggle for home maintenance. Sea voyages and enterprising business journeys. Changes in religious views. A taste for occult and mystical studies, hypnotism, etc.; small persistence therein, however. A discontented partner, causing many troubles in married life. Gain through servants and agencies. Pleasure through psychic matters. Difficulties at the close of life. Gain through mental effort, travel and public concerns; also from relatives. These remarks apply to the whole sign generally, and in a more particular sense to the first decanate (space of 10°.) Mars in the second decanate gives passionate tendencies, with a love of travel and long voyages, also martial inclinations. In the third decanate, a quiet nature, thoughtful and peaceful, and a very inoffensive and harmless disposition.

♂ ♌. Choleric, impulsive, fearless, enterprising, honest. Trouble through inferiors. Secret taste for occult phenomena. Secret alliances; ardent affections, and a partner who reciprocates. Friendship of partners. Hazardous occupations. Gain by government pursuits or responsible posts. Broad religious views, and enthusiastic impulses, or free-thought tendencies. Death while still in office, or labour to the end of life. Peculiar ailments of an inflammatory or tumorous character. A speculative nature, and one fond of adventure ; passionate in both love and pleasure ; fond of music, with some real ability for its study. Financial success at close of life. Idealistic and fond of mental pursuits. Gain through public appointments, or the musical profession. The above applies to the whole sign generally, and in a more particular sense to the first decanate (space of 10°). Mars in the second decanate inclines to travel, independence of action, a taste for philosophical argument, and much religious enthusiasm. In the third decanate it denotes a determined will, a keen sense of justice, love of inventions, ready mechanical ability, and a responsive nature.

♂ ♍. Shrewd, quick-witted and acquisitive. Secret union with inferiors. Death of friends and helpers. Profession abroad, or gain in occupation out of native land. Profit through trading in common things and foreign produce. Orthodox religious views. Gain through insurance and other associations, societies, or public dealings, generally as the result of others' losses. Peculiar ties. Power to resist disease by study of hygiene or care in diet. Gain by speculation and investments, or by keen judgment in Stock Exchange matters. A quiet end, but liable to be affected by relatives, of whom the native usually has many poorer than himself. Has ability to make a fortune by speculation. The above remarks apply to the whole sign generally, and in a more particular sense to the first decanate (space of 10°). Mars in the second decanate gives tact, *finesse*, discrimination and quiet ambition, with ability to make opportunities. In the third decanate it gives a stubborn nature, and very obstinate tendencies with great reserve and pride.

♂ ♎. Clear vision, refined tastes, idealistic temperament. Troubles concerning deaths, and losses of many related to the home circle. Makes many friends of a philosophical or religious type. Succeeds in partnership with others. Follows refined occupations, but suffers through competitors. Pure in religious views. Has the opportunity to become clairvoyant. Survives enemies. Developes much perception. The native finds purification of emotions through marriage and the grave responsibilities it throws upon him. Unfortunate in monetary affairs through servants and inferiors. Many and intelligent children. Pleasures connected with the affairs of relatives. Involved in domestic affairs at the close of life. An intuitive mind of a speculative character. Gain from business and professional pursuits. The foregoing applies to the whole sign generally, and in a more particular sense to the first decanate (space of 10°). Mars in the second decanate is good for associations and societies, out of which the native gains pleasure; it also shows love of humanitarian ideals, and gives refined children. In the third decanate it inclines towards educational pursuits, and quickens the mentality generally.

♂ ♏. Quick and acute in judgment—good or evil according to the quality of the nativity. Intrigues, secret missions, legal troubles. Liability to seclusion or confinement. Government office or work of a peculiar nature in which associates and accomplices are concerned. Prominent in society work or in confederations, or even plots. Sea voyages, in which important work of a private nature or own employment is concerned. Indirectly cause of own death. A designing intellect, and often intense devotion to study, in which magical practices or spiritualistic or mesmeric phenomena play a prominent part. Fond of hazardous enterprises. Gains by public losses. Liability to a sudden or violent end. Unfortunate journeys. Financial gain by marriage. The above remarks apply to the whole sign generally, and in a more particular sense to the first decanate (space of 10°). Mars in the second decanate gives romantic courtship and unfortunate speculations. In the third decanate long journeys, necessitated by domestic conditions; publicity abroad.

♂ ♐. Impulsive in speech and action, enthusiastic, and at times rash and thoughtless. Unprofitable employment, or risk in connection with profession; favourable for professions connected with the occult arts, in which inspirational or prophetic tendencies bring success. Many friends of a refined and intuitive character. Liable to secret scandal and ill-repute, often undeserved. Fond of travel and adventure. Gain by will or legacy, also by marriage. More than one union. Concern regarding health of domestic circle. Fond of pleasure, particularly of outdoor exercise. Improvement of mind by marriage. Gain by social means. Dual experiences at close of life. These remarks apply to the whole sign generally, and in a more particular sense to the first decanate (space of 10°). Mars in the second decanate is exaggerative, and liable to over-estimate and risk too much. In the third decanate it renders the native honest and straightforward, and very ambitious.

♂ ♑. Quietly ambitious, enterprising, industrious and acquisitive.

Involved in difficulties through friends and acquaintances. Liable to suffer in honour through enemies of a secret and designing nature. Honour or fame in profession. Capable of much responsibility and endeavour. A lover of duty. Gain through foreign affairs, also by travel. Survives relatives, but rarely gains through them.' Gains socially through marriage, which produces an important change in the life. Sickly children. Industrious servants. Liable to an early entanglement with an inferior. Marriage greatly affects the close of life. Subtle intellect and gain by intuition. Fond of the occult. Slow to learn, but sure in the assimilation of knowledge. The above applies to the whole sign generally, and in a more particular sense to the first decanate (space of 10°). Mars in the second decanate is good for speculation and acquiring wealth. In the third decanate it bestows good business ability, and a fondness for commerce and science.

♂ ♒. Intellectual, quick-witted, scientific. Interested in humanitarian work, and associated with quiet schemes for public good. Connected with others in hospitable work. Gains many friends in the social world through merit and ability, also in profession, and obtains financial success through public work. Makes a good director, or responsible official in connection with public companies. Capable of blending science and philosophy. Sincere in religion. Gain through parents or relatives. Honourable marriage, and faithful in affections. Refined and faithful servants. Pleasure through union or partnerships. Fond of literature and intellectual studies. Death in a strange land or surrounded by strangers. This applies to the whole sign generally, and in a more particular sense to the first decanate (space of 10°). Mars in the second decanate gives joy in intellectual pursuits, but some danger of gambling tendencies. In the third decanate, success in marriage; high mentality.

♂ ♓. Affectionate, receptive, humane, sympathetic. Occult tendencies, or, if the horoscope denotes it, misfortune. Gain from friends financially. Fond of detail; follows ordinary pursuits but is a true dreamer; many changes either in disposition or in plans and views; pleasure in psychic pursuits; in an evil horoscope death through pleasure. Delays in marriage; two attachments; liable to disappointment in love-affairs, or early death of children. Mental occupation; or some employment requiring uniform. Help from friends. Liable to consumptive tendencies. Uneventful end. The above remarks apply to the whole sign generally, and in a more particular sense to the first decanate (space of 10°). Mars in the second decanate gives joy in psychic or occult pursuits. In the third decanate, liability to early death, or life in foreign lands.

In a depraved horoscope this is an unfortunate position; in a refined horoscope it denotes occult inclinations.

The Aspects of Mars *

♂ and ☉. In any aspect, this increases the animal passions and vigour of the body. In good aspect, the native has much 'fire,' great energy and vigour, and achieves much; he pushes his way with intensity of purpose, and having also much perseverance he is seldom thwarted. He has the ability to command and control others, but more through energy and strength of will than through subtlety of purpose. This position gives ability in games or pursuits involving muscular exercise rather than skill,—although if Mars is in an airy sign this same martial energy may take an intellectual direction: it strongly favours all Mars occupations; also legacy from a parent (probably father); and the birth of sons.

In conjunction or bad aspect, there is likelihood of the death of, separation from or disfavour of a parent (probably father), and a child (probably son). The native is too precipitate, rash, aggressive, proud or over-bearing, and loses the esteem of superiors, parents or the public on this account. In conjunction, may receive a legacy: in bad aspect, less chance of it, and is troubled through the goods of the dead; this latter more especially if one or both planets are in negative signs. His health or life may be in danger from martial diseases, accidents, surgical operations, assaults, quarrels, etc. There is some possibility of heart disease.

If Mars or the Sun be dignified by sign, the evil is lessened, and there is an accession rather of energy and executive power than of destructiveness, quarrelsomeness, or precipitancy.

♂ and ♀. In good aspect this is fortunate for money, whether earned by the native's own exertion, gained by partnership, by association with someone, by marriage, or by legacy. It favours money by

---

* The aspects of Mars to ♆, ♅, ♄, ♃, are given on pp. 234, 238, 247, 258 respectively.

any occupation of the four signs or houses ruled, especially the first and eighth; occupations involving personal energy, personal responsibility, personal initiative; all those ruled by Mars; any occupation connected with the dead or the goods of the dead in any way, or directly or indirectly with marriage. The native will part with money freely in social life and may launch out freely in business, for advertisement, for show, for good fellowship; it is, in fact, apt to be 'easy come, easy go'; money is earned or spent in connection with the opposite sex, ornaments, finery, adornment, art, music, singing, the stage, etc. It is also fortunate for love, marriage, social popularity and attachments in general. The marriage or attachment will be to one signified by either of the two planets, but more especially Mars; and to one following any occupation of the four houses, but more especially those of the first and eighth. The marriage will be either for money, or to a moneyed person, or a marriage of passionate attachment; otherwise, love at first sight, or an early or quick marriage. The native will be very susceptible to the attractions of the opposite sex.

The conjunction is largely evil but not always wholly so; for a good deal depends upon which planet is the stronger, and whether the sign and house harmonise with either of the planets or not.

In bad aspect there will be loss of money from carelessness, extravagance, or dishonesty of some kind, and this may come through any matter signified by the four signs or the houses they occupy in the horoscope; from launching out too freely in enterprises, from the fault or misfortune of the marriage or business partner, or from the dishonesty or misfortune of any person associated with the native. There is likelihood of the loss of a legacy, or money troubles connected with matters pertaining to the dead; the loss of money by marriage or through the opposite sex; or else loss through dissipated habits. It is bad for love and marriage and for all association with the opposite sex; the lover or marriage partner may die, or there will be separation or desertion. In extreme cases, where the rest of the horoscope accords, there will be danger to health or life to or from the opposite sex. The native manifests, or suffers from, jealousy; love turned to hatred; loss and opposition from former friends; or is involved in quarrels and enmity, secret or open. His popularity, social or otherwise, is endangered at times.

♂ and ☿. In good aspect, this combination sharpens the wits.

makes the mind quick, bright, alert and lively, and gives humour, wit, sarcasm and satire.   It throws a great deal of energy, force and activity into all matters signified by the third and sixth houses.   It gives some manual dexterity in the direction of drawing, designing, carving, sculpture, and all that is necessary for music, conjuring, etc., and for many kinds of mechanical work.   It is fortunate for any activity of the third or sixth houses that depends upon energy, activity and individual enterprise ; this combination tending to make such activities arise spontaneously from within the mind rather than impressed from without by force of circumstances.   It gives ability and some inclination for alchemy, chemistry, science, and investigation of the mysteries and secrets of nature, for medicine, drugs, sanitation, engineering.   It is slightly favourable for joining literary or occult societies or associations, or for making friends signified by either of the four signs ruled by the planets.   Legacies may be received from, or money gained through, association with persons signified by the third or sixth houses.   It is good for health and digestion, and the native benefits in health by drugs and sanitary methods, and may be inclined to use them frequently.   The last four sentences apply more especially when the aspect falls from negative signs.

The conjunction is partly good and partly bad ; it partakes to a large extent of the nature of the evil aspects, but may also show much of the good.

In evil aspect, while rendering the mind acute and active, as with the good aspects, and giving wit, dexterity of mind and hand, there is danger of overwork mentally, excitement and rashness.   It gives good intellectual powers, but tends to the matter-of-fact, argumentative, or materialistic, rather than the imaginative or spiritual.   If a writer or speaker he arouses opposition, criticism and ill-will ; sometimes by his sharp tongue or pen or injudicious actions ; sometimes by little apparent fault of his own.   Liable to scandalous reports, discreditable rumours, libel ; or to originate such about other people, according to the general tone of the horoscope.   Likely to disagree or quarrel with brethren, associates, friends.   It brings trouble or obstacles through the affairs governed by the four signs, and accident, disease or malformation of any part of the body signified by these signs, the nervous system especially, such as neuralgia, sleeplessness, headache, etc.   Danger while travelling, whether by land or water ; also from wounds, from surgical operations drugs, tools, instruments, electricity, scientific experiments, etc.; may contract some drug 'habit'; danger from quarrels, and from servants or inferiors; possibility of suicide. Death of brethren, friends, agents, servants. If other influences in the horoscope co-operate, but only in this case, such an aspect as this may unhinge the mind or cause delusions or mania of a violent type.

♂ and ☽. In good aspect, greatly increases the activity, energy and vitality. If there is bad health indicated elsewhere, this will go far to counteract it and to preserve health and life. The native is capable of hard work, and works quickly. He accomplishes his ends more through his energy than subtlety, and influences people more by his activity and pushing ways than through agreeableness or insinuating manner, although all these may be present if indicated elsewhere in the horoscope. Enterprising and fruitful of resource, the native will not shrink from positions of publicity or responsibility. This position brings good fortune through the mother, and the possibility of a legacy or money from her on her side of the family. It is favourable for the dwelling-house and house-property, and for a prosperous close to life; it gives a good deal of activity, intelligence and preservation of the senses to the last in old people. It favours fertility in offspring, and gives strength to the whole system, muscular and circulatory; it is good for those who have to work with their muscles, athletes, labourers, and for occupations carried on in the open air. It gives some likelihood of money or possessions through marriage or partnership. It is good for occupations of the fourth and eighth houses, also for those of the water and the watery element generally, and for martial pursuits. If religion is prominent in the horoscope, this may lend its influence in the same direction, according to its own nature.

In conjunction or bad aspect, the native is imprudent, rash and hasty; his temper is quick, and he says and does things that he soon regrets. He is frequently in mental or physical conflict with other people, and constantly finds himself differing from others and at variance with them, perhaps much to his own surprise and regret. He dislikes being hampered or fettered by restrictions, and often breaks rules and regulations of all kinds, careless of the consequences, inciting others to do the same. This position gives strong and ill-regulated passions, which may bring the native much sorrow; these may act in many directions, but bad temper, drink and sex impulses need specially guarding: he may incur public scandal in some degree in connection with any of these, although sometimes this may be quite as much if not more someone else's fault than his own. It may bring trouble of some kind in the sex relation, whether married or not, and disorders affecting the sex organs, lower bowel, or bladder, also the head or eyes. It brings trouble through the mother and her side of the family, her illness or death, or separation from her; also through the house or dwelling-place, and house property. It may cause maladies affecting the breasts, digestion, head and nervous system, and sometimes cancer. It gives liability to a martial death, one rather sudden, or from fever, accident, excitement, rupture of a blood-vessel, wounds, surgical operations; danger from water and fire, scalding, drowning, burning. Loss of an expected legacy; loss of money through marriage or partnership, through robbery, deceit or the bad advice or action of others. If the aspect is strong the native is likely to arouse enmity and opposition and to incur strong disapproval from many people. It may make him excitable and nervous.

The evil effects, so far as they influence character and disposition, may vary very greatly according to the general condition of the horoscope, the prominence of benefics, the sign rising, etc. With prominent benefics and an otherwise good horoscope, the character may suffer very little, and the effects work out through mere 'bad luck,' fate, or what the Easterns term KARMA.

NOTE.—Mars sometimes seems to act, in good as well as evil, more through the influence of other people and association with them than from the native's own action or initiative; good or evil comes to the native from the action of other people. This is, of course, the female (Scorpio) or negative action of Mars. In its male (Aries) and positive nature, the native influenced by Mars is himself the direct or indirect cause of his own fortune or misfortune, and not other people.

THE INFLUENCE OF VENUS IN THE TWELVE SIGNS

[The following judgments apply more to the planet Venus when Ruler or when in the Seventh than when otherwise placed, although they have a general application also as indicating the subjective ideals.]

♀ ♈. Idealistic, imaginative, affectionate, demonstrative, ardent. Changeable in feelings, romantic in love. Secret attachments, fluctuating finance; friends among relatives. Mental attractions to the opposite sex. Prominent domestic affairs, involving some risks in regard to honour or reputation. Pleasure through foreign travel; philosophical friendships. Financial gain through the death of inferiors, and maternal relatives : happiness and joy in marriage. Liable to strange sicknesses. Pleasure from religious or philosophical studies, also from foreign travel. Feelings affected by the father and his affairs. Intellectual friendships; gain through secret and occult affairs. This position gives an ideal love nature, which seeks union for the realisation of the inner self apart from the senses, and the native is anxious to obtain a mental if not a *Soul Union.*

♀ ♉. Strong feelings and deep emotions. A lover of form, and very responsive to physical attractions ; more intuitive than intellectual. Sorrowful emotions produced by relatives and their restrictions; true friendships and attachments in the domestic circle; honourable love affairs. Orthodox religious tendencies. Loss of marriage partner ; one union. Sickness in travel. Fixed in feelings ; psychic or weird mental conditions. Gain from profession and through personal efforts. *Self-Control* in matters of love is the inward desire.

♀ ♊. Dual love affairs. Gain through relatives. Peculiar love-intrigues necessitated in some manner by home life or domestic ties, many loving friends ; honour affected by inferiors for good or ill. Success with affairs abroad in connection with marriage ; many relatives through marriage ; more than one union. Attachments or marriage to members of the clerical or judicial profession. Sickness through profession or business pursuits ; gain by speculation, through the help and advice of friends. Heart sorrows at the close of life. Travel for pleasure; and gain through secret and obscure methods. *A religious or philosophical love-life* is ever sought rather than the sensual or worldly.

♀ ♋. Fickle love affairs; love of home; affectional attractions. Secret love affairs; friendships amongst inferiors. Honour, fame, or notoriety through marriage; death of partner in a foreign land. Love of mystical religion or partner with occult tendency. A union with one who has repute or social standing. Affection from inferiors, pleasure in psychic things, and gain from unpopular sources or by obscure methods. Power to create own domestic atmosphere; gain through ingenuity or mental receptivity, or by sensing public needs and supplying them. Gifted in the occult arts, or in matters related to the astral or psychic world; fortunate as a medium. The desire nature is polarised towards *Ideal love.*

♀ ♌. Ardent in affection, extravagant, and fond of social display. Secret attachments with inferiors; marriage to a friend or brought about through the influence of friends. Liable to dishonour through jealousy, or failure of duty through attachments. Capable of a soul union or philosophical affection, which is sometimes termed free love. Liable to death in order to save honour. One lasting affection at close of life. Very intuitive where affection is concerned. Fond of speculation, and generally fortunate in speculative ventures when impulse is avoided. Gain through inheritance. Mentally clever or intuitive. Mysterious domestic arrangements at the close of life. The goal sought is *Conjugality*

♀ ♍. Pure in affection; the love of chastity being innate. Secret marriage or *liaison*, intrigue or tragedy in connection with love affairs; honour affected through dual attachments. Travels abroad in connection with business affairs, or to safeguard reputation. Loss of friends by death, causing much sorrow. Marriage to an obscure person, or one who has secret troubles; love-sickness, or entanglements with inferiors. Gain by speculation and the help of partner in monetary affairs. Strange experience at close of life; concern regarding relatives; mind occupied at close of life with affections, which latter occasion much correspondence or perhaps travel. A liability to be always involved in secret attachments or unions that are private and undiscovered. The 'law of opposites' operates here in a marked degree to bring a realisation of the inward purity, which is very difficult to maintain in the outer world owing either to ties of the past or the inner desire to make the *Love universal rather than particular.*

♀ ♎. Pure and refined in affection; a simple love nature; many sorrows through death of loved ones; philosophic friends. Honour or position and social gain through marriage; native survives partner. Love affairs and attachments to cousins or relatives. Marriage for love, and financial sacrifices in consequence, for marriage will bring unusual domestic responsibilities; a fruitful union and intellectual children being however shown. The inner desire is for true *Peace.*

♀ ♏. Jealous love nature. Pride of caste. Probable marriage to one who has been previously married. Risky attachments; self-control in matters connected with the feelings; failure in social affairs. Mystical friends, or friendships with persons of doubtful repute. Attacks upon honour through friends or acquaintances. Sea voyages, and romantic adventures during travel. Liable to death by poison, or by suicide through passion and unhappy alliances. Financial gain through unions; secret enmity of servants or blood relations; death of children or trouble through their affairs. Liable to heart affection at close of life. Power to read character or sit in judgment upon others; gain by secret alliance. The inner desire is for *Purification of the sex-nature.*

♀ ♐. Light-hearted and impressionable; fond of pleasure; much involved in love affairs affecting honour. Powerful friends and lasting affections; hospitable connections, generous and loyal intentions. Gain by legacies and through marriage; more than one union; fond of service in home life. Successful in investments or speculations; loving children, who gain social success. Intellectually improved through marriage; some prophetic tendencies. Strange enemies. A peaceful end. The inner desire is for *Illumination.*

♀ ♑. Ambitious love nature; restricted affections; careful of honour. Liable to treachery through associates; friendly with strange characters, and those who have doubtful reputations. Capable of obtaining fame and distinction through skilful use of affections; gain through diplomatic alliances. Gain through foreign travel. Legacies from relatives. Marriage is often one of convenience or for social standing; there are disappointments in love, and coldness or indifference of partner, intrigues with inferiors and unhealthy attachments; little or no domestic happiness. Mental affliction through secret attractions. Allowances from abroad. The inner desire is for *Excellence.*

♀ ☷. Faithful in affection; platonic unions; romantic and secret attachments. Power to win friends easily, and to form easy acquaintance with strangers. Gain through social affairs and through acquaintances. Philosophical views of love life; reserved in opinions and sincere in religious convictions. Money by inheritance or through public connections. Marriage for pure love; very refined inclinations. Friends amongst inferiors. A happy love attachment, and the probability of a long courtship. Some tragedy or shock at close of life, or change of consciousness of some kind. Fond of mental companionship. Gain indirectly through enemies. The inner desire is for *Soul Communion*.

♀ ♓. Hospitable, sympathetic and easily impressed, philanthropic, or engaged in work connected with institutions; strongly attached to persons weak or afflicted. Gain through friendships: honour amongst relatives. Travel for business purposes. Inspirational or psychic, a true dreamer or medium. Gain from attachments, financially. Discrimination in love affairs; sickness after marriage and liability of affection to one not worthy of support. Gain through the help of friends. A peaceful mind; intuition in business affairs. A good end but somewhat involved. The inner desire is for *Compassion*.

THE ASPECTS OF VENUS *

♀ *and* ☉. In conjunction, the native is a very warm-hearted lover and a general favourite with the opposite sex; he or she probably falls in love 'at first sight,' and usually the marriage is one of affection. Such people seldom remain single; they seem almost invariably to marry, no matter how bad the afflictions may be in other parts of the horoscope. The native is fond of society and friends, and is kind-hearted and sympathetic, but may be too much attached to ease, luxury and comfort. This position is favourable for parents' money, for money derived from parents, and for money earned through business, profession or public occupation. It gives some liking for poetry, music and the fine arts generally, and some ability in this direction. The native is likely to rise in his occupation and to do well by it. He is popular and has many friends; may marry money, though not necessarily *for* money. The semi-square is not very important, but it will co-operate with any

---

* The aspects of Venus to the slower planets are to be found on the following pages :—♅ 235, ♅ 239, ♄ 249, ♃ 261, ♂ 270.

other aspect in causing delay or misfortune in all matters mentioned above. (The ☌ ⋁ and ∠ are of course the only possible aspects.)

♀ *and* ☿. In good aspect or conjunction, this is fortunate for money, property and possessions; and these (to put it briefly) may be obtained through any of the activities of the third or sixth houses. In a secondary degree money may be obtained through pleasure, luxury, the theatre, singing, and through sources of the fifth house generally. It is fortunate for marriage and partnership, which may be with one coming to some extent under the third or sixth house in character or occupation, or to a slighter extent under the ninth or twelfth; and the native may marry twice or have two attachments. It gives fondness for society, an amiable and good-humoured manner, and general popularity, especially with the opposite sex. It is fortunate for all matters of the third house; goodwill between brethren; money earned by the wits, by speaking or writing; it is good for invention, and gives manual dexterity which may be turned to account in any of the arts, drawing, painting, music, sculpture, etc.

It is favourable for intuition and the inspiration of genius, and gives some talent for music, poetry, or kindred pursuits. It gives good brains, wit, mirth, buoyancy, good temper, hopefulness. It is good for all matters of the sixth house; for food, digestion, health; for benefit from doctors or medical affairs, and money therefrom; for good relations with servants and subordinates, also when the native occupies such a position himself; for goodwill between relations (uncles, aunts, cousins, etc.). The native is inclined to marry a cousin or some relation.

The only bad aspect between Mercury and Venus is the semi-square, and this is not important. It may, however, put obstacles in the way of any of the affairs signified by the four signs ruled by the two planets; money, marriage, partnership, writings, brothers, journeys, servants, health, etc., and will reverse or hinder those activities previously referred to under the good aspects.

♀ *and* ☽. In conjunction or good aspect, it is very favourable for all matters signified by the second, fourth, and seventh houses; for money and possessions; for money through a parent or parents (probably from mother); for money through things of the third and eleventh houses; for money through houses, land and fruits of the earth. It is fortunate for friends, partners and marriage, and gives social and general popularity. The occupation will be profitable and yet at the same time either unrefined or of low class or caste, plebeian, or involving secrecy. The partner (business or marriage) will differ in age or social position from the native, but help or approval comes from parents (especially mother).

In bad aspect, it brings trouble and loss through money, possessions and property ; it is bad for parents' money (especially mother), and for any attempt to earn money through the eleventh, third or fourth houses ; money may be lost through such matters. The native may suffer in reputation or pocket through some unpopularity, through some slur being cast upon him, or his business or pursuits ; or through slander or scandal, whether deserved or not ; or through attaching himself to unpopular movements or causes. It brings trouble through partnership, love and marriage ; and the trouble may arise from any of the causes just referred to—social or general unpopularity, disapproval of parents, difference in age or position, or from something arising out of the occupation.

THE INFLUENCE OF MERCURY IN THE TWELVE SIGNS

[The following judgments apply to the mental qualifications quite as much as to the influence of Mercury when Ruler.]

☿ ♈. A quick, active, impulsive and argumentative mind; given to over-estimate or exaggerate, and in making statements to add an unconscious 'colouring'; given also to a change of opinions. It inclines to hasty speech, and rash projects; but it gives clever and inventive methods of thought, with liberal views and expressive characteristics.

☿ ♉. A practical, solid, firm and determined mind, somewhat obstinate and stubborn and inclining to dogmatism or over-fixity of opinion. It denotes decided fancies, and strong likes and dislikes, with, however, much intuition; and it moreover bestows the gift of discreet silence or very diplomatic speech. The mind is generally cheerful, refined and musical.

☿ ♊. A clever, dualistic and inventive mind, with power of clear thinking and freedom from decided bias, or over-much prejudice. It denotes latent wit and humour, and a love of detail, with a fondness for travel and the acquisition of knowledge.

☿ ♋. A discreet, tactful, and diplomatic mind, with ability to change opinions without fear. It gives a clear and well-defined intellect, with the power to argue and reason and also to adapt oneself to conditions and surroundings.

☿ ♌. A determined, governing, organising and controlling mind, with power to take large and extensive views, coupled with a somewhat dogmatic tendency: there is much positive assurance, and a high degree of faith and conviction in noble ideals. It denotes a confident, ambitious, persistent, and at the same time intuitive intellect.

☿ ♍. A good intellect, discriminative, scientific, cautious and prudent. It gives versatility and practicalness, coupled with intuition, and an innate love of mystery; but it tends always towards criticism, and at times scepticism—a desire to know thoroughly before conviction.

☿ ♎. A quiet and dispassionate mind, fond of comparison, and displaying both judgment and temperance. This position refines the mind, and gives a taste for mental pursuits that are broad and catholic in their scope.

☿ ♍. A shrewd, keen and critical mind, curious, suspicious and mistrustful; fond of occult and mystical subjects, but ever intent on gaining knowledge and mental power, which is only acquired when the senses have been purified.

☿ ♐. A prophetic, generous and ambitious mind, which is very independent and often rebellious. It gives a love of philosophising and inclines to great freedom in speech, with some tendency towards rashness and impulse.

☿ ♑. A tactful, suspicious and critical mind, inclined to be discontented, though ever studious and careful. It gives a patient and economical disposition, which is only seen at its best when the mind is active and industrious : it then awakens a keen interest in science and supplies painstaking effort towards perfection of intellect.

☿ ♒. A refined and intuitive mind, faithful and persistent, penetrative, observant and keen in its judgment of human nature, and having considerable powers of concentration and abstract thought. It gives a love of metaphysics, and also humanitarian principles.

☿ ♓. A quiet, flexible and impressionable mind, with great absorbing tendencies and the power to memorise and adapt the mind to requirements. There is, however, little depth or breadth of thought, the mind being more intuitive than actively intellectual. There is a liability to be easily psychologised by becoming over-receptive.

THE ASPECTS OF MERCURY

[Some of these aspects have been treated of before, under the heading of the various planets ; but as the description here given is more especially directed to the *mental* tendencies, they have been included with the others.]

☿ *alone.* When in its own sign, Gemini or Virgo, Mercury might theoretically be supposed to exhibit mind *per se*, uninfluenced by any special mode. In practice, however, this never happens ; because the heavenly body with which it is in closest aspect has then to be taken as significant of the type.

☿ and ♆. The mind gains in receptivity, plasticity, adaptability, and intuition. Any tendencies in the direction of the higher mental emotions and powers of imagination will be increased and may work out in various directions, art, poetry, music, etc., according to the general type of horoscope. Under affliction there may be lack of concentration, absence of mind, dreaminess, or irresolution; but the above-mentioned tendencies may even then show out, nevertheless. With both Uranus and Neptune there will be some psychic or occult inclinations or experiences.

☿ and ♅. In any aspect the mental power is much increased, and may gain either in activity or profundity according to the type of horoscope. There is originality, ingenuity, and inventive ability. Generally some distinct ability for such subjects or pursuits as are indicated by Uranus is shown, and they may be taken up with interest and successfully carried out, unless the aspects are very adverse. It gives a stimulus to literary ability and to almost all Mercurial activities.

☿ and ♄. The effects of this combination may vary a good deal according to the type of horoscope, the aspect, and the relative strength of the two influences. At its best it gives a very comprehensive and profound mind, capable of achieving much in whatever direction it is turned. The memory is good and strong, and the judgment sound and sensible. If the mind is directed outwardly toward the world, it looks for practical results and has abilities suitable for politics, local or municipal, and for large private or general public undertakings, official positions of all kinds, and public appointments. The judgment necessary for dealing in speculative commercial or financial ventures is often present; and there are prudence, caution, and sobriety of judgment. The mind is made up slowly, but there is much strength of will and steady persistence when a determination has been arrived at. When directed inwards, or turned towards more purely intellectual pursuits, similar characteristics are shown along these lines; there is a comprehensive grasp of subject, concentration and continuity of thought, ability for dealing with profound and abstruse subjects, and skill in reducing them to order and system for the use of others. If Mercury is much afflicted these qualities may be lessened and the mind be slow or unpractical, while if Mercury and the Moon are both seriously afflicted by malefics there is danger of mental weakness and instability. Under affliction there may be more or less disappointment, mental gloom, errors of judgment, fear, hesitation, lack of initiative, procrastination, lack of candour, etc.

☿ *and* ♃. This may tend in one or two directions. Firstly, the mind may go out towards mankind, showing interest in all studies, pursuits, or occupations that relate the native to his fellow men. It shows in various ways, from cordiality, sociability, good nature—the prudent adviser, the helpful friend—up to the wider operations of philanthropy and benevolence in the world at large. Secondly, from a more strictly intellectual point of view, there is ability for and a tendency towards religious or philosophical studies, varying, of course, according to opportunity and the degree of cultivation of the mind. At its best, the profoundest philosophy, the most exalted sense of religion, and the widest scientific generalisations can be appreciated. The judgment is ripe, the mind is fruitful, honest and honourable. In less developed souls the same tendencies to human intercourse and to religion or the cultivation of the mind may be exhibited, but in a less exalted degree.

☿ *and* ♂. Here the fire and passion of Mars are blended with the intellect. In undeveloped natures, this means that the reason is constantly in danger of being swept aside by storms of passion, desire, anger, prejudice, or self-will. In higher natures, the mind overcomes such impulses and utilises them as energies to subserve its own ends. It often shows as a restless activity of mind that is never satisfied and never at peace. There is liveliness, resource, wit, irony, sarcasm, ingenuity, and promptness. There may be much strength of will in some cases, but it is usually more due to vigour and energy than to patience and steadfastness. The mind is separative and scattering, but the energies are such that great results can be achieved in a short time. Pride, harsh criticism and fault-finding are sometimes shown, and there is a tendency to exaggeration and even untruthfulness in some cases.

☿ *and* ☉. This is seen when the planet is in Leo or is in close conjunction (say 5°) with the Sun. Strength and vitality are given to the mind as a whole rather than to any subdivision of it. Prompt response to new ideas does not occur so readily as with some of the combinations; but any habit of mind once established is likely to be held tenaciously, faithfully adhered to, not easily given up—never under compulsion, though perhaps under persuasion. Mental firmness, mental continuity, mental conservatism and mental energy are shown. New and unfamiliar modes of thought are apt to be rejected, misunderstood, or entirely overlooked simply because they are new; but if some relation to familiar methods is perceived they are slowly accepted and then very exhaustively examined and held. Some degree of mental dignity or pride is shown, some considerable appreciation of the sublime or the dramatic.

When this type is due to the close conjunction with the Sun, there is practically no danger of mental instability (unless congenital) and the mind remains active and powerful to extreme old age. When it arises from the position of Mercury in Leo, much depends upon aspect. At its best, the mind may exert much control over the body and influence it beneficially in illness.

☿ *and* ♀. This may be taken as a tendency on the part of the mind to combine with the emotions, to be influenced and modified by them, and to harmonise and co-ordinate them in its turn. It lends itself to a variety of uses of all degrees of superficiality or profundity, according to circumstances. Mental buoyancy and hopefulness are generally shown; social qualities are called out and manifested; and the mind has the power to adapt itself to other minds, whether in the limits of family life, or in society, or the world at large. This blend of intellect and feeling may be taken as a type of what, when perfected, becomes the genius of the poet, musician, or artist. At its best, it means that the reason is responsive to impulses superior to reason, as in flashes of genius or the ecstatic vision of the seer. In ordinary humanity it shows companionability and sympathy. This combination lifts the mind higher than any other towards the heaven world.

☿ *and* ☽. There is much less continuity and firmness than with the Sun, but more plasticity, variety, change and adaptability. The mind responds more readily to new ideas; mental habits are less firmly fixed and ingrained; there is a tendency to change opinions, perhaps several times during the life, or even to entertain apparently contradictory ones. Imagination and intuition are increased, also mental sympathy and receptivity.

IMPORTANT NOTE

Due allowance should be made for 'minor' aspects since they have not the same strength and power as the major aspects, which are the opposition, square, trine, and sextile.

Where necessary, it will be needful to make allowance for the contradictions that are sure to occur in the different planetary positions. If unable to blend these, reference should be made to *The Art of Synthesis*, which forms the succeeding volume of this series.

This 'blending' is really the most important as well as the most difficult part of the work of judging a nativity, and calls for natural ability as well as wide experience. But until the *analytical* judgment of the horoscope, the study of which this book is designed to facilitate, has been thoroughly mastered, any attempt at synthesis would be altogether unavailing. In all arts a thorough mastery of the means to be employed—of 'colour values,' as a painter would say—must be gained before any hope of success in achieving a good 'general effect' can be entertained. And the synthesising of a horoscope is essentially an art.

CHAPTER XXI

Concluding Remarks on Judgment

In all cases the 'decanates'* should be studied. If the ascending decanate and its rulers are taken fully into consideration, a great deal of light will be thrown upon the character of the native, and the attitude of mind he will be likely to take under given circumstances.

It is not a good thing to have the Ascendant, Sun, and Moon all in the same triplicity, although at first sight it may appear to be best; for the native would be more likely to become lop-sided—either far too idealistic or, on the other hand, too materialistic and 'practical.'

The Decanates of the signs occupied respectively by both Sun and Moon will modify or expand the influence of the sign, and will help considerably in the judgment as to the value of each polarity. If the Sun were placed in the second decanate of Aries (which gives a Leo influence) and the Moon were in the sign Leo in the first decanate (also a Leo influence) the cultivation of the devotional and higher emotional part of the nature would constitute the ideal of the native's life. Again, if the Sun held the third decanate of Aries (which is of the nature of Sagittarius) and the Moon were placed in the first (♐) decanate of Sagittarius, the trend of the native's desires would be towards prophecy and philosophy, and this would greatly improve the general tone of the horoscope, according to the triplicity in question.

The best polarities are those in which the ascendant and the signs containing the luminaries differ: there is then more adaptability, and less danger of becoming too self-centred and exclusive, too much 'shut up' within.

When the Moon is increasing in light—that is, going from the conjunction to the opposition—the perceptive and objective side of the con-

---

* These, as explained before, are divisions of a sign into three equal parts of 10° each. The three decanates of each sign are ruled thus; Aries, ♈ ♌ ♐; Taurus, ♉ ♍ ♑; Gemini, ♊ ♎ ♒; etc., the first decanate being ever of the nature of the sign itself, the second of the next sign of the same triplicity, and so on.

307

sciousness will be more developed than the subjective or reflective ; while the contrary is the case when the Moon is decreasing or passing from the full to the new. Allowance should be made for this fact when judging the horoscope.

If the Sun meets an important aspect before the Moon, that is, if the Sun is nearer to an aspect of importance than the Moon, then the Individual Character will be as it were ' coloured' by this aspect, and the polarity will be affected by it considerably : in the same way the Personal Disposition will be coloured if the Moon makes the first important aspect. The luminaries *applying* to aspects affect the polarity more than aspects from which they are *separating.*

Another important point to consider is the respective elevation of the luminaries. If the Sun is above the Moon, rising or setting, the Individual Character will be stronger than the personal. If both luminaries are *below* the earth the blending of the luminaries is more potent, and the polarity more complicated. The solar influence is strongest when the ☉ is *above* the earth and the lunar when the ☽ is *below.*

If both are *above* the tendency will be for the Sun to gain the greater power ; if both are *below* the Moon.

The polarity is always stronger when the luminaries are rising (*i.e.,* have not yet reached the point of culmination), and weaker when setting (*i.e.,* the culminating point has been passed). The Individual side of the character is strongest when the Sun applies to the benefics, and the same holds good with regard to the Personality in the case of the Moon.

Much aid will be given to the judgment if the planets ruling the signs holding the luminaries are also studied. If they are in the same signs as the luminaries the polarity is very powerful, and the quality of that sign is much accentuated. For instance, if Mars is also in Aries the influence of the Sun in Aries will partake chiefly of the martial character, no matter what the decanate may be ; but it will denote *strength,* for either good or evil according to the horoscope.

The Polarities of Sun and Moon, etc.

When the separate parts of each horoscope are dissected and the mind has been made familiar with their various portions, an attempt must be made to synthesise the whole, by bringing into unity the quality which every horoscope indicates.

There are six 'pairs of opposites' to be considered before making
the final synthesis, and they represent the positive and negative elements
in every nativity as follows: The Sun and the Moon; Mars and Venus;
Jupiter and Saturn; the positive and negative signs; each house and its
opposite.

The first of these pairs of opposites and the most important is that
constituted by the Sun and Moon, which chiefly tends to determine the
polarity of each horoscope; for it may be considered as synthesising in
itself the pairs of opposites indicated by ♂-♀, ♃-♄.

The Individual and Personal Characters are represented by the Sun
and Moon respectively, and the signs holding these luminaries become
potent and full of meaning when it is understood that the principal part
of the judgment is obtained by a correct knowledge of the polarisation
of the two.   For they represent the higher and lower mind, that part of
the native which is humanising and strictly mental.   The Sun represents
the immortal and real part of the mind, which is as much universal as
it is individual, and the Moon represents a reflected part of the real mind,
being the personal and limited portion, which is expressed through the
brain and which is intimately concerned with all expression on the
physical plane.

Manas, or universal mind, is represented astrologically by the Sun,
and it has six different expressions through the six positive signs of the
Zodiac.   The soul or mind of the world is represented by the Moon and
its six varied expressions through the six negative signs of the Zodiac.
This blending and interblending of the Sun and Moon through the
masculine and feminine signs of the Zodiac form as it were the Shuttle
of Destiny by which the fabric of human fate is woven, and whereby (to
vary the metaphor) matter may be moulded for the wider expression of
the Ego, either individually or personally.

The vitalising power of the Sun upon all that lives upon the earth
is well known to all, therefore but very little expansion of the imagination is required to understand the potent effect the Sun has upon each
sign of the Zodiac.   In fact, as this is the path of the Sun—or, to be
exact, the earth around the Sun—each sign is more complete, more
distinctive and more elastic, so to speak, when the Sun passes (or appears
to pass) through it.   This causes the sign in which the Sun is
placed at birth to be the most actively expressed of the twelve in any
horoscope, all its influence being stamped upon the character of the

native in a very marked and notable degree. For the individual characteristics in every native are shown by the sign which the Solar orb occupied at his birth, and it is therefore necessary, as has been said before, to consider the Sun's position as the most important factor when judging a nativity.

Silence	is	Golden -	-	-	-	☉
Speech	is	Silver -	-	-	-	☽
Thoughts	are	Things -	-	-	-	☿

The 'root of merit' in each individual is astrologically judged by the power, position, and aspects of THE SUN, which represents the Silent Monitor in all. The Sun is silent but potent, it shines on all, good and evil alike, and is the essential 'music of the spheres' out of which all harmony and order are produced.

THE MOON represents the keynote or medium through which the chord of harmony vibrates, and echoes that which has been born in the silence; while MERCURY is, as it were, the string or thread up and down which the silence and the sound are constantly moving as are the pulsations in an organ pipe.

THE SUN is the Source from which the rays of Mercury arise, but the Moon is the lens or reflector which catches and condenses them.

THE SOLAR AND LUNAR POSITIONS AND ASPECTS[*]

With reference to these 'Polarities,' the value of the Sun in each sign as denoting the Individual Characteristics, and similarly also that of the Moon in each sign as relating to the Personal Idiosyncrasies, and the combinations resulting therefrom have each been very fully dealt with in the third revised edition of the first volume of this series, *Astrology for All*, hence it is unnecessary to repeat what has there been said, and it will therefore suffice to give the following brief summary of

THE DISPOSITION PRODUCED BY THE MOON IN PLANETARY SIGNS

In the Sun's Sign (♌).—Honour, self-confidence, self-reliance, dignity, pride, ambition, love of fame, candour, generosity, nobility of

---

[*] The Solar aspects to the various planets are given in Chapter XX

nature, organising ability, tendency to pomp and ceremony.   Evil aspects may not lessen these qualities necessarily, but they are a little apt to turn dignity and pride into conceit, vanity or ostentation.

In the Moon's Sign (♋).—The best side of the Moon's nature shows out here.   Sociability, domesticity, family and parental love, attraction to the mother, accessibility, fellow-feeling, agreeableness, humanity, popularity, love of change.   The feelings and emotions are active, and usually for good.   Bad aspects may not do more than bring ill luck through this side of the nature.

In Mercury's Signs (♊ *and* ♍).—An open and receptive mind, readiness to respond to new ideas and take up new subjects, a fertile fancy, great love of change, and fondness for travel, with a taste for investigating many subjects.   Strengthens the mind and enlivens the intellect, in any direction indicated by the horoscope.   There is ability to learn, memorise, write, speak, acquire education, etc.

In the Signs of Venus (♉ *and* ♎).—Good-humoured, warm-hearted; fond of company, society and amusement; affable, popular, hopeful, mirthful; inclined to friendship, love and marriage.   Appreciation of music, painting, the fine arts, ornamentation, dress, luxury.   Mental refinement, unless badly afflicted.   In Taurus, a tendency to live too much in the feelings, sometimes indulging a morbid approbativeness or jealousy; in Libra sometimes a too complacent nature.

In the Signs of Mars (♈ *and* ♏).—Courage, a positive and forceful nature, enterprise, independence, dislike of control, self-reliance, action, activity, energy, practical ability, will, determination, masterfulness. If there is much affliction by Mars or Saturn, there may be manifested rashness, imprudence, impulsiveness, anger, aggressiveness, rebellion, recklessness, hastiness, pride, intolerance, obstinacy.

In the Signs of Jupiter (♐ *and* ♓).—Good-natured, jovial, social, benevolent, kind, humanitarian, philanthropic, charitable; hopefulness, devotion, faithfulness, openness of mind, inclination to religion or philosophy, imagination, love of beauty and harmony.   In Sagittarius, often somewhat careless, ready in promise or boast but indifferent in performance; in Pisces, sometimes too negative, responding to diseased physical or mental conditions by preference, as it were.

In the Signs of Saturn (♑ *and* ♒).—Gravity, thoughtfulness, steadfastness, patience, self-control, restraint.   A self-contained nature, far-seeing, displaying sobriety of conduct with worldly wisdom; inclination for practical affairs, such as business, politics, etc.; reserve, dignity, ambition, strength of will. Under affliction some of the less favourable qualities may be traced: gloom, despondency, selfishness, hardness, want of hopefulness, lack of enterprise, worldliness, covetousness, coldness of nature, lack of humanity, lack of candour. In Capricorn a tendency to capricious acts. In Aquarius, often a fickle manner, strange tastes, and some aloofness of mind: in either case a subtle and penetrative mind.

The Relationship of the Moon to the Sun by Aspect*

$\odot$ and $\mathbb{D}$. When these are in good aspect, and especially when in conjunction, the individual and personal sides of the nature form a harmonious blend, and the result is decidedly good. It is also good if both are in signs governed by the same planet, or if the lord of the sign containing one is exalted in that containing the other. If either or both are in good aspect to the cusp of the ascendant or to its lord or to a planet in the ascendant, the harmony of the character is considerably increased; and actions, intellect, and feelings will be more in accord than is the case with the average person of to-day.

Aspects to planets, however, must be taken into account to some extent before pronouncing too confident an opinion; for even if the two luminaries are in good aspect to each other, one may be heavily afflicted by planets and the other not; the side of the nature indicated by the planet afflicted will then be much less fortunate than the other. This consideration it is important to bear constantly in mind.

When in conjunction or good aspect, the general strength of character is increased, there is some amount of self-reliance, personal independence, and stability. It promotes usefulness in the home and the world, increases the activity and the will. It is good for all social, benevolent, and utilitarian movements, broadens the sympathies, gives humanitarian impulses, and conduces to popularity and general success. The constitution is strengthened and vitality increased somewhat. There is a likelihood of offspring and of good fortune through them in respect of health, disposition and circumstances. It tends to increase family harmony both in youth and age; is good for parents and children; and

---

* Note.—The aspects of the Moon to the various planets are given in Chapter XX.

favours love, marriage and friendship. It includes the possibility of money and success through a variety of sources, through parents or children, but also and chiefly through occupations or sources indicated by the sign containing the Sun (except when the Moon is the more elevated or the stronger of the two). If both are in one sign, the ruler of that sign will be very important in the character and fortunes; generally for good, unless contradicted elsewhere.

When in bad aspect, more especially in square—for the opposition merely throws the lunar qualities into special prominence—there will be disharmony manifested between the individual and personal characteristics; the one will run counter to the other. Which will prove victor, and whether it will result in a more, or a less, estimable disposition may be judged from the relative power of the luminaries; (1) by mundane position, (2) by zodiacal position, congenial or otherwise, or (3) by the planetary aspects and the power of the planets concerned, whether by position, sign or inherent nature.

The correct judgment of the polarity, in this sense, of the horoscope is really *the key to the reading of the whole nativity*, and the best powers of the student should be concentrated upon it; for it is a subtle and complex problem.

CHAPTER XXII

A SIMPLE WAY OF READING HOROSCOPES

ILLUSTRATED BY REFERENCE TO THE NATIVITY OF THE LATE KING EDWARD VII

IT is far better to make a complete study of a single nativity than to make a desultory examination of a great many. But beginners are often so puzzled as to where to commence, that they are apt to despair of ever completing a systematic study of any horoscope—whether their own or another's. It is hoped that the following hints may be of real help to all students, and especially to beginners.

First of all let us grasp the fact that there are three distinct factors in a horoscope, Planets, Signs and Houses.

THE PLANETS, *per se*, indicate *mind*, or the mental tendencies, inherent mental attributes present as the result of previous activities in past lives.

THE SIGNS OF THE ZODIAC, on the other hand, show the innate feelings; tendencies to respond to particular emotions, love, joy, anger, fear, grief, etc.

THE HOUSES OF THE HOROSCOPE indicate the *senses*, or the matter of this physical planet of which our bodies are built up.

Thus we have the familiar trinity of 'spirit, soul and body,' though differently expressed. The planets themselves and their aspects may be regarded as epitomised in, or synthesised by, the Sun (☉), the motive power; the planets, *as manifesting through the signs*, may be typified by the Moon (☽), the receptive focus; and the houses, as influenced by the signs, by the Earth (⊕), the neutral centre. Again, just as the twelve houses of the horoscope may be regarded as focused in the ascendant; so the signs may be thought of as focused in Aries, the 'first house' of the Zodiac; and the planets in ☿, the 'convertible' planet. It will be useful perhaps to tabulate these, thus

PLANETS *per se* represent *Mind*   and are synthesised in   THE SUN   ☉
SIGNS   „   „   *Feelings*   „   „   „ THE MOON ☽
HOUSES   „   „   *Sense Organs* „   „   „ THE EARTH ⊕
The centre of consciousness (so to speak) of the *Planets* is in ☿
    „   „   „   „   *Signs*   „   ♈
    „   „   „   „   *Houses* „   Ascendant

Having well grounded ourselves in these fundamental ideas, we may now proceed to examine some particular horoscope and see how we can first analyse it into its various factors, and then synthesise the ideas we have gained so as to arrive at a clear understanding of the character and fortune signified.

We will take the late King Edward's horoscope as a suitable example. He was born, according to the official bulletin, 9th November, 1841, at 10.48 a.m., at Buckingham Palace.   Here again we have three essential factors—date, time and place; progressive order of limitations.   The *date* shows us the zodiacal position of the Sun and planets; the *time*, the position of the Moon; and the *place* the position of all these in relation to the celestial 'houses.'   Let us examine them in order.

(1) THE DATE. The Ephemeris shows us that, from 0.0 a.m. to 12 p.m. on 9th November, 1841, the planets were placed as follows:

☉	☽	☿	♀	♂	♃	♄	♅	♆
♏17	♍23°—♎7°	♐2°	♎19°	♑16°	♐22°	♑0°	♓21°	♒15°

This alone tells us a great deal, but we must remember that it will all apply to any person born during the twenty-four hours, and on any part of the globe.   We therefore proceed to study the second limitation.

(2) THE TIME. At 10.48 a.m. G.M.T., on the date in question, we find the planets as in the annexed diagram (*Fig.* 1), which has been purposely drawn with Aries in the place of the ordinary 'first house,' Taurus occupying the second house, and so on.   This diagram gives us a far better idea of the relative sign-positions of the planets, and of their aspects to one another, than any horoscope drawn in the ordinary way. It shows the planetary and zodiacal influences focused upon the earth *as a whole* (irrespective of any particular place), at the precise moment we are considering.   The first thing we notice is that all the planets are, analogically, 'above the Earth'; that is, they are in the latter half of the Zodiac.   Next, we see that both the Moon and Saturn are just on

the 'angles' of the ♎0° and ♑0° (and therefore in square to one another). Two other planets are also 'angular,' two of the four, ♀ and ♄, being in their own houses, and one 'exalted.' This is all testimony of a marked destiny, and of a public position of some kind. The Sun is strong in Scorpio, a fixed sign—the fixed signs being sympathetically related to the Sun—and in trine to Uranus, a planet of power, thus indicating a strong character who will have great sway over his associates. The sextile of Mars supports this, so that the square of Neptune, a baneful influence, is weakened and rendered less harmful.

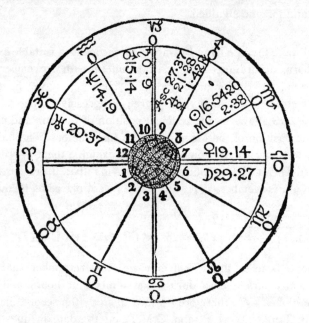

Fig. 1. A ZODIACAL ARRANGEMENT OF THE HOROSCOPE

All the planets being 'above the earth' is evidence of power and influence in the native's own sphere and gives the opportunity of exercising sway. No planets are in Aries, the 'personality' of the Zodiac, but Libra, the 'individuality' (Higher Self) is tenanted by Venus, its ruler. Hence we deduce that the native is not restricted in his views, but broad-minded and sympathetic towards others, a conclusion which is corroborated by Jupiter, representative of the Higher Mind, at home in the 'ninth house' of our symbolical horoscope.

All this, we must remember, would be equally true of *anyone* born on *any* part of the globe at the moment in question, and is therefore not peculiar to our august subject.* Nevertheless, it gives us a very fair idea of what, for want of a better word, we must still call the 'individuality' of any person born at this moment. And we will therefore now proceed to determine how this 'individuality' is likely to be expressed through the personal mould indicated by the Houses of the Horoscope. This leads us to our third and last limitation, namely :

(3) THE PLACE. The second diagram (*Fig.* 2) shows a map of the

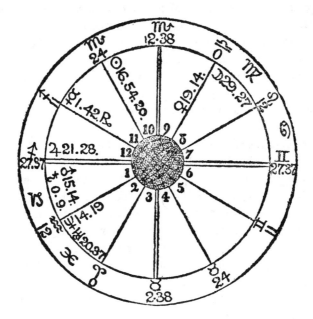

Fig. 2. THE NATIVITY OF THE LATE KING EDWARD VII

heavens calculated for this same minute at Buckingham Palace. Now, in deciding how far destiny will permit of expression in this physical world of the attributes we have deduced from the Zodiacal Horoscope, we first turn to the 'angles' or *cardinal* houses of the figure—houses 1, 4, 7, 10—which, as we know, are concerned more particularly with *manifestation*. Here again we find planets ' angular '—three—all of

* NOTE.—The question of *heredity* will be fully dealt with in the succeeding volume, *The Art of Synthesis*.

them strong (♄ in own house ; ♂ exalted ; ☉ in a fixed sign ⚹ ♂ and △ ♅), and therefore able, we may judge, to overcome the afflictions to the Moon and ruling planet (☽ □ ♄, ♃ □ ♅) ; these three last, ☽, ♃, and ♅, being hidden away in succedent (*fixed*) or cadent (*mutable*) houses. We see that the nature is fairly evenly balanced between ☉, ♄ and ♂, all angular, while the influence of Jupiter, the ruling planet, though weakened by its position in the twelfth, a negative and receptive house, is nevertheless favourable for bringing to naught the malice of enemies, and is potent for deliverance from trouble ; but it somewhat impedes the general good fortune of the royal native. This same remark will also apply to the position of ♆ and ♅, in the second house. Venus, lady of the ninth in the ninth, and in trine to Neptune, indicates the good fortune and peaceable ministrations attendant on foreign travel, of which we have had such abundant instances during the last few years.

This must suffice as to the general principles to be adopted in the judgment of all nativities. In the preceding chapters clear rules have been given and these, coupled with what has been said above, will furnish sufficient basis for further elaboration.

Yet there are those who prefer some method that will shorten the judgment and explain the order in which the delineation should be framed. To satisfy these latter, who will be amateurs in the study of Astrology, the method adopted by the author and used exclusively by him during the past twenty years, is now published for the first time. It is hoped, however, that the simplicity of this plan will not deter the student from using his own judgment, and it should only be used as a system by which the mind can be trained into giving a spontaneous judgment simply and easily.

For the purpose of economising space and avoiding the confusion that many words may produce, the judgments that follow are presented in an epitomised form ; yet although each delineation has been abbreviated to the last degree, the spirit of the judgment is contained in each sentence and by reference to the first part of the work may be extended as fully as the student may desire. The various headings of the horoscope are classified under Roman numerals, and in writing out a *full* delineation it is a good plan to devote about one page, on an average, to each heading. For an elementary delineation, however, if the epitomised judgments are merely copied out, it will serve as a basis for further work—though (as pointed out in the Introduction) it is never wise to copy delineations, since it cramps the judgment.

With a view to making these epitomised judgments more practical they may be referred to the horoscope of KING EDWARD VII, just given.

It should be made quite clear that they have been written with a view to usefulness in a general sense, and not with any special regard to the King's nativity, and that they will therefore require suitable modification in some instances.

The following are the abbreviated delineations arranged under separate headings in the order in which they should be treated in making a detailed judgment of any nativity, each item being numbered for convenience of reference. Those judgments that relate to the King's nativity are tabulated at the conclusion of the chapter, and may thus be read through in the order in which they are numbered.

I. ASCENDANT I.

1. ♈.—The native has a fiery, active, energetic, and somewhat restless body. Disposition: impulsive, enthusiastic, frank, courageous and enterprising; ambitious, independent, adventurous, confident, liberal, responsive, alert, changeable, and fond of pioneering.

2. ♉.—Vital form of body, but stolid, magnetic and sensitive. Disposition: affectionate, fond of pleasure, solid, self-centred, obstinate but practical; persevering, quiet and firm; reserved, decisive; strong bias, keen desires, jealous where affection or honour is concerned.

3. ♊.—Mental temperament; body suitable for mental pursuits, refined, flexible, highly sensitive, nervous. Disposition: restless, irritable, anxious, fond of learning, curious, studental, lacking in continuity, kind, humane, generous and thoughtful.

4. ♋.—Sensitive body, tenacious and receptive. Disposition: imaginative, reserved, impatient, propitious, fond of change, liable to extremes, exacting, timid, retiring, mistrustful, over-cautious, showing strong attachments, over-sensitive and more or less psychic.

5. ♌.—Fiery body, vital temperament, disease-resisting, splendid vitality. Disposition: independent, free, generous, noble-minded, fearless, open and sincere, honourable; proud but magnanimous.

6. ♍.—Sensitive body, mental-motive temperament, usually fairly well balanced. Disposition: flexible, ingenious, studious, practical,

quiet, retiring, modest, yet ambitious of merit; reserved, diffident, sympathetic, but difficult to understand.

7. ♎.—Well balanced temperament. Disposition : gentle, courteous, affable, obliging, intuitive, even, harmonious; keen sense of justice; good comparison ; somewhat indecisive.

8. ♏.—Shortish, somewhat thick but supple body; strong character. Disposition : reserved, proud, determined; acute perception, with keen incisive criticism; fond of the mystic and occult, intelligent, dignified, energetic, self-controlled. Either good or bad, seldom or never ' milk-and-water.'

9. ♐.—Fiery, flexible and wiry body, usually long,* but generally well-proportioned, fond of outdoor sport, exercise and all activities. Disposition : restless, independent, hopeful, philosophical, irrepressible, quick in movement, demonstrative in manner, kind, sympathetic, frank and generous ; fond of freedom.

10. ♑.—Heavy body, usually thin and bony; motive temperament. Disposition : enduring, timid, patient, persistent, restraining, economical, reserved; self-possessed ; ambitious, but pessimistic ; excellent organising ability ; tactful and self-protective.

11. ♒.—Vital-mental type of body, very refined but sensitive. Disposition : humane, faithful, artistic, ingenious, determined and inflexible, self-controlled; mentally refined ; keen student of human nature.

12. ♓.—Plastic, fluidic body ; receptive, mediumistic, and inspirational. Disposition: restless, impressionable, imitative ; hospitable, sympathetic, psychic ; very easily influenced by surrounding conditions.

II. THE RULING PLANET II.

13. ♆.—Denotes transcendentalism, weird tastes and uncommon tendencies, or æsthetic and mystical temperament.

14. ♅.—Denotes originality, unique experiences, leanings towards the occult side of life ; will power, intellectuality ; but when not fully manifest, eccentricity, erratic tendencies, with liability to sudden and unexpected events. Generally gives a nervously organised temperament which is quite uncommon.

---

* NOTE.—In the King's case this is modified by the planets rising, also by the position of the Sun in a fixed sign, which usually tends to shorten the stature, giving more of the ' vital ' temperament.

15. ♄.—Marks limitations, hindrances, obstructions, delays, disappointments; denotes concentration, frugality, perseverance, fortitude, patience, thrift, chastity and a meditative temperament.

16. ♃.—Increases life and vitality; denotes expansion; favours prudence, faith, hope and charity. Stimulates courtesy, temperance and chivalry, and produces good fortune.

17. ♂.—Denotes independence, self-reliance, courage, quick response, self-confidence, ambitious; gives impulse, headstrong and wilful tendencies, with a fighting and combative spirit.

18. ☉.— Self-reliant, strong-minded, strong willed.

19. ♀.—Expressive, lovable, agreeable, artistic and fortunate. Harmonises well with and responds to higher vibrations.

20. ☿.—Depends chiefly upon aspects received from other planets. Being colourless it is absorbent, thus affected by sign occupied. Denotes adaptability, fertility of resource, ingenuity and flexibility of expression.

21. ☽.—Sensitive, fond of form, impressionable and affected by surroundings.

NOTE.—The Sun, Moon, Mercury and Venus as ruling planets depend very much upon the signs they occupy and the aspects they form with regard to their influence.

III. THE RULER'S POSITION III.

22. *In First House.*—Progress, self-control, prosperity from personal effort and merit.*

23. *In Second House.*—Success in financial matters, according to ability; strong thought-force, full of interest in monetary concerns.

24. *In Third House.*—Mental abilities according to talent; greatly concerned with brethren and relatives; much travelling, changes and correspondence, but usually lacking opportunity.

25. *In Fourth House.*—Strong domestic ties; occult or psychic tendencies; affected by parent's influence and often handicapped by environment.

26. *In Fifth House.*—Fond of pleasure, often gains by speculation, or judicious investments; much concern with children or their affairs; plenty of vitality.

---

* In the example map Jupiter has risen above the ascendant but is well within the limits given in the note on p. 90.

27. *In Sixth House.*—Unfavourable position ; handicapped through sickness or misfortune ; best in inferior posts, otherwise gains through servants more than through own ability ; makes a better servant than master.

28. *In Seventh House.*—Fortunate position, some fame in life ; gains best through working with others ; good partnerships, but liable to meet with strong opponents.   Life usually bound up with another's in some special way.

29. *In Eighth House.*—Occult tendencies ; life affected through deaths of others ; gain by legacies, or through co-workers.

30. *In Ninth House.*—Philosophical, good mental abilities, 'a true dreamer' ; fond of travel ; success abroad ; may rise to high and prominent positions.

31. *In Tenth House.*—Rise in life to much higher position than sphere of birth ; achieves honour or fame according to merit, acquires responsibility ; much ambition and aspiring tendencies.   Obtains opportunities.

32. *In Eleventh House.*—Gain through friends ; strong desires and aspirations ; rises in life, makes progress through refinement, and achieves ambition.

33. *In Twelfth House.*—Unfortunate position ; liable to self-undoing ; fond of occultism or spiritualism ; lacks opportunities ; liable to false accusations.   Rises out of sorrows according to merit.

Much of course depends upon nature of ruler, also sign it is in. For fuller information see chapters dealing with these houses.   For Aspects see Chapter IV.

IV. RISING PLANETS* IV.

34. ♆.—Mediumistic and psychic, prone to strange experiences and remarkable episodes.   If given to depravity, becomes a hopeless moral wreck.   When developed, is highly receptive to higher forces.

35. ♅.—A unique character, original, inventive, and unconventional.   Inclines to romance or towards eccentricity and peculiar behaviour.   The undeveloped are abrupt and too independent, the developed are profound occult students.

---

* A planet is considered a 'rising' planet when anywhere between the cusps of the second and twelfth houses.

36. ♄.—Not a fortunate position; is against worldly prosperity, unless very persevering. Denotes obstacles to be overcome, stimulates industry, reserve, prudence and economy. Native often stands in his own light by the exercise of too much caution or fear. Much depends on aspects and sign. (The best signs for this position are ♎ and ♐.)

37. ♃.— Brings good luck, mainly through a generous disposition that is always buoyant, hopeful and aspiring, promises social success, always acts as a preserving influence. The most benefic position, if not in Gemini or Virgo.

38 ♂.—Increases 'vim' and confidence, gives also courage, energy and impulse. Makes the native consequential and inclined to resort to force, with either combative or destructive tendencies.

39. ☉.—Fortunate position; brings dignity and honour, commands respect and good feeling, produces responsible position, gives authority, favours worldly affairs and moral growth. Improves disposition, by enlarging the outlook.

40. ♀.—Favourable position, improves disposition, making it agreeable and cheerful. Gain in life through good fortune, assisted by others. Ability for music, singing or fine arts. Refines nature, gives love of the beautiful, with a tendency to seek pleasure or very refined employment. A most successful position.

41. ☿.—Increases mentality and adaptability; encourages diplomatic tendencies; increases activity and quickness of thought; gives literary ability according to aspects, but denotes fluctuating fortune, sometimes high up and at other times low down.

42. ☽ Disposition mutable, fond of change and novelty; much receptivity; gives popularity, power to sense requirments; love of travel; increases sensitiveness and impressionability. Much depends upon aspects.

V. RISING PLANETS IN SIGNS OF THE ZODIAC V.

See Chapter VI, pp. 105-110. For the RISING PLANET's Aspects see Chapter IV, p. 49 et seq., taking the 'significator' in this case as the Rising Planet.

VI. INDIVIDUALITY VI.

In all delineations THE SUN should be treated as the Individuality and considered as the *background* of the character, characterising the moral nature and the motive power at the back of manifestation. The following are the characteristics.

THE SUN IN THE TWELVE SIGNS

43. ♈.—Enthusiastic, independent, impulsive, energetic, aspiring, idealistic, prophetic, perceptive, loyal, heroic, aspiring and approbative.

44. ♉.—Determined, persistent, patient, enduring, practical, conservative, dogmatic or obstinate. Generous or warm-hearted; reserved, but sympathetic, character exceedingly strong, being dignified, cautious and careful.

45. ♊.—Mentally impulsive, intellectual, literary, ambitious. Restless, nervous, volatile, indecisive, mentally active.

46. ♋.—Reserved, economical, tenacious, sensitive, given to extremes. Strong in caste. Reverence for ancient customs and ancestry. Fond of power and somewhat paradoxical, being persistent, although retiring.

47. ♌.—Strong willed, generous, earnest, sincere, ambitious; proud, or dignified; fond of organising; love of nature; capable of great things.

48. ♍.—Practical, philosophical, constructive, discriminative, critical, self-protective, diplomatic, ingenious; fond of business and generally adaptable.

49. ♎.—Perceptive ability, good powers of comparison, intellectual; love of justice; conscious of trust and confidence, fond of approbation; keen insight; best when associating with others.

50. ♏.—Very determined; strong magnetic power; critical perception, ability to judge; failure through exacting, jealous and proud tendencies. Inclined to be sharp and sarcastic; not over sympathetic. Tenacious and secretive, much self-control; succeeds in government office; much silent force within. A strong and powerful character. When developed, many admirable qualities; but in the undeveloped many vices are exhibited.

51. ♐.—Reliant, prophetic, candid, outspoken, devoted and affectionate; frank, generous, loyal, philosophical; possessed of either a religious or intuitive spirit.

52. ♑.—Ambitious, persistent, industrious, persevering, independent, determined; thrifty, prudent, enduring, capable of responsibility

trustworthy and reliable.   Strong characters are patient and enduring, while the weak are servile, cringing, and bound by custom.

53. ♒.—Faithful, kind, humane, honest and intuitive; equable, dispassionate, constant in affection.   Good judges of character; quiet, unobtrusive, and capable of making high attainments.

54. ♓.—Sympathetic, emotional, lacking in ambition, mediumistic, sociable, hospitable; when developed very honest and trustful, but in the undeveloped there is much weakness.

THE SUN IN THE TWELVE HOUSES need not be specified; for it is only necessary to remember that the Sun quickens and stimulates everything in connection with the house in which it is placed, in other words, it illuminates all the dark places of that house, and brings out all the characteristics denoted by it, usually being fortunate in connection with the house in which it is placed; that is if free from serious afflictions.

The Sun's aspects, however, are very important.   Much information concerning the Sun has been given in the first part of this work (Ch. V). The first major aspect formed by the Sun is always very important, since the planet aspected by the Sun is revivified, as it were, and made more potent in the nativity.   The following are the general aspects formed by the Sun: they are grouped under three heads, ADVERSE ASPECTS, BENEFIC ASPECTS, and CONJUNCTIONS, signified by three letters, A, B, C, an arrangement which will be adhered to throughout the remainder of the chapter.

55. ☉ ♆ A.—Gives a liability to treachery, deceit and grievous disappointments.

56. ☉ ♆ B.—Gives often extraordinary good fortune; a peculiar temperament with a love of mysticism and the possibility of much expansion of consciousness.

57. ☉ ♆ C.—Gives a strange individuality; if developed, clairvoyance or clairaudience or some psychic ability; but in the undeveloped, it tends to produce sexual depravity.

58. ☉ ♅ A.—Is unfortunate and often very disastrous.   Produces estrangements, unforeseen and unexpected events; many changes; often crashes of a severe character.   Nearly always produces unpopularity or notoriety at some period of the life.

59. ☉ ♅ B.—Denotes some genius or originality.   It makes the individual character self-reliant and resourceful, very independent and

broadminded, with philosophical or unconventional tendencies. It
favours popularity.

60. ☉ ♅ C.—Denotes a unique character, with a powerful will,
great constructive ability, much originality, and a commanding
individuality.

61. ☉ ♄ A.—Weakens the constitution, brings many limitations
and disappointments. Health suffers through imperfect circulation, and
if the moral character is not very strong, some mischievous traits of
character are developed, such as selfishness, jealousy, and enmity.

62. ☉ ♄ B.—Denotes success in life through a patient, persevering
and honest character. Shows success in responsible posts, also through
aged persons, and is a very steadying influence, which is felt more
towards the latter part of the life than at the beginning.

63. ☉ ♄ C.—Is neither fortunate nor unfortunate, but tends to stop
the moral growth. Gives power to assume responsibility, and generally
excellent organising ability as well. If used correctly, promises the
accumulation of wealth through economy, patience and perseverance
but increases caution and self-restraining powers.

64. ☉ ♃ A.—Denotes trouble in connection with social affairs;
difficulties in connection with religious matters; health affected through
excesses, and unless strict temperance is observed a tendency towards
extravagance or extremes. In a depraved horoscope this denotes
hypocrisy.

65. ☉ ♃ B.—Promises much good fortune, many social advantages, a religious spirit, much benevolence and sympathy. It gives
prosperity in life, favours health, finance and love affairs.

66. ☉ ♃ C.—Brings many opportunities in life, morally, socially
and physically. It denotes prosperity, expansive sympathies and
nobility of character.

67. ☉ ♂ A.—An unfavourable aspect, since it gives a liability to
feverish tendencies, hasty conduct, and a tendency to become excited
and careless, thus giving liability to accidents and errors of conduct
through the desires being stronger than the will.

68. ☉ ♂ B.—Good for the health and vitality. It strengthens the
constitution, gives much will power, increases the energy and perseverance, causing the individuality to be determined, commanding and
authoritative. It gives strength to the system, and denotes an
enterprising spirit.

69. ☉ ♂ C.—A powerful position, denoting a strong will, but with sometimes a tendency to exhibit passion or anger, with a liability to excess of feeling, and unless self-control is shown by the horoscope there is danger of going to extremes and becoming forceful. It denotes a dominating and powerful will, with abundance of energy behind it.

70. ☉ ♀ A. (∠).—Tends to produce disappointments and often brings social difficulties, and unless the moral character is very strong it weakens the individuality.

71. ☉ ♀ B. (∨): or ☉ ♀ C.—Gives a love of pleasure; stimulates the artistic faculties; refines the individuality, making the life more or less successful. It is generally a fortunate influence, more particularly where pleasures are concerned.

72. ☉ ☿ C.—A doubtful position, sometimes giving good business ability by stimulating the intellectual faculty, although it is more often than not colourless.

73. ☉ ☽ A.—Unfortunate, since it brings obstacles, delays and hindrances. Affects the health more or less, owing to lack of constant recuperative power. Is against fame or popularity. Sometimes affects honour or injures credit. Does not give success with superiors or those in authority, and very often affects the eyesight.

74. ☉ ☽ B.—Improves the horoscope; brings success through the realisation and attainment of desires and wishes. It gives right ambition, and prosperity attending effort. It brings fame and recognition according to the ability. Brings success in matters where feeling is concerned, adding to the general sincerity of the nature.

75. ☉ ☽ C.—Not always a favourable position, except with very advanced individuals, for then the individuality becomes very powerful. The conjunction is always more favourable for males than females.

VII. PERSONALITY VII.

THE MOON is taken as a general significator of the personality, and its position and the sign are important, as the physical activities are mostly denoted by them. For fuller information concerning these positions see pages 79 to 85.

THE MOON IN THE TWELVE SIGNS

76. ☽ ♈.—Denotes a martial and aggressive tendency; inde-

pendence, self-reliance ; sharp, shrewd and observant intellect ; aspiring
nature, hasty in speech ; usually impulsive, with a tendency to rebel
against authority.

77. ☽ ♉.—Reserved, obstinate, persistent ; kind, sociable, dignified,
intuitive and capable of endurance.

78. ☽ ♊.—Literary tastes, active mentally and physically, quick-
witted ; adaptable.   Mental abilities easily developed.

79. ☽ ♋.—Sensitive, imaginative, economical, receptive; tenacious,
with psychic tendencies.

80. ☽ ♌.—Fond of responsibility, persevering, affectionate; faithful and sincere ; honourable and dignified ; kind and affectionate.

81. ☽ ♍.—Critical ; business ability ; love of hygiene ; adaptable,
clear mind, good memory and educatable.

82. ☽ ♎.—Refined tastes, courteous and obliging manners ;
perceptive and equable.

83 ☽ ♏.—Firm, self-reliant ; at times abrupt and masterful ; fond
of secrecy ; interested in plots.   Often mystical and fond of the occult.
At times severely critical, and apt to be revengeful when slighted.

84. ☽ ♐.—Quick and active, fond of demonstration; at times
rebellious ; prophetic tendencies ; fond of dual experiences.

85. ☽ ♑.—Love of fame or recognition ; capable of responsibility ;
often chaste and prudish; fond of economy ; very sensitive to mental
vibrations.

86. ☽ ♒.—Refined, but peculiar tendencies ; sociable, independent;
fond of appreciation ; capable of studying human nature ; fond of secret
things.

87. ☽ ♓.—Very receptive; often mediumistic ; inclined to despond ;
hospitably inclined ; romantic and usually fond of expressing sympathy.

87a. Reference should now be made to the 'Polarities' or the
Combination of the Sun and Moon in Signs to be found in Chapter
XVIII of *Astrology for All*, the first volume of this Series.

The Moon's position in the houses is always an important factor
with regard to inclinations, and the instincts are usually centred in the
house occupied by the Moon.

The Moon in the Twelve Houses

88. ☽ *in the First House.*—Love of fame, activity and change ;

increases the ambition; gives ingenuity for planning; love of novelty and adventure; and some fame or public recognition is acquired, owing to the versatility that it usually produces.

89. ☽ *in the Second House.*—Fluctuating fortune; success in public affairs; commercial instincts; romantic or imaginative mind; the ability to make much out of little, with success in small matters or details.

90. ☽ *in the Third House.*—Love of knowledge; much curiosity; experiences connected with relatives or brethren; successful in intellectual pursuits; somewhat changeable disposition.

91. ☽ *in the Fourth House.*—Interested in all psychic matters; love of home; ability in domestic affairs; links with parents; fond of the occult and mystical; adventures at the close of life.

92. ☽ *in the Fifth House.*—Speculative tendencies; fond of pleasure; ardent affections; romantic experiences; active sensations.

93. ☽ *in the Sixth House.*—Wavering tendencies; lack of opportunities; troubles concerning health; attachments to inferiors; changeable nature where work is concerned; better success in the service of others; usually fond of ceremonies; indifferent fortune.

94. ☽ *in the Seventh House.*—Desire for popularity; active or roving life; fluctuating fortunes; experiences through attachments with others; happy in partnerships, or where dual interests are concerned.

95. ☽ *in the Eighth House.*—Gain through partners and co-workers; occult tendencies; experiences in connection with deaths; usually a notorious or public death.

96. ☽ *in the Ninth House.*—Philosophical tendencies; active mind; prophetic tendencies; fond of travel; mystical, and given to deep studies; peculiar in religious beliefs.

97. ☽ *in the Tenth House.*—Public fame or recognition; fond of changes; ambitious; acquires prominent positions; comes into either fame or notoriety, according to aspects.

98. ☽ *in the Eleventh House.*—Success through friends and acquaintances; experiences connected with associations or societies; strong desires or aspirations; studental tendencies.

99. ☽ *in the Twelfth House.*—Strange and often romantic experiences; liable to extremes, and great changes; often handicapped by surroundings or environment.

The Aspects formed by the Moon are also very important, links being formed and attachments made according to the nature of the aspects and the planets aspected. As before, the first three letters of the alphabet will be used as abbreviations : *A* for adverse, *B* for benefic, *C* for conjunction.

100. ☽ ♅ *A.* Subject to peculiar disappointments ; liable to be victimised or psychologised ; tendency to depravity through either drugs or narcotics ; peculiar mind, often very unreliable.

101. ☽ ♅ *B.*—Inspirational tendencies ; strong sympathies ; sensuous nature ; admiration for physical beauty ; sometimes very artistic, and possessing a charming personality.

102. ☽ ♅ *C.*—A somewhat weird and peculiar nature ; difficult to understand. Often very psychic or ultra-sensitive. Given to many moods and in extreme cases liable to obsession.

103. ☽ ♅ *A.*—An unfortunate aspect, bringing sudden difficulties ; obstinate ; self-willed ; liable to eccentricities ; peculiar moods and erratic tendencies. An undesirable aspect.

104. ☽ ♅ *B.*—Original and inventive nature ; constructive powers ; fond of occult and mystical. Splendid magnetic or healing power ; an eventful though favourable life.

105. ☽ ♅ *C.*—Important changes ; somewhat chequered career ; peculiar disposition ; often abrupt or irritable ; but if free from personal bias or prejudice may manifest genius. It denotes a strong will and powerful magnetism.

106. ☽ ♄ *A.*—Adverse fate ; liable to sorrows and misfortunes ; often discontented or bound by customs ; given to despondency, with many obstacles to thwart the life.

107. ☽ ♄ *B.*—Success in life through perseverance, patience and prudence ; good organising ability, capable of holding responsible posts ; faithful and reliable ; serious and steady ; love of truth and purity. Success follows merit.

108. ☽ ♄ *C.*—Disadvantages through early environment ; sceptical or critical tendencies ; undemonstrative, but usually faithful, sincere and just ; capable in responsibility. But note aspects formed by both to other planets.

109. ☽ ♃ *A.*—Extravagant or careless ; liable to false accusations ; immoderate or wasteful ; liable to be victimised by others.

110. ☽ ♃ *B.*—Fortunate in life ; prosperous ; social advancements ;

hopeful disposition. Honest or religiously minded ; just and sympathetic. Intuitive with a progressive nature.

111. ☽ ♃ C.—Successful life ; good social qualities ; right dignity and power ; attractive magnetism ; powerful friends ; sure rise in life.

112. ☽ ♂ A.—Unfortunate aspect ; trouble in life through impulsive action ; given to exaggeration ; somewhat careless or reckless. Hasty temper and given to anger.

113. ☽ ♂ B.—Fearless, enterprising and courageous ; resolute, with plenty of self-confidence ; enterprising, generous and resolute ; cheerful and hopeful.

114. ☽ ♂ C.—Very impulsive ; ardent in desires ; quick in speech ; over-independent or forceful ; very strong feelings and emotions ; given to rash acts.

115. ☽ ♀ A.—Careless tendencies ; unfavourable attachments ; financial losses ; tendency to be over-liberal.

116. ☽ ♀ B.—Success in life ; refined and artistic tastes ; keen appreciation of the beautiful ; loving disposition ; social success ; ability for music or singing ; honourable attachments.

117. ☽ ♀ C.—Good environment ; fortunate life ; fame or recognition ; makes pleasurable or sociable attachments ; a free and easy mind. But note aspects formed by both to other planets.

118. ☽ ☿ A.—Although an unfortunate position it sharpens the wits, but gives either a liability to sarcasm or irritability through nervous disorders ; it produces criticism, giving liability to errors through extremes or inaccuracy.

119. ☽ ☿ B.—Denotes an active brain, quickness of perception ; ability to make money ; power to study ; gives easy expression of thoughts and ideas.

120. ☽ ☿ C.—Good intellect ; quick and accurate perception ; fond of knowledge ; love of change ; much adaptability.

VIII. MENTAL CHARACTERISTICS VIII.

Mercury stands as an indicator of the mental qualifications, and expresses the wisdom of the native, either through intellect or consciousness in any form, as expressed by the sign, aspects and position by house. It may be considered as a mirror of the mind, just as the Moon is a reflector of the senses.

MERCURY IN THE TWELVE SIGNS

121. ☿ ♈.—Denotes quick mental ability; rapid perception and observation; fertile and inventive brain, but prone to be changeable; easily worried or affected by external conditions.

122. ☿ ♉.—Slow mind, plodding, patient and persevering; mind usually affected by feeling. Hence a love of the arts, music and poetry, but a mind that is apt to be uncompromising; over firm, yet usually just and sincere, although proud and often too rigidly strict.

123. ☿ ♊.—Literary tastes, a variable though expansive mind; versatile, active and alert: a good conversationalist, speaker or entertainer. When well aspected gives splendid facility of expression.

124. ☿ ♋.—Changeable, inquisitive, ingenious, perceptive, psychic, impressionable, tactful and ambitious. Usually an over-sensitive mind.

125. ☿ ♌.—Rational, concentrative; mentally generous; very intuitive; capable of mental responsibility; competent to control, command or manage; usually fond of mental power.

126. ☿ ♍.—Active mind; good and comprehensive memory; mentally practical; good at teaching, book-keeping and all common every-day pursuits of the mind where method, order and classification are required.

127. ☿ ♎.— Eloquent, good comparison and judgment; mentally affable, artistic, orderly, just and persuasive. Keen intuition, with very humane tendencies. Capable orator or literary exponent.

128. ☿ ♏.—Mentally positive; obstinate and difficult to convince; but capable of much enthusiasm or great indignation. Powerful mental attitude; with very keen mental likes and dislikes. Always shrewd, active and secretive. Clever in detection, having much tact and diplomacy. Often witty but sarcastic, with much concentration and power to understand mysteries.

129. ☿ ♐.—Mentally frank, just and straightforward. Often religious-minded or fond of philosophy. Facile in expression, but lacking in continuity. Too out-spoken or over-active mentally, the mind being very dual; sometimes brilliant and given to prophetic utterances.

130. ☿ ♑.—Subtle, cautious, diplomatic; often clever or very resourceful. Ambitious, capable of responsibility or organisation.

Inclined to be sympathetic and orderly. Often methodical, with the ability to study deep and profound subjects.

131. ☿ ♒.—Bright and comprehensive mind; a good memory, capable of great mental culture. Fond of science, literature or religion. Apt to be fixed in opinions and averse to mental changes. Fond of educational pursuits, concentrative, intuitive and usually a student of human nature.

132. ☿ ♓.—Mediumistic or receptive mind, voluble in speech; subject to fits of depression; mind often too negative, but capable of versatility, much depending on education and other aspects, as to the effect of this position.

The Aspects to Mercury are important, since that planet is a mirror of the mind and, being convertible, Mercury is often a duplicate of the aspecting planet.

133. ☿ ♆ A.—An unfavourable aspect for the mind, inclining to vague and unpractical imaginations. Visionary or utopian ideas. A tendency either to deceive or be deceived, with strong inclinations towards the sensuous, and sometimes towards the sensual, side of life from the mental standpoint.

134. ☿ ♆ B.—A mind that is very susceptible to higher influences; inclined towards romantic experiences; broad mental sympathies. Often cultivating high ideals. For the mentally cultured, the power to weave beautiful plots or original designs. A good aspect for a novelist.

135. ☿ ♆ C.—A peculiar type of mind, often developing æsthetic tendencies. Usually a mind that is paradoxical, dreamy, and given to weaving many strange theories that are often more or less unpractical.

136. ☿ ♅ A.—A mind that is usually sarcastic, or inclined to be abrupt or irritable. This aspect disorganises the nervous system, owing to the friction that the aspect produces; gives unpopularity, difficulties in dealing with strangers, and a mental magnetism that is not attractive.

137. ☿ ♅ B.—An original mind, inventive or given to expressions of genius; aptitude in most pursuits, producing a mental outlook of the widest character. It denotes a firm mind; a love of principle; and capable of higher thought than the average. If the analytical ability is strong it gives much inner perception and a good mental grasp of higher subjects.

138. ☿ ♅ C.—This position denotes a great deal of nervous energy, which. inclines towards an abrupt and very independent nature. The mind is liable to change very suddenly, but is always ingenious and inventive. It denotes either a crank or a profound thinker according to the indications of the horoscope as a whole.

139. ☿ ♄ A.—Somewhat limited intellect; inclination to set up barriers, causing lack of breadth; often inclined to be too conservative; generally orthodox. Difficulties in dealings with others. Liable to suffer discredit, and often suffers through an unforgiving and jealous nature.

140. ☿ ♄ B.—Usually a prudent and thoughtful mind, and capable of much mental responsibility. Fond of science and profound thought. Capable of much concentration, usually serious, earnest and sincere, and very faithful in attachments. Highly favourable where a general philosophical attitude is indicated.

141. ☿ ♄ C.—Subtle mind, very concentrative, given to the study of metaphysics and occultism. Capable of deep penetration; able mind, sometimes too severe, critical or exacting. This position may be equally good or bad, according to other aspects.

142. ☿ ♃ A.—Liable to errors of judgment; sometimes prejudiced in regard to religion; oftentimes sceptical. Inclined to create false impressions; sometimes prone to litigation; and liable to be severely criticised.

143. ☿ ♃ B.—Excellent judgment, broad and philosophic mind; mentally intuitive or harmonious; straightforward and conscientious; capable of being wise; very well balanced mentally.

144. ☿ ♃ C.—Joyous and hopeful mental attitude; intuitive and sincere mind, and capable of great mental expansion.

145. ☿ ♂ A.—Impulsive mind; often over-energetic; quick wit; exaggerated imagination; a fearless intellect, with inclination to assert some opinions very freely. It often gives ability to follow scientific pursuits, or intellectual ingenuity, but is against really original work.

146. ☿ ♂ B.—Very energetic mind, acute, sharp and active; much mental force; usually a witty, bright and cheerful outlook. Sometimes gives ability for drawing or designing, and more often than not gives mechanical ability with manual dexterity.

147. ☿ ♂ C.—Quick wit, cheerful mind, materialistic or practical tendencies; socialistic views. Enterprise and business ability; but

often inclined to say more than is wise and to over-estimate or exaggerate. The magnifying ability is very great.

148.   ☿ ♀ *A*.—Usually an unimportant aspect, but prevents intuition or a full development of the artistic tastes.

149.   ☿ ♀ *B*.—The mind is softened, and inclined to be merry, cheerful, bright; gives a love of music or the fine arts; blends mind with feeling.

150.   ☿ ♀ *C*.—A refining position; gives sympathy and appreciation; love of reading; an affable disposition; fond of all sociable and pleasurable conditions.

IX.   THE HOUSES   IX.

The various houses in the horoscope may now be separately studied so far as they affect the fate and fortune of the native.

THE FIRST HOUSE

This house and the planets in it affect the general activities and that which is chiefly concerned with the personality.   It has been already treated with sufficient fulness in Chapter VI.

THE SECOND HOUSE

This is chiefly concerned with finance, means of livelihood, etc., and planets in this house cause a strong interest in money matters throughout the greater part of the native's life.

151.   ♆.—May be either very good or very evil for finance.   Sometimes natives having this position lose through fraud and deception, although money often comes from unexpected sources or through following occupations of an uncommon nature.

152.   ♅.—Denotes sudden changes of fortune, often bringing peculiar and remarkable experiences in financial affairs.   Denotes success in professions connected with curiosities, old books or curious and antique furniture, auctioneering and all matters of an uncommon nature.

153.   ♄.—Not always favourable for money, but denotes gain by perseverance, thrift or carefulness.   If well aspected brings gain through investment in land or property, or through heavy and arduous pursuits. Nevertheless money comes in slowly unless obtained by hereditary right.

154. ♃.—This is the best position for the accumulation of wealth; generally brings money by legacy or the aid of others; brings gain through foreign travel or pursuits connected with land, food or clothing. But it is best for all pursuits of an expansive nature, thus favours money-lenders, bankers, or those who have the handling of much cash.

155. ♂.—Gives success through enterprise; also through legacies and inheritance, but denotes waste of money or extravagance and lack of carefulness. Usually Mars in the second brings money, which, however, is quickly spent.

156. ☉.—Increases financial gain, gives success in government affairs, or concerns where much authority is exercised. It favours expenditure on a large scale for the purpose of big realisations. Thus shows gain by speculation, judicious investments; or gain through superiors and a fixed income.

157. ♀.—Favours acquisition of wealth, denoting good fortune and prosperity in any occupation. But always inclines towards professional pursuits, partnerships and refined employments.

158. ☿.—Gain through literary pursuits, agencies, or where business versatility is necessary, giving success through commission agencies, acting as intermediary, through printing, journalism or any profession where adaptability is necessary.

159. ☽.—Denotes a fluctuating financial condition, monetary prospects waxing and waning like the Moon. It favours success in connection with public commodities, public companies and associations catering and public wants generally, and favours S.P.Q.R. dealing.

159a. When no planets occupy the second house, and it is governed by a CARDINAL SIGN, it denotes gain through ambition; much activity and industry, though there is always a liability to fluctuating fortune and changes where money is concerned. It however favours speculative enterprise, and acquisitiveness is usually well developed.

159b. If a FIXED SIGN occupy the second, the liability to fluctuation is lessened and there is usually a fixed income, much or little according to the position and aspects of its lord or ruler. It denotes gain through investments and favours unearned incomes.

159c. If a MUTABLE SIGN rule the second, finance is prone to fluctuation. It favours professional pursuits but gives some anxiety where finance is concerned. There is apt to be some indifference regarding the accumulation of wealth.

The Third House

The third house concerns matters connected with the lower brain mind, mental disposition, etc., and is chiefly concerned with travel, particularly short journeys; it also affects matters connected with relatives, brothers, sisters, etc.   Any planet in this house accentuates its influence.

160.   ♆.—Indifference to travel; inclines to weird experiences; a skeleton in the cupboard with regard to relatives, and peculiar episodes in connection with brethren.   It gives a peculiar type of mind.

161.   ♅.—Not altogether favourable for travelling, and usually indicates sudden and unexpected journeys.   It produces friction between relatives and brethren, who act in a peculiar and strange manner. Indicates a love of Astrology and all metaphysical subjects.   When well aspected, it is a good influence.

162.   ♄.—Not good for travel, denoting hindrances and delays in connection with journeys.   It is unfavourable for any agreement between relatives, and sorrow often comes through brethren.   Gives a serious type of mind, fond of the occult and mystical, with the ability to study Astrology.

163.   ♃.—Fortunate for travel, which is undertaken either for pleasure or profit.   It indicates successful dealings with kindred, and success in the social world through brethren; gives a religious type of mind.

164.   ♂.—Not good for travelling, denoting liability to accidents while on journeys, which are usually of an enterprising character.   It denotes troubles through relatives; scandal or annoyance through brethren; and a combative or impulsive type of mind.

165.   ☉.—Favourable for travel, although it does not indicate much moving about.   Journeys are generally undertaken for important purposes, and may have far-reaching results.   It denotes a high-spirited mind, the prosperity of brethren, and successful dealings with relatives.

166.   ♀.—Makes travel successful and prosperous, journeys usually being undertaken in order to improve the mind, which is easy-going, pleasure-loving, and more or less artistic.   Brethren rise in life and dealings with relatives are successful and fruitful.

167.   ☿.—Many journeys, with a love of travelling and sightseeing; journeys are also undertaken for business purposes or in search of

information.   It shows a very active mind and indifferent relations with brethren.

168. ☽.—Many short journeys, usually through compulsion, either for business purposes or between two houses, and unless a fixed sign is on the cusp, journeys and changes are frequent.   The mind is more or less changeable, and there are many experiences connected with relatives.

If no planet occupy the third house the quality of the sign occupying the cusp should be studied.

168a. A CARDINAL SIGN denotes much travelling about, a love of change, and many journeys.   The mind is ambitious; close ties are formed with relatives.

168b. A FIXED SIGN gives a disinclination to travel about, and any travel undertaken is usually compulsory.   Tends to make the mind proud or austere, and thus gives a liability of estrangements with relations.

168c. A MUTABLE SIGN shows journeys to be the result of circumstances, and does not denote any definite desire for travel.   Sometimes residence in foreign countries, however.   The mind is usually indecisive.

THE FOURTH HOUSE

The fourth house is usually concerned with the environment, comprising parents, home life, the domicile and domestic affairs generally, also the condition at the close of life.   As in the other houses so here, a planet or planets occupying this house accentuates its influence over the life as a whole.   If no planet *in* the house, that ruling the sign on the cusp should be regarded as the main influence concerned.

169. ♆.—Uncertainty with regard to birth; peculiar environments, probability of unhappiness in the home life, and a strange end.

170. ♅.—Eccentricities in connection with parentage; peculiar environment; dislike for domestic affairs; sudden changes at the close of life; strong leanings towards the occult.

171. ♄.—Usually a poor environment; necessity for economy in domestic affairs; the cultivation of acquisitiveness; with probabilities of an isolated old age.

172. ♃.—A good birth with favourable social environment; more success at home than abroad; domestic happiness; gain by inheritance A prosperous and comfortable end to the life.

173. ♂.—An unfavourable environment; turbulent home life; unfavourable domestic surroundings, and difficulties at the close of life.

174. ☉.—Denotes a good end to the career, a favourable environment, and usually a strong character.

175. ♀.—Good parentage; peaceful environment; harmonious home surroundings; success in the domestic sphere, and a satisfactory finish.

176. ☿.—An unsettled environment; worries in connection with home life and a changeable period at end of life.

177. ☽.—Much attachment to home, many domestic cares and worries; changes and fluctuations in home life; a love of the mystical and occult. But much depends upon aspects.

THE FIFTH HOUSE

The fifth house is connected with enterprise and all matters of a speculative character, which are supposed to be concerned with pleasure and the generative principles. Planets in this house need special study, as it may be taken as showing in a special sense the trend of past lives.

178. ♆.—Grave risks in connection with love affairs, fraudulent enterprises, or troubles in connection with speculation. If well aspected, unexpected gains. This position sometimes favours platonic unions.

179. ♅.—An enterprising and speculative nature. Sudden and unexpected gains and losses. Much romance, but estrangements in love affairs.

180. ♄.—Keen interest in all enterprises, but sorrowful experiences in connection with pleasure, and often indifferent success concerning speculation. Trouble through children.

181. ♃.—Success in speculation; luck in connection with enterprises; fruitful issue; success in all pleasures, and social gain through children.

182. ♂.—Much energy in connection with enterprise; tendency to be rash in speculation, and (especially if afflicted by Jupiter) where a gambling spirit is denoted the 'plunging' element is very strong. It denotes ardent affections, and often entanglements.

183. ☉.—Favourable for all matters of an enterprising nature. The speculative interests are very keen and the capacity for enjoyment very great.

184. ♀.—Enterprises of a successful character; gain through investment or speculation; successful love affairs; a fruitful and happy union; gain through children, with a liability to excesses in pleasure.

185. ☿.—Denotes love of enterprise, mental interests in speculative affairs; some romance; much correspondence connected with love affairs, and generally a love of children.

186. ☽.—While showing an enterprising tendency, sometimes inclines to gambling. Often a love of sensation, with a liability to be easily affected or impressed by others. Usually gives a love of pleasure.

The Sixth House

The sixth house is usually concerned with the state of the health, association with inferiors, servants, and the working capacities. Planets in this house have much to do with matters of hygiene, and if afflicted signify ill-health.

187. ♅.—Peculiar ailments; uncommon disorders; liability to obsession, or to be affected by unhealthy surroundings. Frequently somewhat morbid or hysterical.

188 ♅.—Peculiar and often incurable complaints; dangers through operations; strange illnesses. Sometimes hysterical or hypochondriacal. Sickness generally arises through nervous disorders. Interest in psychic matters.

189. ♄.—Wasting diseases; sickness following colds or chills; bad circulation, and unless the constitution is strong many long and severe illnesses. Industrious worker; trouble in connection with servants or inferiors.

190. ♃.—A speedy and quick recovery from sickness through good and proper nursing. If afflicted, a liability to intemperate living affecting the blood and liver. Faithful servants and success with inferiors.

191. ♂.—Much energy in connection with work; active servants· difficulties with inferiors; illnesses affecting the muscular system. If afflicted by Saturn, rheumatic fevers; generally a tendency to excesses, producing feverish and inflammatory complaints.

192. ☉—Denotes vital strength; constitution able to resist disease; ability to recuperate. It also denotes gain through inferiors; ability to work hard; but it is not a fortunate position for the Sun.

193. ♀.—If afflicted, kidney troubles; sickness through indiscretion in diet, but successful nursing; usually good servants : success in dealing with inferiors.

194. ☿.—Nerves affected, or at least highly sensitive. Ill-health through worry, usually concerning work. Easily influenced by inferiors. Keen psychic impressions, and mental afflictions if badly aspected.

195. ☽.—Disturbs functional arrangements; gives liability to indigestion; sickness through too much bathing or travelling; and a tendency to absorb impure magnetism. If afflicted, liability to tumorous complaints.

If the lord of the Ascendant is in the sixth, much ill-health may be indicated, especially if afflicted there. This position usually produces a prodigious worker, and sometimes gives strong socialistic tendencies.

THE SEVENTH HOUSE

Although the seventh house is chiefly connected with marriage, there are matters governed by it that are explained in the first part of this work (see Chapter XIV). The following, however, are the general indications when planets occupy the seventh ; they will also in many cases apply to the lord of the seventh, if no planets occupy the house.

196. ♆.—Usually unfavourable for marriage, and uncommon experiences generally occur in connection with it. This position is favourable for a platonic union if the horoscope as a whole denotes an advanced character.

197. ♅.—Estrangements and peculiar episodes in connection with marriage, or a union with someone quite out of the common. The position of Uranus in the seventh house is often a dangerous position for marriage unless the senses are well under control by both parties.

198. ♄.—Hinders or delays marriage, but promises a faithful and steady partner; one who is industrious, careful, and thrifty, but not demonstrative, valuing action more than speech.

199. ♃.—Very favourable for a happy union: the partner is generally noble, generous and fortunate. If afflicted, too proud and lofty in manner. In many cases the partner has been married before or had a prior engagement of importance in the past life.

200. ♂.—Denotes much passion, probably a hasty marriage or love at first sight. It always hastens marriage, and although there is generally affection, reactions are more than probable with this influence.

201. ⊙.—Denotes an ambitious partner and one whose influence over the life will be beneficial, promising social and financial gain. If well aspected, the partner will be independent, or of sound moral integrity, seeking to produce harmony and happiness in the marriage state. But if afflicted it denotes trouble through pride, according to the nature of the aspect.

202. ♀.—Promises a happy marriage, benefits both social and financial. A fruitful union is denoted and social success assured after marriage. The union will be fruitful and successful.

203. ☿.—Depends largely upon the aspects which Mercury forms, but the partner is shown to be quick, intelligent, fluent in speech, somewhat critical, and nervous; marriage often takes place to one younger than the native. Worries and anxieties after marriage are usually denoted.

204. ☽.—Indecision with regard to marriage; a partner who is sensitive or liable to many moods, but popular and having general recognition. This position denotes fluctuation in feeling during the marriage state.

If the lords of the first and seventh are in favourable aspect success in marriage is denoted, but if afflicted there is very little harmony. A sure sign of friendship is an exchange of the place of the luminaries, that is, the Sun in one horoscope on the Moon in the other. Successful physical unions occur when Mars is on Venus or *vice versâ*.

The Eighth House

The eighth house is usually connected with legacies, deaths, co-workers and occult matters. Planets occupying this house usually incline to an interest in occult matters, but if untenanted the life gradually tends to run more or less on conventional lines, unless the ruler receives *strong* aspects.

205. ♆.—Probability of money being left that is never recovered; liability to be defrauded of inheritance. Death usually hastened by drugs. Liable to trances or a watery death.

206. ♅.—Unexpected and sudden windfalls; a sudden end to existence; danger of death through operations or among crowds.

207. ♄.—Disappointments in connection with legacies; no financial gain through marriage or partnership. A slow death, or death through old age.

208. ♃.—Certain gain by legacy, or good fortune through marriage and insurance; a natural or peaceful end to life.

209. ♂.—Difficulties concerning wills or legacies, unless well aspected. Generally some sudden or unexpected gain. Usually a sudden end to the existence; and if much afflicted liability to violence or public calamity.

210. ☉—Probability of a legacy from a superior; is favourable for occultism; also brings gain from partners and co-workers. Death is usually attended with honour.

211. ♀.—Almost certain gain by legacies, or through marriage and partnership. Good for insurance, and denotes a peaceful death.

212. ☿.—An indifferent position; usually denotes gain through goods of the dead, but if afflicted trouble in connection with administration or through trustees. Occult tendencies indicated.

213. ☽.—Some slight probability of gain through legacies or through co-workers. Either notoriety or public attention at death.

The Ninth House

The ninth house is usually concerned with what is known as philosophy or the action of the higher mind. It concerns vital things that are not always on the surface, or readily seen. Planets in this house have a strong influence upon the subjective consciousness.

214. ♆.—Peculiar views; strange and weird dreams and usually very peculiar experiences.

215. ♅.—Liable to strange or advanced views. A very inventive or ingenious mind, given to the higher criticism; but much depends upon aspects.

216. ♄.—Fond of science; critical mind; unfavourable position for long journeys or foreign affairs; tendency towards deception; or inclined to be too sceptical in matters of religion or higher thought.

217. ♃.—Fond of science, philosophy, or religion. Great capacity of unfoldment; and usually the acquisition of much learning through an expansive mind, having prophetic tendencies. Generally a 'true dreamer.'

218. ♂.—An enthusiastic mind; too much independence; danger of litigation through disputes; oftentimes religious fervour.

219. ☉.—Denotes a philosophical attitude of mind; deep feelings

with regard to religion; a very broad mind; usually success through legal or foreign affairs.   Probability of some long journeys.

220.   ♀.—Keen intuitions; favourable dreams; philosophic tendencies; religious spirit; gain through relatives after marriage.

221.   ☿.—A very active mind; deep inclination to explore hidden mysteries; quick to learn and appreciate; mind of a metaphysical turn.

222.   ☽.—Peculiar views; sometimes enthusiastic with regard to higher thought matters; but the mind is usually broad, and many long journeys or much travel are denoted.   But much depends upon aspects and the sign the Moon occupies.

When no planets occupy the ninth house note carefully the ruler, also its position and aspects.

The Tenth House

The tenth house has to do with fame, honour and profession, and usually indicates the ambitions and the responsibilites, also the credit and discredit, which are denoted by the occupant of this house or its ruler, and the aspects thereto.

223.   ♆.—Strange and uncommon experiences.

224.   ♅.—Strange and peculiar professions; original methods; subject to popularity and reversals.   Some genius or great talent, with inventive powers.   If free from affliction, a unique reputation; if afflicted, much discredit.

225.   ♄.—Subject to fatalistic tendencies and limitations connected with honour and success.   Position secured only by merit and labour. If afflicted, liable to serious misfortunes and disasters.   If well placed by aspects, etc., responsible positions.   The native is highly ambitious.

226.   ♃.—Excellent for success in life.   Native rises to high positions; obtains honourable distinction and secures social recognition.

227.   ♂.—Some mechanical ability; critical positions; sudden loss of position; danger of scandal or discredit; liable to hold risky positions. If afflicted, will abuse responsibility.

228.   ☉.—Responsible employments; ambitious tendencies, rise in life through honour and integrity.

229.   ♀.—Social success; gain through females; success in life in refined possessions and the help of many friends.

230.   ☿.—Fluctuating tendencies; success in literary, writing or

secretarial work. If afflicted, liable to many fluctuations and changes. If well aspected, improvement of business ability and mental opportunities.

231.   ☽.—Fluctuating fortunes; ambitious tendencies; rise in life. Aspects denote either fame or notoriety, according to the general tenor of the horoscope.

231a.   If no planets occupy the tenth house and a CARDINAL SIGN is on the cusp, some fame or reputation is denoted; responsible posts may be filled, and ambition brings rising fortune.

231b.   If a FIXED SIGN is on the cusp, success through determination and effort, or through steady and fixed pursuits.   Responsible posts are generally held, this position favouring all professions of a permanent character, such as the medical and legal professions, governmental occupations, etc.

231c.   If a MUTABLE SIGN, the career tends to be more or less uncertain, much depending upon the sign occupied by the ruler of this house, its aspects, etc.

THE ELEVENTH HOUSE

The eleventh house is concerned with friends, acquaintances, hopes and aspirations, and is usually a fortunate house.   Planets in or ruling this house are largely concerned with the *ideals*.

232.   ♅.—Weird and queer friendships, usually of an unhealthy character : liable to be imposed upon by friends.

233.   ♅.—Unique and exceptional friendships; usually of a bohemian and remarkable character.   Gain in a sudden and unexpected manner through friends.   As an instance of this may be mentioned the following case: A lady friend of the author's, who was a nurse in the Franco-Prussian War, had attended a dying officer, who before his death gave her certain information which enabled her to realise a fortune in connection with some mining shares.

234.   ♄.—Some faithful and reliable friends, often elderly persons; but usually there are some keen disappointments in connection with personal friendships.

235.   ♃.—Advancement and success through friends; social benefits and financial gain through them.

236.   ♂.—Dangerous friendships which are likely to influence the native adversely.

237. ☉.—Firm and reliable friends; gain through **relatives, and** the realisation of many ambitions.

238　♀.—Much success through friends, also gain socially and financially through them.

239.　☿.—Clever friends and acquaintances, but not much reliance should be placed upon them.

240.　☽.—Many acquaintances and few friends.

NOTE.—The lord of the ascendant in one horoscope in the sign on the cusp of the eleventh of the other is always a sure token of friendship between two people.

THE TWELFTH HOUSE

The twelfth house is considered the most unfortunate, and the term 'self-undoing' is used by the author to describe the change in consciousness that usually takes place when planets are placed in this house. It is the house of *true occultism*. Planets in this house are therefore especially important.

241. ♅.—Strange and peculiar experiences in connection with psychic affairs. It is rarely a favourable position unless very well aspected.

242. ♅.—Good for occult matters, but much depends upon aspects.

243.　♄.—Unfavourable, denoting many sorrows, painful experiences, and unforgiving enemies.

244.　♃.—Favourable for occultism, and the native gains indirectly through his enemies, in fact, he always gains through them more or less.

245.　♂.—Unfavourable in this house, and at some period of the life either a hospital or other public building is occupied. It gives danger of false accusation, and if much afflicted liability to imprisonment. Denotes some powerful enemies.

246. ☉.—Good for occult matters, the native overcomes his enemies; improves his worldly affairs and more often than not rises out of obscurity into prosperity.

247.　♀.—Favourable in the twelfth, as it dissipates the sorrows of this house, giving joy and pleasure in occult affairs. It generally denotes, however, secret and romantic love affairs.

248.　☿.—Favours the investigation of spiritualism and occultism, but denotes danger through treachery or the evil thoughts of others if afflicted.

249. ☽—Is unfavourable; denotes restrictions; sometimes produces confinement, or loss of liberty and freedom.   Enemies are troublesome.

X. SUMMARIES X.

(a) PLANETS RISING, SETTING, ABOVE OR BELOW

ALL horoscopes are best summarised, first by the planetary positions taken as a whole (rising, setting, or culminating), and next with regard to the nature of the signs holding the *majority* of the planets.

250. PLANETS RISING,—*i.e.*, in houses XI, XII, I, II, III,—promise a rise in life through the native's own energy and enterprise, indicate opportunities, a fair amount of self-control, and the ability to make the most of those opportunities.

251. PLANETS SETTING,—*i.e.*, in houses V, VI, VII, VII, IX,—show that the life will be more under the influence of fate, and that the influence of others will play an important part in the life of the native; also that the exercise of the will will not be so manifest.   It denotes a certain lack of opportunity.

252. PLANETS ABOVE THE HORIZON,—*i.e.*, in houses VII, VIII, IX, X, XI, XII,—denotes success in life, also that as much as can be manifest will be exhibited.   They indicate ambition, real ability; a self-reliant, persevering, aspiring and energetic nature.   When the majority are above the earth the native nearly always rises above the sphere of his birth.

253. PLANETS BELOW THE HORIZON,—*i.e.*, in houses I, II, III, IV, V, VI (especially the three last),—promise success in the latter half of life, indicating that there is a great deal latent in the native, but that he will probably pass through life unrecognised and unknown.   It also indicates that the native succeeds better in the employ of others nan by taking responsibility upon himself.

(b) PLANETS IN THE TRIPLICITIES

254. The majority of planets in FIERY signs denotes a spirited and idealistic nature.   It gives the native force and energy; a rich and generous nature; plenty of vitality, hope and enthusiasm; deep emotions and an ardent love nature.   Usually gives a great deal of courage mentally or morally.   Planets in those signs are more active than in others.

255. The majority in AIRY signs denotes an inspirational and artistic temperament.   It endows the native with a refined intellect, pure tastes; high ideals and good social abilities.

256. The majority of planets in WATERY signs denotes a psychic or emotional nature; the instinctual consciousness is very keen: and the native is always more or less receptive or impressionable; often mediumistic, and sometimes passionate; responsive to and usually largely affected by circumstances, surroundings and environment.

257. The majority of planets in EARTHY signs shows a very practical and matter-of-fact nature. The native is either scientifically or commercially inclined, and in any case takes a very solid and concrete view of life. Is rarely quick or brilliant, but more often than not persevering, painstaking and plodding. Generally takes a materialistic view of life, requiring a demonstration of theories before they are accepted. This position gives great power in the material world, and in a strong horoscope would denote a very practical man of affairs.

(c) PLANETS IN THE QUADRUPLICITIES

The next consideration is whether the majority of planets are in Cardinal, Mutable or Fixed signs. The first have to do with ambition, fame and recognition, arising from the Cardinal nature of the signs, while socialistic and sympathetic or fickle tendencies are due to a predominance of the Mutable signs, whereas pride, determination, and love of authority are the result of the Fixed signs.

258. The majority of planets in CARDINAL SIGNS causes the native to hold prominent positions; to exhibit much enterprise and ambition; causing him never to be fully satisfied unless he is at the head of things. He will love change, will be more or less self-assertive, independent and active. Will have many changes in his life, and usually each step in life is on to a higher rung of the ladder. He will have high ideals, and seek to make them practical; a political trend of mind, rarely being satisfied if not ruling others: generally the pioneer spirit will predominate.

259. The majority of planets in FIXED SIGNS denotes determination, firmness, and self-reliance. The native will be either proud or dignified, inclined to be austere or autocratic, but will always be dependable and reliable. He will be capable of patience and endurance, and will rise in life through fixity of purpose and persistent effort.

260. The majority of planets in MUTABLE SIGNS indicates either an indifferent or mediocre life; versatility, often much indecision; a liability to be fickle and discontented; always more or less restless, but with

either intellectual or educational views. The native is always more or less demonstrative and capable of very deep feelings and emotions, but rarely succeeds in life unaided by others. Or if he does succeed, fails to gain sufficient recognition for his labours. Often misses opportunities; is rarely thorough, although often methodical; and seldom if ever achieves fame, although he may be possessed of excellent merit. A great characteristic of this quality is sympathy, and in spite of their unreliability, these people are usually very 'likeable.'

261. When the planets are almost equally distributed throughout the three quadruplicities, a well-balanced and fairly even temperament is denoted, and in this case more attention should be paid to the planetary positions (a) than to the signs they occupy. It is, on the whole, a favourable testimony and generally gives a more or less 'all-round' character, sound common sense, and good judgment.

TABULATION

HOROSCOPE OF KING EDWARD VII.

Description	*Ref. No.*	*Description*	*Ref. No.*
I. RISING SIGN ♐	par. 9	VIII. ☿ IN SIGN	par. 129
DECANATE, 3rd (*p.* 100) ,,	—	,, HOUSE xi. (*p.* 220) ,,	—
II. RULING PLANET ♃ ,,	16	,, ASPECTS ∨ ♄ , ,,	
III. RULER IN SIGN ♐ (*p.* 123) ,,	—	∠ ♂	,,140,145
,, HOUSE i. ,,	22	SOLI-LUNAR POLARITY ,,	87a
,, ASPECTS ♃ ⚹ ♀ ,		IX. FINANCE ♅	,, 151
♃ □ ♅ (*see pp.* 261		X. TRAVEL CARDINAL	,, 168a
and 237) ,,	—	XI. ENVIRONMENT ♀	,, 175
IV. RISING PLANETS ♄ ♂ ,, 36, 38		XII. ENTERPRISE ♀	,, 184
V. ,, PLANET'S SIGN ♑		XIII. SICKNESS ☿	,, 194
(*see pp.* 244 and		XIV. MARRIAGE ☿	,, 203
268) ,,	—	XV. LEGACIES ☉	,, 210
,, ASPECTS ♄ □ ☽ ,		XVI. PHILOSOPHY ♀	,, 220
♂ ⚹ ☉ (*pp.* 253		XVII. PROFESSION ☉	,, 228
and 270 ,,	—	XVIII. FRIENDS ☿	,, 239
VI. ☉ IN SIGN ♏ ,,	50	XIX. ENEMIES ♃	,, 244*
,, ASPECTS □ ♅ , ⚹ ♂ ,, 55, 68		XX. SUMMARIES (*a*)	,, 250
VII. ☽ IN SIGN ♍ ,,	81	,, (*b*)	,, 257
,, HOUSE viii. ,,	95	,, (*c*)	,, 261
,, ASPECTS ∠ ☉, ⚿ ♅ ,,, 73,100			
□ ♄, ⚹ ☿	106,119		

NOTE.—As regards the Summary it will be seen that this is a very well-balanced horoscope, each quality and triplicity being well represented.

---

* Jupiter should here be looked upon rather as the ruler of the twelfth than as occupying it, since it is virtually in the first. See note on p. 90.

If a sheet is prepared in the manner shown, it will be very easy to obtain a classification of the various positions in the horoscope, the numbers showing the particular paragraph to which reference has to be made. In this case the numbers supplied refer to the horoscope given on p. 297 and those paragraphs which have corresponding numbers : a few references are also given to the earlier portion of the book. If by way of exercise the paragraphs here enumerated are copied out, under their respective headings, a skeleton delineation of this nativity will be obtained that will well repay further study. By carefully weighing the contradictory testimonies, in view of King Edward's known character, the development of the student's power of judgment will be very materially aided, and he will find himself soon able to write out, on the plan here laid down, a full delineation of this nativity which shall be clear and consistent.

The student is very strongly urged to adopt this suggestion, rather than to content himself with merely *reading* the paragraphs enumerated. For he can hardly realise until he has done so the benefit that he will derive from this discipline of his powers, which will prove far more valuable to him than any amount of desultory work.

A CENTILOQUY

The ' Centiloquies' of Claudius Ptolemy and others are famous for containing in a short and pithy form the fruit of many years of study. The present Centiloquy is intended simply as a help to the student by which he may fix in his mind the gist of the teachings given in this book, in the form of a hundred brief aphorisms. To each aphorism is added the page on which more detailed information can be found.

I. The 'squares' denote opposition and discord, the 'triangles' peace and harmony (4).

II. Astrological symbology conceals within itself the history of the earth as a planet (6).

III. The Ascendant corresponds to sunrise, and suggests spirit made subject to matter ; the Meridian corresponds to noon, and suggests balance between spirit and matter ; the Descendant corresponds to sunset and suggests the triumph of spirit over matter ; the *Imum Coeli* is the great mystery, the occult centre (7).

IV. The Cardinal Houses indicate physical matters connected with the external life ; the Fixed Houses indicate matters connected with feelings and emotions, not yet ripe, but maturing ; the Mutable Houses indicate matters latent in the mind, and affairs brought over from past lives (8).

V. The Cadent, Succedent and Cardinal divisions represent thought, speech and action, or spirit, soul and body (6).

VI. The six houses above the horizon (xii, xi, x, ix, viii, vii) correspond to the 'life' side of the universe, the six below (vi, v, iv, iii, ii, i) correspond to its 'form' side (6).

VII. There exists an intimate correspondence between the Signs and the Houses (10).

VIII. The Houses relate to *physical* and *etheric* matter, and the Signs to *astral* matter (10).

IX. The influence of the Signs is greater than that of the Houses, and the former will 'overbear' the latter (p. 10).

X. The Houses are like transparent vessels, each having its own pattern ; the Signs supply the contents of such vessels, giving a special substance, colour and quality to each house (12).

XI. The four triplicities are Fire, Air, Water, Earth; or Spirit, Space, Time and Matter. The three qualities are Cardinal, Fixed, and Mutable (14).

XII. The Cardinal Signs govern the head, and their chief characteristic is activity (15).

XIII. The Fixed Signs govern the heart and will, and their chief characteristic is stability (15).

XIV. The Mutable signs govern the limbs, lungs and bowels, and their chief characteristic is adaptability (15).

XV. Odd Signs are all positive, male, day signs; Even Signs are negative, female, night signs (16).

XVI. Positive signs refer to the force or life side of things, negative signs to the matter or form side (16).

XVII. The Fiery Signs as a whole signify energy, vitality and vigour. Aries the originator, Leo the organiser, Sagittarius the executant (17, 18).

XVIII. The Watery Signs as a whole signify mobility and sensation. Cancer the insistent, Scorpio the passionate, Pisces the emotional and sympathetic (19, 20, 21).

XIX. The Airy Signs as a whole signify expansion and mentality. Libra the Woman, Aquarius the Father-Man, Gemini the child (22, 23).

XX. The Earthy Signs as a whole signify completion and achievement. Capricorn the practical idealist, Taurus the concentrator, Virgo the discriminator (24, 25).

XXI. Planets in their exaltation exert a more refined and more powerful influence than elsewhere (28).

XXII. The Sun is the vehicle through which the Solar Logos manifests; in the horoscope it represents the Individuality (29).

XXIII. The Moon is the vehicle of communication between the Sun and each living thing; in the horoscope it represents the Personality (29).

XXIV. Mars is the planet of focussed force and out-going impulse (30).

XXV. Saturn is the planet which binds, limits and crystallises (32).

XXVI. Saturn rules the personal Ego, Mars the animal tendencies (33).

XXVII. Venus and Jupiter are the respective counterparts of Mars and Saturn (33).

XXVIII. Venus is the planet whose force comes from within through the Ego's direct intuitive power (34).

XXIX. Mars is the planet of physical generation, Venus the planet of creation (34)

XXX. Jupiter is the planet of expansion, and rules the 'celestial' body (35).

XXXI. Mercury is the planet of adaptation, and represents in each life the knowledge gained (36).

XXXII. Uranus is the planet which represents the *fully individualised* Ego (36).

XXXIII. Neptune is concerned with psychic evolution (37).

XXXIV. Conjunctions stand symbolically for union and synthesis (40).

XXXV. Oppositions signify antagonism, rivalry and duality (46).

XXXVI. Squares alternately crystallise and limit, and disrupt and shatter (46).

XXXVII. Trines stand for progression and harmony (46).

XXXVIII. In examining aspects, pay attention to the application of the swifter moving planet (63).

XXXIX. If the ruler has just left one aspect and applies to another, give the principal value to the influence forming (p. 63).

XL. Planetary influences are primarily of a super-material nature, and cannot be accurately expressed in words (65).

XLI. The Sun represents the Individuality and corresponds to the Fixed Signs (68).

XLII. The Moon represents the Personality, and corresponds to the Mutable Signs (69).

XLIII. The Ascendant represents the physical body and brain, and corresponds to the Cardinal Signs (71).

XLIV. The Ascendant moves most quickly and corresponds to the Rajasic guna ; the Sun moves most slowly and corresponds to the Tamasic guna ; the Moon is intermediate and corresponds to the Sattvic guna (72).

XLV. Fiery Signs rising denote good vitality, airy signs less vitality but more mentality, watery signs a tendency to weak constitution, and earthy signs good general health but not much vitality (90).

XLVI. Fixed signs rising denote fixity of purpose ; cardinal signs energy ; mutable signs, versatility (91).

XLVII. The expression of the Ascendant is considerably modified or accentuated by the planets rising (91).

XLVIII. Whatever be the Rising Sign, pay especial attention to the corresponding house (92).

XLIX. Aries, Taurus and Gemini belong to the Intellectual Trinity ; their keynote is knowledge and progression through the intellect (95).

L. Cancer, Leo and Virgo belong to the Maternal Trinity, and their keynote is emotion and progression through the moral sentiments (98).

LI. Libra, Scorpio and Sagittarius belong to the Reproductive Trinity and their keynote is Progression through the power to reform and renew (101).

LII. Capricorn, Aquarius and Pisces belong to the Serving Trinity, and their keynote is Service to Humanity (104).

LIII. The general influence of Neptune rising tends to inversion of *motives*; that of Uranus, to inversion of *ideas* (105, 106).

LIV. Saturn rising denotes limitation, and the form side of power; Jupiter rising denotes dignity and the internal power in which the will is exercised (106, 107).

LV. Mars rising denotes a strong desire nature; Venus rising refines and beautifies the love nature (107).

LVI. The Sun rising strengthens the constitution, and gives dignity to the appearance (108).

LVII. The Moon rising influences the temperament, and makes the stamp of heredity more clearly defined (109).

LVIII. Mercury rising is very potent and denotes the mental capacities, but it is greatly affected by the influence of aspects (109).

LIX. The Ruling Planet is either the lord of the ascending sign, or else that planet which is strongest or most prominent in the horoscope (129).

LX. The Sun well aspected and well placed brings success in life (131).

LXI. In considering the question of health, take into consideration Ascendant, Moon and Sun (139).

LXII. If the Sun is afflicted, the flow of the vital energy will be disturbed; if the Moon, the vehicle conveying the life forces is abnormal; if the Ascendant, the health will suffer according to nature of affliction and the rising sign (139).

LXIII. The Hyleg is that point in the horoscope upon which health and life depend (140).

LXIV. Positive Signs rising tend to give vitality, negative signs are not quite so vigorous (141).

LXV. The Apheta is that which supports life, the Anareta that which takes away life (144, 145).

LXVI. The relationship between signs and houses is that of 'correspondence' or analogy (147).

LXVII. In judging the financial prospects in a nativity, study the second house in all its bearings (151).

LXVIII. The Cardinal Signs give money through fame and public recognition, the Fixed Signs through Government or authoritative influence, the Common Signs through service and ordinary means. (157).

LXIX. The third house has a definite influence over the mind and is analogically under the rulership of Mercury (158).

LXX. In judging the mental qualifications consider the luminaries and Mercury, as well as the third house (163).

LXXI. The fourth house relates to the end of life, the environment of the native, and one of the parents (164).

LXXII. The signs on the cusps of the tenth and fourth houses, their rulers and the aspects between them, will denote the attitude of the parents towards each other, and their influence upon the native (170).

LXXIII. In considering the question of parental influence generally, include the Sun and the planet Saturn, with regard to he father, and the Moon and Venus with regard to the mother (169).

LXXIV. The fifth house relates to pleasure, society and social affairs, also to the emotions and feelings (172).

LXXV. The fifth house is an index to the sensations and passional tendencies, the sign upon the cusp indicating past experiences (175).

LXXVI. The first, fifth and ninth houses represent the personal man, showing his present, past and future consciousness symbolically (175).

LXXVII. The sixth house is connected with the mid-heaven and the second house, and relates to work, servants, sickness and the condition of the physical body (178).

LXXVIII. The sixth house indicates the psychic tendencies of the native, and is the house of phenomenal or ceremonial magic (183).

LXXIX. The seventh house is the complement of the first, and represents the unifying of all that is separated or isolated in the ascendant (184).

LXXX. The seventh house signifies the transmutation of the passions into love, the exchange of intellect for wisdom, and the perfect individualisation of the conscious self (184).

LXXXI. Any planet in the seventh house describes the partner, and gives the history of any union (186).

LXXXII. From a higher standpoint, the seventh house may be considered as the house of the Individuality as contrasted with the Personality ; the blending of these two being the true marriage (189).

LXXXIII. If the seventh house and its ruler do not offer a clear judgment in a male horoscope note the application of the Moon, and in a female horoscope, the Sun (189).

LXXXIV. In descriptions of marriage partner, judge according to the planet occupying the seventh, and the sign on the cusp : if no planet in seventh then judge by lord of sign on cusp, and the sign which said planet occupies (191).

LXXXV. The eighth house is the house of death, and all matters connected therewith, and also has relation to some forms of mediumship and occultism (195).

LXXXVI. In all questions of death, the sign upon the cusp of the eighth house, and the signs containing the majority of the planets, must be carefully considered (200).

LXXXVII. The ninth house is the house of philosophy, the higher mind ; the house of the subjective and abstract mind as opposed to the objective and concrete brain mind (202).

LXXXVIII. The ninth house denotes that which is to be the unfolding of what is possible in the future (206).

LXXXIX. All planets in the ninth house have a higher vibration than when placed in any other (206).

XC. The ninth house denotes the unexpressed, the motive behind the act, the thought behind the speech (206).

XCI. The tenth house is the house of honour, reputation, profession or occupation and represents the public standing or worldly position of the native (207).

XCII. In considering a vocation, take careful note of Saturn, the ruler of Capricorn, the natural tenth house in the order of the signs (216).

XCIII. The eleventh house is that of friends, acquaintances, hopes, wishes and aspirations (217).

XCIV. The twelfth house is the house of sorrow—the house of self-undoing (226).

XCV. Luminaries *applying* to aspects affect the polarity more than aspects from which they are separating (288).

XCVI. If the Sun is above the Moon, rising or setting, the Individual character will be stronger than the Personal (288).

XCVII. If both luminaries are below the earth the blending of them is more potent and the polarity more complicated (p. 288).

XCVIII. If both luminaries are above the earth, the Sun gains the greater power ; if both are below, the Moon (p. 288).

XCIX. The polarity is always stronger when the luminaries are rising, and weaker when they are setting (288).

C. If either of the luminaries apply to the benefics, the Individuality is stronger if it be the Sun, the Personality if it be the Moon (288).

THE ALAN LEO ASTROLOGER'S LIBRARY

The most renowned, complete course in Astrology ever to appear! The Alan Leo Astrologer's Library has become the undisputed source for self-instruction in Astrology.

ASTROLOGY FOR ALL $12.95

A concise, easy to understand introduction to astrology, which presents the major astrological principles in a simple and fascinating manner, developed especially for the reader without prior knowledge. This, Leo's most general text, is specifically designed for the beginning student and therefore includes background material, an analysis of the characteristics of each of the signs, a description of the sun and moon through the signs, and of the significance of the planets in each of the signs. The body of the work concerns the influence of the two major luminaries, the sun and moon, on character and offers a complete delineation of the twelve zodiacal types and the 144 sub-types born each year.

CASTING THE HOROSCOPE $12.95

Fundamental to astrology is the horoscope, a map of the heavens for the time and place of an individual's birth, from which astrological interpretation begins. In this book, Leo teaches everything one needs to know to cast a natal horoscope, including calculation of the ascendant, the use of the table of houses, how to read an ephemeris, the conversion of birth time to sidereal time and adjustments of planetary motions. For the more advanced student, there is information on rectification, directions, methods of house division, lessons in astronomy and sample tables. The coverage is comprehensive and includes areas not detailed in other works.

HOW TO JUDGE A NATIVITY $12.95

HOW TO JUDGE A NATIVITY is a storehouse of general information concerning planetary and zodiacal influences. It deals with the nativity almost entirely on a purely practical level, explaining how to assess the occupations and activities of life in great detail, from health, wealth and the home to philosophy and travel. All the necessary rules and references are presented with a view to helping the student learn to give a reliable reading of any nativity. Comprehensive analysis of the individual houses as they relate to chart interpretation is included, as well as planetary positions and aspects.

THE ART OF SYNTHESIS $12.95

In this work, Alan Leo stresses the esoteric and intuitional aspects of astrology, along with the philosophical and psychological. He provides a richly detailed study of the relation between planets and consciousness, based upon first-hand experience. Particularly interesting are the planetary correlations to the types of temperament, e.g. martial, saturnine, jovial, etc., accompanied by illustrations of the types. The triplicities are analysed comprehensively. Twelve sample horoscopes of famous individuals, including Rudolph Steiner, Robespierre and John Ruskin are discussed as examples of how to synthesize the many elements which come into play in a single, natal chart. A handy astro-theosophical dictionary is provided for the reader's convenience. Where HOW TO JUDGE A NATIVITY emphasizes the scientific-technical aspect of astrological interpretation, THE ART OF SYNTHESIS demonstrates the intuitional dimension. Intuition is soul penetration; it sees through the veil that divides the subjective from the objective universe and brings knowledge that the mind alone cannot obtain from the objective world. THE ART OF SYNTHESIS brings this intuitive penetration to astrology.

THE PROGRESSED HOROSCOPE
$12.95

THE PROGRESSED HOROSCOPE is the most comprehensive guide to the system of predicting the future. The methods for drawing up annual forecasts and divining upcoming influences are completely outlined. Included are a detailed and full delineation of every possible progressed aspect; solar, mutual and lunar. Their influences on character and destiny are fully described, enabling the student to form a firm foundation on which to base his judgment of any progressed horoscope he may wish to interpret. There is a lengthy chapter dealing with Transits in their exoteric and esoteric aspects. The last section, "The Art and Practice of Directing" is a complete handbook on "Primary Directions". The YES! Guide calls this "...the most detailed examination of progression available. Includes a great deal of background information on the why of progressions, in addition to detailed instructions on calculating the progressed ascendant, solar and lunar positions and aspects, solar revolutions and transits and primary directions."

THE KEY TO YOUR OWN NATIVITY
$12.95

A complete and comprehensive analysis of all the elements of the horoscope, giving full descriptions of every position in the nativity. With the assistance of this book, any person can learn to interpret a natal chart. Shows where to find indications in the horoscope related to topics such as, finance, travel, environment, enterprise, sickness, marriage, legacies, philosophy, profession, friends, occultism. Here is the master astrologer's easy to follow method for delineation and interpretation. A must for the beginner and an essential reference for the advanced astrologer.

ESOTERIC ASTROLOGY
$12.95

This work deals with Natal Astrology in a manner never before attempted by any writer on Astrology. Divided into three parts, the first part explains the theoretical aspect of Esoteric Astrology; the second demonstrates the practical side of Esoteric Astrology with many examples and complete explanations and the third part deals with the subdivisions of the Zodiac.

For the first time in the history of Astrology, an entirely new method of reading horoscopes is given. The *individual* and *personal* Stars of all persons are explained by a series of *Star Maps,* showing how the age of the soul may be astrologically discovered. It shows how the Horoscope may be changed into a Star Map.

Along with chart interpretation in terms of reincarnation, the methods for the working out of Karma are covered in detail.

THE COMPLETE DICTIONARY OF ASTROLOGY
$12.95

A handy reference text of all the terms and concepts you will need to understand astrology in its technical and philosophical dimensions. Useful for quick reference to the signs, planets, houses, ascendants, aspects, decanates, planetary herbs, etc. An extensive section on Hindu astrology. An analysis of horary astrology. Simple explanations of technical terms. Esoteric interpretation of the different elements of astrology. Indispensable to the study of the other Leo textbooks and a useful companion to any study of astrology.

These and other titles in the Alan Leo Astrologer's Library are available at many fine bookstores or, to order direct, send a check or money order for the total amount, plus $2.00 shipping and handling for the first book and 75¢ for each additional book to:

Inner Traditions International
P.O. Box 1534
Hagerstown, MD 21741

To order with a credit card, call toll-free:

1-800-638-3030

For a complete catalog of books from Inner Traditions International, write to:

Inner Traditions International
One Park Street
Rochester, VT 05767